Advances in Mathematical, Numerical and Artificial Intelligence Methods in Rock Engineering Applications

Advances in Mathematical, Numerical and Artificial Intelligence Methods in Rock Engineering Applications

Guest Editors

Xin Cai
Shaofeng Wang
Yu Wang
Xueming Du

Basel • Beijing • Wuhan • Barcelona • Belgrade • Novi Sad • Cluj • Manchester

Guest Editors

Xin Cai
School of Resources and
Safety Engineering
Central South University
Changsha
China

Shaofeng Wang
School of Resources and
Safety Engineering
Central South University
Changsha
China

Yu Wang
Department of Civil
Engineering
University of Science and
Technology Beijing
Beijing
China

Xueming Du
School of Water Conservancy
and Transportation
Zhengzhou University
Zhengzhou
China

Editorial Office
MDPI AG
Grosspeteranlage 5
4052 Basel, Switzerland

This is a reprint of the Special Issue, published open access by the journal *Mathematics* (ISSN 2227-7390), freely accessible at: https://www.mdpi.com/si/mathematics/9MY2F06TNX.

For citation purposes, cite each article independently as indicated on the article page online and as indicated below:

Lastname, A.A.; Lastname, B.B. Article Title. *Journal Name* **Year**, *Volume Number*, Page Range.

ISBN 978-3-7258-4257-5 (Hbk)
ISBN 978-3-7258-4258-2 (PDF)
https://doi.org/10.3390/books978-3-7258-4258-2

© 2025 by the authors. Articles in this book are Open Access and distributed under the Creative Commons Attribution (CC BY) license. The book as a whole is distributed by MDPI under the terms and conditions of the Creative Commons Attribution-NonCommercial-NoDerivs (CC BY-NC-ND) license (https://creativecommons.org/licenses/by-nc-nd/4.0/).

Contents

Preface vii

Xin Cai, Shaofeng Wang, Yu Wang and Xueming Du
Editorial: Advances in Mathematical, Numerical and Artificial Intelligence Methods in Rock Engineering Applications
Reprinted from: *Mathematics* **2025**, *13*, 1632, https://doi.org/10.3390/math13101632 1

Zilong Zhou, Hang Yuan and Xin Cai
Rock Thin Section Image Identification Based on Convolutional Neural Networks of Adaptive and Second-Order Pooling Methods
Reprinted from: *Mathematics* **2023**, *11*, 1245, https://doi.org/10.3390/math11051245 4

Amichai Mitelman and Alon Urlainis
Investigation of Transfer Learning for Tunnel Support Design
Reprinted from: *Mathematics* **2023**, *11*, 1623, https://doi.org/10.3390/math11071623 31

Zhe Liu, Jianhong Chen, Yakun Zhao and Shan Yang
A Novel Method for Predicting Rockburst Intensity Based on an Improved Unascertained Measurement and an Improved Game Theory
Reprinted from: *Mathematics* **2023**, *11*, 1862, https://doi.org/10.3390/math11081862 46

Lu Chen, Xiangxi Yu, Ron Luo, Ling Zeng and Hongtao Cao
High Steep Rock Slope Instability Mechanism Induced by the Pillar Deterioration in the Mountain Mining Area
Reprinted from: *Mathematics* **2023**, *11*, 1889, https://doi.org/10.3390/math11081889 64

Xianhui Mao, Ankui Hu, Rui Zhao, Fei Wang and Mengkun Wu
Evaluation and Application of Surrounding Rock Stability Based on an Improved Fuzzy Comprehensive Evaluation Method
Reprinted from: *Mathematics* **2023**, *11*, 3095, https://doi.org/10.3390/math11143095 78

Jianhong Chen, Yakun Zhao, Zhe Liu, Shan Yang and Zhiyong Zhou
Prediction of Rockburst Propensity Based on Intuitionistic Fuzzy Set—Multisource Combined Weights—Improved Attribute Measurement Model
Reprinted from: *Mathematics* **2023**, *11*, 3508, https://doi.org/10.3390/math11163508 97

Yingjie Xia, Bingchen Liu, Tianjiao Li, Danchen Zhao, Ning Liu, Chun'an Tang and Jun Chen
Numerical Simulation of Failure Modes in Irregular Columnar Jointed Rock Masses under Dynamic Loading
Reprinted from: *Mathematics* **2023**, *11*, 3790, https://doi.org/10.3390/math11173790 119

Wei Shao, Wenhan Yue, Ye Zhang, Tianxiang Zhou, Yutong Zhang, Yabin Dang, et al.
The Application of Machine Learning Techniques in Geotechnical Engineering: A Review and Comparison
Reprinted from: *Mathematics* **2023**, *11*, 3976, https://doi.org/10.3390/math11183976 144

Bo Zhang, Long Shi, Wenxuan Zhang, Chao Huan, Yujiao Zhao and Jingyu Wang
Numerical Investigation on the Performance of Horizontal Helical-Coil-Type Backfill Heat Exchangers with Different Configurations in Mine Stopes
Reprinted from: *Mathematics* **2023**, *11*, 4173, https://doi.org/10.3390/math11194173 160

Weiguang Ren, Chaosheng Wang, Yang Zhao and Dongjie Xue
Research on Precursor Information of Brittle Rock Failure through Acoustic Emission
Reprinted from: *Mathematics* **2023**, *11*, 4210, https://doi.org/10.3390/math11194210 181

Jianchun Ou, Enyuan Wang and Xinyu Wang
Time-Frequency Response of Acoustic Emission and Its Multi-Fractal Analysis for Rocks with Different Brittleness under Uniaxial Compression
Reprinted from: *Mathematics* **2023**, *11*, 4746, https://doi.org/10.3390/math11234746 . . . . **197**

Min Wang, Yakun Tian, Zhijun Zhang, Qifeng Guo and Lingling Wu
Dynamic Evolution of Coal Pore-Fracture Structure and Its Fractal Characteristics under the Action of Salty Solution
Reprinted from: *Mathematics* **2024**, *12*, 72, https://doi.org/10.3390/math12010072 . . . . **209**

Jing Zhou, Lang Liu, Yuan Zhao, Mengbo Zhu, Ruofan Wang and Dengdeng Zhuang
An Improved Rock Damage Characterization Method Based on the Shortest Travel Time Optimization with Active Acoustic Testing
Reprinted from: *Mathematics* **2024**, *12*, 161, https://doi.org/10.3390/math12010161 . . . . **230**

Preface

In the field of rock engineering, landscape studies have been greatly transformed by the increasing number of projects constructed in complex geological settings, extreme temperature conditions, high-pressure water environments, seismically active areas, and deep underground sites. Rock, a heterogeneous and anisotropic material full of multi-scale defects, spanning tiny particles to large-scale fractures, fissures, joints, stratifications, and faults, displays complex behaviors. These are greatly affected by the stress–physical–chemical coupling processes taking place within these defects. As a result, non-traditional rock failures like collapse, rockburst, and large-scale deformation occur more frequently, posing a significant threat to the safety and stability of rock engineering projects.

Traditional laboratory testing methods have been shown to be insufficient in clarifying the complex rock mechanics and disaster mechanisms under such difficult conditions. This inadequacy has thus led to an urgent need for new methods. The aim of this reprint, "Advances in Mathematical, Numerical and Artificial Intelligence Methods in Rock Engineering Applications", is to fill this knowledge and methodological void.

This reprint planed to collect research and review articles that thoroughly cover the latest laboratory or in situ experiments, mathematical models, theoretical analyses, numerical simulations, and artificial intelligence-based methods related to rock mechanics and rock engineering. The 13 articles included in this reprint represent praiseworthy efforts in using these advanced methods to address the long-standing challenges in rock mechanics and rock engineering.

We are convinced that this collection will not only deepen the understanding of rock behavior at a basic level but will also serve as an invaluable reference point for researchers and engineers in the field. This reprint is anticipated to stimulate further innovation and drive the development of more effective and reliable solutions in rock engineering applications.

Xin Cai, Shaofeng Wang, Yu Wang, and Xueming Du
Guest Editors

Editorial

Editorial: Advances in Mathematical, Numerical and Artificial Intelligence Methods in Rock Engineering Applications

Xin Cai [1,*], Shaofeng Wang [1], Yu Wang [2] and Xueming Du [3]

1. School of Resources and Safety Engineering, Central South University, Changsha 410083, China; sf.wang@csu.edu.cn
2. Department of Civil Engineering, School of Civil and Resource Engineering, University of Science and Technology Beijing, Beijing 100083, China; wyzhou@ustb.edu.cn
3. School of Water Conservancy and Transportation, Zhengzhou University, Zhengzhou 450001, China; 2007-dxm@163.com
* Correspondence: xincai@csu.edu.cn

MSC: 65S11; 68U11; 74R11; 74S11; 74F11

1. Introduction

This editorial presents 12 research articles published in the Special Issue entitled "Advances in Mathematical, Numerical and Artificial Intelligence Methods in Rock Engineering" of the MDPI Mathematics journal. The twelve studies collectively advance rock engineering through experimental, numerical, and AI-driven approaches, focusing on structural stability, failure prediction, and system optimization. Common themes include analyzing damage mechanisms (e.g., chemical degradation, dynamic stress effects) via fractal analysis, acoustic emission, and finite element modeling, alongside hybrid frameworks integrating fuzzy logic and machine learning for enhanced predictive accuracy. Distinctive contributions span diverse applications: pore-fracture evolution in coal, thermal efficiency in heat exchangers, and AI innovations such as CNNs for image classification and transfer learning for tunnel design. Methodological uniqueness lies in novel hybrid models (e.g., intuitionistic fuzzy sets, game theory) addressing rockburst propensity and instability, highlighting interdisciplinary synergy in addressing geotechnical challenges.

2. Overview of the Published Papers

Dynamic Evolution of Coal Pore-Fracture Structure and Its Fractal Characteristics under the Action of Salty Solution (by M. Wang, Y. Tian, Z. Zhang, Q. Guo and L. Wu) investigates the influence of salt solution immersion on coal pore structure by analyzing the porosity evolution under varying immersion times and concentrations. The study reveals that prolonged exposure to salt solutions increases coal porosity and deteriorates its structural integrity, providing insights into the damage mechanisms of coal properties under chemical interactions.

Time–Frequency Response of Acoustic Emission and Its Multi-Fractal Analysis for Rocks with Different Brittleness under Uniaxial Compression (by J. Ou, E. Wang and X. Wang) employs acoustic emission (AE) monitoring and multifractal analysis to explore the correlation between rock brittleness and AE time–frequency characteristics during uniaxial compression. The results demonstrate that brittleness is directly proportional to the parameter $\Delta\alpha$ (data uniformity) and inversely proportional to Δf (frequency difference), with abrupt changes in these parameters serving as precursors to rock failure.

Research on Precursor Information of Brittle Rock Failure through Acoustic Emission (by W. Ren, C. Wang, Y. Zhao and D. Xue) proposes a rock failure prediction method using triaxial experiments on granite, integrating the b-value and correlation dimension calculated via the G-P algorithm. The study identifies decreasing trends in both parameters as reliable indicators of impending rock damage, offering a framework for estimating surrounding rock stability.

Numerical Investigation on the Performance of Horizontal Helical-Coil-Type Backfill Heat Exchangers with Different Configurations in Mine Stopes (by B. Zhang, L. Shi, W. Zhang, C. Huan, Y. Zhao and J. Wang) utilizes the COMSOL software platform to simulate 3D unsteady heat transfer in spiral-type horizontal backfill heat exchangers (BFHEs). The results highlight that spiral tube arrangements and optimized pitch-to-diameter ratios enhance thermal efficiency and heat storage capacity, providing guidelines for BFHE design optimization.

Numerical Simulation of Failure Modes in Irregular Columnar Jointed Rock Masses under Dynamic Loading (by Y. Xia, B. Liu, T. Li, D. Zhao, N. Liu, C. Tang and J. Chen) applies the finite element method (FEM) to analyze dynamic failure modes of irregular columnar jointed rock masses (CJRMs) at varying dip angles. The study reveals that increasing dip angles shift failure modes from tension–compression–shear to pure tension, with higher stress wave amplitudes accelerating crack propagation.

Prediction of Rockburst Propensity Based on Intuitionistic Fuzzy Set—Multisource Combined Weights—Improved Attribute Measurement Model (by J. Chen, Y. Zhao, Z. Liu, S. Yang and Z. Zhou) introduces a rockburst prediction model combining intuitionistic fuzzy sets, multisource weighting, and improved attribute measurement. The model outperforms existing methods in accuracy by incorporating parameters such as uniaxial compressive strength, tensile stress, and elastic deformation coefficients.

Evaluation and Application of Surrounding Rock Stability Based on an Improved Fuzzy Comprehensive Evaluation Method (by X. Mao, A. Hu, R. Zhao, F. Wang and M. Wu) develops an improved fuzzy comprehensive evaluation method (IFCEM) integrating analytic hierarchy process (AHP) and coefficient of variation (CV) to assess surrounding rock stability. The results demonstrate enhanced accuracy through game theory-based weight optimization, offering a robust tool for engineering applications.

High Steep Rock Slope Instability Mechanism Induced by the Pillar Deterioration in the Mountain Mining Area (by L. Chen, X. Yu, R. Luo, L. Zeng and H. Cao) establishes a numerical model to investigate slope instability mechanisms caused by pillar deterioration in mountain mining areas. The study emphasizes the critical role of pillars in controlling slope deformation and failure progression, providing practical insights for slope stability management.

A Novel Method for Predicting Rockburst Intensity Based on an Improved Unascertained Measurement and an Improved Game Theory (by Z. Liu, J. Chen, Y. Zhao and S. Yang) proposes a rockburst intensity prediction method combining enhanced unascertained measurement and game theory-based weight integration. The results validate its superior accuracy over traditional models, highlighting its applicability in geotechnical risk assessment.

Investigation of Transfer Learning for Tunnel Support Design (by A. Mitelman and A. Urlainis) explores transfer learning to address data scarcity in tunnel support design. By training artificial neural networks (ANNs) on large datasets and fine-tuning with smaller datasets, the method effectively optimizes support parameters, demonstrating adaptability to unstudied geological conditions.

Rock Thin Section Image Identification Based on Convolutional Neural Networks of Adaptive and Second-Order Pooling Methods (by Z. Zhou, H. Yuan and X. Cai) introduces a convolutional neural network (CNN) model (ASOPCNN) incorporating adaptive and second-order pooling layers to enhance rock thin section image identification. The results confirm improved feature representation and classification accuracy, establishing ASOPCNN as a reliable tool for geological analysis.

The Application of Machine Learning Techniques in Geotechnical Engineering: A Review and Comparison (by W. Shao, W. Yue, Y. Zhang, T. Zhou, Y. Zhang, Y. Dang, H. Wang, X. Feng and Z. Chao) reviews machine learning algorithms, including SVM, ANN, and random forest (RF), in geotechnical applications. The study highlights RF's efficacy in soil classification, SVM's precision in rock deformation prediction, and the suitability of ANNs for strength and settlement forecasting.

Conflicts of Interest: The authors declare no conflict of interest.

List of Contributions:

1. Wang, M.; Tian, Y.; Zhang, Z.; Guo, Q.; Wu, L. Dynamic Evolution of Coal Pore-Fracture Structure and Its Fractal Characteristics under the Action of Salty Solution. *Mathematics* **2024**, *12*, 72. https://doi.org/10.3390/math12010072.
2. Ou, J.; Wang, E.; Wang, X. Time-Frequency Response of Acoustic Emission and Its Multi-Fractal Analysis for Rocks with Different Brittleness under Uniaxial Compression. *Mathematics* **2023**, *11*, 4746. https://doi.org/10.3390/math11234746.
3. Ren, W.; Wang, C.; Zhao, Y.; Xue, D. Research on Precursor Information of Brittle Rock Failure through Acoustic Emission. *Mathematics* **2023**, *11*, 4210. https://doi.org/10.3390/math11194210.
4. Zhang, B.; Shi, L.; Zhang, W.; Huan, C.; Zhao, Y.; Wang, J. Numerical Investigation on the Performance of Horizontal Helical-Coil-Type Backfill Heat Exchangers with Different Configurations in Mine Stopes. *Mathematics* **2023**, *11*, 4173. https://doi.org/10.3390/math11194173.
5. Xia, Y.; Liu, B.; Li, T.; Zhao, D.; Liu, N.; Tang, C.; Chen, J. Numerical Simulation of Failure Modes in Irregular Columnar Jointed Rock Masses under Dynamic Loading. *Mathematics* **2023**, *11*, 3790. https://doi.org/10.3390/math11173790.
6. Chen, J.; Zhao, Y.; Liu, Z.; Yang, S.; Zhou, Z. Prediction of Rockburst Propensity Based on Intuitionistic Fuzzy Set—Multisource Combined Weights—Improved Attribute Measurement Model. *Mathematics* **2023**, *11*, 3508. https://doi.org/10.3390/math11163508.
7. Mao, X.; Hu, A.; Zhao, R.; Wang, F.; Wu, M. Evaluation and Application of Surrounding Rock Stability Based on an Improved Fuzzy Comprehensive Evaluation Method. *Mathematics* **2023**, *11*, 3095. https://doi.org/10.3390/math11143095.
8. Chen, L.; Yu, X.; Luo, R.; Zeng, L.; Cao, H. High Steep Rock Slope Instability Mechanism Induced by the Pillar Deterioration in the Mountain Mining Area. *Mathematics* **2023**, *11*, 1889. https://doi.org/10.3390/math11081889.
9. Liu, Z.; Chen, J.; Zhao, Y.; Yang, S. A Novel Method for Predicting Rockburst Intensity Based on an Improved Unascertained Measurement and an Improved Game Theory. *Mathematics* **2023**, *11*, 1862. https://doi.org/10.3390/math11081862.
10. Mitelman, A.; Urlainis, A. Investigation of Transfer Learning for Tunnel Support Design. *Mathematics* **2023**, *11*, 1623. https://doi.org/10.3390/math11071623.
11. Zhou, Z.; Yuan, H.; Cai, X. Rock Thin Section Image Identification Based on Convolutional Neural Networks of Adaptive and Second-Order Pooling Methods. *Mathematics* **2023**, *11*, 1245. https://doi.org/10.3390/math11051245.
12. Shao, W.; Yue, W.; Zhang, Y.; Zhou, T.; Zhang, Y.; Dang, Y.; Wang, H.; Feng, X.; Chao, Z. The Application of Machine Learning Techniques in Geotechnical Engineering: A Review and Comparison. *Mathematics* **2023**, *11*, 3976. https://doi.org/10.3390/math11183976.

Article

Rock Thin Section Image Identification Based on Convolutional Neural Networks of Adaptive and Second-Order Pooling Methods

Zilong Zhou, Hang Yuan * and Xin Cai *

School of Resources and Safety Engineering, Central South University, Changsha 410083, China
* Correspondence: 205511039@csu.edu.cn (H.Y.); xincai@csu.edu.cn (X.C.)

Abstract: In order to enhance the ability to represent rock feature information and finally improve the rock identification performance of convolution neural networks (CNN), a new pooling mode was proposed in this paper. According to whether the pooling object was the last convolution layer, it divided pooling layers into the sampling pooling layer and the classification pooling layer. The adaptive pooling method was used in the sampling pooling layer. The pooling kernels adaptively adjusted were designed for each feature map. The second-order pooling method was used by the classification pooling layer. The second-order feature information based on outer products was extracted from the feature pair. The changing process of the two methods in forward and back propagation was deduced. Then, they were embedded into CNN to build a rock thin section image identification model (ASOPCNN). The experiment was conducted on the image set containing 5998 rock thin section images of six rock types. The CNN models using max pooling, average pooling and stochastic pooling were set for comparison. In the results, the ASOPCNN has the highest identification accuracy of 89.08% on the test set. Its indexes are superior to the other three models in precision, recall, F1 score and AUC values. The results reveal that the adaptive and second-order pooling methods are more suitable for CNN model, and CNN based on them could be a reliable model for rock identification.

Keywords: rock; rock thin section image; rock identification; convolution neural networks; pooling layer

MSC: 68T07

1. Introduction

Rock identification is a basic and prerequisite work of geological engineering [1]. For instance, geologists need lithological type information to infer the history of regional geological evolution, judge types of deep mineral resources, as well as oil and gas resources, and invert reserve information of various resources [2,3]. Engineers need lithological type information to guide and design the construction of geotechnical engineering, such as mining and tunnelling [4,5]. Insufficient rock type information may lead to a series of engineering disasters, including landslide, collapse, and settlement [6,7]. Hence, it is necessary to study how to identify rock types accurately and quickly.

Many scholars have conducted lots of research on rock identification and put forward many methods, which can be summarized into the following four types: microscopic observation, experimental tests, statistics and learning, and deep learning [8].

Microscopic observation and experimental tests belong to manual identification methods. They observe rock characteristics through optical microscopes, and analyze compositions and structures of rocks and minerals with the help of X-ray Diffraction (XRD), Electron Microprobe Analysis (EMPA), etc. Zhang [9] introduced the identification principle and process of rock microscopic observation in combination with cases. In order to identify acid volcanic rocks, Liu et al. [10] used X-ray Fluorescence Spectroscopy (XRF) to analyze the principal components of rocks and EMPA to check and show the minerals. Manual identification methods have achieved certain results; however, they are time-consuming, labor-intensive, costly, subjective, and greatly affected by professional levels of observers as well as professionalism of instruments. It is not applicable for rock identification of large-scale stratums in engineering.

The automatic identification methods based on rock features and machine learning have gradually gained the favor of scholars [11,12]. Chatterjee et al. [13] input color, shape and texture features extracted from rock images into SVM to identify rock types, and finally achieved an accuracy of 96.2%. Patel et al. [14] extracted nine color histogram features from rock images and input them into the probabilistic neural network. They successfully identified limestone types, with an error rate of less than 6%. Zhang et al. [15] used five machine learning models to identify rock and mineral images, and then selected three models with the best performance to stack. The stacked model effectively improved model performance. Machine learning methods can realize automatic identification of rock types. However, features required to classify still need to be selected subjectively by professionals. Feature types selected usually are few [8]. In addition, features of different lithology have different preferences, resulting in many problems in practical application.

In recent years, artificial intelligence (AI) methods and technologies have developed rapidly [16–20]. As a core method in the field of target detection, target identification and target segmentation, deep learning has been gradually applied to geological and rock engineering [21–26].

As a visual model of deep learning, convolutional neural networks (CNN) can automatically select the most suitable features to distinguish different type rocks. Rock type identification using CNN is usually based on rock thin section images. Rock thin sections are rock slices, which are observed and studied under the polarizing microscope. The rock slices are made from large rock samples through cutting, grinding and other operations, and they are about 60 mm × 60 mm in size and about 0.3 mm in thickness. Many scholars have performed lots of innovative research on rock thin section image identification. Polat et al. [27] used DenseNet121 and ResNet50 to identify six types of volcanic rock and tested the impact of four different optimizers on model accuracy. Alzubaidi et al. [28] used the architecture of ResNeXt-50 to identify the rock types of oil and gas reservoir logging core images, and the final accuracy reached 93.12%. In order to improve the identification accuracy, Liu et al. [29] built a mineral image identification model based on ResNet, embedding four visual attention blocks. Ma et al. [30] proposed the MaSE-ResNeXt model to enhance feature connectivity between different channels, and the identification accuracy on three kinds of rock thin section images finally reached 90.89%. Li et al. [8] researched the influence of three different optimization algorithms and two attenuation methods of learning rate on identification performance. Dos Anjos et al. [31] believed that the existing CNN needed to unify the input image size, which would lose the original image information inevitably. Their research work proposed a CNN based on a pyramid pooling layer. The image was down sampled according to the pyramid layering mode, which can process input images of all sizes. The final research showed that this method can improve the identification accuracy to a certain extent. Su et al. [32] believed that different shooting types of rock images had an impact on the final accuracy. Their research work inputted three types of rock images into three identical CNN, respectively, including the plane polarized light image, the cross polarized light image and the image after principal component analysis. The final rock type was determined through the maximum likelihood method based on the results of three CNN. The final accuracy reached 89.97%. Seo et al. [33] researched the impact of local images on the identification accuracy. They believed that the features in local areas in the rock image were more representative and definite. They proposed a model based on image segmentation. The large image was divided into several small parts, which were input into CNN in turn. The final lithology category was the one with the highest quantity of local identification results. Xu et al. [34] researched the impact of the fusion of image and data features on rock identification. Their research work proposed a fusion identification method, which inputs image features and parts of lithological data into the full connection layer of CNN. The final results showed that this method can improve the identification accuracy. Zhang et al. [15] researched the effect of different classifiers on the performance of rock identification models. They identified and classified the rock image features extracted from CNN by using five classifiers: logical regression (LR), support vector machine (SVM), random forest (RF), k-nearest neighbors (KNN), multilayer perceptron (MLP) and gaussian naive Bayes (GNB). The final result showed that the classification performance of the logistic regression, support vector machine and multilayer perceptron was better than other methods. However, the above research still has some deficiencies. Current research mainly focuses on the function of convolution layers, full connection layers and optimization algorithms of CNN, ignoring the effect of pooling layers on the performance of rock identification. Current pooling layers only play the role of down sampling. The current pooling methods used are main max pooling and average pooling. They are static and can only extract less information about rock features. Max pooling is sensitive to mutation of pixels, so it can retain texture features of rocks, as well as shape and size features of minerals to the maximum extent [35]. Average pooling pays more attention to preserving overall feature information of input images. It can better preserve color features, background features and global combination features of mineral composition in location and content [29]. However, internal structures and mineral morphology of rocks contain dozens or even hundreds of features, and the features required to distinguish different rocks are distinctive. Static pooling methods cannot select the best pooling method according to different lithological characteristics. At the same time, current pooling methods can only obtain first-order feature information from a single feature map, ignoring the relationship between feature pairs. Adequate exploration of feature distributions is important for realizing the full potentials of CNN [36].

Therefore, the functions of pooling layers were divided into two types: down sampling and classification, and the adaptive and second-order pooling methods were designed and respectively applied in this paper. The adaptive pooling set pooling kernels for each feature map. The parameters in pooling kernels participated in the training process, and finally they were configured by error feedback. During the process of the second-order pooling, the second-order feature information based on outer products between feature pairs was extracted and finally input into a classifier. After deducing the changing process of forward and back propagation, the proposed pooling methods were embedded into CNN to build an identification model of rock thin section images. Another three models using traditional pooling methods were used for comparison. The performance was comprehensively evaluated with multiple indicators to provide a reliable model for rock identification.

2. Data Collection

The rock thin section images used in this paper were from the symposium on Microscopic Images of Rocks in the open-source database, China Scientific Data [37–42]. There were 3374 images collected from the open-source database. Six kinds of common rocks were selected for experiment, including wackestone, granite, schist, quartz sandstone, conglomerate and crystalline dolomite. The sites of rock samples and the production process of rock thin section images were shown in Figure 1a. As shown in Figure 1b, these rock samples came from geological drillings in different regions of China. Through the steps in Figure 1c, rock samples were cut, polished and stuck into rock thin sections, and then they were photographed under polarizing microscopes to obtain microscopic images. Wackestone is a kind of sedimentary rock. The matrix filling of it is plaster, and the particles are mainly bioclasts and cuttings of rocks. Granite is a kind of igneous rock with holocrystalline structures. Its main mineral compositions are quartz, feldspar, and a small amount of mica. Schist is a kind of metamorphic rock with lamellar structures. Its common mineral compositions include quartz, quartzite, and mica. Quartz sandstone is a kind of sedimentary rock with clastic structures. Its mineral composition is mainly quartz, containing a small amount of feldspar. The cement between minerals is calcareous. The diameter of mineral particles is mostly between 0.2 mm and 2 mm. Conglomerate is a kind of sedimentary rock with clastic structures. Its mineral compositions are mainly quartz and feldspar and contains some cuttings of rocks. The cement between minerals is siliceous. The diameter of mineral particles is mostly between 2 mm and 5 mm. Crystalline dolomite is a kind of sedimentary rock with recrystallized structures. The crystalline minerals are mostly quartz, with diameters ranging from 0.005 mm to 0.03 mm. The cement between minerals is siliceous.

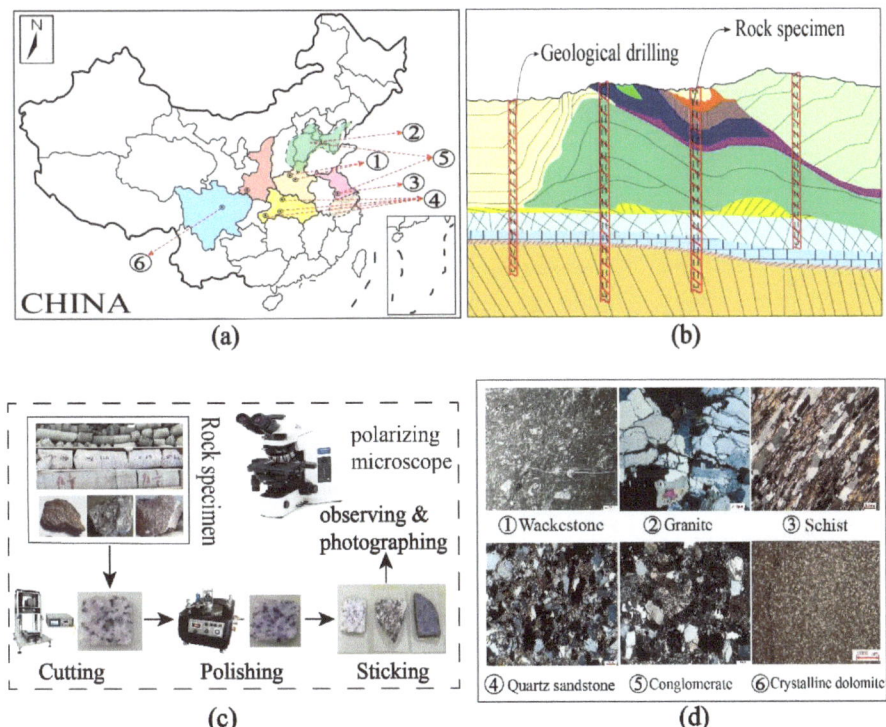

Figure 1. The sites of rock samples and the production process of rock thin section images; (**a**) Rock sample acquisition area; (**b**) Lithological map of different stratum; (**c**) Manufacturing process of rock thin sections; (**d**) Rock thin section image set.

To prevent over fitting in the training process and increase robustness of results, several commonly used image enhancement technologies were used to expand the image set, including image rotation, image flip, brightness change, noise addition and histogram equalization [30,33]. The image set contained 5998 images after enhancement. It was roughly divided into the training set, validation set and test set with the ratio of 7:2:1. The specific division details can be seen in Table 1. The pixels of the images in the original set were not uniform, while the CNN model required the input images to be consistent in size, so the bilinear interpolation algorithm was used to unify the image size to 227 × 227 pixels. The process of bilinear interpolation was shown in Figure 2. According to the coordinate defined in Figure 2, the pixel values of the interpolation points can be calculated by Equations (1) and (2); the pixel value of the target point can be calculated by Equation (3).

$$f(x, y_0) = \frac{x_1 - x}{x_1 - x_0} f(x_0, y_0) + \frac{x - x_0}{x_1 - x_0} f(x_1, y_0) \qquad (1)$$

$$f(x, y_1) = \frac{x_1 - x}{x_1 - x_0} f(x_0, y_1) + \frac{x - x_0}{x_1 - x_0} f(x_1, y_1) \quad (2)$$

$$f(x, y) = \frac{y_1 - y}{y_1 - y_0} f(x, y_0) + \frac{y - y_0}{y_1 - y_0} f(x, y_1) \quad (3)$$

where $f(x,y)$ is the pixel value of the target point; $f(x,y_0)$, $f(x,y_1)$ are pixel values of the interpolation point; $f(x_0,y_0)$, $f(x_1,y_0)$, $f(x_0,y_1)$, $f(x_1,y_1)$ are pixel values of the original points.

Table 1. Rock thin section image set.

Rock Type	Training Set	Validation Set	Test Set	Total
Wackestone	636	180	103	919
Granite	732	216	92	1040
Schist	672	192	89	953
Quartz sandstone	756	216	102	1074
Conglomerate	768	216	104	1088
Crystalline dolomite	648	180	96	924
Total	4212	1200	586	5998

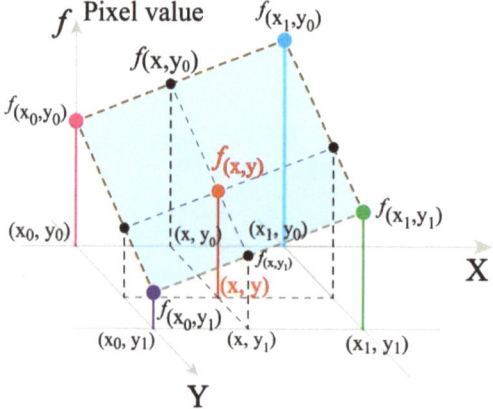

Figure 2. The calculation process of the bilinear interpolation algorithm.

3. Proposed Method

3.1. Basic CNN Model

The structure of CNN can be divided into two modules: feature extraction and feature classification, and its overall workflow can be divided into two processes: forward propagation and back propagation (parameters updating). Its basic structure was shown in Figure 3.

Images to be identified were input into the feature extraction module, which was stacked by multiple convolution layers and pooling layers. The module was used to extract the underlying features of images. Then, the extracted features were input into the feature classification module, which was composed of full connection layers and a softmax layer. Its function was to classify the input features. The final output was a vector, in which each element value represented the probability that the image belonged to the corresponding category. Through this process, a forward propagation was completed. Then the sum of the error between calculated results and real values was taken as the total loss of CNN. The partial derivatives of the total loss to parameters were taken as the error sensitivity. The error sensitivity of each layer was calculated by back propagation. Then the parameter values were optimized by optimizers. Through this process, a back propagation process was completed. The gradient descent method was usually used as the optimizer in CNN. Its calculation process was shown in Equation (4). The CNN model completed an iteration through forward and backward propagation. The specific function of each layer was introduced below.

$$new(w) = old(w) - \eta \delta w \quad (4)$$

where δw was the error sensitivity of weight parameter w; η was the learning rate.

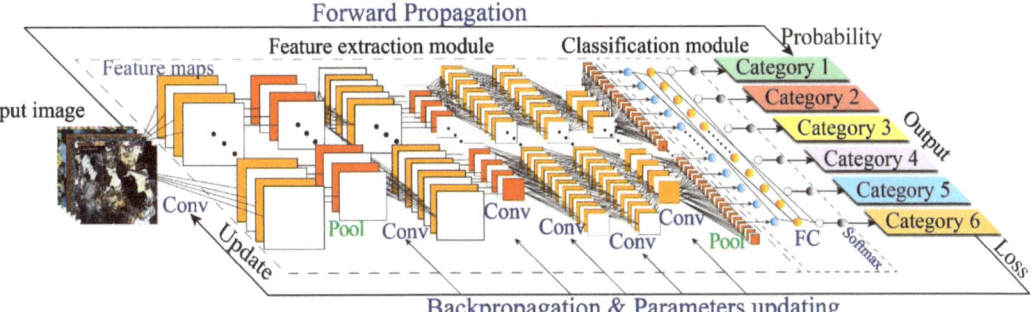

Figure 3. The structure and workflow of CNN model.

The function of convolution layers is to extract feature maps. Convolution kernels slide across the input images from left to right and top to bottom. At each sliding position, the sub-region elements and convolution kernels perform convolution operations as shown in Equation (5). The output results constitute feature maps.

$$X_j^l = f\left(\sum_{i \in M_j} X_i^{l-1} \otimes k_{ij}^l + b_j^l\right) \quad (5)$$

where X_j^l is the jth feature map of the lth layer, k_{ij}^l is the convolution kernel of the lth layer, $\otimes$ is the convolution operation symbol, which represents the sum of the multiplication of corresponding position elements of two matrixes. The function of activation layers is to increase the nonlinearity of output and make multi-layer stacking meaningful. The commonly used activation functions include ReLU and Sigmoid. The function of pooling layers is to reduce the size of the feature maps. Pooling layers output results through a sliding window similar to convolution layers. Each sliding outputs a special value of the corresponding sub-region. The function of the full connection layers is to classify the input feature data. It can map the input features to the sample tag space and obtain the values of the sample belonging to each category. The calculation process is shown below.

$$X_j^l = f\left(\sum_i X_i^{l-1} \cdot W_i + b_j^l\right) \quad (6)$$

The function of the softmax layer is to convert the results from full connection layers into probabilities between 0 and 1. The calculation process is shown below.

$$p(x_i) = \frac{e^{x_i}}{\sum_{j=1}^{K} e^{x_j}} \quad (7)$$

3.2. Rock Thin Section Image Identification Model

In this section, the pooling layers were first divided into the sampling pooling layer and the classification pooling layer according to whether the pooling object was the last convolution layer. Then, the adaptive pooling method was designed for the sampling pooling layer, and the second-order pooling method was designed for the classification pooling layer. Then based on the Alexnet [43] framework, these two pooling methods were embedded to design a rock thin section image identification model. Alexnet is a classic CNN model, which won the championship in the IMAGENET-2012 competition. It was widely used in rock image identification because of its small model and fast computation [44], the adaptive pooling and second-order pooling methods were embedded to build a feature extractor, and then the feature extractor was combined with a classifier to construct a rock thin section image identification model (ASOPCNN). The overall structure of the model was shown in Figure 4. Rock thin section images with 227 × 227 pixels were input into the feature extractor, which included 5 convolution layers, 2 adaptive pooling layers and 1 s-order pooling layer. The detailed parameters of the convolution and pooling layers were shown in left bottom of Figure 4. The parameter table in the convolution layer successively represented the kernel size and number, the layer name, the moving step and padding value. The parameter table in the pooling layer successively represented the kernel size and number, the layer name and the pooling step. The second-order pooling layer specifically included five layers as shown in lower right corner of Figure 4. In order to speed up the training process, the 2nd, 4th and 5th convolution layers were set as the upper and lower parts, using two GPU for parallel computing. The activation function used the ReLU. The rock features extracted were input into the classifier. The classifier contained 3 full connection layers and 1 softmax layer. The numbers of neurons in the full connection layer were 4096, 4096, 6, respectively. The probability values belonging to each rock category were output as the results.

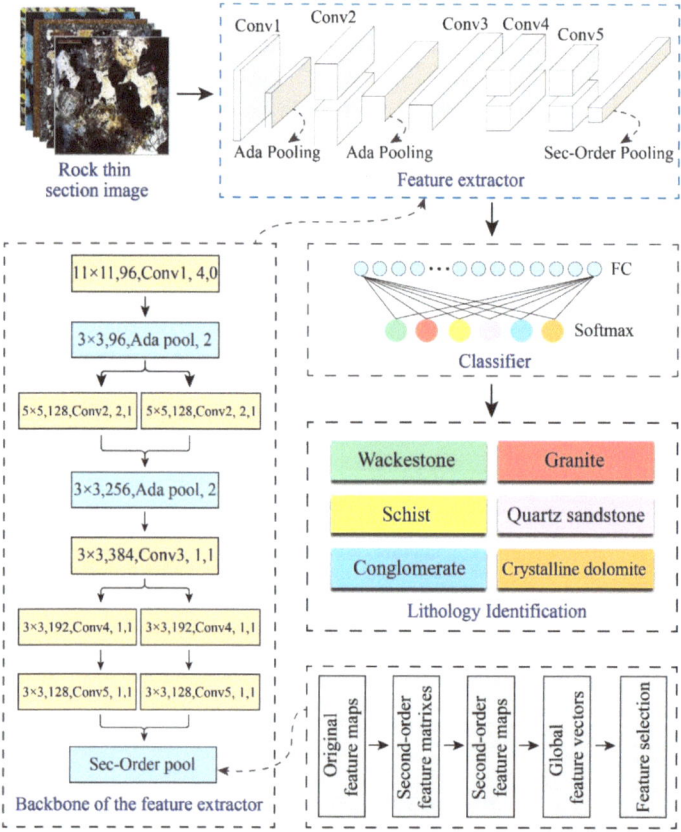

Figure 4. The structure of rock thin section image identification model (ASOPCNN).

3.3. Adaptive Pooling Method

The purpose of sampling pooling layers is to reduce the size of feature maps [45]. The traditional pooling methods are mainly max pooling, mean pooling and stochastic pooling. Their pooling processes were shown in Figure 5. With max pooling, the maximum value of each region was output. The average value of each region was output through average pooling. With stochastic pooling, the probability of each element in the region was calculated, and then the output was selected randomly according to the magnitude of probability [20]. However, pooling methods have certain selectivity in the process of representing rock features. Figure 6 shows the selectivity of two pooling methods. It can be seen in Figure 6a that texture features became more prominent after max pooling, while the number of textures decreased, and the structure becomes fuzzy after average pooling. It showed that max pooling had a strengthening effect on texture features, while average pooling had a restraining effect. Figure 6b shows the pooling process of wackestone. From the color histogram, we can see that color values of the original image were concentrated in the range of 50 to 200 but are relatively dispersed. After average pooling, the value range remained unchanged, and the aggregation degree was higher. It indicated that some disturbing color information was lost after average pooling. However, the color range changed after max pooling. It indicated that the original color feature had been lost, which also proved the inapplicability of max pooling to color features.

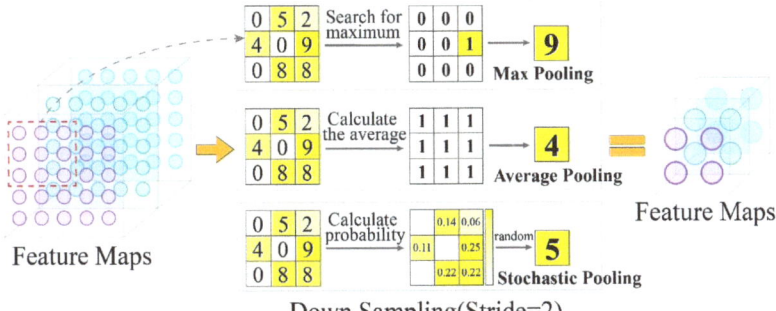

Figure 5. Process of traditional pooling methods, including max pooling, average pooling and stochastic pooling.

No matter what traditional pooling method is used, all feature maps use a single sampling way, which will inevitably cause loss of feature information and affect performance of CNN. An adaptive pooling method was proposed in this paper, and its pooling process was shown in Figure 7. For input feature maps, firstly, the pooling kernels were deployed for each feature map; each kernel was independent of each other. Then, initial values were set randomly between 0 and 1 for each kernel. Finally, convolutional results were calculated between the feature maps and the pooling kernels through Equation (8).

$$O = \frac{\sum_{i=1}^{m}\sum_{j=1}^{n} I_{ij} \cdot W_{ij}}{\sum_{i=1}^{m}\sum_{j=1}^{n} W_{ij}} \tag{8}$$

where O was the output value; I was the input value; W was the parameter of pooling kernels. The parameters were adaptively adjusted, and the process can be divided into the following four steps, as shown in the right side of Figure 7.

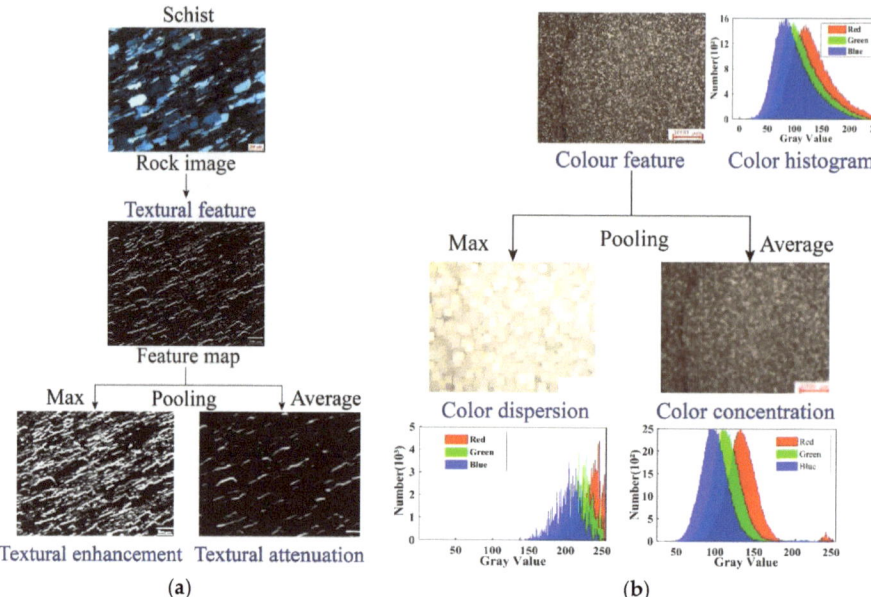

Figure 6. (a) The selectivity of textural features in the pooling process; (b) The selectivity of color features in the pooling process.

Step 1: Calculate total loss L. The total loss was the difference between real values and actual output values.

Step 2: Calculate partial derivatives. The partial derivatives of total loss to each parameter of pooling kernels were calculated layer-by-layer through back propagation.

Step 3: Update parameters. According to the partial derivatives and the learning rate, new parameters were calculated through the gradient descent method.

Step 4: Limit parameter boundary. If the calculated parameter was bigger than 1, then it was equal to 1; if the calculated parameter was smaller than 0, then it was equal to 0.

The adaptive pooling method affected the forward and back propagation process of CNN. Its forward propagation was the convolutional calculation of the target feature maps with the pooling kernels. The result feature maps can be calculated by Equation (9).

$$y_{i,j} = \sum_{m=1}^{b} \sum_{n=1}^{b} w_{m,n} \cdot x_{s \cdot (i-1)+m, s \cdot (j-1)+n} \tag{9}$$

where $x_{i,j}$ and $y_{i,j}$, respectively, represented the values in row i and column j of the target feature maps and the result feature maps; $w_{m,n}$ represented the value in row m and column n of pooling kernels; b represented the size of pooling kernels; s represented the step size.

The back propagation process needed to calculate $\delta x_{i,j}$ and $\delta w_{i,j}$ through Equations (10) and (11). $\delta x_{i,j}$ was the error sensitivity of target feature maps, which represented the partial derivative of the total loss to each element in the target feature maps. In the same way, $\delta w_{i,j}$ was the error sensitivity of pooling kernels, which was used to calculate error sensitivity of front layers.

$$\delta x_{i,j} = \sum_{m=1}^{c} \sum_{n=1}^{c} \delta y_{m,n} \cdot w_{i-s \cdot m+s, j-s \cdot n+s} \cdot f[i - s \cdot (m-1)] \cdot f[j - s \cdot (n-1)] \tag{10}$$

$$\delta w_{i,j} = \sum_{m=1}^{c} \sum_{n=1}^{c} \delta y_{m,n} \cdot x_{s \cdot (m-1)+i, s \cdot (n-1)+j} \tag{11}$$

where $\delta y_{m,n}$ was the error sensitivity of the result feature map; c was the size of the result feature maps. $f(x)$ was a judgement function, which equaled to 1 while $0 < x < b$ and equaled to 0 for else. The detailed derivation process of forward and back propagation can be seen in Appendix A.

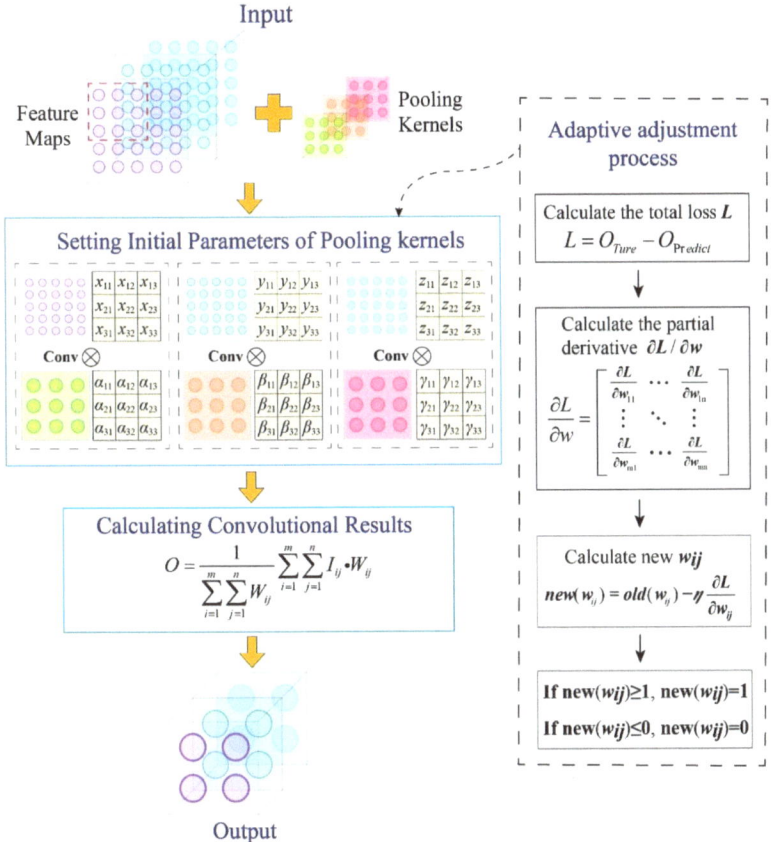

Figure 7. Process of the adaptive pooling method.

3.4. Second-Order Pooling Method

The classification pooling layer is connected behind the last convolution layer. Its purpose is to integrate feature maps into a compact global feature. Then the global feature is input into a full connection layer for classification. The process of integrating feature maps for traditional pooling methods was shown in Figure 8. Each feature map was expanded into a vector after down sampling, then all vectors were connected to form a global feature vector in turn. However, this method only counted first-order feature information. Because in the integration process, each feature map was independent and uncorrelated. As a result, the ability of feature representation was limited.

Carreira et al. [46] proposed a method based on outer products to extract second-order feature information. However, they only used it for image segmentation. Based on their work of them, the second-order pooling method was proposed in this paper by embedding the second-order information extraction process into CNN and deriving its forward and back propagation. The process of the second-order pooling was shown in Figure 9. The whole process can be divided into the following six steps.

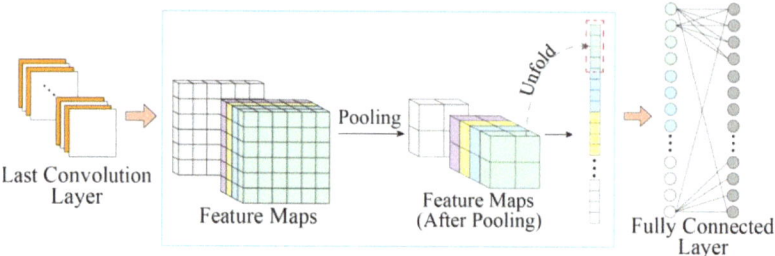

Figure 8. Process of integrating feature maps of traditional pooling methods.

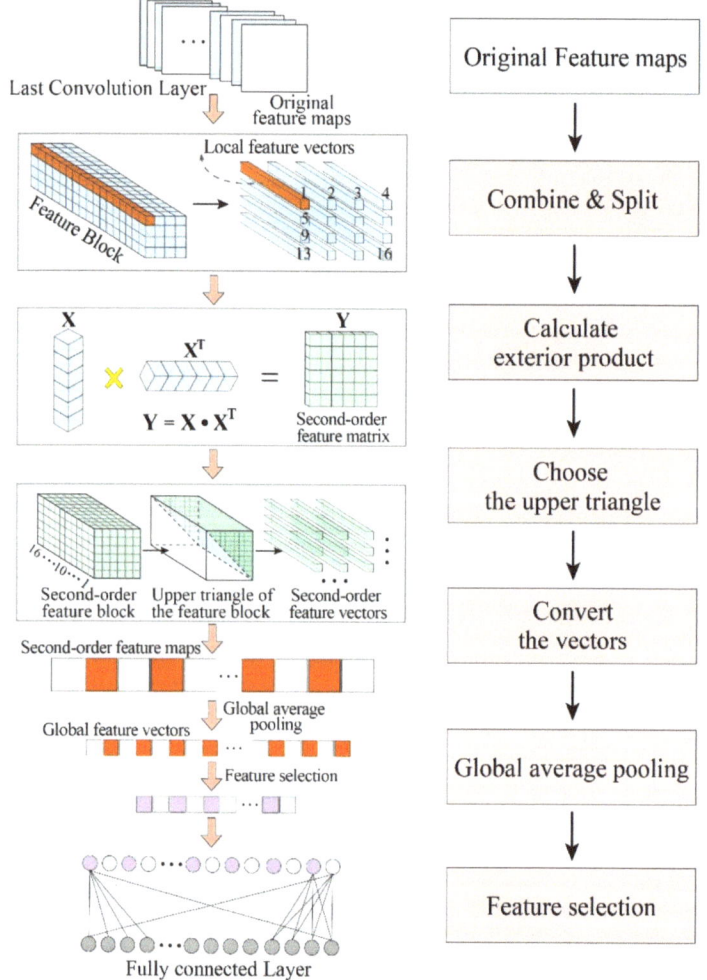

Figure 9. The process of the second-order pooling method.

Step 1: Combine and split. For feature maps of the last convolution layer, they were combined to form a feature block; then, the feature block was divided into local feature vectors in sequence from left to right and top to bottom according to the element position. The local feature vectors contained information of all feature maps at a single position.

Step 2: Calculate outer products. The local feature vectors were taken as the main body, then outer products of each local feature vector were calculated to obtain the second-order feature matrixes.

Step 3: Choose upper triangle part. All second-order feature matrixes were combined to form a second-order feature block, and then the block was divided into second-order feature vectors in sequence from left to right and top to bottom according to the element position. To avoid duplication, only the upper triangle part of the block was retained. Each second-order feature vector contained information of all positions in each original feature map.

Step 4: Convert vectors into matrixes. Each second-order feature vector was converted into a second-order feature map in sequence from left to right and top to bottom according to the size of the original feature map.

Step 5: Global average pooling. The second-order feature maps were down sampled to obtain the global feature vector through global average pooling.

Step 6: Feature selection. Because the positive excitation function, such as ReLU and Sigmoid functions, was generally used in the process of feature extraction, the numerical difference of elements can reflect the importance of feature information. The second-order pooling can further expand this difference. In order to reduce the number of parameters and speed up the training process, a part of feature information was selected in sequence from large to small according to the importance of feature information. The number of features as a super parameter needed to be preset.

The second-order pooling method affected forward and back propagation of CNN. In forward propagation process, the elements in the second-order feature matrixes, second-order feature maps and global feature vectors can be, respectively, obtained by Equations (12)–(14).

$$y_{i,j,k} = \sum_{m=1}^{a}\sum_{n=1}^{a} x_{m,n,i} \cdot x_{m,n,j} \cdot I[a(m-1)+n=k] \tag{12}$$

$$z_{\alpha,\beta,\gamma} = \sum_{k=1}^{a^2}\sum_{i=1}^{b}\sum_{j=1}^{b} y_{i,j,k} \cdot I[b(i-1)+j-\frac{i^2-i}{2}=\gamma] \cdot I[c(\alpha-1)+\beta=\gamma] \tag{13}$$

$$Z_p = \frac{\sum_{\alpha=1}^{c}\sum_{\beta=1}^{c} z_{\alpha,\beta,p}}{\alpha \cdot \beta} \tag{14}$$

where $x_{m,n,l}$ represented the element in row m and column n of the ith original feature map; $y_{i,j,k}$ represented the element in row I and column j of the kth second-order feature matrix; $z_{\alpha,\beta,\gamma}$ represented the element in row α and column β of the γth second-order feature map; Z_p represented the value of the pth element in the global feature vector; a, b, c, respectively, represented the size of the original feature maps, the second-order feature matrixes and the second-order feature maps; I (condition) was a judgment function; if the condition was met, then $I = 1$, otherwise $I = 0$.

In the back propagation process, since there were no parameters to be updated, only elements of error sensitivity were required to calculate. The error sensitivity of the second-order feature maps, the second-order feature matrixes and the original feature maps can be, respectively, obtained by Equations (15)–(17).

$$\delta z_{\alpha,\beta,\gamma} = \frac{\delta Z_\gamma}{\alpha \cdot \beta} \tag{15}$$

$$\delta y_{i,j,k} = \sum_{\alpha=1}^{c}\sum_{\beta=1}^{c} \delta z_{\alpha,\beta,b \cdot (i-1)+j-(i^2-i)/2} \cdot I[b(\alpha-1)+\beta=k] \tag{16}$$

$$\delta x_{m,n,l} = \sum_{i=1}^{b}\sum_{j=1}^{b} \delta y_{i,j,s_2 \cdot (m-1)+n} \cdot x_{m,n,j} \cdot I(i=l) \cdot [I(i=m) \cdot I(j=n)+1] \tag{17}$$

where δZ_γ represented the error sensitivity of the global feature vector; $\delta z_{\alpha,\beta,\gamma}$ represented the error sensitivity of the second-order feature maps; $\delta y_{i,j,k}$ represented the error sensitivity of the second-order feature matrixes; $\delta x_{m,n,l}$ represented the error sensitivity of the original feature maps. The detailed derivation process of the forward and back propagation can be seen in Appendix B.

3.5. Evaluation Metrics

In order to effectively evaluate classification performance of CNN models, several indicators were used, including accuracy rate (ACC), precision rate (PRE), recall rate (REC), F1 score (F1), confusion matrix and the receiver operating characteristic curve (ROC) [47–49]. The confusion matrix was shown in Figure 10, through which the identification effect of CNN models can be observed intuitively. In the confusion matrix, each row is the prediction labels of samples, and each column is the real labels of samples. P (Positive) represents the prediction label is positive; N (Negative) represents the prediction label is negative; T (Ture) represents the sample is predicted correctly; F (False) represents the sample is predicted wrongly.

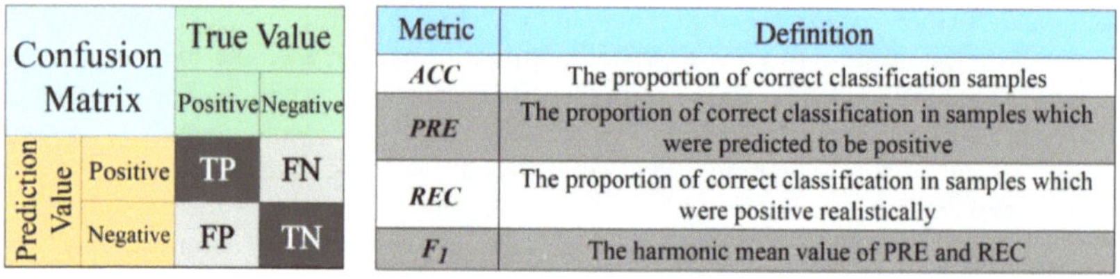

Confusion Matrix		True Value	
		Positive	Negative
Prediction Value	Positive	TP	FN
	Negative	FP	TN

Metric	Definition
ACC	The proportion of correct classification samples
PRE	The proportion of correct classification in samples which were predicted to be positive
REC	The proportion of correct classification in samples which were positive realistically
F1	The harmonic mean value of PRE and REC

Figure 10. Schematic of the confusion matrix.

The accuracy rate (ACC) represents the proportion of correct classification, which can be calculated by Equation (18). The precision rate (PRE) represents the proportion of correct classification in labels which were predicted to be positive, which can be calculated by Equation (19). The recall rate (REC) refers to the proportion of correct classification in labels which were realistically positive, which can be calculated by Equation (20). F1 score is the harmonic mean value of PRE and REC, which can be calculated by Equation (21).

$$ACC = \frac{TP + TN}{TP + TN + FP + FN} \tag{18}$$

$$PRE = \frac{TP}{TP + FP} \tag{19}$$

$$REC = \frac{TP}{TP + FN} \tag{20}$$

$$F_1 = \frac{2TP}{2TP + FP + FN} \tag{21}$$

The receiver operating characteristic curve (ROC) can show the performance of models under different classification thresholds. The ROC curve uses the false positive rate (FPR) as the abscissa and the true rate (TPR) as the ordinate, which can be calculated by Equations (22) and (23), respectively. AUC is the area under the curve, and large AUC value indicates good performance of models. When AUC ≤ 0.5, prediction result is less effective than random guess, and the model has no predictive worth.

$$FPR = \frac{FP}{TN + FP} \tag{22}$$

$$TPR = \frac{TP}{TP + FN} \tag{23}$$

4. Results and Discussions

The program of the proposed model was written based on Matlab language and the deep learning library in Matlab 2021b. It was 32 k in size. The experimental process was carried out on the server with a 64-core CPU, a 192 G RAM and the Linux operating system, which belonged to the Super Cloud Computing Center in Beijing, China. The average cost of per image during training was 1.257 s. In order to verify the effectiveness of the adaptive and second-order pooling methods, the original model of Alexnet, which used max pooling, was used for comparative verification. It was recorded as MAXCNN. On this basis, all pooling layers of the Alexnet were replaced with average pooling and stochastic pooling respectively to build another 2 models, which were recorded as MEACNN and STOCNN respectively. The structures of four models were shown in Table 2. The experiment mainly included the following three aspects: (1) the identification results on the training and validation set; (2) the identification results on the test set; (3) identification performance of various models in each rock category.

Table 2. Model structure configuration.

ASOPCNN	MAXCNN	MEACNN	STOCNN
Convolution 11 × 11-96 filters	Convolution 11 × 11-96 filters	Convolution 11 × 11-96 filters	Convolution 11 × 11-96 filters
Adaptive pooling	Max pooling	Mean pooling	Stochastic pooling
2 Group convolution	2 Group convolution	2 Group convolution	2 Group convolution
5 × 5-128 filters	5 × 5-128 filters	5 × 5-128 filters	5 × 5-128 filters
Adaptive pooling	Max pooling	Mean pooling	Stochastic pooling
Convolution 3 × 3-384 filters	Convolution 3 × 3-384 filters	Convolution 3 × 3-384 filters	Convolution 3 × 3-384 filters
2 Group convolution	2 Group convolution	2 Group convolution	2 Group convolution
3 × 3-192 filters	3 × 3-192 filters	3 × 3-192 filters	3 × 3-192 filters
2 Group convolution	2 Group convolution	2 Group convolution	2 Group convolution
3 × 3-128 filters	3 × 3-128 filters	3 × 3-128 filters	3 × 3-128 filters
Second order pooling	Max pooling	Mean pooling	Stochastic pooling
3 Fully Connected 4096 4096 6	3 Fully Connected 4096 4096 6	3 Fully Connected 4096 4096 6	3 Fully Connected 4096 4096 6
Softmax	Softmax	Softmax	Softmax

In order to speed up the training process, the initial parameters were set by means of transfer learning. The pre-training parameters in the original Alexnet were applied to the convolution layers of the four models. The training set contained 4212 pictures, and the validation set contained 1200 pictures. Mini-batch method was used in the training process, and mini-batch gradient descent method was used to update parameters. 70 pictures were trained in each batch, with 60 iterations in each round. one verification operation was performed every 10 iterations. The learning rate was set to 5×10^{-4}. The feature selection number of second-order pooling layer was set to 9216. A total of 30 cycles, 1800 iterations, were conducted in the whole process.

4.1. Training and Validation Results

The total loss is a non-negative function used to measure the difference between predicted values and real values. The smaller the total loss is, the better the training effect and robustness are. Figure 11 showed the loss decline of four models in the training process. In order to compare different decline processes conveniently, the initial loss of ASOPCNN was taken as the benchmark, and the loss values of the other models were divided by the benchmark value for unified processing. It can be seen from Figure 11a that the total loss of ASOPCN on the training and verification sets was the smallest, indicating that the training effect of ASOPCN was the best. It can be seen from Figure 11b that the difference between ASOPCN and the other three models was that the loss fluctuation was more obvious. This was because the pooling layers of ASOPCN contained random initial parameters. The quality of these parameters had a greater impact on the training performance. Figure 12 showed the changing process of model accuracy. It can be seen that the change rate of

ASOPCNN was slower than that of STOCNN at the initial stage. With the increase in the iteration number, the rate of ASOPCNN exceeded that of the other three models and became the largest. In order to quantitatively compare the final convergence accuracy, the mean accuracy of the last round was taken as the final accuracy, and the results were shown in Table 3. The ASOPCNN model had the highest accuracy on both training and verification sets, which were 0.9286 and 0.8671, respectively. It showed that adaptive and second-order pooling methods were helpful for optimization of training process.

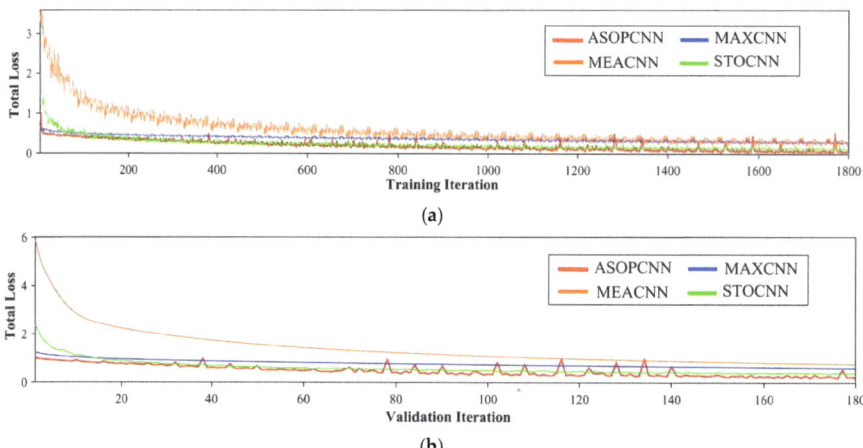

Figure 11. (**a**) The loss decline process of four models on the training set; (**b**) the loss decline process of four models on the verification set.

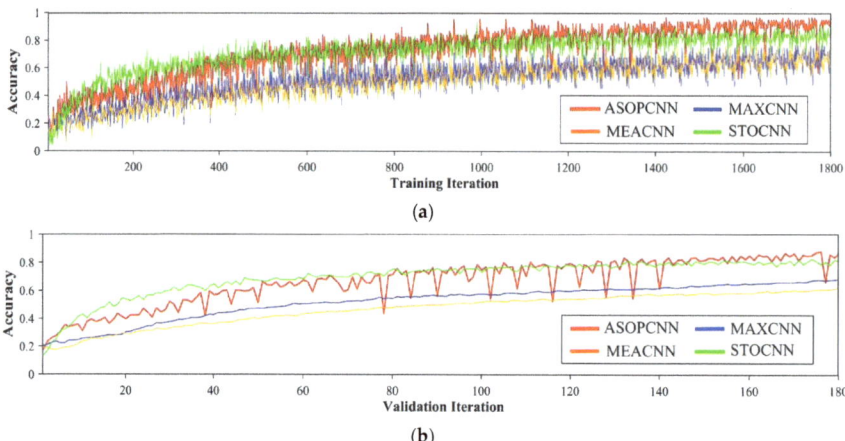

Figure 12. (**a**) The changing process of model accuracy on the training set; (**b**) the changing process of model accuracy on the verification set.

Table 3. The final accuracy on training and verification sets.

Model	ASOPCNN	MAXCNN	MEACNN	STOCNN
Training set	0.9286	0.7086	0.6657	0.8412
Validation set	0.8671	0.6808	0.6163	0.8075

4.2. Testing Results

The performance of models on unknown test sets can represent their actual application effects. There were 586 images of six rock types in the rock image test set. Figure 13 showed the accuracy of the four models on the test set. The accuracy of ASOPCNN was 0.8908, higher than MAXCNN (0.6911), MEACNN (0.6297) and STOCNN (0.7696), indicating that the adaptive and second-order pooling methods were more suitable for CNN than traditional pooling methods. In order to visualize identification results, we randomly selected an image from each rock type in the test set for display, as shown in Figure 14. The identification probability corresponding to each image was shown in Table 4. It can be seen that the identification accuracy of each type of rock images was higher than 0.8, which indicated that the ASOPCN had high identification confidence coefficients and can be used as a reliable model for rock thin section image identification.

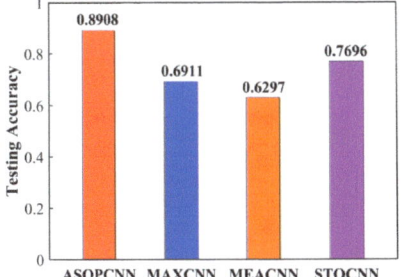

Figure 13. Accuracy of each model on the test set.

Figure 14. Prediction results of partial images on the test set; (**a**) wackestone; (**b**) granite; (**c**) schist; (**d**) quartz sandstone; (**e**) conglomerate; (**f**) crystalline dolomite.

Confusion matrixes can show the identification performance of each specific category. The confusion matrix obtained by the four models was shown in Figure 15. The elements on the diagonal line were correct identification numbers of each rock type. The correct number of rock images identified by ASOPCNN for each type were 99, 81, 76, 83, 90 and 93, which were higher than the other three models. From color depths of elements in the confusion matrix, it can be seen that the probability of misclassification between conglomerate and quartz sandstone was greater. From Figure 14d,e, conglomerate and quartz sandstone were very similar. Their main mineral compositions were quartz and feldspar, and their structures were clastic structures. The main difference was the mineral particle size. The numbers of misclassified samples in each category of the ASOPCNN were less than that of the other three models, indicating that the ASOPCNN can distinguish some image samples that were difficult for the others to a certain extent.

Table 4. Identification probability of rock images in Figure 14, the meaning of digits: 1- wackestone, 2-granite; 3-schist, 4-quartz sandstone, 5-conglomerate, 6-crystalline dolomite.

Rock Category	Wackestone	Granite	Schist	Quartz Sandstone	Conglomerate	Crystalline Dolomite
1	0.9241	0.0156	0.0326	0.0123	0.0062	0.0092
2	0.0658	0.8606	0.0369	0.0223	0.0056	0.0088
3	0.0033	0.0015	0.9341	0.0061	0.0089	0.0461
4	0.0031	0.0026	0.0011	0.9073	0.0030	0.0829
5	0.0023	0.1356	0.0011	0.0010	0.8483	0.0117
6	0.0033	0.0011	0.0010	0.0010	0.0918	0.9028

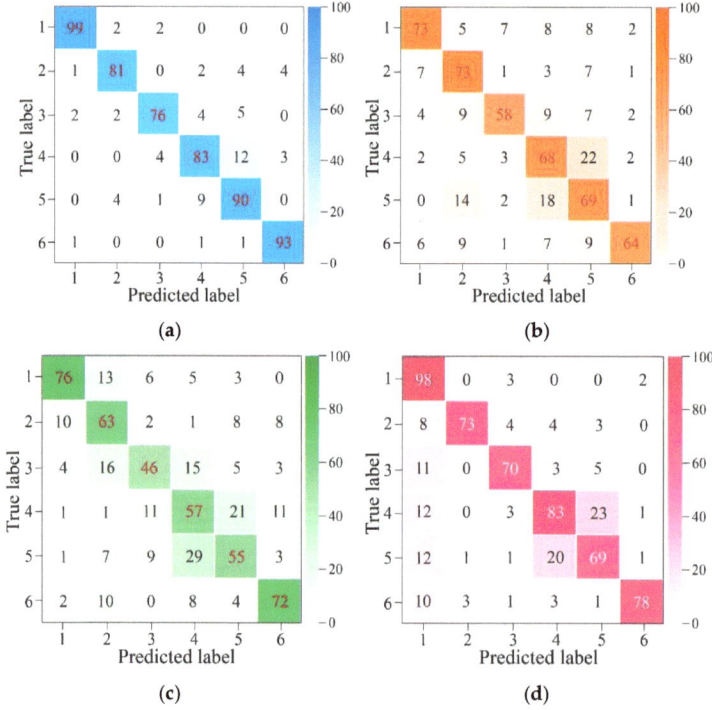

Figure 15. Confusion matrixes of each identification model on the test set, the meaning of digits: 1-wackestone, 2-granite, 3-schist, 4-quartz sandstone, 5-conglomerate, 6-crystalline dolomite. (a) ASOPCNN; (b) MAXCNN; (c) MEACNN; (d) STOCNN.

Figure 16 showed the comparison of the precision, recall and f1 score on the test set. It can be seen that the evaluation indicators of all models showed a similar trend of first falling and then rising, which indicated that the wackestone and crystalline dolomite were easier to identify than the other four types. In Figure 16a, ASOPCNN showed better performance in the recall rate. From Figure 16b, we can see that the precision rates of ASOPCNN in wackstone, schist, sandstone and conglomerate were higher. Figure 15c showed that ASOPCCNN was higher in F1 score. From the above results, it can be seen that ASOPCCNN had superior classification performance on the whole. Figure 17 showed the ROC curve of the four models on six rock categories. It can be seen that the AUC value of the ASOPCN was the highest in the categories of wackestone, schist, quartz sandstone, conglomerate and crystalline dolomite. It indicated that the ASOPCNN had the better performance. In Figure 17b, although the AUC value of the ASOPCNN was lower than that of the STOCNN for the granite category, the correct identification number was greater in Figure 15a,d. It indicated that the identification probability values of ASOPCNN were slightly lower than that of STOCNN.

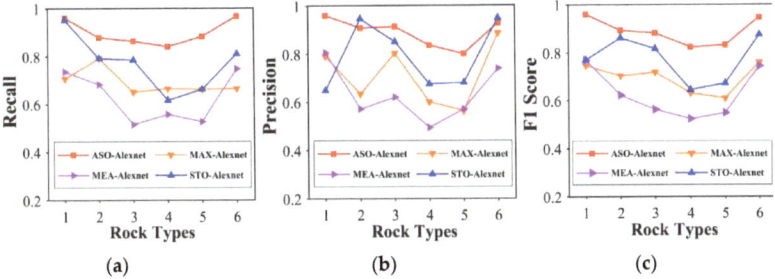

Figure 16. Performance of various rock types evaluated by different metrics, the meaning of digits: 1-wackestone, 2-granite, 3-schist, 4-quartz sandstone, 5-conglomerate, 6-crystalline dolomite. (**a**) Recall rate; (**b**) precision rate; (**c**) F1 score.

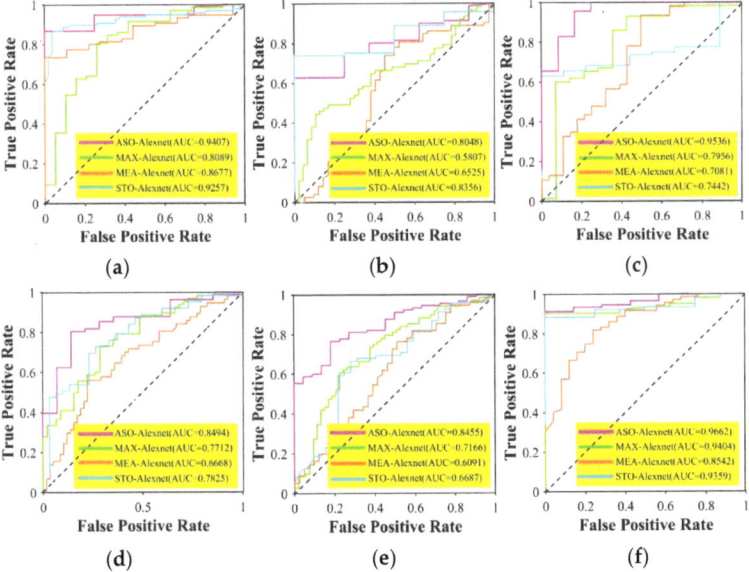

Figure 17. The ROC and AUC values of the four models for six rock categories. (**a**) wackestone; (**b**) granite; (**c**) scholar; (**d**) quartz sandstone; (**e**) conglomerate; (**f**) crystalline dolomite.

4.3. Discussion and Analysis

According to the above results, the pooling layers of CNN can be divided into sampling pooling layers and classification pooling layers, and the adaptive pooling and second-order pooling methods can be used respectively. It can provide better performance than using traditional pooling methods. This was the explain of experimental results. In fact, from the theoretical analysis, the performance of adaptive and second-order pooling methods was generally not worse than traditional pooling methods. This is because the adaptive pooling method can be transformed into the traditional pooling methods through training, and the second-order pooling method completely contains all the information of the traditional pooling methods.

Adaptive pooling can be seen as a collection of multiple pooling methods. In the adaptive pooling method, a pooling kernel was configured for each feature map. The calculation process is expressed as Equation (8). The parameters in the pooling kernel can be adjusted according to propagation errors. When the parameters are equal, the Equation (8) can transform into the Equation (24), representing the average pooling.

$$O = \frac{\sum_{i=1}^{m} \sum_{j=1}^{n} I_{ij}}{m * n} \qquad (24)$$

When there was only one non-zero value in pooling kernels, if the non-zero value corresponded to the maximum value, then the Equation (8) can transform into the Equation (25), representing the max pooling.

$$O = \max\{I_{ij}\}, (i = 1, 2, \ldots, m; j = 1, 2, \ldots, n) \qquad (25)$$

When the non-zero value did not correspond to the maximum value, the Equation (8) can transform into the Equation (26), representing the stochastic pooling.

$$O = rand\{I_{ij}\}, (i = 1, 2, \ldots, m; j = 1, 2, \ldots, n) \qquad (26)$$

When the parameter had more than one non-zero value, the adaptive pooling can also be regarded as other non-special pooling methods. Therefore, the adaptive pooling method can be transformed into the traditional pooling methods through training.

The purpose of classification pooling layer is to integrate feature map information to form a global vector. The integration process of the traditional pooling methods was shown in Figure 8. It only counted first-order feature information. Each feature map was independent and uncorrelated. The integration process of the second-order pooling methods was shown in Figure 18. Second-order pooling was to add more feature information on the basis of guaranteeing the original first-order feature information. Outer products between feature pairs were calculated to obtain second-order correlation. As shown in the yellow diagonal part of the second-order feature block, the diagonal elements were the square of the original first-order feature elements, the feature information carried by them remained unchanged. It can be seen that the first-order feature information extracted by the traditional methods took a small proportion of the information extracted by the second-order pooling method. The upper triangle part of the second-order feature block carried the second-order feature information of feature pairs, which had better feature representation ability than first-order feature information [50]. Therefore, the second-order pooling method completely contained all the information of the traditional pooling methods.

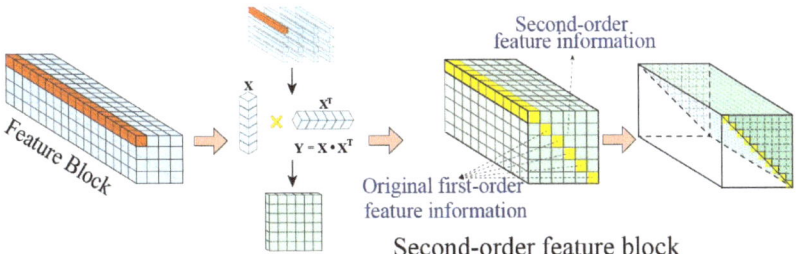

Figure 18. Second-order pooling contained the feature information of traditional pooling methods.

5. Conclusions

In this paper, the shortcomings of traditional pooling methods in the process of rock identification were analyzed, and the adaptive pooling and second-order pooling methods were proposed. The theoretical advantages of these two pooling methods applied to the CNN were analyzed, and then the changing process of forward and back propagation of these two pooling methods was deduced. On the basis of a visual CNN framework, Alexnet, a rock identification model called ASOPCNN was constructed by using the two pooling methods. There were 5998 images for model training, including 6 common rock categories. The rock images were collected from the symposium on Microscopic Images of Rocks in the open-source database, China Scientific Data. Three models were set for comparison, which respectively used the max pooling, average pooling and stochastic pooling methods. The accuracy rate, precision rate, recall rate, F1 score, and AUC values were used to evaluate the model performance. In the results, the total loss of the ASOPCNN is minimum when the training process converges, and the accuracy of ASOPCNN model in training and validation sets are 92.86% and 86.71%, respectively. In the test set of 586 pictures, the identification accuracy of ASOPCNN reaches 89.08%. It is at least 12% higher than the models using traditional pooling methods. The precision rate, recall rate, F1 score and AUC values of the ASOPCNN are 89.33%, 89.07%, 0.8914 and 0.8934, respectively. The experimental results show that the performance of the ASOPCNN is better than the other three models using traditional pooling methods. It also shows that the ASOPCNN could be a reliable model in rock identification of rock thin section images. In addition, among the six rock types in this paper, the wackestone and crystalline dolomite are easier to distinguish than granite, schist, conglomerate and quartz sandstone. Conglomerate and quartz sandstone are more likely to be misclassified because they are similar in mineral compositions and structures. The adaptive and second-order pooling methods were generally not worse than the traditional pooling methods. This is because the adaptive pooling method can be transformed into the traditional pooling methods through training, and the second-order pooling method completely contains all the information of the traditional pooling methods.

Author Contributions: Conceptualization, Z.Z.; Methodology, H.Y.; Supervision, Z.Z. and X.C.; Data curation, H.Y.; Formal analysis, H.Y.; Funding acquisition, Z.Z. and X.C.; Validation, Z.Z. and X.C.; Writing—original draft, H.Y. All authors have read and agreed to the published version of the manuscript.

Funding: This research was supported by the National Key Research and Development Program of China (Grant No.: 2022YFC2903901) and the National Natural Science Foundation of China (Grant No.: 52274249).

Institutional Review Board Statement: Not applicable.

Informed Consent Statement: Not applicable.

Data Availability Statement: The data used in this paper can be obtained from the symposium on Microscopic Images of Rocks in the open-source database, China Scientific Data.

Acknowledgments: We would like to acknowledge the editors and reviewers for their invaluable comments.

Conflicts of Interest: The authors declare no conflict of interest.

Appendix A

The specific derivation process of forward and back propagation of adaptive pooling method is as follows. Since each feature map performs independent but identical pooling operations, only a single feature map is calculated. The feature map

$$x = \begin{bmatrix} x_{11} & x_{12} & \cdots & x_{1a} \\ x_{21} & x_{22} & & x_{2a} \\ \cdots & \cdots & \ddots & \cdots \\ x_{a1} & x_{a2} & \cdots & x_{aa} \end{bmatrix},$$

called the target feature map, is obtained from the convolution layer. The size of the target feature map is a. The adaptive pooling method is used for down sampling operation. The pooling kernel is

$$w = \begin{bmatrix} w_{11} & \cdots & w_{1b} \\ \cdots & \ddots & \cdots \\ w_{b1} & \cdots & w_{bb} \end{bmatrix},$$

where b is the size of the pooling kernel. The result feature map obtained after pooling operation is

$$y = \begin{bmatrix} y_{11} & y_{12} & \cdots & y_{1c} \\ y_{21} & y_{22} & \cdots & y_{2c} \\ \cdots & \cdots & \ddots & \cdots \\ y_{c1} & y_{c2} & \cdots & y_{cc} \end{bmatrix},$$

where c is the size of the result feature map. The element of y can be calculated by Equation (A1).

$$\begin{aligned} y_{11} &= w_{11}x_{11} + w_{12}x_{12} + w_{13}x_{13} + \cdots + w_{33}x_{33} + \cdots\cdots + w_{bb}x_{bb} \\ y_{12} &= w_{11}x_{1,1+s} + w_{12}x_{1,2+s} + w_{13}x_{1,3+s} + \cdots + w_{33}x_{3,3+s} + \cdots\cdots + w_{bb}x_{b,b+s} \\ y_{21} &= w_{11}x_{1+s,1} + w_{12}x_{1+s,2} + w_{13}x_{1+s,3} + \cdots + w_{33}x_{3+s,3} + \cdots\cdots + w_{bb}x_{b+s,b} \\ y_{22} &= w_{11}x_{1+s,1+s} + w_{12}x_{1+s,2+s} + w_{13}x_{1+s,3+s} + \cdots + w_{33}x_{3+s,3+s} + \cdots\cdots + w_{bb}x_{b+s,b+s} \end{aligned} \quad \text{(A1)}$$

The above equations can be equivalently rewritten as a convolution calculation equation as follows.

$$y_{i,j} = \sum_{m=1}^{b} \sum_{n=1}^{b} w_{m,n} \cdot x_{s \cdot (i-1)+m, s \cdot (j-1)+n} \quad \text{(A2)}$$

where x is regarded as a Convolution operator; $y_{i,j}$ represents the element in the row i and column j of the result feature map. During the back propagation, the partial derivative matrix of total loss L to elements of pooling kernels is

$$\delta w_{i,j} = \begin{bmatrix} \delta w_{11} & \cdots & \delta w_{1b} \\ \cdots & \ddots & \cdots \\ \delta w_{b1} & \cdots & \delta w_{bb} \end{bmatrix}.$$

Variables

$$\delta y_{i,j} = \begin{bmatrix} \delta y_{11} & \delta y_{12} & \cdots & \delta y_{1c} \\ \delta y_{21} & \delta y_{22} & \cdots & \delta y_{2c} \\ \cdots & \cdots & \ddots & \cdots \\ \delta y_{c1} & \delta y_{c2} & \cdots & \delta y_{cc} \end{bmatrix} \text{ and } \delta x_{i,j} = \begin{bmatrix} \delta x_{11} & \delta x_{12} & \cdots & \delta x_{1a} \\ \delta x_{21} & \delta x_{22} & \cdots & \delta x_{2a} \\ \cdots & \cdots & \ddots & \cdots \\ \delta x_{a1} & \delta x_{a2} & \cdots & \delta x_{aa} \end{bmatrix}$$

can be obtained from similar definitions. The Equation (A3) can be obtained from the chain derivation rule.

$$\frac{\partial L}{\partial w_{i,j}} = \frac{\partial L}{\partial y_{i,j}} \cdot \frac{\partial y_{i,j}}{\partial w_{i,j}} \quad \text{(A3)}$$

The relationship between $y_{i,j}$ and $w_{i,j}$ is shown in Equation (A1). After the derivation of both sides of Equation (A1), Equation (A4) can be obtained by combining Equation (A3).

$$\begin{aligned}
\delta w_{11} &= \delta y_{11} x_{11} + \delta y_{12} x_{1,1+s} + \delta y_{21} x_{1+s,1} + \delta y_{22} x_{1+s,1+s} + \cdots \\
\delta w_{12} &= \delta y_{11} x_{12} + \delta y_{12} x_{1,2+s} + \delta y_{21} x_{1+s,2} + \delta y_{22} x_{1+s,2+s} + \cdots \\
\delta w_{13} &= \delta y_{11} x_{13} + \delta y_{12} x_{1,3+s} + \delta y_{21} x_{1+s,3} + \delta y_{22} x_{1+s,3+s} + \cdots \\
&\cdots \\
\delta w_{33} &= \delta y_{11} x_{33} + \delta y_{12} x_{3,3+s} + \delta y_{21} x_{3+s,3} + \delta y_{22} x_{3+s,3+s} + \cdots \\
&\cdots \\
\delta w_{bb} &= \delta y_{11} x_{bb} + \delta y_{12} x_{b,b+s} + \delta y_{21} x_{b+s,b} + \delta y_{22} x_{b+s,b+s} + \cdots
\end{aligned} \quad (A4)$$

Equation (A4) can be equivalently written as the following matrix form.

$$\begin{bmatrix} \delta w_{11} & \cdots & \delta w_{1b} \\ \cdots & \ddots & \cdots \\ \delta w_{b1} & \cdots & \delta w_{bb} \end{bmatrix} = \begin{bmatrix} x_{11} & x_{12} & \cdots & x_{1a} \\ x_{21} & x_{22} & \cdots & x_{2a} \\ \cdots & \cdots & \ddots & \cdots \\ x_{a1} & x_{a2} & \cdots & x_{aa} \end{bmatrix} \otimes \begin{bmatrix} \delta y_{11} & 0 & \cdots & 0 & \delta y_{12} & \cdots & \delta y_{1c} \\ 0 & 0 & \cdots & 0 & 0 & \cdots & 0 \\ \cdots & \cdots & \cdots & \cdots & \cdots & \cdots & \cdots \\ 0 & 0 & \cdots & 0 & 0 & \cdots & 0 \\ \delta y_{21} & 0 & \cdots & 0 & \delta y_{22} & \cdots & \delta y_{2c} \\ \cdots & \cdots & \cdots & \cdots & \cdots & \cdots & \cdots \\ \delta y_{c1} & 0 & \cdots & 0 & \delta y_{c2} & \cdots & \delta y_{cc} \end{bmatrix} \quad (A5)$$

The upper equation is recorder as $\delta w_{i,j} = \delta y_{i,j} \otimes A$, where $\otimes$ is the convolution operation symbol. Matrix A is a convolution operator. It is formed by inserting zero vectors with the same dimension between each row and column of the matrix. The number of inserting zero vectors was $s-1$. Through induction and summary, Equation (A5) can be equivalent to the following equation.

$$\delta w_{i,j} = \sum_{m=1}^{c} \sum_{n=1}^{c} x_{s \cdot (m-1)+i, s \cdot (n-1)+j} \cdot \delta y_{m,n} \quad (A6)$$

where $\delta y_{m,n}$ is the convolution operator. Parameters of the pooling kernel can be updated by gradient descent algorithm as follows.

$$w_{i,j} = w_{i,j} - \eta \cdot \delta w_{i,j} \quad (A7)$$

where η is the learning rate. If $w_{i,j} \geq 1$, then $w_{i,j} = 1$; if $w_{i,j} \leq 0$, then $w_{i,j} = 0$. The Equation (A8) can be obtained from the chain derivation rule.

$$\frac{\partial L}{\partial x_{i,j}} = \frac{\partial L}{\partial y_{i,j}} \cdot \frac{\partial y_{i,j}}{\partial x_{i,j}} \quad (A8)$$

To facilitate inductive solution, let $s = 2$. After the derivation of both sides of Equation (A1), Equation (A9) can be obtained by combining Equation (A8).

$$\begin{aligned}
\delta x_{11} &= \delta y_{11} w_{11} \\
\delta x_{12} &= \delta y_{11} w_{12} \\
\delta x_{13} &= \delta y_{11} w_{13} + \delta y_{12} w_{11} \\
&\cdots \\
\delta x_{21} &= \delta y_{11} w_{21} \\
\delta x_{22} &= \delta y_{11} w_{22} \\
\delta x_{23} &= \delta y_{11} w_{23} + \delta y_{12} w_{21} \\
&\cdots \\
\delta x_{31} &= \delta y_{11} w_{31} + \delta y_{21} w_{11} \\
\delta x_{32} &= \delta y_{11} w_{32} + \delta y_{21} w_{12} \\
\delta x_{33} &= \delta y_{11} w_{33} + \delta y_{12} w_{31} + \delta y_{21} w_{13} + \delta y_{22} w_{11} \\
&\cdots \cdots
\end{aligned} \quad (A9)$$

Through induction and summary, Equation (A9) can be equivalently rewritten as the following matrix form in the case of $s = 2$.

$$\begin{bmatrix} \delta x_{11} & \delta x_{12} & \cdots & \delta x_{1a} \\ \delta x_{21} & \delta x_{22} & \cdots & \delta x_{2a} \\ \cdots & \cdots & \ddots & \cdots \\ \delta x_{a1} & \delta x_{a2} & \cdots & \delta x_{aa} \end{bmatrix} = \begin{bmatrix} 0 & 0 & 0 & \cdots & 0 & 0 & 0 \\ 0 & 0 & 0 & \cdots & 0 & 0 & 0 \\ 0 & 0 & w_{11} & \cdots & w_{1b} & 0 & 0 \\ 0 & 0 & \cdots & \ddots & \cdots & 0 & 0 \\ 0 & 0 & w_{b1} & \cdots & w_{bb} & 0 & 0 \\ 0 & 0 & 0 & 0 & 0 & 0 & 0 \\ 0 & 0 & 0 & 0 & 0 & 0 & 0 \end{bmatrix} \otimes \begin{bmatrix} \delta y_{cc} & \cdots & \delta y_{c2} & 0 & \delta y_{c1} \\ \cdots & \ddots & \cdots & & \cdots \\ \delta y_{2c} & \cdots & \delta y_{22} & 0 & \delta y_{21} \\ 0 & & 0 & 0 & 0 \\ \delta y_{1c} & \cdots & \delta y_{12} & 0 & \delta y_{11} \end{bmatrix} \quad (A10)$$

The upper equation is recorded as $\delta x_{i,j} = B \otimes C$. Matrix B is composed of matrix W with an appropriate number of 0 in the outer circle. Matrix C is a convolution operator. It was formed by rotating the matrix elements by 180 degrees and then inserting an appropriate number of zero vectors between every two columns as same as every two rows. The numbers of zero filling in the outer of matrix B and zero vectors inserted in matrix C are related to the pooling step s and the size c of the result feature map. The calculation formula is as follows.

$$\alpha = s(c-1)$$
$$\beta = s-1 \quad (A11)$$

Through induction and summary, Equation (A10) can be equivalent to the Equation (A12).

$$\delta x_{i,j} = \sum_{m=1}^{c} \sum_{n=1}^{c} w_{i-s\cdot m+s, j-s\cdot n+s} \cdot \delta y_{m,n} \cdot f[i - s\cdot(m-1)] \cdot f[j - s\cdot(n-1)] \quad (A12)$$

where $f(x)$ is the judgement function, which equals to 1 while $n < x < b$ and equals to 0 for else.

Appendix B

The specific derivation process of forward and back propagation of second-order pooling method is as follows. The lth original feature map calculated from the last convolution is $x_l = \begin{bmatrix} x_{1,1,l} & x_{1,2,l} & \cdots & x_{1,a,l} \\ x_{2,1,l} & x_{2,2,l} & \cdots & x_{2,a,l} \\ \cdots & \cdots & \ddots & \cdots \\ x_{a,1,l} & x_{a,2,l} & \cdots & x_{a,a,l} \end{bmatrix}$, $(l = 1,2,3,\ldots,s_1)$, where a is the size of the original feature maps; s_1 is the number of feature maps contained. The original feature maps are split from left to right and top to bottom. Then the elements at the same position in all the original feature maps are integrated to form the local first-order feature vector, which is recorded as $A = (x_{i,j,1}, x_{i,j,2}, x_{i,j,3}, \ldots, x_{i,j,s_1})$, $(i,j = 1,2,\ldots,a)$. The outer products of all local first-order feature vectors are calculated according to the following equation.

$$\begin{bmatrix} x_{i,j,1}^2 & x_{i,j,1}x_{i,j,2} & x_{i,j,1}x_{i,j,3} & \cdots & x_{i,j,1}x_{i,j,s_1} \\ x_{i,j,2}x_{i,j,1} & x_{i,j,2}^2 & x_{i,j,2}x_{i,j,3} & \cdots & x_{i,j,2}x_{i,j,s_1} \\ x_{i,j,3}x_{i,j,1} & x_{i,j,3}x_{i,j,2} & x_{i,j,3}^2 & \cdots & x_{i,j,3}x_{i,j,s_1} \\ \vdots & \vdots & \vdots & \ddots & \vdots \\ x_{i,j,s_1}x_{i,j,1} & x_{i,j,s_1}x_{i,j,2} & x_{i,j,s_1}x_{i,j,3} & \cdots & x_{i,j,s_1}x_{i,j,s_1} \end{bmatrix} = (x_{i,j,1},\ldots,x_{i,j,s_1})^T \cdot (x_{i,j,1},\ldots,x_{i,j,s_1}), (i,j = 1,2,\ldots,a) \quad (A13)$$

The above equation is recorded as $y = A^T A$. y is the outer product of the local first-order feature vector, called the second-order feature matrix. The kth second-order feature matrix can also be recorded as $y_k = \begin{bmatrix} y_{1,1,k} & y_{1,2,k} & y_{1,3,k} & \cdots & y_{1,b,k} \\ y_{2,1,k} & y_{2,2,k} & y_{2,3,k} & \cdots & y_{2,b,k} \\ y_{3,1,k} & y_{3,2,k} & y_{3,3,k} & \cdots & y_{3,b,k} \\ \vdots & \vdots & \vdots & \ddots & \vdots \\ y_{b,1,k} & y_{b,2,k} & y_{b,3,k} & \cdots & y_{b,b,k} \end{bmatrix}$,

($k = 1, 2, 3, \ldots, s_2$), where b is the size of the second-order feature matrix; s_2 is the number of feature maps contained. Combining Equation (A13), the relationship between the second-order feature matrixes and the original feature maps can be constructed as follows.

$$y_{i,j,k} = \sum_{m=1}^{a} \sum_{n=1}^{a} x_{m,n,i} \cdot x_{m,n,j} \cdot I[a(m-1) + n = k], (i,j = 1, 2, \ldots, b; k = 1, 2, \ldots, s_2) \quad (A14)$$

where $I(\text{condition})$ is the judgment function. If the condition is met, then $I = 1$; otherwise $I = 0$. It is not difficult to see the following variable relations.

$$\begin{aligned} b &= s_1 \\ s_2 &= a^2 \end{aligned} \quad (A15)$$

The second-order feature matrixes are split from left to right and top to bottom. Then the elements at the same position in all second-order feature matrices are integrated to form the second-order feature vectors, which can be recorded as $B = (y_{i,j,1}, y_{i,j,2}, y_{i,j,3}, \ldots, y_{i,j,s_2})$ ($i, j = 1, 2, 3, \ldots, b$). According to Equation (A15), all second-order feature vectors can be rewritten into matrix form as follows. Because the second-order feature matrixes are symmetric, only the upper triangular part is converted into the corresponding second-order feature vectors.

$$(y_{i,j,1}, y_{i,j,2}, y_{i,j,3}, \ldots, y_{i,j,s_2}) \rightarrow \begin{bmatrix} y_{i,j,1} & y_{i,j,2} & y_{i,j,3} & \cdots & y_{i,j,a} \\ y_{i,j,a+1} & y_{i,j,a+2} & y_{i,j,a+3} & \cdots & y_{i,j,2a} \\ y_{i,j,2a+1} & y_{i,j,2a+2} & y_{i,j,2a+3} & \cdots & y_{i,j,3a} \\ \vdots & \vdots & \vdots & \ddots & \vdots \\ y_{i,j,a(a-1)+1} & y_{i,j,a(a-1)+2} & y_{i,j,a(a-1)+3} & \cdots & y_{i,j,a^2} \end{bmatrix} \quad (A16)$$

The matrix transformed from the second-order feature vector is called the second-order feature map, and the γth second-order feature maps can be recorded as

$$z_\gamma = \begin{bmatrix} z_{1,1,\gamma} & z_{1,2,\gamma} & z_{1,3,\gamma} & \cdots & z_{1,c,\gamma} \\ z_{2,1,\gamma} & z_{2,2,\gamma} & z_{2,3,\gamma} & \cdots & z_{2,c,\gamma} \\ z_{3,1,\gamma} & z_{3,2,\gamma} & z_{3,3,\gamma} & \cdots & z_{3,c,\gamma} \\ \vdots & \vdots & \vdots & \ddots & \vdots \\ z_{c,1,\gamma} & z_{c,2,\gamma} & z_{c,3,\gamma} & \cdots & z_{c,c,\gamma} \end{bmatrix}, (\gamma = 1, 2, 3, \ldots, s_3),$$ where c is the

size of the second-order feature maps; s_3 is the number of feature maps contained. The relationship between the second-order feature maps and the second-order feature matrixes can be constructed by combining Equation (A16).

$$z_{\alpha,\beta,\gamma} = \sum_{k=1}^{s_2} \sum_{i=1}^{b} \sum_{j=1}^{b} y_{i,j,k} \cdot I[b(i-1) + j - \frac{i^2 - i}{2} = \gamma] \cdot I[c(\alpha - 1) + \beta = \gamma], (\alpha, \beta = 1, 2, \ldots, c; \gamma = 1, 2, \ldots, s_3) \quad (A17)$$

It is not difficult to see the following variable relations.

$$\begin{aligned} c &= a \\ s_3 &= \frac{b^2 + b}{2} \end{aligned} \quad (A18)$$

The second order feature matrixes are down sampling to obtain the global feature vector. It can be recorded as $Z = (Z_1, Z_2, Z_3, \ldots, Z_{s_4})$, where s_4 is the number of vectors contained. The calculation equation is as follows.

$$Z_p = \frac{\sum\limits_{\alpha=1}^{c} \sum\limits_{\beta=1}^{c} z_{\alpha,\beta,p}}{\alpha \cdot \beta}, (p = 1, 2, 3, \ldots, s_4) \quad (A19)$$

In the back propagation process, since the entire pooling process doesn't contain parameters, only the derivative of the total loss to each feature map is required. The derivative of the total loss to the global feature vector is $\delta Z = (\delta Z_1, \delta Z_2, \delta Z_3, \ldots, \delta Z_{s_4})$, which is obtained through the fully connected layer. The error of the global feature vector is back propagated to the second-order feature matrixes, and the relationship between them is shown in Equation (A19). Then the error sensitivity in the second-order feature maps, recorded as $\delta z_\gamma = \begin{bmatrix} \delta z_{1,1,\gamma} & \delta z_{1,2,\gamma} & \delta z_{1,3,\gamma} & \cdots & \delta z_{1,c,\gamma} \\ \delta z_{2,1,\gamma} & \delta z_{2,2,\gamma} & \delta z_{2,3,\gamma} & \cdots & \delta z_{2,c,\gamma} \\ \delta z_{3,1,\gamma} & \delta z_{3,2,\gamma} & \delta z_{3,3,\gamma} & \cdots & \delta z_{3,c,\gamma} \\ \vdots & \vdots & \vdots & \ddots & \vdots \\ \delta z_{c,1,\gamma} & \delta z_{c,2,\gamma} & \delta z_{c,3,\gamma} & \cdots & \delta z_{c,c,\gamma} \end{bmatrix}, (\gamma = 1, 2, 3, \ldots, s_3)$, can be calculated as follows.

$$\delta z_{\alpha,\beta,\gamma} = \frac{\delta z_\gamma}{\alpha \cdot \beta}, (\alpha, \beta = 1, 2, 3, \ldots, c; \gamma = 1, 2, 3, \ldots, s_3) \quad (A20)$$

It can be seen from Equation (A16) that the second-order feature maps need to convert into vectors when the error is transmitted from them to the second-order feature vectors. Therefore, the second-order feature maps are converted into the second-order feature vectors in the following way.

$$\begin{bmatrix} \delta z_{1,1,\gamma} & \delta z_{1,2,\gamma} & \delta z_{1,3,\gamma} & \cdots & \delta z_{1,c,\gamma} \\ \delta z_{2,1,\gamma} & \delta z_{2,2,\gamma} & \delta z_{2,3,\gamma} & \cdots & \delta z_{2,c,\gamma} \\ \delta z_{3,1,\gamma} & \delta z_{3,2,\gamma} & \delta z_{3,3,\gamma} & \cdots & \delta z_{3,c,\gamma} \\ \vdots & \vdots & \vdots & \ddots & \vdots \\ \delta z_{c,1,\gamma} & \delta z_{c,2,\gamma} & \delta z_{c,3,\gamma} & \cdots & \delta z_{c,c,\gamma} \end{bmatrix} \rightarrow (\delta z_{1,1,\gamma}, \delta z_{1,2,\gamma}, \ldots, \delta z_{c,c,\gamma}), (\gamma = 1, 2, 3, \ldots, s_3) \quad (A2)$$

All the second-order feature vectors are combined into the second-order feature matrixes in order, and the error remains unchanged. Because the second-order feature matrixes are symmetric and the elements of the lower triangular part of the matrixes are not involved in the calculation, the error of the elements of the lower triangular part equals to 0. The equation for calculating the error sensitivity of the second-order feature matrixes can be deduced as follows by replacing δz with δy in Equation (A22).

$$\delta y_{i,j,k} = \begin{cases} \sum\limits_{\alpha=1}^{c} \sum\limits_{\beta=1}^{c} \delta z_{\alpha,\beta,b(i-1)+j-(i^2-i)/2} \cdot I[b(\alpha-1)+\beta=k], i < j \\ 0, i > j \end{cases} \quad (A22)$$

The second-order feature matrixes back propagate the error to the local first-order feature vectors. The relationship between them is shown in Equation (A13). The error sensitivity of the local first-order feature vectors can be obtained by derivation of Equation (A13). In the process of transforming the local first-order feature vectors into the original feature maps, the element value does not change but the position changes. Finally, the relationship between the error sensitivity of the second-order feature matrixes and original feature maps can be established as follows.

$$\delta x_{m,n,l} = \sum_{i=1}^{b}\sum_{j=1}^{b} \delta y_{i,j,s_2\cdot(m-1)+n} \cdot x_{m,n,j} \cdot I(i=l) \cdot [I(i=m)\cdot I(j=n)+1], (m,n=1,2,\ldots,a; l=1,2,\ldots,s_1) \qquad (A23)$$

References

1. Xu, Z.; Ma, W.; Lin, P.; Hua, Y. Deep learning of rock microscopic images for intelligent lithology identification: Neural network comparison and selection. *J. Rock. Mech. Geotech. Eng.* **2022**, *14*, 1140–1152. [CrossRef]
2. Liu, N.; Huang, T.; Gao, J.; Xu, Z.; Wang, D.; Li, F. Quantum-Enhanced Deep Learning-Based Lithology Interpretation from Well Logs. *IEEE Trans. Geosci. Remote Sens.* **2022**, *60*, 4503213. [CrossRef]
3. Pi, Z.; Zhou, Z.; Li, X.; Wang, S. Digital image processing method for characterization of fractures, fragments, and particles of soil/rock-like materials. *Mathematics* **2021**, *9*, 815. [CrossRef]
4. Zhou, Z.; Lu, J.; Cai, X.; Rui, Y.; Tan, L. Water saturation effects on mechanical performances and failure characteristics of rock-concrete disc with different interface dip angles. *Constr. Build. Mater.* **2022**, *324*, 126684. [CrossRef]
5. Yin, J.; Lu, J.; Tian, F.; Wang, S. Pollutant Migration Pattern during Open-Pit Rock Blasting Based on Digital Image Analysis Technology. *Mathematics* **2022**, *10*, 3205. [CrossRef]
6. Zhou, Z.; Zang, H.; Cao, W.; Du, X.; Chen, L.; Ke, C. Risk assessment for the cascading failure of underground pillar sections considering interaction between pillars. *Int. J. Rock. Mech. Min. Sci.* **2019**, *124*, 104142. [CrossRef]
7. Xue, Y.; Li, X.; Li, G.; Qiu, D.; Gong, H.; Kong, F. An analytical model for assessing soft rock tunnel collapse risk and its engineering application. *Geomech. Eng.* **2020**, *23*, 441–454.
8. Li, D.; Zhao, J.; Ma, J. Experimental Studies on Rock Thin-Section Image Classification by Deep Learning-Based Approaches. *Mathematics* **2022**, *10*, 2317. [CrossRef]
9. Zhang, B. Application of thin section micro-image in identification of rock. *Petrochemical. Ind. Technol.* **2016**, *23*, 108.
10. Xu, C.; Li, L.; Zhang, J.; He, L.; Zhang, G.; Wang, Y. Application of X-ray Fluorescence Spectrometry and Electron Microprobe in the Identification of Intermediate-Felsic Volcanic Rocks. *Rock. Miner. Anal.* **2016**, *35*, 626–633.
11. Singh, N.; Singh, T.; Tiwary, A.; Sarkar, K. Textural identification of basaltic rock mass using image processing and neural network. *Comput. Geosci.* **2010**, *14*, 301–310. [CrossRef]
12. Mlynarczuk, M.; Gorszczyk, A.; Slipek, B. The application of pattern recognition in the automatic classification of microscopic rock images. *Comput. Geosci.* **2013**, *60*, 126–133. [CrossRef]
13. Chatterjee, S. Vision-based rock-type classification of limestone using multi-class support vector machine. *Appl. Intell.* **2013**, *39*, 14–27. [CrossRef]
14. Patel, A.; Chatterjee, S. Computer vision-based limestone rock-type classification using probabilistic neural network. *Geosci. Front.* **2016**, *7*, 53–60. [CrossRef]
15. Zhang, Y.; Li, M.; Han, S.; Ren, Q.; Shi, J. Intelligent Identification for Rock-Mineral Microscopic Images Using Ensemble Machine Learning Algorithms. *Sensors* **2019**, *19*, 3914. [CrossRef] [PubMed]
16. Schmidhuber, J. Deep learning in neural networks: An overview. *Neural Netw.* **2015**, *61*, 85–117. [CrossRef]
17. LeCun, Y.; Bengio, Y.; Hinton, G. Deep learning. *Nature* **2015**, *521*, 436–444. [CrossRef] [PubMed]
18. Esteva, A.; Kuprel, B.; Novoa, R. Dermatologist-level classification of skin cancer with deep neural networks. *Nature* **2017**, *542*, 115–118. [CrossRef]
19. Pan, S.; Yang, Q. A Survey on Transfer Learning. *IEEE Trans. Knowl. Data Eng.* **2010**, *22*, 1345–1359. [CrossRef]
20. Gu, J.; Wang, Z.; Kuen, J.; Ma, L.; Shahroudy, A.; Shuai, B.; Liu, T.; Wang, X.; Wang, G.; Cai, J. Recent advances in convolutional neural networks. *Pattern Recognit.* **2018**, *77*, 354–377. [CrossRef]
21. Bamford, T.; Esmaeili, K.; Schoellig, A. A deep learning approach for rock fragmentation analysis. *Int. J. Rock. Mech. Min. Sci.* **2021**, *145*, 104839. [CrossRef]
22. Wang, P.; Wang, S.; Zhu, C.; Zhang, Z. Classification and extent determination of rock slope using deep learning. *Geomech. Geophys. Geo.* **2020**, *6*, 33. [CrossRef]
23. Li, H.; Hu, Q.; Mao, Y.; Niu, F.; Liu, C. Deep Learning-based Model for Automatic Salt Rock Segmentation. *Rock. Mech. Rock. Eng.* **2022**, *55*, 3735–3747. [CrossRef]
24. Zhao, J.; Wang, F.; Cai, J. 3D tight sandstone digital rock reconstruction with deep learning. *J. Pet. Sci. Eng.* **2021**, *207*, 109020. [CrossRef]
25. Cao, D.; Ji, S.; Cui, R.; Liu, Q. Multi-task learning for digital rock segmentation and characteristic parameters computation. *J. Pet. Sci. Eng.* **2022**, *208*, 109202. [CrossRef]
26. Li, D.; Zhao, J.; Liu, Z. A Novel Method of Multitype Hybrid Rock Lithology Classification Based on Convolutional Neural Networks. *Sensors* **2022**, *22*, 1574. [CrossRef]
27. Polat, O.; Polat, A.; Ekici, T. Automatic classification of volcanic rocks from thin section images using transfer learning networks. *Neural Comput. Appl.* **2021**, *33*, 11531–11540. [CrossRef]
28. Alzubaidi, F.; Mostaghimi, P.; Swietojanski, P.; Clark, S.; Armstrong, R. Automated lithology classification from drill core images using convolutional neural networks. *J. Pet. Sci. Eng.* **2021**, *197*, 107933. [CrossRef]

29. Liu, Y.; Zhang, Z.; Liu, X.; Wang, L.; Xia, X. Deep Learning Based Mineral Image Classification Combined with Visual Attention Mechanism. *IEEE Access* **2021**, *9*, 98091–98109. [CrossRef]
30. Ma, H.; Han, G.; Peng, L.; Zhu, L.; Shu, J. Rock thin sections identification based on improved squeeze-and-Excitation Networks model. *Comput. Geosci.* **2021**, *152*, 104780. [CrossRef]
31. dos Anjos, C.; Avila, M.; Vasconcelos, A.; Neta, A.; Medeiros, L.; Evsukoff, A.; Surmas, R.; Landau, L. Deep learning for lithological classification of carbonate rock micro-CT images. *Comput. Geosci.* **2021**, *25*, 971–983. [CrossRef]
32. Su, C.; Xu, S.; Zhu, K.; Zhang, X. Rock classification in petrographic thin section images based on concatenated convolutional neural networks. *Earth Sci. Inform.* **2020**, *13*, 1477–1484. [CrossRef]
33. Seo, W.; Kim, Y.; Sim, H.; Song, Y.; Yun, T. Classification of igneous rocks from petrographic thin section images using convolutional neural network. *Earth Sci. Inform.* **2022**, *15*, 1297–1307. [CrossRef]
34. Xu, Z.; Shi, H.; Lin, P.; Liu, T. Integrated lithology identification based on images and elemental data from rocks. *J. Pet. Sci. Eng.* **2021**, *205*, 108853. [CrossRef]
35. Saeedan, F.; Weber, N.; Goesele, M.; Roth, S. Detail-Preserving Pooling in Deep Networks. In Proceedings of the IEEE Computer Society Conference on Computer Vision and Pattern Recognition, Salt Lake City, UT, USA, 18–23 June 2018.
36. Li, P.; Xie, J.; Wang, Q.; Zuo, W. Is Second-order Information Helpful for Large-scale Visual Recognition. In Proceedings of the 2017 IEEE International Conference on Computer Vision, Venice, Italy, 22–29 October 2017.
37. Ma, R.; Liu, C.; Yang, J.; Wang, Y.; Liu, J. A Carbonate Microscopic Image Dataset of the Permo-Carboniferous Taiyuan Formation in the Southern Margin of the North China Block. Science Data Bank. Available online: https://www.scidb.cn/en/detail?dataSetId=727517165267189760 (accessed on 15 October 2022).
38. Liu, Y.; Hou, M.; Liu, X.; Qi, Z. A Micrograph Dataset of Buried Hills and Overlying Glutenite in Bozhong Sag, Bohai Bay Basin. Science Data Bank. Available online: https://www.scidb.cn/en/detail?dataSetId=752623639467130880 (accessed on 15 October 2022).
39. Lai, W.; Jiang, J.; Qiu, J.; Yu, J.; Hu, X. Photomicrograph Dataset of Rocks for Petrology Teaching in Nanjing University. Science Data Bank. Available online: https://www.scidb.cn/en/detail?dataSetId=732953783604084736 (accessed on 15 October 2022).
40. Qi, Z.; Hou, M.; Xu, S.; He, L.; Tang, Z.; Zhang, M. A Carbonate Microscopic Image Dataset of Sinian Dengying Period Northwestern Margin of Sichuan Basin. Science Data Bank. Available online: https://www.scidb.cn/en/detail?dataSetId=73212342660399104 (accessed on 15 October 2022).
41. Ma, Q.; Chai, R.; Yang, J.; Du, Y.; Dai, X. A microscopic Image Dataset of Mesozoic Metamorphic Grains Bearing Sandstones from Mid-Yangtze, China. Science Data Bank. Available online: https://www.scidb.cn/en/detail?dataSetId=7275250430634885 (accessed on 15 October 2022).
42. Cai, W.; Hou, M.; Chen, H.; Liu, Y. A Micrograph Dataset of Terrigenous Clastic Rocks of Upper Devonian Lower Carboniferous Wutong Group in Southern Lower Yangtze. Science Data Bank. Available online: https://www.scidb.cn/en/detail?dataSetId=2987889075355648 (accessed on 15 October 2022).
43. Krizhevsky, A.; Sutskever, I.; Hinton, G. ImageNet Classification with Deep Convolutional Neural Networks. *Commun. ACM* **2017**, *60*, 84–90. [CrossRef]
44. Yang, Z.; He, B.; Liu, Y.; Wang, D.; Zhu, G. Classification of rock fragments produced by tunnel boring machine using convolutional neural networks. *Autom. Constr.* **2021**, *125*, 103612. [CrossRef]
45. Yu, Z.; Dai, S.; Xing, Y. Adaptive Salience Preserving Pooling for Deep Convolutional Neural Networks. In Proceedings of the 2019 IEEE International Conference on Multimedia and Expo Workshops, Shanghai, China, 8–12 July 2019.
46. Carreira, J.; Caseiro, R.; Batista, J.; Sminchisescu, C. Free-form region description with second-order pooling. *IEEE Trans. Pattern Anal. Mach. Intell.* **2015**, *37*, 1177–1189. [CrossRef]
47. Zhou, J.; Huang, S.; Wang, M.; Qiu, Y. Performance evaluation of hybrid GA–SVM and GWO–SVM models to predict earthquake-induced liquefaction potential of soil: A multi-dataset investigation. *Eng. Comput.* **2021**, *38*, 4197–4215. [CrossRef]
48. Zhou, J.; Huang, S.; Zhou, T.; Armaghani, D.; Qiu, Y. Employing a genetic algorithm and grey wolf optimizer for optimizing RF models to evaluate soil liquefaction potential. *Artif. Intell. Rev.* **2022**, *55*, 5673–5705. [CrossRef]
49. Zhou, J.; Huang, S.; Qiu, Y. Optimization of random forest through the use of MVO, GWO and MFO in evaluating the stability of underground entry-type excavations. *Tunn. Undergr. Space. Technol.* **2022**, *124*, 104494. [CrossRef]
50. Li, P.; Xie, J.; Wang, Q.; Gao, Z. Towards Faster Training of Global Covariance Pooling Networks by Iterative Matrix Square Root Normalization. In Proceedings of the IEEE Computer Society Conference on Computer Vision and Pattern Recognition, Salt Lake City, UT, USA, 18–23 June 2018.

Disclaimer/Publisher's Note: The statements, opinions and data contained in all publications are solely those of the individual author(s) and contributor(s) and not of MDPI and/or the editor(s). MDPI and/or the editor(s) disclaim responsibility for any injury to people or property resulting from any ideas, methods, instructions or products referred to in the content.

Article

Investigation of Transfer Learning for Tunnel Support Design

Michai Mitelman and Alon Urlainis *

Department of Civil Engineering, Ariel University, Ariel 40700, Israel
* Correspondence: alonu@ariel.ac.il

Abstract: The potential of machine learning (ML) tools for enhancing geotechnical analysis has been recognized by several researchers. However, obtaining a sufficiently large digital dataset is a major technical challenge. This paper investigates the use of transfer learning, a powerful ML technique, used for overcoming dataset size limitations. The study examines two scenarios where transfer learning is applied to tunnel support analysis. The first scenario investigates transferring knowledge between a ground formation that has been well-studied to a new formation with very limited data. The second scenario is intended to investigate whether transferring knowledge is possible from a dataset that relies on simplified tunnel support analysis to a more complex and realistic analysis. The technical process for transfer learning involves training an Artificial Neural Network (ANN) on a large dataset and adding an extra layer to the model. The added layer is then trained on smaller datasets to fine-tune the model. The study demonstrates the effectiveness of transfer learning for both scenarios. On this basis, it is argued that, with further development and refinement, transfer learning could become a valuable tool for ML-related geotechnical applications.

Keywords: artificial neural networks; geotechnical engineering; machine-learning; transfer learning; tunnel support

MSC: 00A69

1. Introduction

The extent of support in tunneling projects has a major impact on overall project costs [1]. However, tunnel support analysis still relies on rather crude estimations, due to the current knowledge gaps in geological engineering [2]. The potential of machine learning (ML) for revolutionizing various engineering disciplines has garnered significant attention in recent research. ML is well suited for increasing predictive power by detecting hidden patterns in large datasets [3]. Indeed, a growing number of papers on ML applications for tunnel applications have been published.

Despite their promise, ML methods have significant limitations. The amount of data required cannot be determined beforehand, and it is required to collect, train, and test data until ML model performance is deemed satisfactory [4]. As a result, stakeholders may be reluctant to invest in large-scale ML research projects as results cannot be guaranteed. For geotechnical applications it is difficult to obtain high-quality data, as monitoring devices that deliver reliable data are costly. In addition to the cost of instrumentation, handling the data requires managerial efforts and costs, including careful labeling of all data, inspection, and interpretation.

Another significant shortcoming of ML models is that they perform poorly when used outside the range of data they have been trained on. Therefore, a fundamental question remains regarding the prospect of extrapolating knowledge from one study to other sites and projects. The pressure induced upon tunnel support is impacted by numerous geological phenomena, such as tectonic pressures, folds, shear zones, groundwater, and more [5]. Due to the heterogeneous nature of geological materials, this question holds even for a single tunneling project, as uncertainty remains for each advancement step of tunneling.

Considering these two limitations of ML, the concept of transfer learning is of primary interest. Transfer learning is a novel ML technique where an existing model based on a large dataset is used for a related but different task [6]. Currently, transfer learning is used primarily for image recognition tasks via deep learning [7].

In this paper, the implementation of transfer learning is investigated in the context of tunnel engineering for two objectives. The first is the simulation of a sudden change in ground conditions during a tunneling project, as illustrated conceptually in Figure 1. For this scenario, it is assumed that the initial ground has been sufficiently monitored and studied, and only a limited amount of data has been collected for the newly encountered (unstudied) ground. Accordingly, it is investigated whether transfer learning can overcome the shortage of data for the unstudied ground.

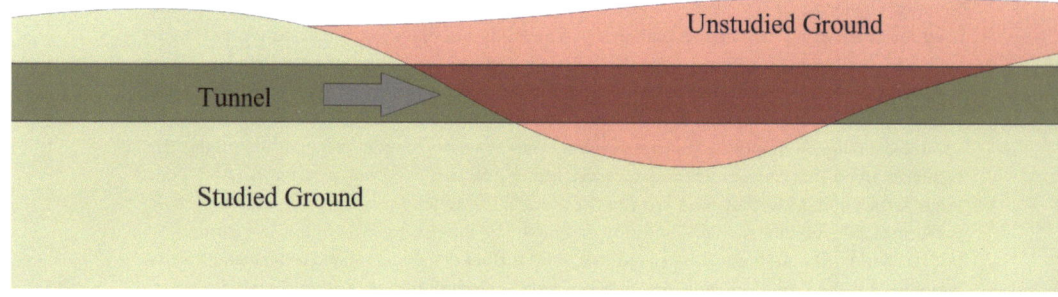

Figure 1. Illustration of sudden change in ground conditions.

The second study aims to investigate whether learning can be transferred from simple to more complex data. For this purpose, two datasets are created: (1) a large dataset from a simplified hydrostatic stress field analysis, and (2) a small dataset from a more complex and realistic non-hydrostatic loading. Successful implementation of transfer learning on these tasks can be interpreted as an indication that simpler artificial data can be used to augment the more complex real-world data, as illustrated in Figure 2. Potentially, data generated via numerical simulations could be used to pre-train an initial ML-model and transferred to learn the data collected in-situ. This could help overcome the technical limitation of the size of data needed for ML, as a vast amount of artificial data can be generated from FE models with minimal costs. As stated in Figure 2, whether the results of the current study apply to the transfer of knowledge to real-world settings requires further work.

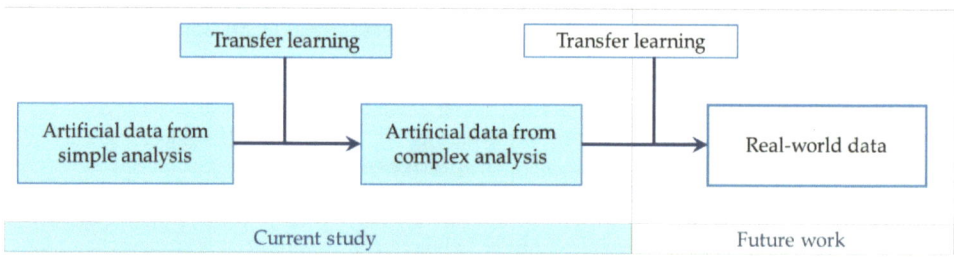

Figure 2. Illustration of the potential of the current study for future application to real-world settings.

Hereinafter, the paper is organized as the following:
- First, a brief review of the relevant background information for tunnel support analysis and ML is provided.
- Second, the methodology and implementation of transfer learning for the simulation of the first scenario of a change in ground conditions is presented.

- Third, following the same methodology as the first scenario, the implementation of transfer learning from simple to complex tunnel support analysis is presented.
- Fourth, the results of both investigations are presented and discussed.
- Finally, the conclusions and limitations of the current work are summarized.

2. Background Information

2.1. Tunnel Support Analysis

A number of different approaches are regularly used in conjunction for the stability analysis of tunnels, including analytical, empirical, and numerical methods. Analytical methods are limited to a set of simplifying assumptions that allow for a precise mathematical solution, and empirical methods are limited to the settings of their case studies [8]. In contrast, numerical methods based on the finite-element (FE) method are capable of simulating irregular geometries and complex material models. However, the assessment of ground strength parameters often relies on empirical methods and subjective judgment.

An analytical approach which is widely studied and used for tunnel support analysis is the convergence-confinement (CC) method. The CC method is based on three main independent components:

1. The ground convergence curve
2. The support curve (confinement)
3. Initial displacement prior to the support

Numerous solutions for ground (or tunnel) convergence curves and for support response have been published ([9–11]). These solutions assume mainly elastoplastic Mohr–Coulomb behavior and vary primarily by their post-peak behavior, as well as modifications for other unique conditions. The CC method is used primarily for weak rock tunneling, but can be applied to other interaction problems, such as room and pillar mining [12].

Once both the tunnel convergence and support curves are plotted, their point of intersection shows the final displacement of the supported tunnel. Inevitably, some displacement occurs prior to support installation. This initial displacement occurs mainly on the longitudinal distance between the tunnel face and point of support installation. In the CC plot, this initial displacement dictates the origin of the support curve. For the current work, it has been assumed that the support is installed at the tunnel face. Note that some initial displacement occurs even at the tunnel face [13]. Figure 3 shows an example of a CC plot, where the point of curve intersection defines the system-equilibrium displacement by its reflection on the horizontal axis. This figure has been generated via the commercial program RocSupport which relies on the CC approach [14]. The parameters that dictate the slope of the ground response curve are the ground's Young's-modulus and uniaxial strength. The former determines the initial slope of the curve, and the latter dictates the point of transition to a non-linear curve. Post-peak behavior is computed according to the development of a plastic radius around the tunnel contour.

In order to obtain closed-form solutions of GRCs, the simplifying assumption of axisymmetric conditions is made. The axisymmetric assumption requires that the shape of the tunnel is circular and that the in-situ stress field is hydrostatic (i.e., the vertical stresses are equal to the horizontal stresses). Hence, the displacement of the tunnel is uniform. While many tunnels are circular, the assumption of a hydrostatic stress field is an over-simplification of reality, as it neglects significant phenomena such as ground arching and liner bending [15]. Figure 4 shows an example of the stress field and deformation for hydrostatic and non-hydrostatic loading conditions, generated via the RS2 program.

Compared to FE modeling, the CC approach has the advantage of explicitly providing a factor of safety, which is useful for design purposes. However, there are available methods for enhancing FE analysis to include stability assessment, such as the FE limit analysis [16,17].

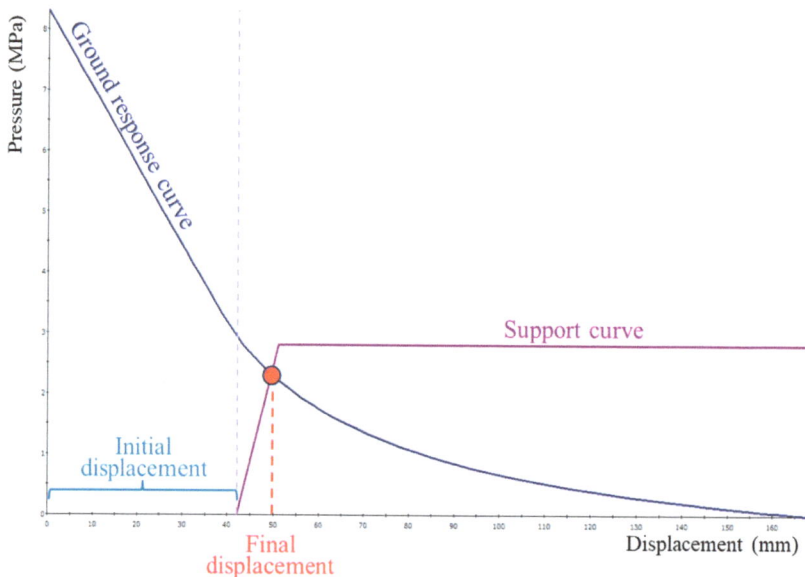

Figure 3. Example of CC plot generated via the program RocSupport.

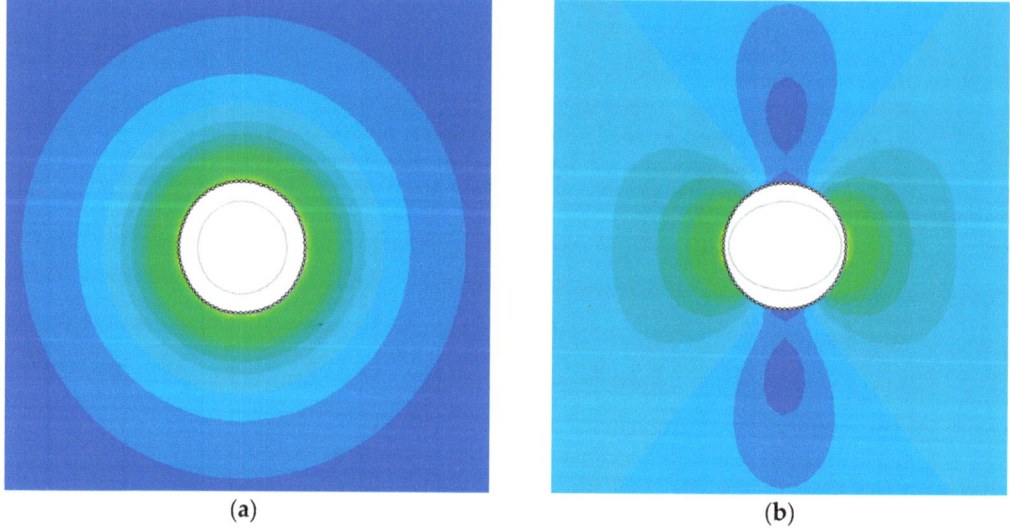

Figure 4. Stress distribution and tunnel deformation for (**a**) hydrostatic loading, and (**b**) non-hydrostatic loading.

2.2. Machine-Learning

The immense advancement of computing power and digital data ML algorithms have emerged as powerful computational tools for applications that require the analysis of large sets of data. ML has been recognized as a potential tool for revolutionizing the field of geological engineering by collecting extensive field data via digital instrumentation and correlating it to various measurable ground responses [18]. The main obstacles of actualizing many potential applications of ML for such research projects is related to the acquisition of data. The cost of monitoring device installation is great and, in many projects, limited reliable data are generated. Moreover, the generated data often require extensive efforts to prepare the data for ML.

Another potential use of ML involves coupling it with artificial data generated by numerical modeling. This type of coupling is often referred to as surrogate modeling. An excellent review of the concept of surrogate models is presented by [19]. Surrogate models allow for fast and rigorous data analysis and help provide insights that may otherwise remain unrecognized.

There are many available models for ML, each with pros and cons. Artificial neural networks (ANNs) are a collection of nodes that receive input numbers and pass on some other number to the subsequent nodes on the network. Using a training process referred to as back-propagation, the values in each node are adjusted to minimize the error between the inputs and outputs. ANNs allow for the identification of subtle patterns in large and complex datasets. However, ANNs generally perform poorly on small datasets and simpler ML methods, such as random forest (RF), are more suitable for training small datasets [20]. RF is an ensemble method where multiple decision trees are assessed, and the correlation between input and output data is established according to a majority vote. RFs are robust methods and have been found to perform well for small datasets [21]. Another advantage of RFs compared to ANNs is that they are less sensitive to hyper-parameters and therefore require less fine-tuning.

Transfer learning is a technique in ML that allows for extracting knowledge obtained from a large dataset and transferring it to different but related task with a smaller dataset. Ref. [22] provide an intuitive illustration of this concept: learning how to play the piano would demand less effort if the person already knows to play the guitar. The major benefit of this technique is overcoming the limitation of dataset size. There are other benefits to transfer learning, including reducing overfitting and decreasing the time and computational resources required to train a model. Transfer learning is regularly achieved by freezing the initial ANN. Subsequently, the training process for the smaller dataset is executed either by starting with the initialized weights and biases from the original model or by adding an additional layer and fitting it to the new data. For the current paper, the second method is used.

Different researchers have demonstrated the use of coupling ML tools with geotechnical analysis. For example, ref. [23] analyzed numerical models of tunnels with ANNs in order to investigate the stability of the tunnel face. Ref. [19] used ML models to investigate different problems with rock mechanics. However, it is important to remember the limitations of such applications, as ML is used to enhance and accelerate numerical modeling, rather than discovering new knowledge. Ref. [18] discusses the opportunities of utilizing in-situ data from tunnels and mines for overcoming knowledge gaps in rock mechanics.

Transfer learning has been applied to several fields [22]. A number of researchers have recently published works where transfer learning is used for tunnel engineering applications. Zhou et al. [24] proposed applying transfer learning for predicting tunneling-induced surface settlements. Ref. [25] used a transfer learning technique to extract knowledge from historical databases for predicting cutterhead torque in TBMs. Ref. [26] studied the application of transfer learning for an image recognition task to classify cracks in tunnel liners.

3. Transfer Learning for Change in Ground Conditions

In order to examine the problem described in the introduction and illustrated in Figure 1, the following scenario was assumed. A circular tunnel with a 14 m diameter is to be driven through weak ground. Tunnel liner elements are 450 mm thick and made of concrete with 45 MPa uniaxial strength. While the majority of the ground is anticipated to be from a single geological formation, it is likely that unknown formations will be encountered. In this case, it is important to respond promptly and implement the appropriate measure (e.g., reinforcement of the ground or support, stopping excavation, etc.). The in-situ stresses are mainly tunnel depth and soil weight and are assumed to vary as well.

Table 1 lists the statistics (minimum, mean, and maximum) of the soil input parameters used for three datasets, denoted DS1, DS2, and DS3. These datasets represent three varying soil formations according to the following rationale:

- DS1—represents a soil where a significant amount of data has been collected and consists of 200 rows of input parameters.
- DS2—represents a new soil formation with only 25 rows of input parameters. This soil is slightly weaker than DS1, with a significant overlap of parameter range compared to DS1.
- DS3—represents a new soil with a small dataset, similar to DS2. In contrast to DS2, DS3 has very little overlap with DS1 parameters.

Table 1. Dataset #1 (DS1), #2 (DS2), and #3 (DS3) input parameter range and tunnel displacements computed via the CC method.

		Friction Angle	Cohesion	In-Situ Stress	Uniaxial Strength	Young's Modulus	Tunnel Displacement
	Units:	Degrees	MPa	MPa	Mpa	Mpa	mm
DS1 (n = 200)	Min.	22.5	0.35	8	1.05	524	34
	Mean	30	0.5	10	1.73	1053	122
	Max.	37.5	0.65	12	2.64	1582	504
DS2 (n = 25)	Min.	20	0.3	8	0.86	383	124
	Mean	25	0.35	9	1.08	510	308
	Max.	30	0.4	10	1.37	660	627
DS3 (n = 25)	Min.	40	0.1	6	0.43	339	43
	Mean	45	0.15	7	0.72	574	97
	Max.	50	0.2	8	1.10	809	190

With respect to the soil parameters listed in Table 1, the friction angle, cohesion, and in-situ stress are assumed, and the uniaxial strength and Young's modulus are computed according to the relationships given in Equations (1) and (2):

$$\sigma = \frac{2 * c * \cos\varnothing}{1 - \sin\varnothing} \quad (1)$$

$$E = MR * \sigma \quad (2)$$

where σ is the soil uniaxial strength, c is the cohesion, $\varnothing$ is the friction angle, E is the Young's modulus, and MR is an empirical modulus ratio. Note that a modulus ratio is usually used for rock mechanics applications [27], and laboratory and field tests are usually used for Young's modulus estimation for soil. This simple linear relationship is used here for the sake of simplicity. However, in order to add another degree of noise, MR is randomly varied using different ranges for each dataset.

The tunnel displacements are computed using the CC method. The commercial program RocSupport was developed to allow for rapid calculation of tunnel displacements and support pressures according to different conditions and methods [28]. A Python script was written to automate the computation process of this program and calculate the tunnel displacements for each set of input parameters. The solution derived by [29] is used for the ground response curves. As part of the CC solving process, the plastic radius around the tunnel is computed. The mathematical derivation of the plastic radius is given by [13]. Ultimately, each dataset consists of an input matrix of four parameters in each row: in-situ stress, uniaxial strength, Young's modulus, and the resultant plastic radius. The output parameter is a column vector that consists of the corresponding tunnel displacements.

All ML programming is carried out in Python via the Keras open-source library [7]. In order to investigate the effect of transfer learning, an initial ANN referred to as NN1 is trained on DS1, to be later modified to predict the smaller datasets DS2 and DS3. This training process involves fitting the input parameter matrix to the tunnel displacement column vector. Subsequently, NN2 and NN3 are created in order to transfer the learning from DS1 to DS2 and DS3, respectively.

The technical procedure for transfer learning undertaken in this paper is illustrated in Figure 5. Figure 5a shows the four nodal inputs, which are the input parameters from each row of DS1. These inputs are passed to the hidden nodes. The arrows in the figure represent dense connections, i.e., the output of each neuron in the subsequent layer is based on the input from each neuron in the preceding layer. In ML practice, the optimal number of hidden neurons cannot be pre-determined. Therefore, it is customary to compare different network architectures and select the one that is most accurate. After the hidden nodes and other hyper-parameters are fine-tuned and the accuracy of ANN is found to be sufficient, NN1 is stored in its final numerical configuration.

Figure 5b shows the second ANN, NN2, for the transfer learning task. For the current analysis, the blue nodes (sometimes referred to as neurons) represent the network components of the smaller dataset, i.e., DS2 or DS3. A new ANN for transfer learning is created and referred to as NNT. For this purpose, the inputs and outputs for the smaller dataset are connected through NN1 and an additional hidden layer that precedes the output node. NN1 is frozen in its original state, whereas the additional layer is subject to fine-tuning.

In order to investigate the effect of noisy data, a Gaussian generator was used. After computing results with no noise, the computation was repeated with noise standard deviations (NSD) of 5% and 10% that were added to all inputs and outputs in each dataset.

A number of metrics are available for evaluating ML performance, including the coefficient of determination, mean absolute error, and root-mean-square error (RMSE), among others. For example, RMSE = 50 mm would indicate that, on average, the model's predictions deviate by 50 mm from the actual results. In order to provide an intuition for ML model performance and RMSE, a model that always predicts the mean displacement is generated and the corresponding RSME is found to equal approximately 70 mm.

Fine-tuning ANN architecture and hyper-parameters is a subject of ongoing research [30]. Hyper-parameters are the parameters that are not part of the studied problem but impact the learning process. There are different methods for selecting the optimal combination of hyper-parameters, the simplest being manual tweaking. However, manual adjustments based on trial and error are time consuming and are also less likely to lead to optimal results. A grid search is a rigorous method where different combinations of hyper-parameters are examined. Advanced methods include the application of optimization algorithms, such as the genetic algorithm. The effort invested in the fine-tuning process is dependent on the level of accuracy required for the specific application. For the current work, the objective of the analysis is largely for the sake of evaluating transfer learning success rather than obtaining very high accuracy. The method used was a random search where, through an iterative process, the ANN was repeatedly computed with randomly varied hyper-parameters. The number of layers, number of nodes in each layer, learning rate, batch size, activation function, and regularization strength were varied in each iteration, and the corresponding RMSE was found. In this study, a single hidden layer of nodes performed better than two and three layers. The hyper-parameters selected for NN1 with no noise were 16 nodes, a learning rate of 0.001, a regularization strength of 1%, a batch size of 32, and the softplus activation function. These hyper-parameters were slightly modified for the noisy datasets. For NT, where an additional layer was added, minimal fine-tuning was carried out, as only the number of nodes and batch size were altered.

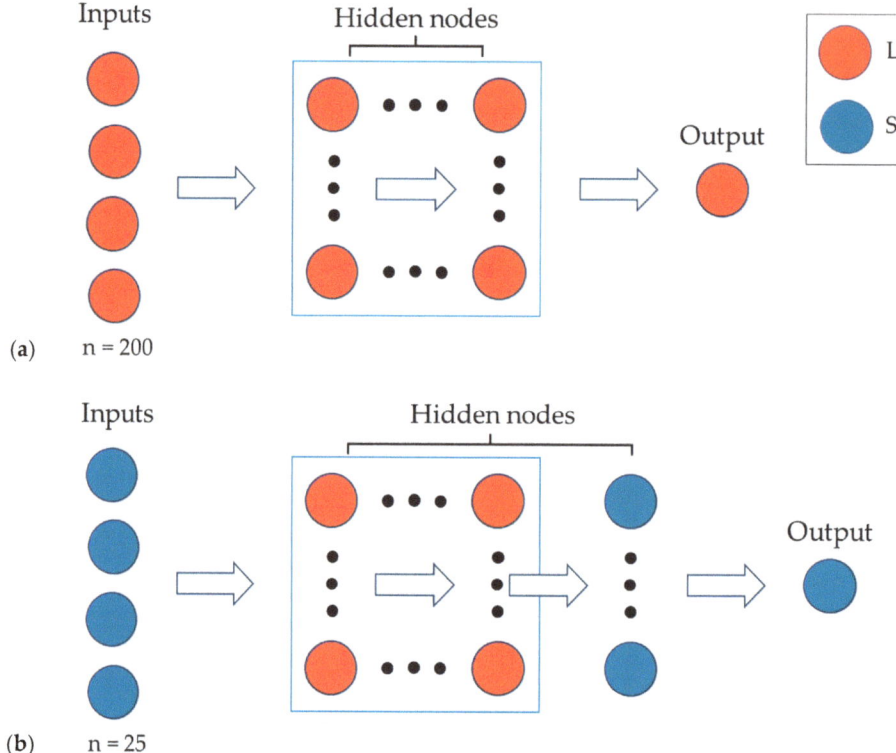

Figure 5. Illustration of (**a**) original ANN (NN1) and (**b**) NN1 transferred and modified to a new ANN (NNT). The red and blue nodes represent the network components of the large and small datasets, correspondingly.

4. Transfer Learning for Simple to Complex Analysis

The hydrostatic assumption (i.e., horizontal to vertical stress ratio $K = 1$) made for the CC method is a significant simplification with respect to reality, as discussed in Section 2.1. In this section, a large dataset, DS1, made of 200 rows, is created according to the hydrostatic loading assumption, representative of simplistic analysis. Similar to the previous section, two small datasets of 25 rows are created where more realistic non-hydrostatic loading conditions are applied. For both small datasets, DS2 and DS3, the K ratio varies from 0.3 to 0.7. With respect to the ground strength parameters, DS2 is identical to the large dataset DS1, and DS3 consists of a different range of strength parameters. Table 2 shows the variation of the input parameters and displacements for the datasets.

Displacement results computed with the CC method and from FE models with hydrostatic loading may differ for various reasons. Hence, for the current analysis, all the results were computed with the commercial FE code RS2 [28]. Figure 6 shows the model geometry and mesh. For all datasets, the tunnel diameter is 14 m, the liner thickness is 450 mm, and the vertical stress is 10 MPa. In order to account for the initial displacement prior to support installation, the FE model loading is staged, where 30% (i.e., 3 MPa) of the load is applied upon the unsupported tunnel in the first stage, and 70% (i.e., 7 MPa) is activated on the supported tunnel in the second stage.

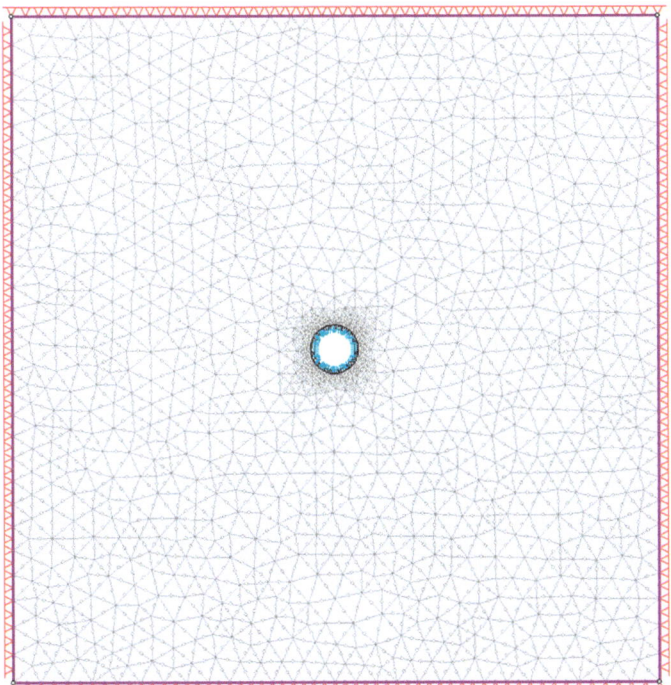

Figure 6. FE model geometry.

Table 2. Range of input parameters and tunnel displacement for the datasets.

		Friction Angle	Cohesion	Young's Modulus	Tunnel Displacement
Units:		Degrees	MPa	MPa	mm
DS1 (n = 200) DS2 (n = 25)	Min.	20	0.35	500	35
	Mean	30	0.5	1000	64
	Max.	40	0.65	1500	139
DS3 (n = 25)	Min.	20	0.15	1000	37
	Mean	30	0.3	1500	71
	Max.	40	0.45	2000	140

Ultimately, each dataset consists of an input matrix of four parameters in each row: in-situ stress, uniaxial strength, Young's modulus, and the K ratio. Note that the plastic radius is not included as a feature for this analysis because this parameter is only valid for hydrostatic loading. For the non-hydrostatic loading, the plastic zone around the tunnel is not circular. In addition, for non-hydrostatic loading, the displacements vary along the tunnel contour. The maximum displacements occur at the tunnel crown and are passed to the output column vector.

The methodology for ML analysis undertaken in the previous section is generally repeated for the current investigation. In brief, DS1 is trained with NN1, and transfer learning is carried out with NNT. NNT is created by freezing NN1 and adding an additional layer. The process for adding noise is identical to the previous section. In order to gain an intuition of the RMSE, a model that predicts the mean displacement for every instance was generated, and an RMSE of 55 mm was yielded.

Based on a randomized search, hyper-parameters were selected for NN1. In this process, it was found that two hidden layers perform better than a single hidden layer. Accordingly, the following hyper-parameters were selected for the ANN with no noise: 32 nodes for the first and second hidden layer, a learning rate of 0.0001, a batch size of 16, and the ReLU and Tanh activation functions. The hyper-parameters selected for NNT are 16 nodes in the additional layer and a batch size of four. These hyper-parameters were slightly modified for the noisy datasets.

5. Results

In order to determine whether transfer learning is effective, two conditions must be satisfied:
1. The accuracy of N1 predictions on the small datasets DS2 and DS3
2. The accuracy of a new ML model for predicting DS2 and DS3

With respect to the first condition, it was found that even after fine-tuning of the hyper-parameters, ANNs failed to provide valid predictions for the smaller datasets in both investigated scenarios. In addition, RF models, considered ideal for small datasets, also performed poorly on this task.

In order to examine whether the second condition is satisfied, the RMSE was computed for DS2 and DS3 with NN1 and NNT. Since small datasets are prone to high variance, two additional datasets of 25 rows were generated, and the mean RMSE was taken according to an average of both results.

The results of the analysis for the first scenario (i.e., change in ground conditions) are listed in Table 3. Results demonstrate that implementation of transfer learning leads to a significant improvement in accuracy for both datasets and under every NSD. Figure 7a,b show the predictions and actual displacements for a sample of 10 rows from DS3 with NSD = 5% computed with NN1 (without transfer learning) and NT (with transfer learning), respectively.

Table 3. Summary of performance of ANNs under different noise standard deviations (NSD).

		RMSE [mm]		
ML-Model	Dataset	NSD = 0%	NSD = 5%	NSD = 10%
NN1	DS1	14	16	19
NN1	DS2	102	95	106
NNT	DS2	41	56	65
NN1	DS3	37	40	39
NNT	DS3	21	22	24

As mentioned, it is important to bear in mind that ANNs are susceptible to errors and inconsistencies, as they are highly influenced by hyper-parameters [7]. Moreover, other sources of randomness (e.g., random weight initialization) may alter the results of ANNs, even without changing hyper-parameters. Such inconsistencies can be observed in Table 3 itself, as the RMSE is expected to increase with increasing noise, yet this is not always the case.

For the second scenario (i.e., learning from hydrostatic to non-hydrostatic conditions) results are listed in Table 4. Results show that transfer learning improves ML performance for both datasets and for every NSD. Compared to the analysis conducted for the first scenario, the relative RMSE of the small datasets is greater (see Table 3). A possible explanation for the greater error in the current analysis is that the tunnel behavior is substantially different under hydrostatic conditions. In contrast, in the previous analysis only the ground properties were changed. In addition, the omission of the plastic radius feature that does not apply to the current analysis may also have a negative impact on ML performance.

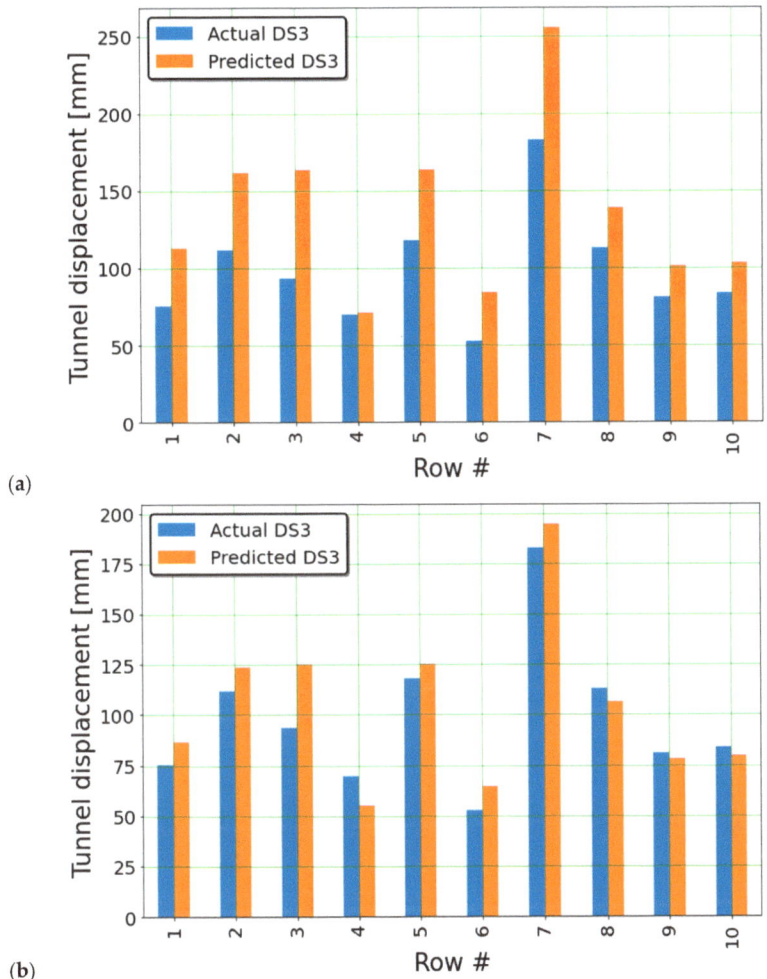

Figure 7. Prediction vs. actual tunnel displacements for DS3 with NSD = 5% computed with (**a**) NN1, i.e., no transfer learning, and (**b**) NNT, i.e., with transfer learning.

Comparing the RMSE of NN1 and NNT for DS2 and DS3 shows that transfer learning brings improved correlation in of the instances. Figure 8 shows an example of predictions vs. actual displacements with and without transfer learning for DS3 with NSD = 10%. The benefit of transfer learning is apparent in the figure. This finding indicates that there is potential for artificial data to enhance real-world data. However, these results should be interpreted with caution, as real-world data is likely noisier and more complex compared to the current data. Indeed, more work is required where artificial data and real-world data are analyzed.

Comparing NNT performance on DS2 and DS3, the latter was found to be more accurate. This is somewhat counter-intuitive, as different ground parameters are assigned to DS3. This reflects upon the black-box nature of ML, as the internal learning process of ANNs is not interpretable to the user.

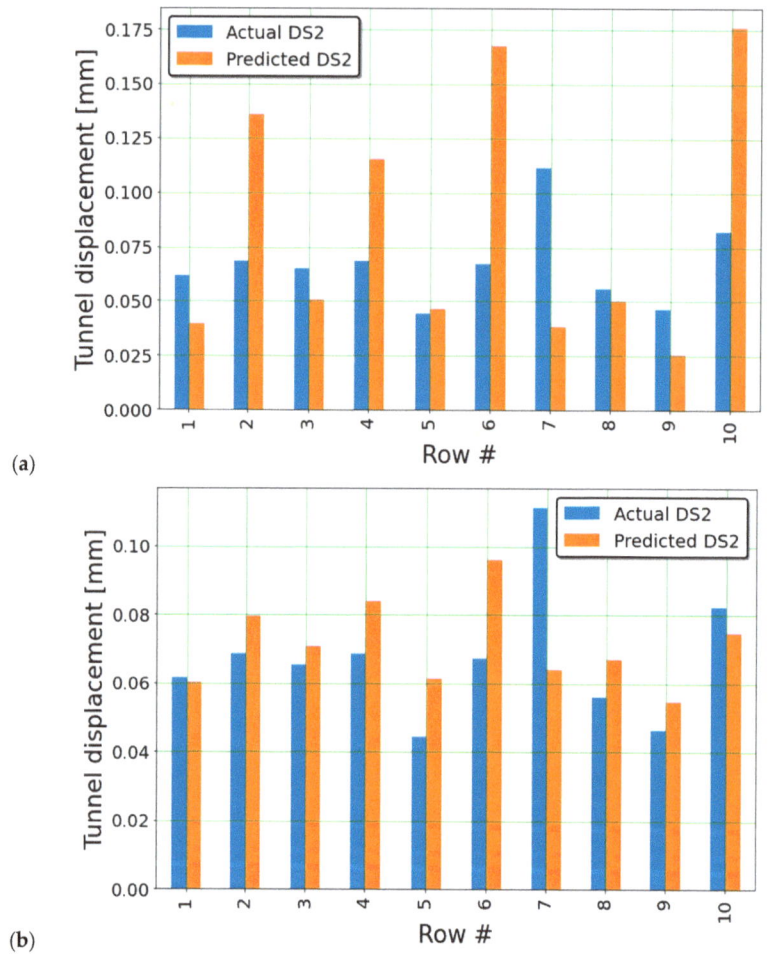

Figure 8. Prediction vs. actual tunnel displacements for DS3 with NSD = 10% computed with (**a**) NN1, i.e., no transfer learning, and (**b**) NNT, i.e., with transfer learning.

Table 4. Summary of performance of ANNs under different noise standard deviations (NSD).

		RMSE [mm]		
ML-Model	Dataset	NSD = 0%	NSD = 5%	NSD = 10%
NN1	DS1	2	3	7
NN1	DS2	40	51	59
NNT	DS2	26	29	33
NN1	DS3	41	37	54
NNT	DS3	14	18	20

6. Summary and Conclusions

In order to investigate the implementation of transfer learning for tunnel support analysis, two scenarios were investigated: (1) transferring knowledge between different ground formations, and (2) transferring knowledge from simplified hydrostatic loading to a more complex and realistic non-hydrostatic stress field. The objective of the second scenario is to examine the potential of enhancing real-world data with data generated via numerical simulations (see illustration in Figure 2).

The technical process for implementing transfer learning involved training an ANN on an initial large dataset with a size of 200 rows, and then adding an additional layer and training it on small datasets of 25 rows. Subsequently, the ANNs were tested on unseen data, and the RMSE was computed. In order to conclude that transfer learning is effective, two conditions were checked: (1) the RMSE from transfer learning is lower than the RMSE from an RF model trained solely on the small datasets, and (2) the RMSE from transfer learning is lower compared to predictions made with the original ANN trained on the large dataset. In order to better mimic reality, numerical noise was added to the datasets. The analysis was repeated for each of the scenarios for varying degrees of noise.

As expected, increasing the degree of noise caused the RMSE to increase. Nevertheless, the improvement due to transfer learning was consistent throughout all investigations of both scenarios. A comparison of the results of the two scenarios shows that lower accuracy is achieved for the second task. The apparent explanation for this is that transferring knowledge between analyses with different tunnel behavior is less effective than transferring knowledge between identical behavior with different strength parameters.

To summarize, the findings in this paper highlight the potential of transfer learning as a powerful technique for overcoming dataset size limitations. The results demonstrate the effectiveness of this technique and suggest that it would be possible to synthesize artificial data with real-world data. The prospect of transfer learning should motivate researchers, engineers, and other stakeholders to invest in in-situ data collection for the sake of ML analysis. The general methodology presented in this paper could be applied and further modified for the analysis of other applications. For this reason, we have made our data and code available online [31]. It is anticipated that, following further development and refinement, transfer learning will become a fundamental part of ML-related works in geotechnical applications.

7. Limitations

It is important to acknowledge the limitations of the current study. Firstly, the fields of data science and artificial intelligence are rapidly advancing, with transfer learning being in its nascent state. Hence, technical details and results (e.g., size of datasets, ANN architecture, and hyper-parameters) should be interpreted with caution. Each case study requires special analysis and judgment regarding optimal ML analysis procedures while staying up to date with the latest developments in this field.

Secondly, the current analyses rely on artificial data. While the addition of noise generally assists in bridging the gap from model to reality, there is still a lack of research that provides guidelines for selecting signal-to-noise ratios that are representative of geological materials.

Finally, integrating ML tools with geotechnical analysis is still in its infancy. As a result, there are no available guidelines for the implementation of ML in compliance with standard design procedures. The execution and evaluation of ML algorithms implicitly impacts the assessment of safety factors. Further research is necessary for developing procedures for the proper integration of ML with established design procedures.

Author Contributions: Conceptualization, A.M. and A.U.; Methodology, A.M. and A.U.; Software, A.M.; Validation, A.M.; Formal analysis, A.M.; Investigation, A.M. and A.U.; Writing—original draft, A.M.; Writing—review & editing, A.U.; Visualization, A.M. and A.U. All authors have read and agreed to the published version of the manuscript.

Funding: This research received no external funding.

Data Availability Statement: Data is available online: https://github.com/AlonU1/Numerical-Investigation-of-Transfer-Learning-for-Tunnel-Support-Design.

Conflicts of Interest: The authors declare no conflict of interest.

References

1. Paraskevopoulou, C.; Benardos, A. Assessing the Construction Cost of Greek Transportation Tunnel Projects. *Tunn. Undergr. Space Technol.* **2013**, *38*, 497–505. [CrossRef]
2. Elmo, D.; Mitelman, A.; Yang, B. Examining Rock Engineering Knowledge through a Philosophical Lens. *Geosciences* **2022**, *12*, 1. [CrossRef]
3. Yarkoni, T.; Westfall, J. Choosing Prediction Over Explanation in Psychology: Lessons From Machine Learning. *Perspect. Psych. Sci.* **2017**, *12*, 1100–1122. [CrossRef]
4. Balki, I.; Amirabadi, A.; Levman, J.; Martel, A.L.; Emersic, Z.; Meden, B.; Garcia-Pedrero, A.; Ramirez, S.C.; Kong, D.; Moody A.R.; et al. Sample-Size Determination Methodologies for Machine Learning in Medical Imaging Research: A Systematic Review. *Can. Assoc. Radiol. J.* **2019**, *70*, 344–353. [CrossRef]
5. Diwakar, K.; Gautam, K.; Dangi, H.; Kadel, S.; Hu, L. Challenges in Tunneling in the Himalayas: A Survey of Several Prominent Excavation Projects in the Himalayan Mountain Range of South Asia. *Geotechnics* **2022**, *2*, 802–824. [CrossRef]
6. West, J.; Ventura, D.; Warnick, S. Spring Research Presentation: A Theoretical Foundation for Inductive Transfer. Brigham Young University, College of Physical and Mathematical Sciences. *J. Softw. Eng. Appl.* **2007**, *12*, 11.
7. Géron, A. *Hands-On Machine Learning with Scikit-Learn and TensorFlow*, 3rd ed.; O'Reilly Media: Newton, MA, USA, 2022; ISBN 9781098125974.
8. Yang, B.; Mitelman, A.; Elmo, D.; Stead, D. Why the Future of Rock Mass Classification Systems Requires Revisiting Their Empirical Past. *Q. J. Eng. Geol. Hydrogeol.* **2022**, *55*, qjegh2021-039. [CrossRef]
9. Vrakas, A.; Anagnostou, G. A Finite Strain Closed-Form Solution for the Elastoplastic Ground Response Curve in Tunnelling. *Int. J. Numer. Anal. Methods Geomech.* **2014**, *38*, 1131–1148. [CrossRef]
10. Carranza-Torres, C. Elasto-Plastic Solution of Tunnel Problems Using the Generalized Form of the Hoek-Brown Failure Criterion. *Int. J. Rock Mech. Min. Sci.* **2004**, *41*, 629–639. [CrossRef]
11. Hoek, E. Support for Very Weak Rock Associated with Faults and Shear Zones. In *Rock Support and Reinforcement Practice in Mining*; Routledge: London, UK, 2018; pp. 19–32.
12. Mitelman, A.; Elmo, D.; Stead, D. Development of a Spring Analogue Approach for the Study of Pillars and Shafts. *Int. J. Min. Sci. Technol.* **2018**, *28*, 267–274. [CrossRef]
13. Oreste, P. The Convergence-Confinement Method: Roles and Limits in Modern Geomechanical Tunnel Design. *Am. J. Appl. S.* **2009**, *6*. [CrossRef]
14. Rocscience Inc. *OcSupport—Rock Support Interaction and Deformation Analysis for Tunnels in Weak Rock Ver 3 Tutorial Manual*; Rocscience Inc.: Toronto, ON, Canada, 2005.
15. Mitelman, A.; Elmo, D. Analysis of Tunnel-Support Interaction Using an Equivalent Boundary Beam. *Tunn. Undergr. Space Technol.* **2019**, *84*, 218–226. [CrossRef]
16. Fraldi, M.; Guarracino, F. Limit Analysis of Collapse Mechanisms in Cavities and Tunnels According to the Hoek-Brown Failure Criterion. *Int. J. Rock Mech. Min. Sci.* **2009**, *46*, 665–673. [CrossRef]
17. Keawsawasvong, S.; Ukritchon, B. Design Equation for Stability of a Circular Tunnel in Anisotropic and Heterogeneous Clay. *Undergr. Space* **2022**, *7*, 76–93. [CrossRef]
18. Morgenroth, J.; Khan, U.T.; Perras, M.A. An Overview of Opportunities for Machine Learning Methods in Underground Rock Engineering Design. *Geosciences* **2019**, *9*, 504. [CrossRef]
19. Furtney, J.K.; Thielsen, C.; Fu, W.; Le Goc, R. Surrogate Models in Rock and Soil Mechanics: Integrating Numerical Modeling and Machine Learning. *Rock Mech. Rock Eng.* **2022**, *55*, 2845–2859. [CrossRef]
20. Kelleher, J.D.; Tierney, B. *Data Science*; MIT Press: Cambridge, MA, USA, 2018; ISBN 9780262535434.
21. Breiman, L. Random Forests. *Mach. Learn* **2001**, *45*, 5–32. [CrossRef]
22. Weiss, K.; Khoshgoftaar, T.M.; Wang, D.D. A Survey of Transfer Learning. *J. Big Data* **2016**, *3*, 9. [CrossRef]
23. Ngamkhanong, C.; Keawsawasvong, S.; Jearsiripongkul, T.; Cabangon, L.T.; Payan, M.; Sangjinda, K.; Banyong, R.; Thongchom, C. Data-Driven Prediction of Stability of Rock Tunnel Heading: An Application of Machine Learning Models. *Infrastructures* **2022**, *7*, 148. [CrossRef]
24. Zhou, Q.; Shen, H.; Zhao, J.; Xiong, X. Tunnel Settlement Prediction by Transfer Learning. *J. ICT Res. Appl.* **2019**, *13*, 118–1. [CrossRef]
25. Fu, T.; Zhang, T.; Song, X. A Novel Hybrid Transfer Learning Framework for Dynamic Cutterhead Torque Prediction of the Tunnel Boring Machine. *Energies* **2022**, *15*, 2907. [CrossRef]
26. O'Brien, D.; Andrew Osborne, J.; Perez-Duenas, E.; Cunningham, R.; Li, Z. Automated Crack Classification for the CERN Underground Tunnel Infrastructure Using Deep Learning. *Tunn. Undergr. Space Technol.* **2023**, *131*, 104668. [CrossRef]
27. Hoek, E.; Diederichs, M.S. Empirical Estimation of Rock Mass Modulus. *Int. J. Rock Mech. Min. Sci.* **2006**, *43*, 203–215. [CrossRef]
28. Rocscience Phase2 Version 6.020; Toronto. 2007. Available online: https://www.rocscience.com/software/rs2 (accessed on March 2023).
29. Fama, M.E.D. Numerical Modeling of Yield Zones in Weak Rock. In *Rock Mechanics Continuum Modeling*; Elsevier: Amsterdam, The Netherlands, 1993; ISBN 978-0-08-040615-2.

Yu, T.; Zhu, H. Hyper-Parameter Optimization: A Review of Algorithms and Applications. *arXiv* **2020**, arXiv:2003.05689, Preprint. [CrossRef]

Mitelman, A.; Urlainis, A. Available online: https://github.com/AlonU1/Numerical-Investigation-of-Transfer-Learning-for-Tunnel-Support-Design (accessed on 1 March 2023).

Disclaimer/Publisher's Note: The statements, opinions and data contained in all publications are solely those of the individual author(s) and contributor(s) and not of MDPI and/or the editor(s). MDPI and/or the editor(s) disclaim responsibility for any injury to people or property resulting from any ideas, methods, instructions or products referred to in the content.

Article

A Novel Method for Predicting Rockburst Intensity Based on an Improved Unascertained Measurement and an Improved Game Theory

Zhe Liu, Jianhong Chen, Yakun Zhao and Shan Yang *

School of Resources and Safety Engineering, Central South University, Changsha 410083, China
* Correspondence: yangshan@csu.edu.cn

Abstract: A rockburst is a dynamic disaster that may result in considerable damage to mines and pose a threat to personnel safety. Accurately predicting rockburst intensity is critical for ensuring mine safety and reducing economic losses. First, based on the primary parameters that impact rockburst occurrence, the uniaxial compressive strength (σ_c), shear–compression ratio (σ_θ/σ_c), compression–tension ratio (σ_c/σ_t), elastic deformation coefficient (W_{et}), and integrity coefficient of the rock (K_V) were selected as the evaluation indicators. Second, an improved game theory weighting method was introduced to address the problem that the combination coefficients calculated using the traditional game theory weighting method may result in negative values. The combination of indicator weights obtained using the analytic hierarchy process, the entropy method, and the coefficient of variation method were also optimized using improved game theory. Third, to address the problem of subjectivity in the traditional unascertained measurement using the confidence identification criterion, the distance discrimination idea of the Minkowski distance was used to optimize the identification criteria of the attributes in an unascertained measurement and was applied to rockburst prediction, and the obtained results were compared with the original confidence identification criterion and the original distance discrimination. The results show that the improved game theory weighting method used in this model makes the weight distribution more reasonable and reliable, which can provide a feasible reference for the weight determination method of rockburst prediction. When the Minkowski distance formula was introduced into the unascertained measurement for distance discrimination, the same rockburst predictions were obtained when the distance parameter (p) was equal to 1, 2, 3, and 4. The improved model was used to predict and analyze 40 groups of rockburst data with an accuracy of 92.5% and could determine the rockburst intensity class intuitively, providing a new way to analyze the rockburst intensity class rationally and quickly.

Keywords: improving game theory; combination weights; improving unascertained measurement; distance discrimination; rockburst prediction

MSC: 28E99

1. Introduction

It is well known that underground space engineering, such as mining and tunnel transportation, is constantly extending deeper into the earth [1–3]. However, with the deepening of underground engineering, the probability of engineering disasters also increases, especially that of rockbursts induced by high geo-stress [1]. Rockbursts, which are sudden releases of energy and rock ruptures caused by external disturbances under conditions of high ground stress, have been called a geological "cancer". They are a relatively common engineering geohazard during the excavation and construction of deeply buried underground structures and are characterized by high risk, suddenness, and unpredictability [4–8]. For instance, a severe rockburst that happened on 28 November 2009 at the Jinping II hydropower facility in China caused seven fatalities, one major injury, and the destruction of a tunnel-boring machine [9]. In November 2011, a catastrophic rockburst at the Qianqiu Mine in Henan Province killed 10 miners and injured 64 more [10]. On 31 May 2015, a rockburst at the Neelum–Jhelum Hydropower Project in Pakistan resulted in the deaths of three workers and the destruction of a TBM [11]. This type of disaster causes significant economic damage and casualties and poses a serious threat to the safety of construction personnel and equipment. In severe cases, it can even induce earthquakes. During construction, various techniques can be used to reduce the harm caused by rockbursts, such as improving the stress on the wall rock, improving the nature of the wall rock, and maintaining the integrity of the wall rock by using controlled blasting techniques, water spraying, water injection, enhanced support or advanced support, and other technical means [12]. However, due to the uncertainty of rockbursts, the prediction of rockburst probability and intensity classification has been a worldwide problem in the field of rock engineering, with positive implications for practical construction [13–16].

Rockburst criteria can typically be classified into two categories: single-indicator empirical criteria and multi-factor empirical evaluation criteria [1,4,17,18]. The commonly used single-indicator criteria include Turchaninov's criterion [19], Russenes' criterion [20], Barton's criterion [21], Hoek's criterion [22], and the rock elastic energy index [23], among others. However, these criteria usually only consider one or two influencing factors. Because the mechanism behind rockbursts is complex, multiple factors affect their occurrence. Therefore, these single-indicator criteria have limitations when predicting rockbursts [1]. Recognizing these limitations, some scholars have attempted to use key factors that influence rockburst occurrence as evaluation indicators [24]. Wang [25] was the first to propose a multi-factor rockburst prediction model through the lens of fuzzy mathematical theory, which offers a new comprehensive approach for predicting rockbursts. Many scholars have since begun to combine multi-factor indicators and mathematical methods to develop suitable mathematical models or empirical evaluation systems for integrated rockburst prediction in some underground engineering projects. The multi-factor rockburst prediction models are mainly divided into uncertainty evaluation models and intelligent optimization evaluation models. In the field of rockburst prediction uncertainty evaluation, there are several models available, including the distance discrimination method [26,27], the cloud model [28,29], extenics [30,31], the rough set theory [32], the efficacy coefficient method [33,34], set pair analysis [18,35], the attribute measure [36], the ideal point method [24,37], TOPSIS [38,39], fuzzy set theory [40,41], etc. All of these models consider a combination of rockburst indicators and their non-linear relationships with rockburst risk. However, there are still challenges in terms of selecting appropriate model functions, handling multi-source data with multiple indicators and indicator weights, and the critical issue of determining the weights of rockburst correlation indicators and their influencing factors while avoiding subjective decision making [1,24]. Intelligent optimization algorithms are novel methods that have been proposed to solve complex optimization problems. They were inspired by the principles of biological evolution and some physical phenomena. Among the mainstream intelligent optimization algorithms are PSO [16,42,43], BP neural networks [44,45], Bayesian networks [46,47], random forests [48,49], genetic algorithms [50], support vector machines [51], decision tree models [52,53], and so on. These algorithms have shown excellent performances in handling complex problems and exhibit high computational efficiency. However, the accuracy of their evaluation depends to some extent on the quality of the training sample. Moreover, they are also computationally expensive [54].

Unascertained measurement is a method that can effectively deal with fuzzy and uncertain information [55]. However, the traditional unascertained measurement approach uses a confidence criterion for calculations [56–61], which introduces some subjectivity. To ensure the objectivity of discrimination results, the idea of distance discrimination can be introduced to optimize an attribute recognition model. Additionally, the game theory method resolves the contradiction between subjective and objective empowerment methods, ensuring the accuracy of quantitative analyses and the scientificity of qualitative analyses. To avoid the unreasonable phenomenon of negative values for combined weight coefficients that may arise from the traditional game theory calculation method, constraints were introduced to the existing formula, and an improved game theory weighting method was applied for the first time in the field of rockburst prediction. A flow chart of this paper is shown in Figure 1.

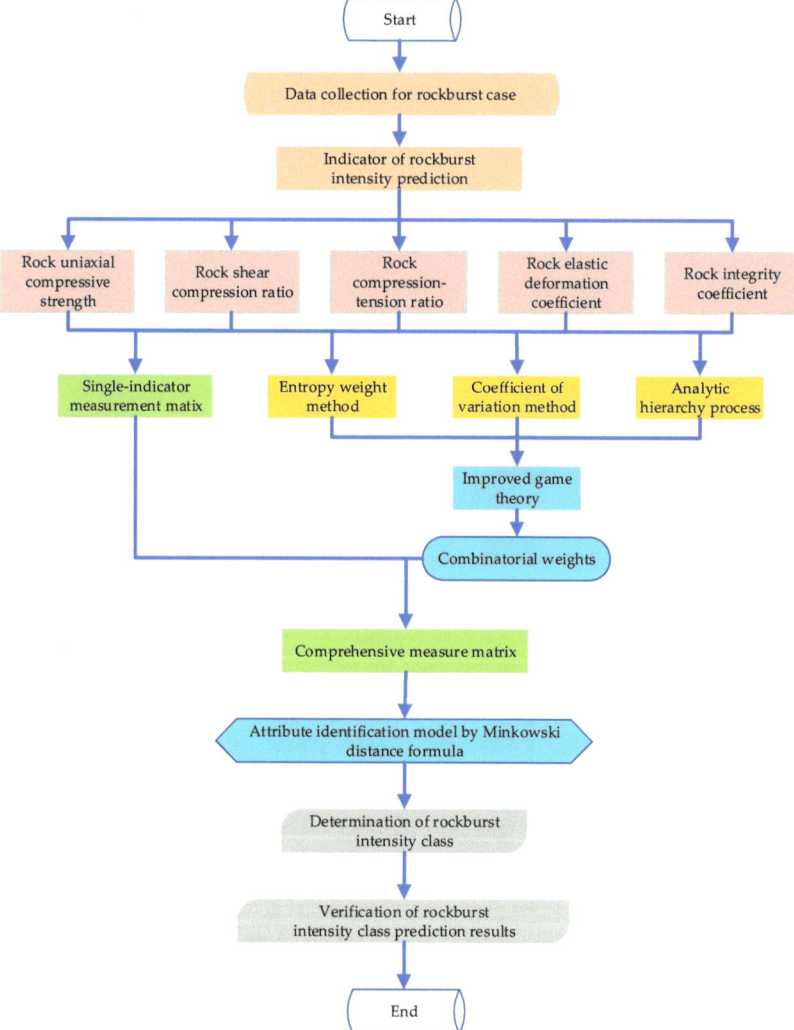

Figure 1. Model framework for predicting rockburst intensity.

2. Weighting Calculation Method

The indicator weights play a crucial role in rockburst prediction and evaluation, as they reflect the relative contribution of each indicator to the evaluated object, mainly including subjective and objective weighting methods [55]. The subjective weighting method mainly assesses the weight of each indicator in the decision-making process by evaluating the experience and attitude of the decision maker, thereby determining the level of importance of each indicator to the final decision, while the objective weighting method obtains relatively objective calculation results by using mathematical algorithms based on all the information contained in the raw data.

2.1. Subjective Weighting Method

The analytic hierarchical process (AHP) is a comprehensive evaluation method for system analysis and decision making that was proposed by T. LSaaty [62]. AHP is a subjective assignment method based on a priority judgment matrix of pairwise comparisons of indicators. It organically integrates quantitative analysis and qualitative analysis to systematically and hierarchically analyze decision problems. In this study, a judgment matrix is constructed using the 9-level scale method to calculate the indicator's subjective weight coefficient, denoted as W_1, and the matrix is tested for consistency.

The consistency index (CI) is calculated as follows:

$$CI = \frac{\lambda_{\max} - n}{n - 1} \quad (1)$$

where CI is the consistency index; $\lambda_{\max}$ denotes the maximum eigenvalue of the judgment matrix; and n is the order of the judgment matrix.

The value of the random consistency indicator RI of the matrix is judged, as shown in Table 1.

Table 1. Dimensions and corresponding RI values [36].

Dimensions	1	2	3	4	5	6	7	8	9	10
RI	0	0	0.52	0.89	1.12	1.26	1.36	1.41	1.46	1.49

The consistency ratio (CR) is calculated as follows:

$$CR = \frac{CI}{RI} \quad (2)$$

If $CR < 0.1$, it means that the judgment matrix meets the consistency requirement with the normalized feature vector as the weight vector; otherwise, the judgment matrix would need to be readjusted.

The factors involved in the rockburst prediction criterion can be broadly classified into three categories: rock mechanics properties, rock stress conditions, and surrounding rock conditions. To evaluate the rockburst risk, these key influencing factors are hierarchically divided, and the relevant target layer, guideline layer, and plan layer are determined, as shown in Figure 2.

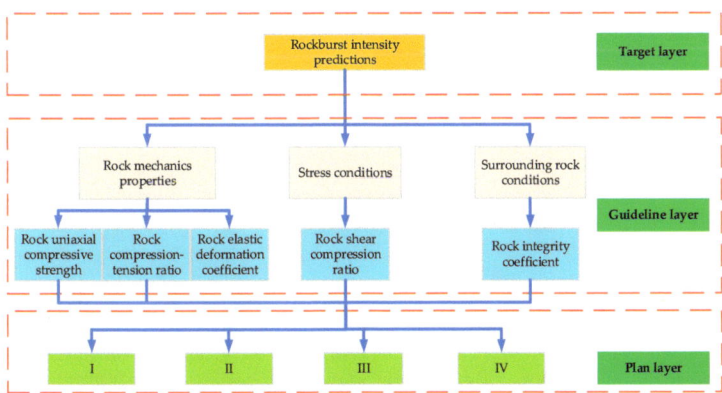

Figure 2. A diagram of the evaluation indicator hierarchy.

2.2. Objective Weighting Method
2.2.1. Entropy Weight Method

The mathematician Shannon introduced the concept of thermodynamic entropy into information theory in 1948 to measure the uncertainty of a system [63]. The "entropy" approach calculates indicator weights based on the information utility provided by each indicator, making it an objective weighting method. Indicators with smaller entropy values contain more information and contribute less uncertainty to the system [64]. The weight (W_2) calculated by the entropy weighting method can effectively avoid the subjective influence of weighting decisions with more objective results.

Suppose there are m objects to be evaluated and each has t evaluation indicators. Let the jth index of the ith objects take the value x_{ij}, forming the original evaluation index data matrix as

$$X = (x_{ij})_{m \times t} \tag{3}$$

Step 1: normalization process:
For benefit-based indicators:

$$b_{ij} = \frac{x_{ij} - \min_j(x_{ij})}{\max_j(x_{ij}) - \min_j(x_{ij})} \tag{4}$$

For cost-based indicators:

$$b_{ij} = \frac{\max_j(x_{ij}) - x_{ij}}{\max_j(x_{ij}) - \min_j(x_{ij})} \tag{5}$$

where $\max_j(x_{ij})$ and $\min_j(x_{ij})$ denote the maximum and minimum values of the jth column of matrix X, respectively.

Step 2: calculate the entropy value of each indicator:

$$E_j = \frac{-\sum\limits_{j=1}^{m} F_{ij} \ln F_{ij}}{\ln m} \tag{6}$$

where

$$F_{ij} = \frac{1 + b_{ij}}{\sum\limits_{j=1}^{m}(1 + b_{ij})} \tag{7}$$

when $f_{ij} = 0$, E_i is 0. where b_{ij} is the value of the indicator normalized according to Equations (4) and (5).

Step 3: determine the indicator weight:

$$\lambda_i = \frac{1 - E_i}{t - \sum\limits_{j=1}^{t} E_i} \quad (i = 1, 2, \cdots, t) \tag{8}$$

Therefore, the weights $W_2 = (\lambda_1, \lambda_2, \cdots, \lambda_m)$ are calculated using the entropy weight method.

2.2.2. Coefficient of Variation Method

The coefficient of variation method (CV) is utilized to measure the degree of variation in the values taken by each indicator through the coefficient of variation of each indicator. The higher the degree of variation, the greater the degree of importance of an indicator, and the higher the weight of an indicator [65]. The weights calculated using this method can eliminate the influence of the evaluation indicator system on the calculation process caused by the different quantitative units and orders of magnitude of each indicator, providing an objective and dynamic weighting method [31]. The steps involved in this method are as follows:

$$\delta_j = \sigma_j / h_j \tag{9}$$

$$v_j = \frac{\delta_j}{\sum_{j=1}^{t} \delta_j} \tag{10}$$

where σ_j is the coefficient of variation of the indicator; σ_j is the standard deviation; h_j is the mean of the indicator; and v_j is the weight of the indicator.

Therefore, the weights $W_3 = (v_1, v_2, \cdots, v_t)$ are calculated using the coefficient of variation method.

2.3. Improved Game Theory Combination Weighting Method

The fundamental principle of the game theory weighting method is to seek linear combination coefficients so that the deviation between the combination weights and the weights calculated using different methods is minimized. However, the combination coefficients calculated using the traditional game theory weighting method may have negative values, which is inconsistent with the actual situation [66]. Therefore, some scholars [67] have proposed improvements to the game theory weighting method by introducing a constraint function to ensure that the combination coefficients are non-negative. The improved game theory can be used to calculate the combined weight (W_C). The specific steps for calculating the combined weights using the improved game theory are as follows:

Let the weights of the evaluation indicators be calculated by K methods and then establish the linear combination of the integrated weight (W_C) for the K weights, as shown in Equation (11):

$$W_C = \sum_{i=1}^{K} \alpha_i w_i^T \tag{11}$$

where α_i is the linear combination coefficient, $\alpha_i > 0$, and w_i^T is the transpose of the weight row vector calculated using the ith method.

The countermeasure model of the optimal solution of W_C is established to minimize the deviation of the integrated weight from all w_i values, as shown in Equation (12):

$$\text{Min} \left\| \sum_{i=1}^{K} \alpha_i w_i^T - w_r \right\|_2, r = 1, 2, \cdots, K \tag{12}$$

The optimal condition of Equation (12) can be derived from the differential properties of the matrix, as shown in Equation (13):

$$\underset{\alpha_1, \alpha_2, \cdots, \alpha_l}{\text{Min}} g = \sum_{i=1}^{K} \left| \left(\sum_{j=1}^{K} \alpha_j w_i w_j^T \right) - w_i w_i^T \right| \tag{13}$$

To ensure that the calculated combination coefficients are greater than 0, an optimization model is established with the addition of constraints, as shown in Equation (14):

$$\begin{cases} \underset{\alpha_1, \alpha_2, \cdots, \alpha_l}{\text{Min}} g = \sum_{i=1}^{K} \left| \left(\sum_{j=1}^{K} \alpha_j w_i w_j^T \right) - w_i w_i^T \right| \\ s.t. \sum_{j=1}^{n} \alpha_j^2 = 1, \alpha_j > 0, j = 1, 2, \cdots, K \end{cases} \tag{14}$$

To solve the model, the following Lagrangian function (Equation (15)) is established:

$$L(a_j, \lambda) = \sum_{i=1}^{K} \left| \left(\sum_{j=1}^{K} a_j w_i w_j^T \right) - w_i w_i^T \right| + \frac{\lambda}{2} \left(\sum_{j=1}^{K} a_j^2 - 1 \right) \tag{15}$$

The optimal solution of the combination coefficient $\alpha_j (\alpha_j > 0)$ is calculated by solving Equation (16), as shown in Equation (17):

$$\alpha_j = \frac{\sum_{i=1}^{K} w_i w_j^T}{\sqrt{\sum_{j=1}^{K} \left(\sum_{i=1}^{K} w_i w_j^2 \right)^2}} \tag{16}$$

$$\alpha_j^* = \frac{\sum_{i=1}^{K} w_i w_j^T}{\sum_{j=1}^{K} \sum_{i=1}^{K} w_i w_j^T} \tag{17}$$

This value can be substituted into Equation (11), which can be solved to obtain the combined weight (W_C), followed by normalization, as shown in Equation (18):

$$W = \sum_{j=1}^{K} \alpha_j^* w_j^T \tag{18}$$

3. Evaluation Method

3.1. Multi-Indicator Comprehensive Measurement

Unascertained measurement, a mathematical method for dealing with uncertain information, was first proposed by Professor Wang [68]. Based on this study, Liu [69] proposed a mathematical theory of unascertained measurement and first applied it to the evaluation problem. After years of unremitting research by many experts and scholars, its theoretical system has gradually matured and has been applied in many fields [57,70,71].

There are m samples of object X to be evaluated, and for each evaluated object ($X = \{X_1, X_2, \cdots, X_m\}$) there are k single evaluation index spaces, denoted as $R = \{R_1, R_2, \cdots, R_t\}$. Let X_i be denoted as a t-dimensional vector ($X_i = \{x_{i1}, x_{i2}, \cdots, x_{it}\}$), where x_{ij} denotes the measurement of the evaluation object (X_i) with respect to the evaluation index (R_j). For each subtest (x_{ij}) with k evaluation levels, assume that the evaluation space (P) has k evaluation levels, denoted as $P = \{P_1, P_2, \cdots, P_k\}$. The tth evaluation class (P_t) is the class value of x_{ij}. Let class P_{i+1} be "higher" or "lower" than class P_i, denoted as $P_{i+1} > P_i$. If $P_k > P_{k-1} > \cdots > P_2 > P_1$ is satisfied, then $\{P_1, P_2, \cdots, P_k\}$ is called an ordered partition class of the evaluation class space (P).

$\mu_{ijt} = \mu(x_{ij} \in P_t)$ denotes the degree to which observation x_{ij} belongs to the tth assessment class (P_t), with μ being satisfied as follows:

$$0 \leq \mu(x_{ij} \in P_l) \leq 1 \quad (i = 1, 2, \cdots, m; j = 1, 2, \cdots, t; l = 1, 2, \cdots, k) \tag{19}$$

$$\mu(x_{ij} \in P) = 1 \tag{20}$$

$$\mu\left(x_{ij} \in \bigcup_{l=1}^{k} P_l\right) = \sum_{i=1}^{k} \mu(x_{ij} \in P_i) \tag{21}$$

where Equation (19) is called non-negative boundedness, Equation (20) is called normalizability, Equation (21) is called additivity, and μ satisfied by Equations (19)–(21) at the same time is called an unascertained measurement.

There are many ways to construct single-indicator measure functions, but linear measure functions are considered to be the simplest and most widespread in application [58,60].

$$\left(\mu_{ijl}\right)_{t\times k} = \begin{bmatrix} \mu_{i11} & \mu_{i12} & \cdots & \mu_{i1k} \\ \mu_{i21} & \mu_{i22} & \cdots & \mu_{i2k} \\ \vdots & \vdots & \ddots & \vdots \\ \mu_{it1} & \mu_{it2} & \cdots & \mu_{itk} \end{bmatrix} \quad (22)$$

The weighted comprehensive measure matrix (C) of multiple indicators can be calculated using Equations (18) and (22).

$$C = W \cdot \begin{bmatrix} \mu_{i11} & \mu_{i12} & \cdots & \mu_{i1k} \\ \mu_{i21} & \mu_{i22} & \cdots & \mu_{i2k} \\ \vdots & \vdots & \ddots & \vdots \\ \mu_{it1} & \mu_{it2} & \cdots & \mu_{itk} \end{bmatrix} \quad (23)$$

3.2. Improving the Attribute Recognition Model Using Distance Discrimination

The characteristics of things are divided into k categories: $F_1, F_2, \cdots, F_k$. Correspondingly, the m factors are also classified into k categories. Then, the sample mean of each category is determined as the classification center of k classification patterns $(F_1, F_2, \cdots, F_k)$, so the unascertained measurements are $f_1 = [1, 0, 0, \cdots, 0]$, $f_2 = [0, 1, 0, \cdots, 0]$, $\cdots$, $f_k = [0, 0, 0, \cdots, 1]$, respectively.

The distance discrimination method is used as the attribute identification criterion so that the distance ($L_{p,k}$) calculated using Minkowski's distance formula is the distance from the comprehensive multi-indicator measure (μ_{ijk}) to the classification class (v_k). The formula is shown below.

$$L_{p,k} = \left(\sum_{i=1}^{n} |x_{ijk} - f_k|^p\right)^{\frac{1}{p}} \quad (24)$$

When $p = 1$, the Minkowski distance formula is the Manhattan distance.

$$L_{1,k} = \sum_{i=1}^{n} |x_{ijk} - f_k| \quad (25)$$

When $p = 2$, the Minkowski distance formula is the Euclidean distance.

$$L_{2,k} = \sqrt{\sum_{i=1}^{n} (x_{ijk} - f_k)^2} \quad (26)$$

For convenience of calculation in engineering applications, this paper compares the magnitude of each unascertained measurement distance ($L_{p,j}(j = 1, 2, \cdots, k)$) by taking p = 1, 2, 3, and 4, as shown in Equation (27):

$$d_{p,\min} = \text{Min}(L_{p,1}, L_{p,2}, \cdots, L_{p,k}) \quad (27)$$

If $d_{p,\min} = L_{p,k}$, it indicates that the sample (p) to be predicted is closest to class k and thus could be classified into class k.

4. Rockburst Intensity Class Prediction

From the study of most of the discrimination indicators of rockburst prediction [25,31,36,55], the five indicators of rock uniaxial compressive strength (σ_c), the ratio of rock uniaxial compressive strength to tensile strength (σ_θ/σ_c), the ratio of rock uniaxial compressive strength to tensile strength (σ_c/σ_t), rock elastic deformation indicator (W_{et}), and the rock integrity coefficient (K_V) contain the main information for predicting rockbursts. By classifying rocks, it is possible to gain more valuable insights into them [72]. Take {no rockburst, low rockburst, medium rockburst, heavy rockburst} = {I,II,III,IV}. Each evaluation indicator classification was established, as shown in Table 2, and a single-indicator measurement chart is shown in Figure 3.

Table 2. Single-indicator classification standards for rockburst intensity.

Evaluation Indicators	σ_c (MPa)	σ_θ/σ_c	σ_c/σ_t	W_{et}	K_V
No rockburst (I)	0–80	0–0.3	40–53	0–2.0	0–0.55
Low rockburst (II)	80–120	0.3–0.5	26.7–40	2.0–3.5	0.55–0.65
Medium rockburst (III)	120–180	0.5–0.7	14.5–26.7	3.5–5.0	0.65–0.75
Heavy rockburst (IV)	180–320	0.7–1.0	0–14.5	5.0–10.0	0.75–1.0

To verify the reasonableness and validity of the improved rockburst intensity prediction model, 40 sets of typical rockburst example data from the literature [25,32,36,55,73–76] were counted, and detailed indicators of the measured values and actual rockburst classes are shown in Table 3.

The weights W_1 = [0.1429,0.1429,0.1429,0.2857,0.2857] were calculated according to the AHP evaluation method, the weights W_2 = [0.2403,0.2560,0.1019,0.2323,0.1695] of the entropy weight method were calculated according to Equations (3)–(8), and the weights W_3 = [0.2255,0.2283,0.1404,0.2220,0.1839] of the coefficient of variation method were calculated according to Equations (9) and (10). Then, the combination weights of each indicator were calculated using the improved game theory method (Equations (17) and (18)) to be Equation (28), as shown in Table 4 and Figure 4.

$$W = [0.2028, 0.2090, 0.1283, 0.2467, 0.2132] \tag{28}$$

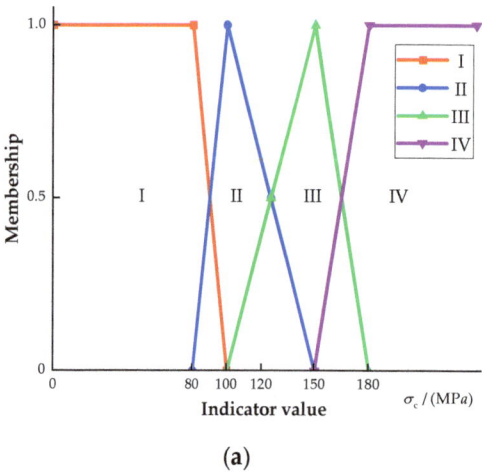
(a)

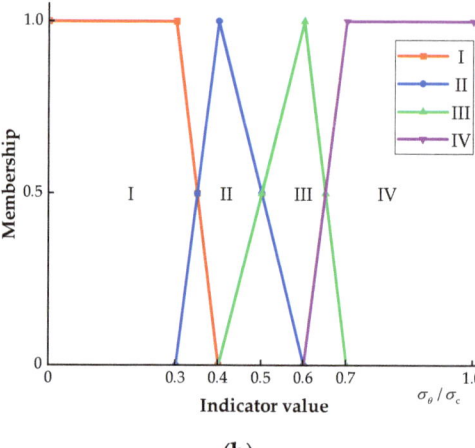
(b)

Figure 3. Cont.

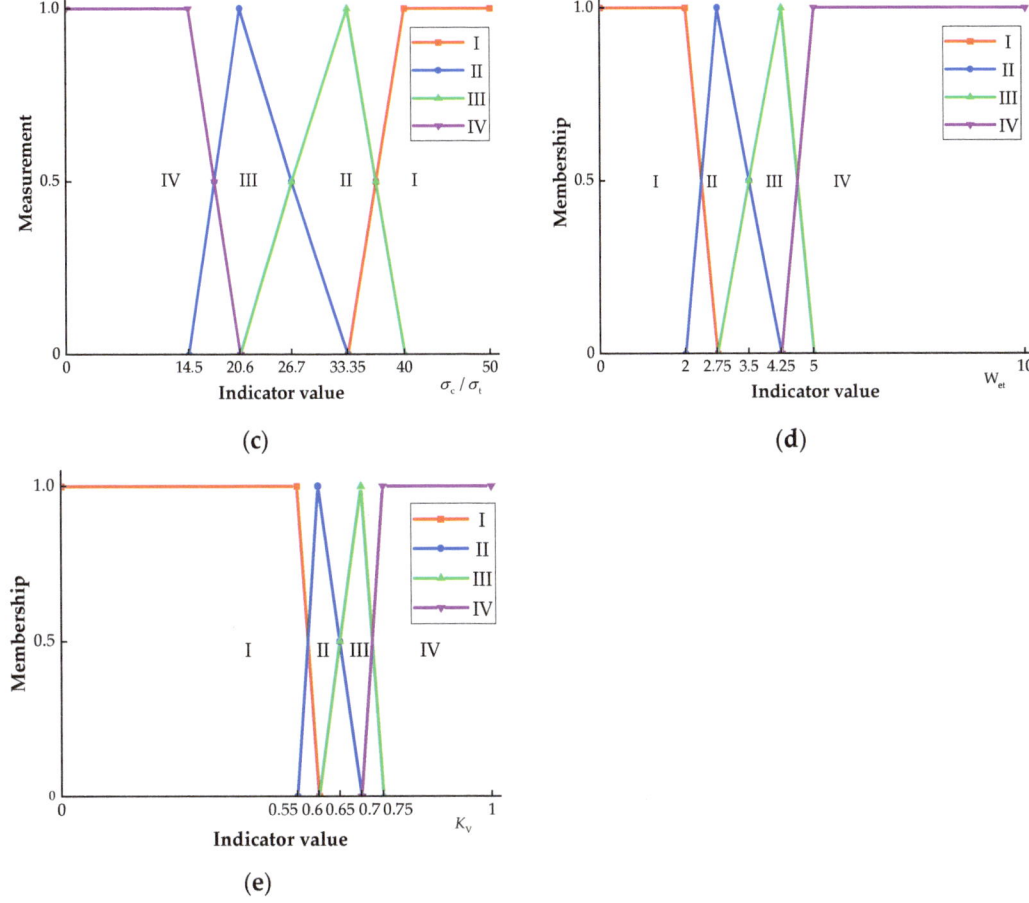

Figure 3. Single-indicator measurement functions for rockbursts. (**a**) Measurement function of rock uniaxial compressive strength. (**b**) Measurement function of rock shear to compressive strength ratio. (**c**) Measurement function of rock compressive strength–tensile strength ratio. (**d**) Measurement function of rock elastic deformation coefficient. (**e**) Measurement function of rock integrity coefficient.

Table 3. Indicators and classes of actual rockburst intensity.

Sample	Actual Data for Rockburst Indicators					Classification
	σ_c (MPa)	σ_θ/σ_c	σ_c/σ_t	W_{et}	K_V	
1	148.40	0.45	17.46	5.10	0.68	III
2	157.60	0.58	13.24	6.30	0.79	IV
3	107.50	0.20	41.35	1.70	0.50	I
4	167.20	0.66	13.17	6.80	0.82	IV
5	170.00	0.53	15.04	6.50	0.70	III
6	181.00	0.42	21.81	4.50	0.67	III
7	130.00	0.38	19.70	5.00	0.69	III
8	215.00	0.30	24.00	6.60	0.73	III
9	153.00	0.38	22.10	5.10	0.72	III
10	173.00	0.42	21.70	5.20	0.74	III

Table 3. Cont.

Sample	Actual Data for Rockburst Indicators					Classification
	σ_c (MPa)	σ_θ/σ_c	σ_c/σ_t	W_{et}	K_V	
11	156.00	0.20	11.20	3.60	0.44	I
12	172.00	0.77	17.50	5.50	0.82	IV
13	121.00	0.72	13.90	9.05	0.91	IV
14	124.00	0.64	14.40	7.74	0.96	IV
15	120.00	0.52	18.60	4.16	0.87	III
16	157.63	0.58	13.18	6.27	0.79	IV
17	132.05	0.39	20.86	4.63	0.65	III
18	127.93	0.28	28.90	3.67	0.60	II
19	96.41	0.19	47.93	1.87	0.43	I
20	167.19	0.66	13.20	6.83	0.82	IV
21	118.46	0.22	33.75	2.89	0.54	II
22	148.52	0.66	22.30	3.23	0.88	III
23	162.33	0.72	13.20	5.23	0.71	IV
24	116.78	0.37	29.73	3.52	0.68	II
25	109.33	0.42	32.77	2.97	0.71	II
26	98.56	0.28	42.73	2.17	0.49	I
27	156.73	0.49	20.13	3.82	0.91	III
28	100.32	0.38	28.77	3.02	0.70	II
29	142.20	0.72	27.52	4.30	0.73	III
30	160.32	0.69	16.55	5.72	0.90	IV
31	97.60	0.42	15.50	3.20	0.62	II
32	106.32	0.22	36.42	1.75	0.46	I
33	146.75	0.62	19.35	4.50	0.88	III
34	160.75	0.65	12.36	5.41	0.91	IV
35	146.72	0.59	18.75	4.20	0.84	III
36	162.70	0.73	29.70	3.82	0.70	III
37	157.60	0.58	13.20	6.30	0.79	IV
38	132.10	0.39	20.90	4.60	0.65	III
39	107.50	0.20	41.00	1.70	0.50	I
40	167.20	0.66	13.20	6.80	0.82	IV

Table 4. The weights of each indicator of rockburst intensity.

Methods	σ_c (MPa)	σ_θ/σ_c	σ_c/σ_t	W_{et}	K_V
AHP	0.1429	0.1429	0.1429	0.2857	0.2857
EWM	0.2403	0.2560	0.1019	0.2323	0.1695
CV	0.2255	0.2283	0.1404	0.2220	0.1839
GT	0.2028	0.2090	0.1283	0.2467	0.2132

Sample 1 is used as an example in this paper, while the computational process of the remaining 39 groups of samples was the same as that of sample 1. Therefore, only the computational results are listed (see Table 5), and the detailed computational process is not repeated.

Table 5. Statistics of the predicted results of the case samples.

Sample	I-1	I-2	I-3	I-4	C-0.6	C-0.7	MD-1	MD-2	Actual Class
1	III	III	III	III	III	IV•	III	III	III
2	IV	IV	IV	IV	IV	IV	III•	III•	IV
3	I	I	I	I	I	I	II•	II•	I
4	IV	IV	IV	IV	IV	IV	III•	IV	IV
5	IV•	IV•	IV•	IV•	IV•	IV•	III	III	III

Table 5. Cont.

Sample	I-1	I-2	I-3	I-4	C-0.6	C-0.7	MD-1	MD-2	Actual Class
6	III	III	III	III	III	III	III	III	III
7	III	III	III	III	III	III	III	III	III
8	IV•	IV•	IV•	IV•	IV•	IV•	III	III	III
9	III	III	III	III	III	IV•	III	III	III
10	IV•	IV•	IV•	IV•	IV•	IV•	III	III	III
11	I	I	I	I	III•	III•	II•	II•	I
12	IV	IV	IV	IV	IV	IV	IV	III•	IV
13	IV	IV	IV	IV	IV	IV	IV	IV	IV
14	IV	IV	IV	IV	IV	IV	IV	IV	IV
15	III	III	III	III	III	III	III	III	III
16	IV	IV	IV	IV	IV	IV	III•	III•	IV
17	III	III	III	III	III	III	III	III	III
18	II	II	II	II	II	III•	II	II	II
19	I	I	I	I	I	I	II•	I	I
20	IV	IV	IV	IV	IV	IV	III•	IV	IV
21	II	II	II	II	II	II	II	II	II
22	III	III	III	III	III	IV•	III	III	III
23	IV	IV	IV	IV	IV	IV	III•	III•	IV
24	II	II	II	II	III•	III•	II	II	II
25	II	II	II	II	II	III•	II	II	II
26	I	I	I	I	I	I	II•	II•	I
27	III	III	III	III	III	III	III	III	III
28	II	II	II	II	II	III•	II	II	II
29	III	III	III	III	III	IV•	III	III	III
30	IV	IV	IV	IV	IV	IV	IV	IV	IV
31	II	II	II	II	II	II	II	II	II
32	I	I	I	I	I	I	I	II•	I
33	III	III	III	III	III	IV•	III	III	III
34	IV	IV	IV	IV	IV	IV	III•	IV	IV
35	III	III	III	III	III	III	III	III	III
36	III	III	III	III	III	III	III	III	III
37	IV	IV	IV	IV	IV	IV	III•	III•	IV
38	III	III	III	III	III	III	III	III	III
39	I	I	I	I	I	I	II•	II•	I
40	IV	IV	IV	IV	IV	IV	III•	IV	IV

In the table, I-1 indicates an improved unascertained measurement with $p = 1$; C-0.6 indicates an unascertained measurement with a credibility degree of 0.6; MD-1 and MD-2 denote the distance discriminants of the Manhattan distance and Euclidean distance, respectively; and • indicates a misjudgment.

According to Equations (19)–(21), the single-indicator measure matrix was:

$$\mu = \begin{bmatrix} 0 & 0.032 & 0.968 & 0 \\ 0 & 0.750 & 0.250 & 0 \\ 0 & 0 & 0.485 & 0.515 \\ 0 & 0 & 0 & 1 \\ 0 & 0.200 & 0.800 & 0 \end{bmatrix} \tag{29}$$

According to Equations (23), (28), and (39), the comprehensive weight was:

$$C = \begin{bmatrix} 0 & 0.206 & 0.481 & 0.313 \end{bmatrix} \tag{30}$$

According to Equation (25), when $p = 1$, unascertained measurement distance L can be calculated:

$$\begin{aligned} L_{1,1} &= |0-1| + |0.206-0| + |0.481-0| + |0.313-0| = 2.000 \\ L_{1,2} &= |0-0| + |0.206-1| + |0.481-0| + |0.313-0| = 1.588 \\ L_{1,3} &= |0-0| + |0.206-0| + |0.481-1| + |0.313-0| = 1.038 \\ L_{1,4} &= |0-0| + |0.206-0| + |0.481-0| + |0.313-1| = 1.374 \end{aligned} \quad (31)$$

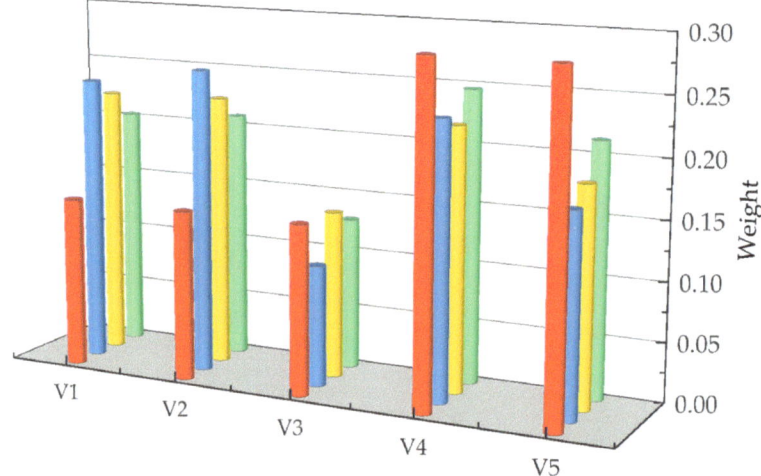

Figure 4. Visual comparison of indicator weights. In the figure, V1, V2, V3, V4, and V5 represent σ_c, σ_θ/σ_c, σ_c/σ_t, W_{et}, and K_V and AHP, EWM, CV, and GT represent the analytic hierarchy process, the entropy method, the coefficient of variation method, and the improved game theory, respectively.

The shortest distance d_{min}^1 was determined:

$$d_{1,min} = \text{Min}\{L_{1,1}, L_{1,2}, L_{1,3}, L_{1,4}\} = L_{1,3} = 1.038 \quad (32)$$

According to Equation (26), when $p = 1$, sample 1 could be calculated using the distance discriminant method to predict rockburst class III, which belongs to the medium rockburst classification.

$$\begin{aligned} L_{2,1} &= \sqrt{(0-1)^2 + (0.206-0)^2 + (0.481-0)^2 + (0.313-0)^2} = 1.171 \\ L_{2,2} &= \sqrt{(0-0)^2 + (0.206-1)^2 + (0.481-0)^2 + (0.313-0)^2} = 0.980 \\ L_{2,3} &= \sqrt{(0-0)^2 + (0.206-0)^2 + (0.481-1)^2 + (0.313-0)^2} = 0.640 \\ L_{2,4} &= \sqrt{(0-0)^2 + (0.206-0)^2 + (0.481-0)^2 + (0.313-1)^2} = 0.864 \end{aligned} \quad (33)$$

The shortest distance $d_{2,min}$ was determined:

$$d_{2,min} = \text{Min}\{L_{2,1}, L_{2,2}, L_{2,3}, L_{2,4}\} = L_{2,3} = 0.640 \quad (34)$$

When $p = 2$, sample 1 could be calculated using the distance discriminant method to predict rockburst class III, which belongs to the medium rockburst classification. Likewise, for $p = 3$ and 4, it was possible to calculate rockburst intensity class III according to the same method.

The credibility degree was set at 0.6 and 0.7 when calculated using the confidence criterion [57,60]. It was compared with the attribute identification model optimized using the Minkowski distance discrimination criterion. Then, the accurate judgments and misjudgments of the predicted rockburst intensity were calculated for each model (see Table 5).

As shown in Table 6 and Figure 5, the accuracy of the prediction results using the improved unascertained measurement was 92.5%, and the prediction evaluation results were the same when $p = 1, 2, 3$, and 4. Accordingly, on one hand, the accuracy values of the prediction results when calculated using the confidence criterion with the credibility degree set at 0.6 and 0.7 were 87.5% and 67.5%, respectively. On the other hand, the accuracy values calculated solely using the Manhattan distance and Euclidean distance methods were 67.5% and 75.0%, respectively. Compared to the other models, the improved unascertained measurement proposed in this paper had higher accuracy, with more accurately judged cases than the other models and a smaller number of misjudged cases. Therefore, it was demonstrated that the model is more accurate and reliable in practical engineering applications. Furthermore, the predicted rockburst results of the model were higher than the actual classes, even in the case of misjudgment, which means that the use of the model's predictions to prevent the occurrence of rockburst hazards provides a greater assurance of safety.

Table 6. Rockburst prediction results of each model.

Sample	I-1	I-2	I-3	I-4	C-0.6	C-0.7	MD-1	MD-2
Accurate	37	37	37	37	35	27	27	30
Lower than reality	0	0	0	0	0	0	8	5
Misjudged	3	3	3	3	5	13	13	10
Accuracy	92.5%	92.5%	92.5%	92.5%	87.5%	67.5%	67.5%	75.0%

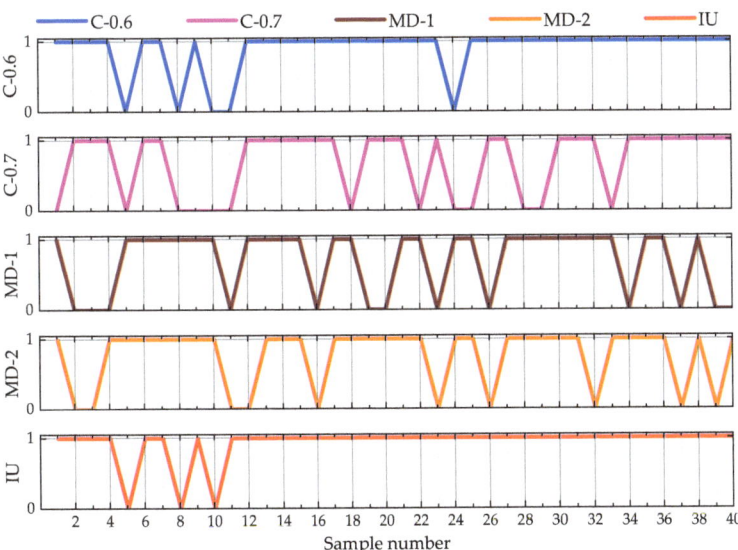

Figure 5. Comparison of prediction results of different models, where IU stands for the improved unascertained measurement obtained using the Minkowski distance formula in this paper, while 0 and 1 represent misjudgments and correct judgments, respectively.

5. Conclusions

In this work, considering the mechanism of rockbursts and the influencing factors, the five factors of the uniaxial compressive strength, the shear to compression ratio, the compression to tension ratio, the elastic deformation coefficient, and the integrity coefficient of the rock were selected as evaluation indexes. A new model for rockburst prediction was proposed by comprehensively analyzing the shortcomings of the existing rockburst criteria. The main conclusions are as follows:

1. By introducing constraints to improve the game theory combination weighting method and then combining the analytic hierarchy process, the entropy method, and the coefficient of variation method, the combination weights of each indicator affecting rockbursts were calculated. This methodology effectively addresses the inadequacies of a singular weighting method by overcoming the one-sidedness of indicator weights and resolving the potential for negative combination coefficients.
2. Based on the unascertained measurement, the Minkowski distance formula was introduced for attribute identification, eliminating the error of discrimination results caused by different credibility degrees, which not only reduced the effect of high subjectivity due to the confidence criterion but also improved the discriminatory accuracy of the model.
3. A novel model for rockburst prediction based on improved game theory and improved unascertained measurement was proposed. Forty sets of typical rockburst cases were selected from around the world, and the improved model was compared to the unimproved model. The accuracy rate of the improved model was 92.5%, which was higher than the other methods, indicating that this method is effective and reliable.

Author Contributions: Conceptualization, Y.Z.; methodology, Y.Z.; data curation, Y.Z. and S.Y.; formal analysis, Y.Z. and J.C.; validation, J.C.; resources, J.C. and S.Y.; writing—original draft preparation, Y.Z. and Z.L.; writing—review and editing, Y.Z. and Z.L.; project administration, S.Y. All authors have read and agreed to the published version of the manuscript.

Funding: This research was funded by the National Natural Science Foundation Project of China under Grant No. 72088101, No. 52274163 and No. 51404305.

Data Availability Statement: Data is contained within the article.

Acknowledgments: The authors would like to express their thanks to the National Natural Science Foundation.

Conflicts of Interest: The authors declare no conflict of interest.

Abbreviations

σ_c	uniaxial compressive strength
σ_θ/σ_c	shear–compression ratio
σ_c/σ_t	compression–tension ratio
W_{et}	elastic deformation coefficient
K_V	integrity coefficient of the rock
CI	the consistency index
RI	the random consistency indicator of the matrix
CR	the consistency ratio
AHP	the analytic hierarchical process
CV	the coefficient of variation method
EWM	the entropy weight method
GT	the improved game theory

References

1. Zhou, J.; Li, X.; Mitri, H.S. Evaluation method of rockburst: State-of-the-art literature review. *Tunn. Undergr. Space Technol.* 201 81, 632–659. [CrossRef]
2. Zhou, Z.; Cai, X.; Li, X.; Cao, W.; Du, X. Dynamic Response and Energy Evolution of Sandstone Under Coupled Static–Dynam Compression: Insights from Experimental Study into Deep Rock Engineering Applications. *Rock Mech. Rock Eng.* 2020, 5 1305–1331. [CrossRef]
3. Liu, Z.X.; Han, K.W.; Yang, S.; Liu, Y.X. Fractal evolution mechanism of rock fracture in undersea metal mining. *J. Cent. Sou Univ.* 2020, 27, 1320–1333. [CrossRef]

Yang, B.; He, M.; Zhang, Z.; Chen, Y. A new criterion of strain rockburst in consideration of the plastic zone of tunnel surrounding rock. *Rock Mech. Rock Eng.* **2022**, *55*, 1777–1789. [CrossRef]

Qian, Q. Definition, mechanism, classification and quantitative forecast model for rockburst and pressure bump. *Rock Soil Mech.* **2014**, *35*, 1–6. (In Chinese) [CrossRef]

Cai, X.; Cheng, C.; Zhou, Z.; Konietzky, H.; Song, Z.; Wang, S. Rock mass watering for rock-burst prevention: Some thoughts on the mechanisms deduced from laboratory results. *Bull. Eng. Geol. Environ.* **2021**, *80*, 8725–8743. [CrossRef]

Vižintin, G.; Kočjančič, M.; Vulić, M. Study of Coal Burst Source Locations in the Velenje Colliery. *Energies* **2016**, *9*, 507. [CrossRef]

Yang, Z.; Liu, C.; Zhu, H.; Xie, F.; Dou, L.; Chen, J. Mechanism of rockburst caused by fracture of key strata during irregular working face mining and its prevention methods. *Int. J. Min. Sci. Technol.* **2019**, *29*, 889–897. [CrossRef]

Liu, G.F.; Feng, X.T.; Feng, G.L.; Chen, B.R.; Chen, D.F.; Duan, S.Q. A Method for Dynamic Risk Assessment and Management of Rockbursts in Drill and Blast Tunnels. *Rock Mech. Rock Eng.* **2016**, *49*, 3257–3279. [CrossRef]

Pu, Y.; Apel, D.; Xu, H. Rockburst prediction in kimberlite with unsupervised learning method and support vector classifier. *Tunn. Undergr. Space Technol.* **2019**, *90*, 12–18. [CrossRef]

Naji, A.M.; Rehman, H.; Emad, M.Z.; Yoo, H. Impact of Shear Zone on Rockburst in the Deep Neelum-Jehlum Hydropower Tunnel: A Numerical Modeling Approach. *Energies* **2018**, *11*, 1935. [CrossRef]

Kaiser, P.K.; Moss, A. Deformation-based support design for highly stressed ground with a focus on rockburst damage mitigation. *J. Rock Mech. Geotech. Eng.* **2022**, *14*, 50–66. [CrossRef]

Du, K.; Tao, M.; Li, X.B.; Zhou, J. Experimental study of slabbing and rockburst induced by true-triaxial unloading and local dynamic disturbance. *Rock Mech. Rock Eng.* **2016**, *49*, 3437–3453. [CrossRef]

Cai, M. Prediction and prevention of rockburst in metal mines—A case study of Sanshandao gold mine. *J. Rock Mech. Geotech. Eng.* **2016**, *8*, 204–211. [CrossRef]

Bukowska, M. The rockbursts in the Upper Silesian Coal Basin in Poland. *J. Min. Sci.* **2012**, *48*, 445–456. [CrossRef]

Xue, Y.; Bai, C.; Qiu, D.; Kong, F.M.; Li, Z.Q. Predicting rockburst with database using particle swarm optimization and extreme learning machine. *Tunn. Undergr. Space Technol.* **2020**, *98*, 103287. [CrossRef]

He, M.; Zhang, Z.; Zheng, J.; Chen, F.; Li, N. A new perspective on the constant mi of the Hoek–Brown failure criterion and a new model for determining the residual strength of rock. *Rock Mech. Rock Eng.* **2020**, *53*, 3953–3967. [CrossRef]

Zhou, Y.; Wang, W.; Lu, X.; Wang, K. Combination weighting prediction model and application of rockburst disaster based on game theory. *China Saf. Sci. J.* **2022**, *32*, 105–112. (In Chinese)

Turchaninov, I.A.; Markov, G.A.; Gzovsky, M.V.; Kazikayev, D.M.; Frenze, U.K.; Batugin, S.A.; Chabdarova, U.I. State of stress in the upper part of the Earth's crust based on direct measurements in mines and on tectonophysical and seismological studies. *Phys. Earth Planet. Inter.* **1972**, *6*, 229–234. [CrossRef]

Russenes, B.F. Analysis of Rock Spalling for Tunnels in Steep Valley Sides. Master Thesis, Norwegian Institute of Technology, Trondheim, Norway, 1974.

Barton, N.; Lien, R.; Lunde, J. Engineering classification of rock masses for the design of tunnel support. *Rock Mech.* **1974**, *6*, 189–236. [CrossRef]

Hoek, E.; Brown, E.T. Practical estimates of rock mass strength. *Int. J. Rock Mech. Min. Sc.* **1997**, *34*, 1165–1186. [CrossRef]

Kidybiński, A. Bursting liability indices of coal// International journal of rock mechanics and mining sciences & Geomechanics Abstracts. *Pergamon* **1981**, *18*, 295–304. [CrossRef]

Zhou, H.; Liao, X.; Chen, S.; Feng, T.; Wang, Z. Rockburst risk assessment of deep lying tunnels based on combination weight and unascertained measure theory: A case study of Sangzhuling tunnel on Sichuan-tibet traffic corridor. *Earth Sci.* **2022**, *47*, 2130–2148. (In Chinese) [CrossRef]

Wang, Y.; Li, W.; Li, Q.; Xu, Y.; Tan, G. Method of fuzzy comprehensive evaluations for rockburst prediction. *Chin. J. Rock Mech. Eng.* **1998**, *17*, 493–501. (In Chinese)

Gong, F.; Li, X. A distance discriminant analysis method for prediction of possibility and classification of rockburst and its application. *Chin. J. Rock Mech. Eng.* **2007**, *26*, 1012–1018. (In Chinese)

Wang, J.; Li, X.; Yang, J. A weighted mahalanobis distance discriminant analysis for predicting rock-burst in deep hard rocks. *J. Min. Saf. Eng.* **2011**, *28*, 395–400. (In Chinese)

Liu, R.; Ye, Y.; Hu, N.; Chen, H.; Wang, X. Classified prediction model of rockburst using rough sets-normal cloud. *Neural Comput. Appl.* **2019**, *31*, 8185–8193. [CrossRef]

Wang, M.; Liu, Q.; Wang, X.; Shen, F.; Jin, J. Prediction of rockburst based on multidimensional connection cloud model and set pair analysis. *Int. J. Geomech.* **2020**, *20*, 04019147. [CrossRef]

Chen, J.; Chen, Y.; Yang, S.; Zhong, X.; Han, X.A. Prediction model on rockburst intensity grade based on variable weight and matter-element extension. *PLoS ONE* **2019**, *14*, e0218525. [CrossRef]

Zhang, L.; Zhang, X.; Wu, J.; Zhao, D.; Fu, H. Rockburst prediction model based on comprehensive weight and extension methods and its engineering application. *Bull. Eng. Geol. Environ.* **2020**, *79*, 4891–4903. [CrossRef]

Xue, Y.; Li, Z.; Li, S.; Qiu, D.; Tao, Y.; Wang, L.; Yang, W.; Zhang, K. Prediction of rockburst in underground caverns based on rough set and extensible comprehensive evaluation. *Bull. Eng. Geol. Environ.* **2019**, *78*, 417–429. [CrossRef]

Wang, Y.; Shang, Y.; Sun, H.; Yan, X. Study of prediction of rockburst intensity based on efficacy coefficient method. *Rock Soil Mech.* **2010**, *31*, 529–534. (In Chinese)

34. Wang, Y.; Jing, H.; Ji, X.; Mou, T.; Zhang, C. Model for classification and prediction of rock burst intensity in a deep underground engineering with rough set and efficacy coefficient method. *J. Cent. South Univ. Sci. Technol. Ed.* **2014**, *45*, 1992–1997. (In Chinese)
35. Jia, Q.; Wu, L.; Li, B.; Chen, C.; Peng, Y. The Comprehensive Prediction Model of Rockburst Tendency in Tunnel Based on Optimized Unascertained Measure Theory. *Geotech. Geol. Eng.* **2019**, *37*, 3399–3411. [CrossRef]
36. Zhao, Y.; Chen, J.; Yang, S.; Liu, Z. Game Theory and an Improved Maximum Entropy-Attribute Measure Interval Model for Predicting Rockburst Intensity. *Mathematics* **2022**, *10*, 2551. [CrossRef]
37. Xu, C.; Liu, X.; Wang, E.; Zheng, Y.; Wang, S. Rockburst prediction and classification based on the ideal-point method of information theory. *Tunn. Undergr. Space Technol.* **2018**, *81*, 382–390. [CrossRef]
38. Xue, Y.; Bai, C.; Kong, F.; Qiu, D.; Li, L.; Su, M.; Zhao, Y. A two-step comprehensive evaluation model for rockburst prediction based on multiple empirical criteria. *Eng. Geol.* **2020**, *268*, 105515. [CrossRef]
39. Peng, T.; Deng, H. Comprehensive evaluation on water resource carrying capacity in karst areas using cloud model with combination weighting method: A case study of Guiyang, southwest China. *Environ. Sci. Pollut. Res.* **2020**, *27*, 37057–3707. [CrossRef]
40. Wang, X.; Li, S.; Xu, Z.; Xue, Y.; Hu, J.; Li, Z.; Zhang, B. An interval fuzzy comprehensive assessment method for rockburst in underground caverns and its engineering application. *Bull. Eng. Geol. Environ.* **2019**, *78*, 5161–5176. [CrossRef]
41. Liang, W.; Zhao, G.; Wang, X.; Zhao, J.; Ma, C. Assessing the rockburst risk for deep shafts via distance-based multi-criteria decision making approaches with hesitant fuzzy information. *Eng. Geol.* **2019**, *260*, 105211. [CrossRef]
42. Xu, F.; Xu, W. Projection pursuit model based on particle swarm optimization for rockburst prediction. *Chin. J. Geotech. Eng.* **2013**, *3*, 718–723.
43. Liu, Y.; Hou, S. Rockburst Prediction Based on Particle Swarm Optimization and Machine Learning Algorithm. In *Information Technology in Geo-Engineering. ICITG 2019*; Correia, A., Tinoco, J., Cortez, P., Lamas, L., Eds.; Springer: Cham, Switzerland, 2020. [CrossRef]
44. Wang, X.F.; Li, X.H.; Gu, Y.L.; Jin, X.; Kang, Y.; Li, D. Application of BP neural network into prediction of rockburst in tunneling. In Proceedings of the 2004 International Symposium on Safety Science and Technology, Shanghai, China, 5–10 October 2004; Volume 4, pp. 617–621.
45. Zhang, M. Prediction of rockburst hazard based on particle swarm algorithm and neural network. *Neural Comput. Appl.* **2022**, *3*, 2649–2659. [CrossRef]
46. Li, X.; Mao, H.; Li, B.; Xu, N. Dynamic early warning of rockburst using microseismic multi-parameters based on Bayesian network. *Eng. Sci. Technol. Int. J.* **2021**, *24*, 715–727. [CrossRef]
47. Ke, B.; Khandelwal, M.; Asteris, P.G.; Skentou, A.D.; Mamou, A.; Armaghani, D.J. Rock-Burst Occurrence Prediction Based on Optimized Naïve Bayes Models. *IEEE Access* **2021**, *9*, 91347–91360. [CrossRef]
48. Dong, L.; Li, X.; Kang, P. Prediction of rockburst classification using Random Forest. *Trans. Nonferrous Met. Soc. China* **2013**, *2*, 472–477. [CrossRef]
49. Li, D.; Liu, Z.; Armaghani, D.J.; Xiao, P.; Zhou, J. Novel Ensemble Tree Solution for Rockburst Prediction Using Deep Forest. *Mathematics* **2022**, *10*, 787. [CrossRef]
50. Li, T.; Li, Y.; Yang, X. Rockburst prediction based on genetic algorithms and extreme learning machine. *J. Cent. South Univ.* **2017**, *24*, 2105–2113. [CrossRef]
51. Guo, J.; Guo, J.; Zhang, Q.; Huang, M. Research on Rockburst Classification Prediction Based on BP-SVM Model. *IEEE Access* **2022**, *10*, 50427–50447. [CrossRef]
52. Pu, Y.; Apel, D.B.; Lingga, B. Rockburst prediction in kimberlite using decision tree with incomplete data. *J. Sustain. Min.* **2018**, *17*, 158–165. [CrossRef]
53. Ghasemi, E.; Gholizadeh, H.; Adoko, A.C. Evaluation of rockburst occurrence and intensity in underground structures using decision tree approach. *Eng. Comput.* **2020**, *36*, 213–225. [CrossRef]
54. Zhou, J.; Li, E.; Yang, S.; Wang, M.; Shi, X.; Yao, S.; Mitri, H. Slope stability prediction for circular mode failure using gradient boosting machine approach based on an updated database of case histories. *Saf. Sci.* **2019**, *118*, 505–518. [CrossRef]
55. Wu, S.; Yang, S.; Huo, L. Prediction of rockburst intensity based on unascertained measure-intuitionistic fuzzy set. *Chin. J. Rock Mech. Eng.* **2020**, *39* (Suppl. S1), 2930–2939.
56. Gong, F.; Li, X.; Dong, L.; Liu, X. Underground goaf risk evaluation based on uncertainty measurement theory. *Chin. J. Rock Mech. Eng.* **2008**, *27*, 323–330. (In Chinese)
57. Zhou, J.; Chen, C.; Khandelwal, M.; Tao, M.; Li, C. Novel approach to evaluate rock mass fragmentation in block caving using unascertained measurement model and information entropy with flexible credible identification criterion. *Eng. Comput.* **2021**, *3*, 3789–3809. [CrossRef]
58. Zhou, J.; Chen, C.; Du, K.; Armaghani, D.; Li, C. A new hybrid model of information entropy and unascertained measurement with different membership functions for evaluating destressability in burst-prone underground mines. *Eng. Comput.* **2022**, *3* (Suppl. S1), 381–399. [CrossRef]
59. Huang, C.; Li, Q.; Wu, S.; Liu, Y. Subgrade Stability Evaluation in Permafrost Regions Based on Unascertained Measurement Model. *Geotech. Geol. Eng.* **2019**, *37*, 707–719. [CrossRef]
60. Qiansheng, C. Attribute sets and attribute synthetic assessment system. *Syst. Eng.-Theory Pract.* **1997**, *17*, 1–8.

1. Zhou, J.; Chen, C.; Armaghani, D.J.; Ma, S. Developing a hybrid model of information entropy and unascertained measurement theory for evaluation of the excavatability in rock mass. *Eng. Comput.* **2022**, *38*, 247–270. [CrossRef]
2. Saaty, T.L. Modeling unstructured decision problems—The theory of analytical hierarchies. *Math. Comput. Simul.* **1978**, *20*, 147–158. [CrossRef]
3. Shannon, C.E. A mathematical theory of communication. *Bell Syst. Tech. J.* **1948**, *27*, 379–423. [CrossRef]
4. Wang, C.; Wu, A.; Lu, H.; Bao, T.; Liu, X. Predicting rockburst tendency based on fuzzy matter–element model. *Int. J. Rock Mech. Min. Sci.* **2015**, *75*, 224–232. [CrossRef]
5. Li, M.; Li, K.; Liu, Y.; Wu, S.; Qin, Q.; Wang, H. Rockburst prediction based on coefficient of variation and sequence analysis-multidimensional normal cloud model. *Chin. J. Rock Mech. Eng.* **2020**, *39* (Suppl. S2), 3395–3402. (In Chinese) [CrossRef]
6. Lorenzini, G. Simplified modelling of sprinkler droplet dynamics. *Biosyst. Eng.* **2004**, *87*, 1–11. [CrossRef]
7. Li, A. *Research on Safety Evaluation Method of Quayside Container Crane*; Wuhan University of Technology: Wuhan, China, 2017. (In Chinese)
8. Wang, G. Unascertained information and its mathematical treatment. *J. Harbin Univ. Archit. Civ. Eng.* **1990**, *23*, 1–9. (In Chinese)
9. Liu, K.; Pang, Y.; Sun, G.; Yao, L. The unascertained measurement evaluation on a city's environmental quality. *Syst. Eng.-Theory Pract.* **1999**, *19*, 52–58. (In Chinese)
10. Wu, X.; Xu, F. Detection Model for Unbalanced Bidding in Railway Construction Projects: Considering the Risk of Quantity Variation. *J. Constr. Eng. Manag.* **2021**, *147*, 04021055. [CrossRef]
11. Zhong, Y.; Liang, X. Using CNN-VGG 16 to detect the tennis motion tracking by information entropy and unascertained measurement theory. *Adv. Nano Res.* **2022**, *12*, 223–239. [CrossRef]
12. Cai, M.; Kaiser, P. Visualization of rock mass classification systems. *Geotech. Geol. Eng.* **2006**, *24*, 1089–1102. [CrossRef]
13. Zhang, J.; He, C.; Yan, J. Discussion on the applicability of XGBoost algorithm based on cross validation in prediction of rockburst intensity classification. *Tunnel Construct.* **2020**, *40* (Suppl. S1), 247–253. (In Chinese)
14. Wang, Y.; Xu, Q.; Chai, H.; Liu, L.; Xia, S. Rockburst prediction in deep shaft based on RBF-AR model. *J. Jilin Univ. (Earth Sci. Ed.)* **2013**, *43*, 1943–1949. (In Chinese)
15. Zhang, L.W.; Zhang, D.Y.; Qiu, D.H. Application of extension evaluation method in rockburst prediction based on rough set theory. *J. Chin. Coal. Soc.* **2010**, *35*, 1461–1465. (In Chinese)
16. Guo, J.; Zhang, W.X.; Zhao, Y. A multidimensional cloud model for rockburst prediction. *Chin. J. Rock Mech. Eng.* **2018**, *37*, 1199–1206. (In Chinese)

Disclaimer/Publisher's Note: The statements, opinions and data contained in all publications are solely those of the individual author(s) and contributor(s) and not of MDPI and/or the editor(s). MDPI and/or the editor(s) disclaim responsibility for any injury to people or property resulting from any ideas, methods, instructions or products referred to in the content.

Article

High Steep Rock Slope Instability Mechanism Induced by the Pillar Deterioration in the Mountain Mining Area

Lu Chen [1], Xiangxi Yu [1], Ron Luo [2,3,*], Ling Zeng [1] and Hongtao Cao [1]

[1] College of Civil Engineering, Changsha University of Science & Technology, Changsha 410110, China
[2] School of Resource Environment and Safety Engineering, University of South China, Hengyang 421001, China
[3] Periodical Press, Changsha University of Science & Technology, Changsha 410110, China
* Correspondence: luorong-lr@stu.usc.edu.cn

Abstract: In hilly regions, landslides or slope failures are very common phenomena, when underground mineral resources are excavated. In this study, some landslide disasters in a mountain mining area were analyzed. The engineering geological and instability reason were investigated. The numerical simulation of a high steep rock slope disturbed by a room and pillar mine was established. The failure process of a high steep rock slope induced by the pillar deterioration was analyzed to reveal the characteristics of deformation and sliding. The results show that the pillar plays an important role in maintaining the stability of the slope, if the pillar can support the overlying rock mass, only a tiny deformation will be induced. When the pillar fails and the roof caves, the overlying rock mass above the room and pillar goaf will rapidly subside, and the crack evolution of slope is induced, forming the potential slip surface. The landslide mass gradually moves. When the rock mass at the middle and lower of the slope is squeezed out, slope sliding will be induced. The failure process can be divided into four stages as follow: tiny displacement is caused by the mining, roof collapse is caused by the pillar failure, the potential slip surface is formed from the crack evolution; the slope sliding is induced by the fracturing of rock mass at the middle and lower of the slope.

Keywords: rock slope; goaf; pillar deterioration; crack evolution; slope instability

MSC: 65-04

1. Introduction

Mineral resources exploitation has made important contributions to the country's economic development in China. However, when resources are excavated in mountainous areas such as Guizhou and Guangxi Province, the subsidence and instability of overlying strata above the goaf can easily induce mountain cracking and landslide disasters, which seriously affect the safety of people's lives and property in the mountain mining areas [1–7]. Therefore, many scholars have investigated the influence of underground deposit mining on mountain stability. Fan, et al. [8] used field measurement, UAV aerial photography and remote sensing image methods to describe the characteristics of the collapse in the Pusa, a village in the County of Nayong (Guizhou Province, China), the dynamic process and formation mechanism of the collapse are then investigated. Dai et al. [9] analyzed the influence of underground mining disturbance on the deformation and failure of bedding rock slopes using a similar model test method. On this basis, the weakening phenomenon and weakening coefficient were defined, and the stability of the bedding rock slope affected by mining was studied by the limit equilibrium method. Salmi et al. [10] use the discrete element UDEC software to investigate the mechanism of mining-induced landsliding at NattaiNorth, NSW. The outcomes of numerical modeling showed that underground mining will cause the redistribution of stress within the rock mass, resulting in the weakening of the basement rock and the occurrence of shear failure. The failure of the collapsed bedrock of the overlying strata has been the main reason for large-scale landslides, and the instability mode is mainly controlled by the joints and fissures in the rock mass. Zhao et al. [11] studied the failure mechanism of the Madaling landslide 2006 in Guizhou Province, revealing that the slope experienced four stages of failure mechanisms, and the run-out behaviors of the landslide were analyzed. Zheng et al. [12] analyzed the failure process and mechanism associated with underground mining activities, based on field investigation and laboratory experimental study. The rockfalls are classified into one of three failure modes: crack–toppling, crack–sliding, and crack–slumping. In which the failures are governed by the corresponding characteristics of the rock mass structure. Zhong et al. [13] studied the formation mechanism of a slightly inclined bedding mudstone landslide in Tanshan Coal Mine in Ningxia by numerical simulation. It was found that the formation of the landslide is mainly affected by the geological factors of the mountain, coal mining and rainfall. The landslide process can be divided into four stages: slope creep, slope deformation, landslide movement and landslide accumulation. Yang et al. [14] simulated the deformation trend, mechanical behavior, fracture evolution process and deformation and failure mechanism of mining slope under different free surface characteristics by PFC 2D software. the deformation and failure process of the slope is divided into three stages: caving and sinking deformation stage-crack deformation stage-creep deformation stage. Zhang et al. [15] established a mining landslide sensitivity evaluation model based on transfer learning based on typical landslides, analyzing the main influencing factors of landslides in mining areas. Wang et al. [16] analyzed the behavior and characteristics of shallow failure of weak rock slopes through theoretical analysis, numerical simulation and field monitoring. It is found that the mechanical parameters of rock mass strength on the surface of weak rock slopes are quite different from those of the original rock after mining disturbance. The deformation of the lower part of the slope is three to five times that of the upper part, and its failure mode is creep crack.

The previous research shows that the instability and collapse of the slope is easily caused by the mining activity. Moreover, the outcomes have offered critical insight into the mechanism of the mining landslide [17–19]. However, researchers focus on the mechanical deformation characteristics and landslide formation mechanism, and the key role of the pillar in maintaining the stability of goaf is ignored. Some researchers have revealed that the collapse of goaf can be induced by the failure of the pillar [20–23]. To reveal the high steep rock slope instability mechanism induced by the pillar deterioration, some landslide disasters in mining areas were analyzed. Moreover, the numerical simulation of a high steep rock slope impacted by a room and pillar mine was established. The failure process of a rock high steep slope induced by the pillar deterioration was analyzed to reveal the characteristics of deformation and sliding.

2. Cases of High Steep Rock Slope Instability in Mining Area

2.1. Landslide in Pusa, Guizhou

2.1.1. Overview of Landslide

At about 10:40 on 28 August 2017, an extremely large landslide disaster occurred in the Laoyingyan Mountain in Pusa Village, Zhangjiawan Town, Nayong County, Guizhou Province as shown in Figure 1 [24]. The length of the landslide body was about 840 m, the width is about 410 m, and the landslide volume was about 6×10^5 m^3. It destroyed the local forest and cultivated land along the way and buried some houses in the Dashujiao Formation of Pusa Village, resulting in a total of 35 deaths [8].

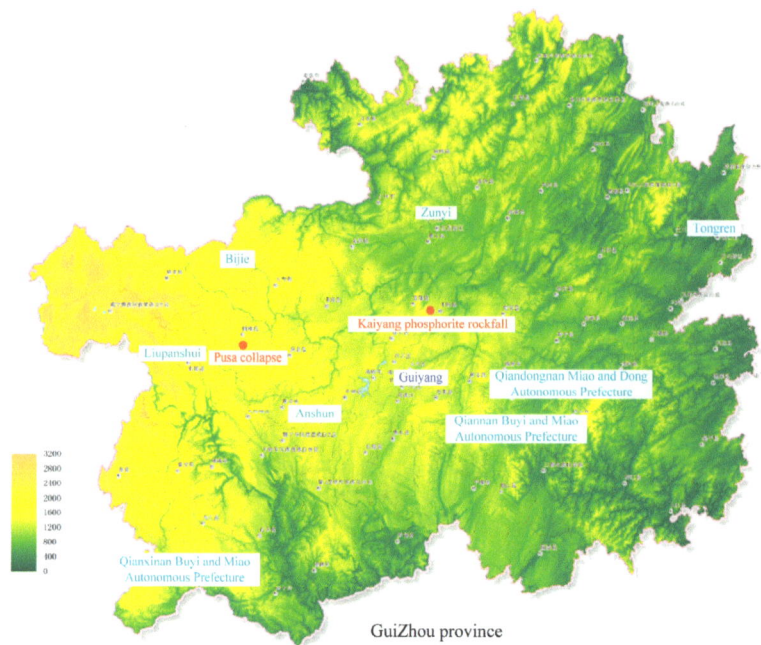

Figure 1. Location of the slope instability [24].

2.1.2. Engineering Geological Condition

The collapse area was located in the upper part of the slope with a natural slope of 55~75°, and the lower part of the slope was a gentle slope with a slope of 10~25°. The dominant surrounding area was dry land. The exposed stratigraphic lithology includes as follows: limestone, silty mudstone and argillaceous siltstone in the Lower Triassic Yelang Formation(T1y); silty mudstone, limestone and argillaceous siltstone in the Upper Permian Changxing-Dalong Formation(P2c + d); the coal line of argillaceous siltstone, carbonaceous mudstone and coal seam in Longtan Formation (P2l). The lithology of the collapse area in Pusa Village is limestone, silty mudstone and argillaceous siltstone of the Lower Triassic Yelang Formation(T1y). The occurrence of the rock stratum is N80°E/SE∠5°~10°. The direction of the cliff wall is N40°~50° E, and the rock stratum is inclined to the slope [8]. The geological profile of the main sliding direction of the collapse in Nayong County, Guizhou Province is shown in Figure 2.

The collapsed area of the Pusa Village is characterized by a monoclinic structure. Moreover, the slope is constituted of a soft and hard interbedded structure rock mass. The limestone layer and marl layer are relatively hard. However, the argillaceous siltstone layer and silty mudstone layer are relatively weak. There are two faults (F1 and F2) in the mining area, which are located in the middle and front of the slope at the lower part of the cliff in the collapse source area. The coal seam in the mining area is fractured by those faults. However, the collapse source area is not impacted directly, as the dip direction of the fault is opposite to that of the rock stratum. Earthquake activity has not been found in this area and adjacent areas in recent years.

The lower part of the collapsed body is the mining area of the Pusa Coal Mine. Which mainly mines the coal seam of the Upper Permian Longtan Formation(P2l), the mind area is about 0.96 km². The dip angle of the mining coal seam is 7~12°. Among them, there are six coal seams, which are the M6, M10, M14, M16, M18 and M20 from top to bottom, with an average thickness of 1.6 m.

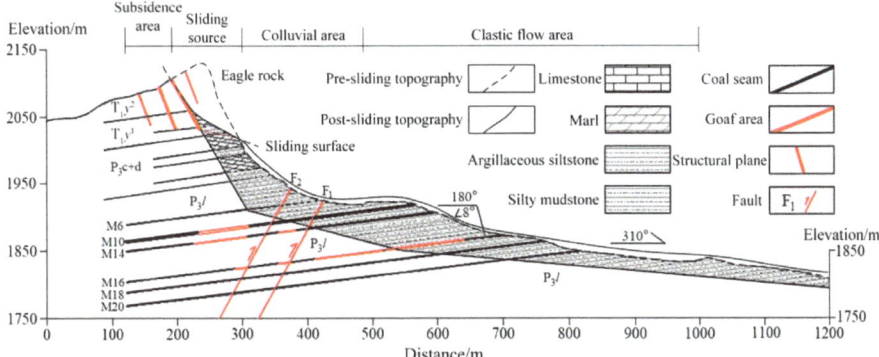

Figure 2. Geological profile of collapse at main sliding direction in Nayong County, Guizhou Province.

2.1.3. Instability Reason Speculation

The main factors causing landslide can be described as follows: the mining activities of the coal seam will affect and change the stress environment of the mountain, reducing the stability of the upper rock and soil. The structural plane, which is not conducive to the stability of rock mass, provides the natural conditions for mountain crack propagation. The dissolution and weathering of limestone rock mass accelerate the crack evolution, and the rainfall in the early stage deteriorates the geological conditions, as the strength of the rock will be weakened by the water [25,26].

2.2. Rockfall in the Kaiyang Phosphorite, Guizhou

2.2.1. Overview of Rockfall

The Kaiyang Phosphate Mine is located in Jinzhong, north of Guiyang, Guizhou Province as shown in Figure 1. According to the field investigation, a certain scale of collapse occurred frequently in the mining area. More than 80 times of collapses and landslides were induced with a total volume of more than 2.8×10^6 m^3. The geological section of the main sliding direction of a typical collapse in the Kaiyang Phosphate Mine is shown in Figure 3.

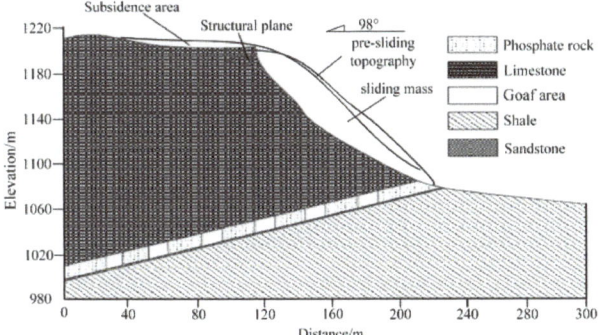

Figure 3. Geological Profile of Typical Collapse at Main Slip Direction in the Kaiyang Phosphate Mine.

2.2.2. Engineering Geological Condition

The terrain of the collapse area is high in the south and low in the north. The highest point of the Langjiling is 1203 m. The slope is steep, the gradient is 45~65°, and the occurrence of rock stratum is N13°E/SE∠30°. The strike of the slope is basically the same as that of the rock stratum, the direction of the dip is opposite, which belongs to the reverse layered structure slope [27].

The slope strata in the collapse area mainly include the Lower Cambrian Qingxudong Formation (ε1q) limestone, the Jindingshan Formation (ε1m) shale intercalated sandstone, the Mingxinsi Formation (ε1j) argillaceous sandstone, the Niutitang Formation (ε1n) carbonaceous shale, the Upper Sinian Dengying Formation (Zbdn) light gray thick dolomite, the Upper Sinian Doushantuo Formation (Zbd) phosphate rock and thin quartz sandstone and the Upper Sinian Nantuo Formation (Zann) purple red shale.

There are three groups of dominant structural planes in the collapse area. The structural plane J1 (N5°E/NW∠75°) constitutes the trailing edge boundary of the collapse area. The structural plane J2 (N15°E/NW∠47°) provides the bottom slip surface of the collapse. The structural plane J3 (N85°E/NW∠75°) is located downstream of the Yangshui River, which constitutes the lateral cutting surface of the collapse. Furthermore, unloading cracks inclined to the outside of the slope can be found in the slope.

2.2.3. Instability Reason Speculation

The long wall mining method is used in the rockfall area, and the regular pillars are retained to support the roof and stratum. The mining sequence is from top to bottom. A large mined-out area has been formed as long-term mining, and the overlying strata have been bent and sunk, inducing tensile cracks on the top and surface of the slope. As the steep and discussions of the slope, the potential sliding surface is easily caused. Furthermore, the rainfall is mainly concentrated from June to July. A large amount of rainwater infiltrates into the slope along the cracks on the top of the slope. While the rock mass is weakened, and the water pressure is produced. Those may induce to collapse of the slope in a critical state.

2.3. Weima Landslide, Shanxi

2.3.1. Overview of Landslide

On 16 August 2013, a landslide occurred at the crest of the Weima Mountain in Shanxi, China. The geological section of the main sliding direction is shown in Figure 4. The highest point elevation is 1471 m, the lowest point is located at the bottom of the slope, the elevation is 1436 m, the height difference is 35 m, and the landslide shear outlet elevation is 1437 m. The plane shape of the sliding body is an irregular oval. The length and width of the sliding body are about 62 m and 101 m, respectively, and the thickness is 5~13 m. The volume is about 5.6×10^4 m^3 which is considered a small bedrock landslide.

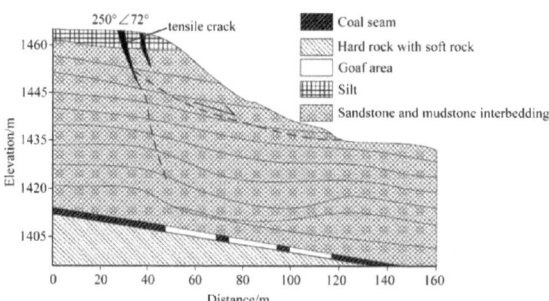

Figure 4. Geological Profile of landslide at Main Slide Direction in the Weima.

2.3.2. Engineering Geological Condition

The upper part of the slope in the landslide area is steep, with a slope angle of about 34°, and the lower part is gentle, with a slope of about 25°. The top layer of the slope is the quaternary silt with a thickness of about 3.15 m. The lower part of the slope is composed of sandstone, mudstone and coal. The occurrence of rock stratum is 165°∠10°, which is a bedding slope. Two groups of the 'X' type conjugate joints LX1 (330°∠80°) and LX2 (250°∠72°) are developed in the slope. The joint surface of LX1 is straight and smooth, and the joint surface of LX2 is serrated, with an opening width of 0.5–22.5 cm [28].

2.3.3. Instability Reason Speculation

The slope was disturbed by underground mining activity, and the underground coal mining in the landslide area can be traced back to the 1990s. The average thickness of the mined coal seam is 1.56 m, the buried depth is about 30~62 m, the short-wall blasting mining method is used, and the roof is managed by all caving methods. When the ore body is mined, a large area of goaf is formed, which causes the overlying rock mass to fall under the action of gravity, and the crack at the position of the trailing edge of the slope is induced as shown in Figure 1. Furthermore, the slope is also impacted by continuous heavy rainfall, the rainwater flows along the cracks, weakening the slope. Ultimately, the sliding is caused.

3. Numerical Simulation Analysis

3.1. Scheme of Numerical Simulation

In order to explore the instability mechanism of the high steep rock slope induced by the weakening of pillar in goaf, the PFC 2D (Particle Flow Code) discrete element software is used to study the mechanical behavior, revealing the dynamic instability mechanism of landslide in the mountain mining area. The length and width of the model are 450 m and 300 m, respectively. The thicknesses of limestone, marl, silty mudstone, coal seam, and argillaceous siltstone are 165 m, 15 m, 30 m, 9 m and 81 m, respectively. The parallel bond model is selected for coal and rock mass, the smooth joint model is selected for rock interface, and the Mohr–Coulomb criterion is used. The strength and deformation parameters in the numerical model (Tables 1 and 2) are determined by the previous research and rock mechanics test [29–33].

Table 1. Rock and coal parameters.

Parameters	Limestone	Marl	Silty Mudstone	Coal	Argillaceous Siltstone
Porosity/%	10	10	10	10	10
Particle density/(kg/m3)	2700	2650	2600	1350	2560
Effective modulus/GPa	10	8	7	3.84	5.6
Normal-to-shear stiffness ratio/k^*	1	1	1	1	1
Bond effective modulus/GPa	10	7	5	3.84	4.6
Bond normal-to-shear stiffness ratio/$\bar{k}^*$	1	1	1	1	1
Bond tensile strength/MPa	15	12.5	10.2	5.5	8
Bond cohesion/MPa	25	18.1	15.4	8	14.45
Bond friction angle/°	33	41	35.8	48	30.1

Table 2. Bedding planes parameters.

Parameters	Rock Interface	Coal Seam Interface
Bond effective modulus/GPa	2.9	1.5
Bond normal-to-shear stiffness ratio/$(\bar{k}^*)$	1	1
Bond tensile strength/MPa	0.15	0.1
Bond cohesion/MPa	0.2	0.13
Bond friction angle/(°)	22	15

According to the engineering geological profile, a two-dimensional numerical model is established as shown in Figure 5. The horizontal displacement of the left and right boundaries is limited; the vertical displacement of the bottom boundary is also limited. The deformation and crack will be caused near the goaf first during the excavating, and the mining response propagates to the surface. The movement of the roof and overlying strata are monitored. In addition, this study focuses on the stability of the high and steep slope disturbed by mining activity, the deformation and crack evolution are analyzed, and the monitoring points at the top and the surface of the slope are arranged. Hence, twenty monitoring points are arranged at the top of the slope, the slope surface, the overlying rock mass and the roof of the goaf, those are divided into four groups as shown in Figure 5. The negative value of horizontal displacement indicates the monitoring point moves to the left of the mode, and the positive value of the horizontal displacement indicates that it moves to the right of the mode or the slope. The height of the mining is 5 m, and the spacing of the mining zone is 45 m. The mining sequence of the numerical model is from the M−1 to the M−3, and the calculation of stress balance is carried out after the mining of each working face.

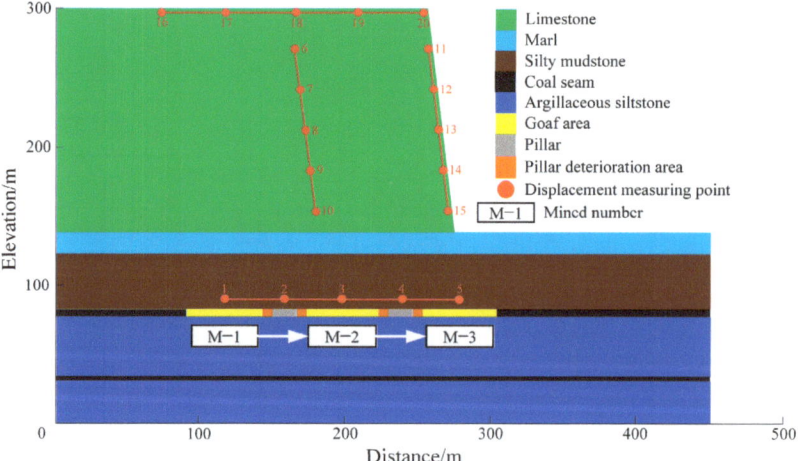

Figure 5. Numerical model and layout of monitoring points.

3.2. Analysis of the Failure Process

The process of cracking evolution and contact force characteristics of the numerical model are shown in Figure 6. When the coal seam is mined, the original stress state of the model is changed, which causes the stress redistribution of the surrounding rock, and the stress concentration occurs at the top of pillar and the boundary of the roof, resulting in cracks in the roof and the underlying weak rock mass as shown in Figure 6a. When the weakening pillar lost the bearing capacity, the roof deformation is caused due to the loss of support. Then, the roof sinks towards the goaf, and the shear crack of the roof is induced at the boundary of the goaf. When the stress of the roof strata in the goaf exceeds its ultimate bearing capacity, that will be gradually broken and then caved. In the process of roof caving, the overlying stratum also bends and sinks. Due to the roof caving, the subsidence of the overlying stratum is also caused, and a tensile fracture is formed inside the overlying rock mass as shown in Figure 6b. Then, the goaf is filled by the caved stratum, and the fracture and stress arch is formed in the slope. A collapse pit on the surface is formed at the top of the slope, accompanied by the visible deep cracks as shown in Figure 6c. When the pillar and roof collapse, the rock mass in the subsidence area is also broken due to the gravity of the overlying stratum. The uneven settlement continues to expand, resulting in the crack evolution of the slope. The slope body located at the right side of the macroscopic cracking dumps generally to the dip direction, and the rock mass at the foot of the slope is subjected to stress concentration due to the movement of the slope body as shown in Figure 6d. With the continuous expansion of cracks, the potential sliding surface is formed in the slope. The rock mass at the middle and foot of the slope is continuously broken, and then squeezed out, the overburden slips downward due to the loss of support. The middle part of the slope is also cracked. With the continuous dumping of the slope, the sliding surface is penetrated, forming a potential landslide area. Ultimately, the sliding surface is connected, and a landslide is induced as shown in Figure 6e,f.

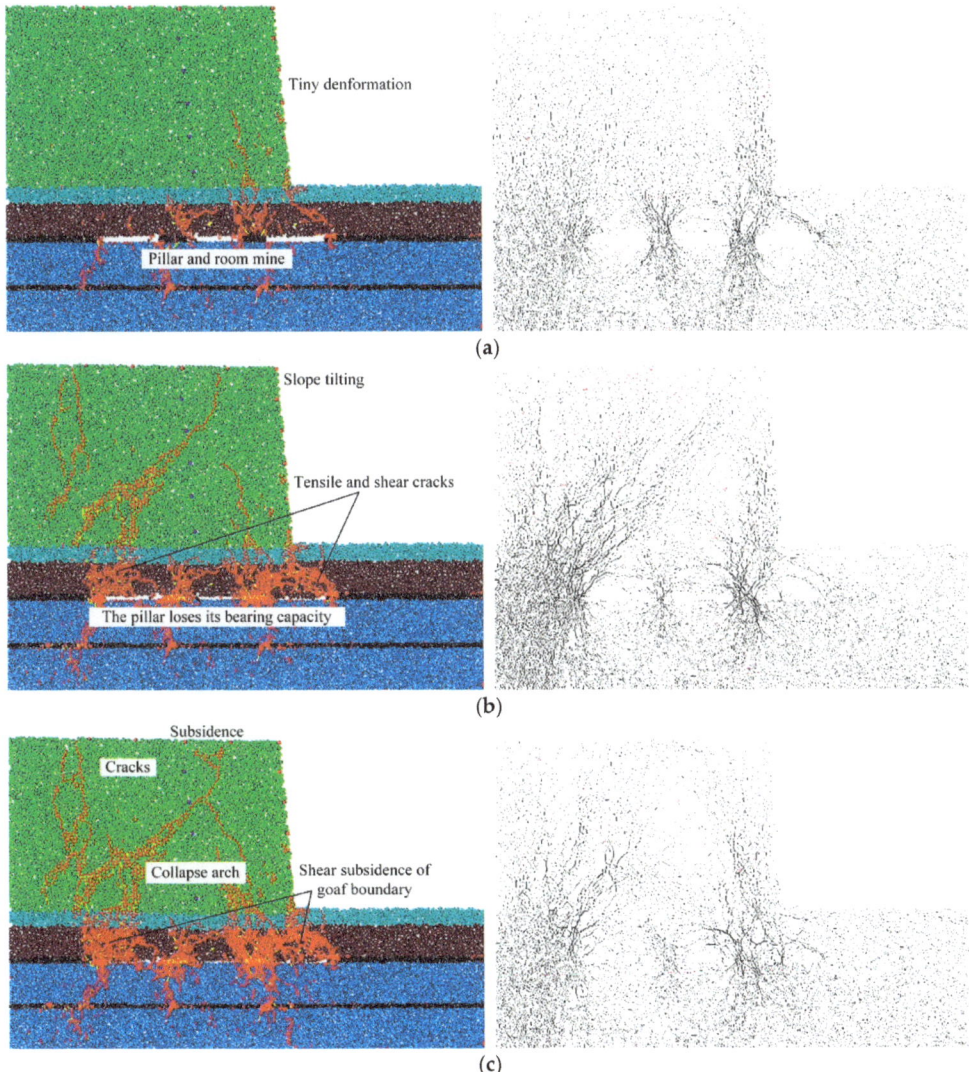

Figure 6. *Cont.*

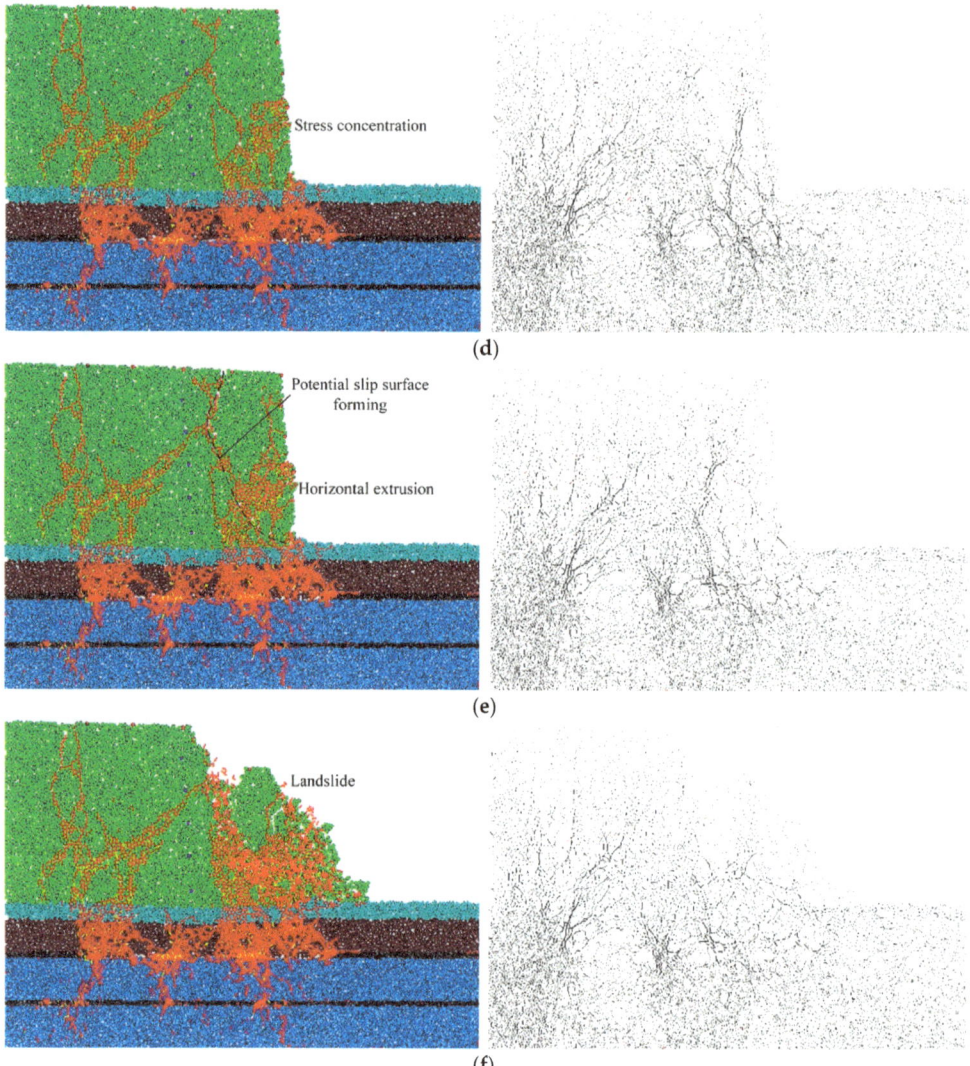

Figure 6. The process of cracking evolution and contact force characteristics. (**a**) mining; (**b**) pillar deterioration; (**c**) roof collapse and goaf filled; (**d**) rock mass spalling at slope; (**e**) potential slip surface forming; (**f**) landslide.

3.3. Analysis of Displacement Characteristics

The displacement laws of monitoring points arranged in roof are shown in Figure 7. When the areas of the M−1 and the M−2 are mined, a tiny displacement is induced. The downward deformation occurs firstly at the measuring point #1, followed by the #2 and #3. When the M−3 is mined, the negative displacement of the #1, #2 and #3 and the positive displacement of the #4 and #5 are induced. The vertical displacement of each measuring point in the roof maintains a small growth rate. Those indicate the measuring points of #1, #2 and #3 moved to the left of the model, and the measuring points of #4 and #5 moved to the right. The roof bends and sinks at the center of the goaf as a symmetrical point. Then, the vertical displacement of the roof increases sharply. Measuring point #5 moves fast to the slope. Both measuring points #3 and #4 move to the left first, and then to right. Those indicate the rapid subsidence of the roof has been induced by the degradation of the pillar. During the rapid subsidence process, the overlying strata are also toppling outward to the slope. Until the roof collapses and the overlying rock mass fills the goaf, the displacement of the measuring point stop growth.

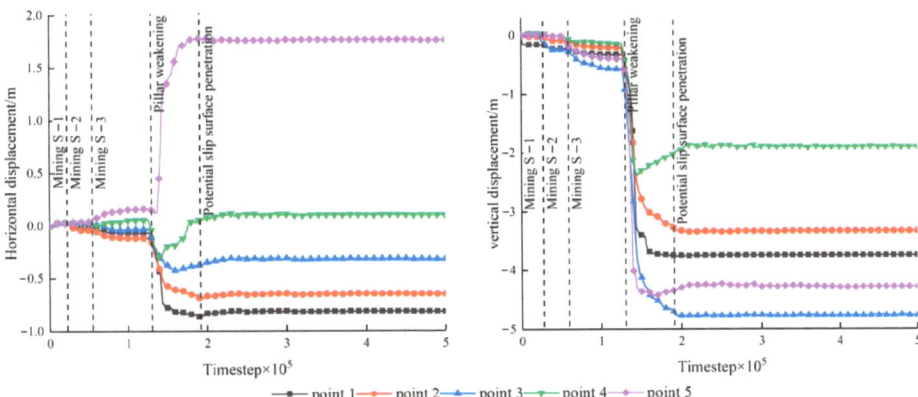

Figure 7. The displacement of the roof of pillar and room goaf.

The displacement laws of the measuring points above the M−2 are shown in Figure 8. It can be found that the tiny vertical displacement is caused by the mining activity, while the pillar has enough bearing capacity to support the overlying rock mass. However, the displacement of each measuring point changes greatly resulting from the deterioration of the pillar. The horizontal displacement develops positively, and the vertical displacement increases negatively. This indicates the rock mass above the M−2 moves to the slope and the goaf when the pillar lost its bearing capacity and the roof collapses. As the rock mass fills the goaf, the displacement of the measuring points also stops growth, indicating that the overlying strata above the M−2 keep stable after the subsidence.

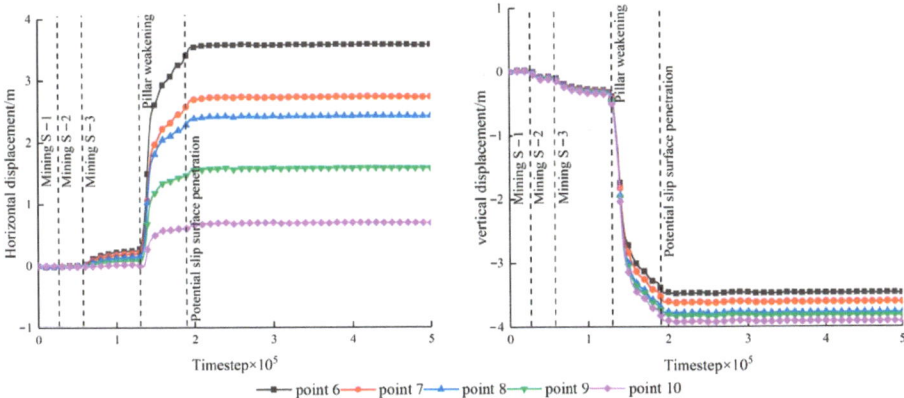

Figure 8. The displacement of strata above the M-2.

The horizontal and vertical displacement at the surface of slope are shown in Figure 9. A tiny displacement is caused during the mining process of the M−1, M−2 and M−3. However, a significant change appears after the pillar deterioration. The horizontal and vertical displacements increase rapidly at the same time, indicating the slope body tends to move to the dip direction of the slope. The horizontal displacement of measuring points #13 and #14 changed earlier than other measuring points. Those show that the rock mass in the middle and lower part of the slope is squeezed out firstly during the settlement deformation of the strata. As the distance between measuring point #15 and the bottom of the slope is small, the displacement value changes little during the process of slope instability. Moreover, the displacement stops changing when that rolls to the bottom of the slope.

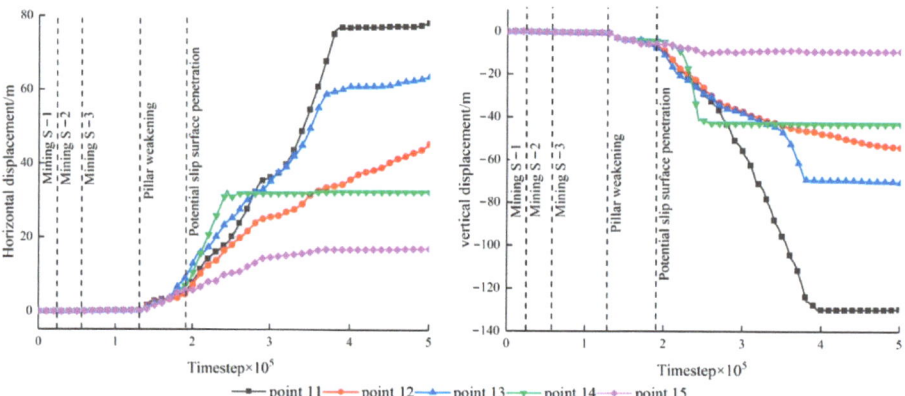

Figure 9. The displacement at the surface of slope.

The horizontal and vertical displacement at the top of the slope is shown in Figure 10. The displacement almost cannot be induced at the top of the slope during the mining process of the M−1, M−2 and M−3. When the bearing capacity of the pillar decreases, some measuring points start moving. The measuring points #16, #17 and #18 moved to the slope, caused by the deterioration of the pillar, and then stopped moving. However, measuring points #19 and #20 speedily moved again at the 1.1×10^5 timestep. Those indicate the slipping has been caused at the monitoring area of points #19 and #20. Moreover, the potential slip surface is located between monitoring points #18 and #19.

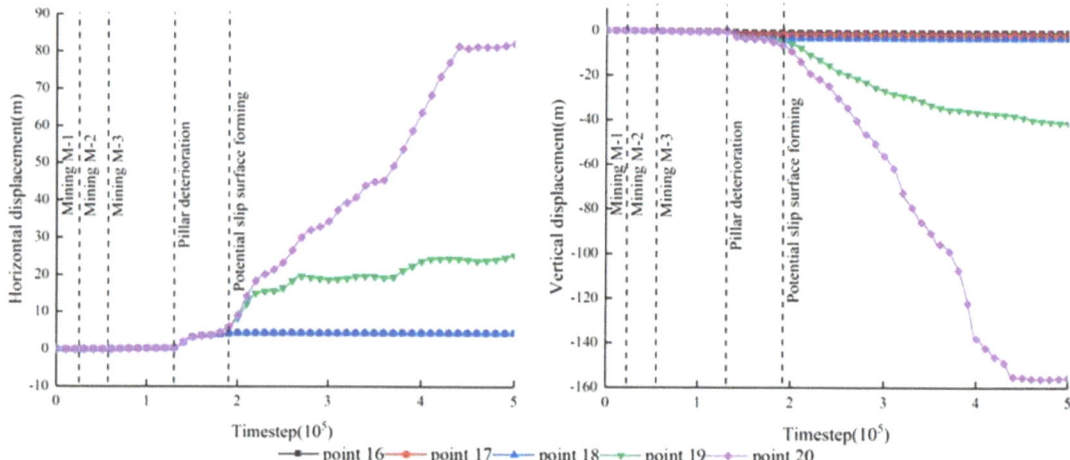

Figure 10. The displacement at the top of slope.

4. Slope Instability Mechanism Induced by the Pillar Deterioration

The failure process of landslide is shown in Figure 11. When the pillar and room goaf is formed, the stress of slope body is redistributed. Moreover, stress concentration occurs, resulting in the cracks evolution of rock mass in the slope. Before the pillar lost its bearing capacity, a tiny displacement is induced. However, when the pillar fails to bear the weight of the overlying rock mass, it causes subsidence in the roof. Moreover, the shear dislocation subsidence occurs at the goaf boundary near the slope toe. As the roof caves gradually, the tensile shear cracks at the boundary gradually expand upward, forming a collapsed arch. The overlying rock mass inclines outward to the dip direction of the slope with the collapsing of the goaf. Moreover, the serious stress concentration occurs at the rock mass in the middle and lower part of the slope. That rock mass is firstly destabilized and squeezed out. As a result, the overlying rock layer loses its support and also dumps outward. In this process, the overlying rock mass gradually breaks and forms the potential sliding surface, and finally slides out on the outside of the slope. Therefore, the instability mechanism of rock slope induced by the pillar deterioration can be summarized as follows:

(I) Tiny displacement is caused by the mining (Figure 11a).
(II) Roof collapse is caused by pillar failure (Figure 11b).
(III) Macro-crack of the slope is induced by the overburdened rock movement, forming the potential slip surface (Figure 11c).
(VI) The rock mass at the middle and lower of the slope is squeezed out, inducing the slope sliding (Figure 11d).

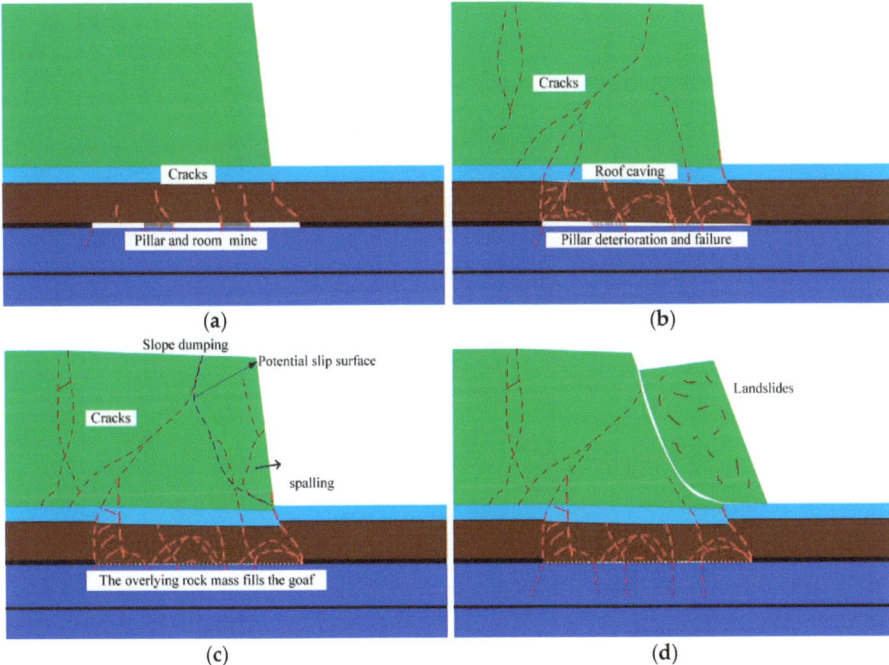

Figure 11. Failure process. (**a**) mining; (**b**) pillar deterioration; (**c**) potential slip surface forming; (**d**) landslide.

5. Discussion and Conclusions

(1) The stability of high steep rock slope is significantly disturbed by mining activity. Especially, the crack and the overall deformation of the slope will be caused by the failure of pillar. When the overburden rock subsides and the slope gradually topples to dip the

direction of the slope. The stability of the slope is greatly affected. The slope sliding is easily induced by the changing external environment conditions.

(2) The pillar may play an important role in process of the deformation and failure of the slope. When the mined-out area is formed, if the pillar can bear the weight of the overlying rock mass, only a tiny deformation can be induced. The impact of slope stability disturbed by mining will be restricted, and the slope will form a new stable state. With the passing of time, if the bearing capacity of the pillar is reduced due to the spalling and strength deterioration, when the pillar is destroyed, the overlying rock mass above the goaf will rapidly subside, which is considered to be responsible for the deformation and instability of the slope.

(3) The failure process of rock slope induced by pillar degradation in goaf can be divided into four stages in this study. (I) Tiny displacement is caused by mining. (II) Roof collapse is caused by pillar failure. (III) The potential slip surface formed results from the crack evolution. (IV) The slope sliding is induced by the fracturing of rock mass at the middle and lower of the slope.

Author Contributions: Conceptualization, L.C.; Data curation, X.Y.; Formal analysis, R.L.; Funding acquisition, L.C.; Investigation, R.L.; Methodology, X.Y.; Project administration, X.Y.; Resources, X.Y. and H.C.; Software, X.Y. and H.C.; Supervision, L.C. and L.Z.; Validation, L.C. and L.Z.; Visualization, R.L.; Writing—original draft, X.Y. All authors have read and agreed to the published version of the manuscript.

Funding: This research was funded by the National Natural Science Foundation of China (52004036, 52078066 and 52078067); the National Natural Science Foundation of Hunan Province (2021JJ40572 and 2021JJ40579), and the Postgraduate Scientific Research Innovation Project of Changsha University of Science & Technology (CX2021SS23).

Data Availability Statement: Data sharing not applicable. The data and materials are contained within the article.

Acknowledgments: We would like to acknowledge the editors and reviewers for their invaluable comments.

Conflicts of Interest: The authors declare no conflict of interest.

References

1. Yu, X.; Mao, X. A preliminary discrimination model of a deep mining landslide and its application in the Guanwen coal mine. *Bull. Eng. Geol. Environ.* **2020**, *79*, 485–493.
2. Yang, Y.; Xu, Y.; Shen, S.; Yuan, Y.; Yin, Z. Mining-induced geo-hazards with environmental protection measures in Yunnan, China: An overview. *Bull. Eng. Geol. Environ.* **2015**, *74*, 141–150. [CrossRef]
3. Zhong, Z.; Xu, Y.; Wang, N.; Liu, X.; Gao, G. Environmental characteristics and unified failure mode classification system for mining landslides in the karst mountainous areas of southwestern China. *Carbonates Evaporites* **2023**, *38*, 2. [CrossRef]
4. Chen, L.; Zhao, C.; Li, B.; He, K.; Ren, C.; Liu, X.; Liu, D. Deformation monitoring and failure mode research of mining-induced jianshanying landslide in karst mountain area, China with ALOS/PALSAR-2 images. *Landslides* **2021**, *18*, 2739–2750. [CrossRef]
5. Cheng, X.; Qi, W.; Huang, Q.; Zhao, X.; Fang, R.; Xu, J. Typical geo-hazards and countermeasures of mines in Yunnan province, southwest China. *IOP Conf. Ser. Earth Environ. Sci.* **2016**, *44*, 022008. [CrossRef]
6. Tong, L.; Liu, L.; Yu, Q. Highway construction across heavily mined ground and steep topography in southern China. *Bull. Eng. Geol. Environ.* **2014**, *73*, 43–60. [CrossRef]
7. Xiao, J. Analysis of the main causes of a composite landslide in Guizhou province. *J. Transp. Sci. Eng.* **2020**, *36*, 40–44. (In Chinese)
8. Fan, X.; Xu, Q.; Scaringi, G.; Zheng, G.; Huang, R.; Dai, L.; Ju, Y. The "long" runout rock avalanche in Pusa, China, on august 28 2017: A preliminary report. *Landslides* **2019**, *16*, 139–154. [CrossRef]
9. Dai, Z.; Zhang, L.; Wang, Y.; Jiang, Z.; Xu, S. Deformation and failure response characteristics and stability analysis of bedding rock slope after underground adverse slope mining. *Bull. Eng. Geol. Environ.* **2021**, *80*, 4405–4422. [CrossRef]
10. Salmi, E.; Nazem, M.; Karakus, M. Numerical analysis of a large landslide induced by coal mining subsidence. *Eng. Geology* **2017**, *217*, 141–152. [CrossRef]
11. Zhao, J.; Xiao, J.; Lee, M.; Ma, Y. Discrete element modeling of a mining-induced rock slide. *Springer Plus* **2016**, *5*, 1633. [CrossRef] [PubMed]
12. Zheng, D.; Frost, J.D.; Huang, R.Q.; Liu, F.Z. Failure process and modes of rockfall induced by underground mining: A case study of Kaiyang phosphorite mine rockfalls. *Eng. Geol.* **2015**, *197*, 145–157. [CrossRef]

Zhong, J.; Mao, Z.; Ni, W.; Zhang, J.; Liu, G.; Zhang, J.; Geng, M. Analysis of formation mechanism of slightly inclined bedding mudstone landslide in coal mining subsidence area based on finite–discrete element method. *Mathematics* **2022**, *10*, 3995. [CrossRef]

Yang, C.; Shi, W.; Peng, X.; Zhang, S.; Wang, X. Numerical simulation of layered anti-inclined mining slopes based on different free face characteristics. *Bull. Eng. Geol. Environ.* **2022**, *81*, 359. [CrossRef]

Zhang, Y.; Yang, Y.; Zhang, J.; Wang, Y. Sensitivity study of multi-field information maps of typical landslides in mining areas based on transfer learning. *Front. Earth Sci.* **2023**, *11*, 1105985. [CrossRef]

Wang, W.; Yan, Y.; Qu, Y.; Wang, P. Shallow failure of weak slopes in Bayan Obo west mine. *Int. J. Environ. Res. Public Health.* **2022**, *19*, 9755. [CrossRef]

Nie, L.; Li, Z.; Zhang, M.; Xu, L. Deformation characteristics and mechanism of the landslide in west open-pit mine, Fushun, China. *Arab. J. Geosci.* **2015**, *8*, 4457–4468. [CrossRef]

Li, J.; Li, B.; He, K.; Gao, Y.; Wan, J.; Wu, W.; Zhang, H. Failure mechanism analysis of mining-induced landslide based on geophysical investigation and numerical modelling using distinct element method. *Remote Sens.* **2022**, *14*, 6071. [CrossRef]

Li, J.; Li, B.; Gao, Y.; Cui, F.; He, K.; Li, J.; Li, H. Mechanism of overlying strata migration and failure during underground mining in the mountainous carbonate areas in southwestern China. *Front. Earth Sci.* **2022**, *10*, 498. [CrossRef]

Cao, Z.; Zhou, Y. Research on coal pillar width in roadway driving along goaf based on the stability of key block. *CMC-Comput. Mater. Contin.* **2015**, *48*, 77–90.

Guo, J.; Cheng, X.; Lu, J.; Zhao, Y.; Xie, X. Research on factors affecting mine wall stability in isolated pillar mining in deep mines. *Minerals* **2022**, *12*, 623. [CrossRef]

Reed, G.; Mctyer, K.; Frith, R. An assessment of coal pillar system stability criteria based on a mechanistic evaluation of the interaction between coal pillars and the overburden. *Int. J. Min. Sci. Technol.* **2017**, *27*, 9–15. [CrossRef]

Zhou, Z.; Cai, X.; Li, X.; Cao, W.; Du, X. Dynamic response and energy evolution of sandstone under coupled static–dynamic compression: Insights from experimental study into deep rock engineering applications. *Rock Mech. Rock Eng.* **2020**, *53*, 1305–1331. [CrossRef]

China Geological Survey. Topographic Map of Guizhou Province. (2018-10-31). Available online: https://geocloudproducts.cgs.gov.cn/dzzlfw/idx/fileView.do?dzcp_id=d9b9919f3f0b4d709b073fb85ae37188&path=https%3A%2F%2Fgeocloudproducts.cgs.gov.cn%2Fdzxxcp%2Fadmin_file%2Fcore%2Ffile%2FtoView.do%3Fid%3Df6852a644b6a4d3aa06c1036e9db5f1a%26t%3Ddeepzoom&providerid=4028803a518fe41c0151a47891240027 (accessed on 31 March 2023).

Cai, X.; Zhou, Z.; Zang, H.; Song, Z. Water saturation effects on dynamic behavior and microstructure damage of sandstone: Phenomena and mechanisms. *Eng. Geol.* **2020**, *276*, 105760. [CrossRef]

Fu, Y.; Liu, Z.; Zeng, L.; Gao, Q.; Luo, J.; Xiao, X. Numerical analysis method that considers weathering and water-softening effects for the slope stability of carbonaceous mudstone. *Int. J. Environ. Res. Public Health.* **2022**, *19*, 14308. [CrossRef] [PubMed]

Huang, G.; Zheng, D. The formation mechanism and numerical simulation of the collapse of Kaiyang phosphate mine in Guizhou. *Chin. J. Geol. Hazard Control.* **2013**, *24*, 46–50+55. (In Chinese)

Duan, P. Analysis on the formation mechanism of overlying landslide in goaf. *Min. Technol.* **2019**, *19*, 68–71. (In Chinese)

Zhou, Z.; Chen, L.; Zhao, Y.; Zhao, T.; Cai, X.; Du, X. Experimental and numerical investigation on the bearing and failure mechanism of multiple pillars under overburden. *Rock Mech. Rock Eng.* **2017**, *50*, 995–1010. [CrossRef]

Zhou, Z.; Zhao, Y.; Cao, W.; Chen, L.; Zhou, J. Dynamic response of pillar workings induced by sudden pillar recovery. *Rock Mech. Rock Eng.* **2018**, *51*, 3075–3090. [CrossRef]

Qiu, Y.; Shang, Y. Analysis of progressive failure mechanism of loose slope under seismic load. *J. China Foreign Highw.* **2022**, *42*, 15–21. (In Chinese)

Zhao, Q.; Yang, Z.; Jiang, Y.; Liu, X.; Cui, F.; Li, B. Discrete element analysis of deformation features of slope controlled by karst fissures under the mining effect: A case study of Pusa landslide, China. *Geomat. Nat. Hazards Risk* **2023**, *14*, 1–35. [CrossRef]

Wang, N.; Zhong, Z.; Liu, X.; Gao, G. Failure mechanism of anti-inclined karst slope induced by underground multiseam mining. *Geofluids* **2022**, *2022*, 1302861. [CrossRef]

Disclaimer/Publisher's Note: The statements, opinions and data contained in all publications are solely those of the individual author(s) and contributor(s) and not of MDPI and/or the editor(s). MDPI and/or the editor(s) disclaim responsibility for any injury to people or property resulting from any ideas, methods, instructions or products referred to in the content.

Evaluation and Application of Surrounding Rock Stability Based on an Improved Fuzzy Comprehensive Evaluation Method

Xianhui Mao [1], Ankui Hu [1,2,3,*], Rui Zhao [1,2,3], Fei Wang [1,2,3] and Mengkun Wu [1]

1. School of Energy and Power Engineering, Xihua University, Chengdu 610039, China
2. Key Laboratory of Fluid Machinery and Engineering, Xihua University, Chengdu 610039, China
3. Key Laboratory of Fluid and Power Machinery, Xihua University, Ministry of Education, Chengdu 610039, China
* Correspondence: stefanhu2016@mail.xhu.edu.cn; Tel.: +86-151-9662-9973

Abstract: Ensuring the stability of surrounding rock is crucial for the safety of underground engineering projects. In this study, an improved fuzzy comprehensive evaluation method is proposed to accurately predict the stability of surrounding rock. Five key factors, namely, rock quality designation, uniaxial compressive strength, integrality coefficient of the rock mass, strength coefficient of the structural surface, and groundwater seepage, are selected as evaluation indicators, and a five-grade evaluation system is established. An improved analytic hierarchy process (IAHP) is proposed to enhance the accuracy of the evaluation. Using interval numbers rather than real numbers in constructing an interval judgment matrix can better account for the subjective fuzziness and uncertainty of expert judgment. Subjective and objective weights are obtained through IAHP and coefficient of variation, and the comprehensive weight is calculated on the basis of game theory principles. In addition, trapezoidal and triangular membership functions are employed to determine the membership degree, and an improved fuzzy comprehensive evaluation model is constructed. The model is then used to determine the stability of the surrounding rock based on the improved criterion. It is applied to six samples from an actual underground project in China to validate its effectiveness. Results show that the proposed model accurately and effectively predicts the stability of surrounding rock, which aligns with the findings from field investigations. The proposed method provides a valuable reference for evaluating surrounding rock stability and controlling construction risks.

Keywords: surrounding rock stability; IAHP; fuzzy comprehensive evaluation; coefficient of variation

MSC: 91A86

1. Introduction

The accelerated exploitation of underground resources has led to increased construction of underground engineering projects. The 21st century has been dubbed the "century of underground space" as more people live or work in such environments. Therefore, ensuring the safe construction of underground engineering is of paramount importance [1]. During the nonlinear excavation process of underground engineering, the stress field of the rock undergoes disturbance and redistribution [2]. These factors can lead to geological hazards, including rock burst, collapse, and water inrush. Determining the stability of the surrounding rock is a critical issue for construction safety [3]. It directly affects the economy, safety, and construction schedule of underground projects. Therefore, accurately assessing surrounding rock stability is vital for underground engineering.

The analysis of surrounding rock stability finds widespread application in water conservancy and hydropower engineering, mining engineering, and traffic engineering [4]. Numerous scholars have developed different evaluation methods based on various theories, which can be classified into analytical, numerical, and machine-learning approaches.

Analytical methods include the Protodyakonov coefficient (f), rock quality designation (RQD), Q, and rock mass rating (RMR) method [5]. The Protodyakonov coefficient is simple but may introduce errors due to changes in stress states resulting from laboratory measurements [6]. RQD, proposed by Deere [7], offers a convenient indicator of rock quality. Beniawski developed the RMR system based on six parameters [8]. Barton proposed the Q system that evaluates rock mass quality using six different parameters [9]. However, these methods involve numerous parameters, some of which are difficult to determine accurately, leading to uncertainties regarding the mechanical properties of rock masses.

Other analytical methods include the Technique for Order Preference by Similarity to an Ideal Solution (TOPSIS) [10], the ideal point method [11], the matter-element method [12], and the cloud model approach [13]. Each of these methods has made remarkable contributions to the field. TOPSIS and the ideal point method calculate the closeness degree to obtain the results and address the quantification of indicator effects, which is a challenge for other methods. However, their results may fall between two grades. The matter-element method can ignore important constraints, leading to discrepancies between evaluation results and actual results. Cloud models construct a cloud generator to address the conversion of qualitative and quantitative data and consider the interaction of indicators. However, constructing cloud models is complex and challenging. Moreover, the evaluation index varies for different geotechnical projects [14].

Numerical methods include analytical fractal methods and numerical boundary element methods [15–17]. These approaches treat rock as porous media and examine its stability through the characterization of its complex structure. However, building fractal or numerical models is complex and time-consuming.

Many machine learning techniques, such as backpropagation (BP), Bayes, support vector machine (SVM), and random forest (RF), have been applied in the field of surrounding rock stability analysis [18,19]. Artificial intelligence algorithms possess strong nonlinear mapping capabilities and are widely used in engineering applications due to their effectiveness in regression prediction. Heuristic optimization algorithms, such as particle swarm optimization, genetic algorithms, gray wolf optimization, and Harris hawks optimizer methods, have been employed to enhance these techniques [20]. Machine learning methods utilize characteristic parameters of the rock mass as input to predict its stability by establishing a complex mapping relationship. This method improves the efficiency of stability prediction, reduces subjective judgment, and addresses parameter uncertainties associated with traditional methods. However, machine learning methods have certain drawbacks. They can be slow to converge, require long training cycles, and are susceptible to local optima. Moreover, these methods require a large number of practical engineering samples for training, and their accuracy is influenced by the data dimension and the volume of data. In addition, machine learning methods are often regarded as black boxes, leading to uncertainty in the output results.

In practical underground engineering, determining the stability of surrounding rock quickly and accurately within limited measured samples and time presents challenges. This study proposes an improved fuzzy comprehensive evaluation method (IFCEM) for determining surrounding rock stability. The method uses the improved analytic hierarchy process (IAHP) and coefficient of variation (CV) to determine the subjective weights (SW) and objective weights (OW) of evaluation indicators. Additionally, game theory is employed to determine the comprehensive weights (CW) of these indicators. Based on fuzzy theory, the proposed method establishes a mathematical model, determines membership functions, improves the traditional judgment criterion, and uses the confidence criterion to assess the stability of surrounding rock. The effectiveness of the method is validated through an underground project in China. The model enables rapid and objective determination of rock mass stability, aligning with the actual situation.

The structure of this article is as follows. Section 1 presents the research background. Section 2 introduces the methods employed. Section 3 determines the evaluation system for surrounding rock stability. Section 4 establishes the fuzzy comprehensive model and presents an engineering case study. Section 5 discusses the results. Section 6 provides the conclusion.

2. Methods

2.1. Improved Analytic Hierarchy Process

The AHP method proposed by Saaty is a commonly used approach to determine SW [21,22]. It is simple, practical, and widely used. In this method, the weights are calculated on the basis of a judgment matrix, and a consistency test is conducted [23].

In the traditional AHP, determining the scale of pairwise comparisons is crucial. During the process of comparison, experts may have limitations in their knowledge, leading to judgments that involve uncertainty. To address this issue, this study proposes an IAHP method that considers the importance of interval numbers in pairwise comparisons. This approach better aligns with the thinking of experts, resulting in weight outcomes that meet the requirements. The steps involved in the IAHP are as follows:

(1) Construction of judgment matrix

Let the interval number a be defined as $a = [a^-, a^+]$, and multiple interval numbers are used to form a judgment matrix A. Experts are invited to provide the upper and lower limits of the interval numbers a^+ and a^- and for pairwise comparisons between the two indexes. The values for the interval numbers are shown in Table 1.

Table 1. Importance scale.

Scale	Definition
1	equal
3	slightly
5	obvious
7	strong
9	extreme

The importance scale for index comparison [24] is defined as follows: a scale of 1 indicates that the index is equally important to other indexes. A scale of 9 signifies that the index is much more important than the other indexes. The interval judgment matrix A is constructed as follows [25]:

$$A = [A_{ij}]_{m \times m} = [a_{ij}^-, a_{ij}^+] = \begin{pmatrix} [1,1] & [a_{12}^-, a_{12}^+] & \cdots & [a_{1m}^-, a_{1m}^+] \\ [\frac{1}{a_{12}^+}, \frac{1}{a_{12}^-}] & [1,1] & \cdots & [a_{2m}^-, a_{2m}^+] \\ [\frac{1}{a_{1m}^+}, \frac{1}{a_{1m}^-}] & [\frac{1}{a_{2m}^+}, \frac{1}{a_{2m}^-}] & \cdots & [1,1] \end{pmatrix} \quad (1)$$

where m is the number of assessment indexes.

(2) Calculation of weight vectors X^- and X^+

Supposing $A = [A^-, A^+]$, the weight vectors X^- and X^+ for A^- and A^+ can be obtained by [26]:

$$X_i^- = \frac{\left(\prod_{j=1}^{m} a_{ij}^-\right)^{\frac{1}{m}}}{\sum_{i=1}^{m}\left(\prod_{j=1}^{m} a_{ij}^-\right)^{\frac{1}{m}}} \quad (2)$$

$$X_i^+ = \frac{\left(\prod_{j=1}^{m} a_{ij}^+\right)^{\frac{1}{m}}}{\sum_{i=1}^{m}\left(\prod_{j=1}^{m} a_{ij}^+\right)^{\frac{1}{m}}} \quad (3)$$

where the symbols have the same meaning as described above.

(3) Consistency test

During the process of comparison, checking for inconsistent judgments is important. Therefore, a consistency test is conducted. This test is solved using two coefficients as follows [27]:

$$\lambda = \sqrt{\sum_{j=1}^{m} \frac{1}{\frac{1}{m}\sum_{i=1}^{m} a_{ij}^{+}}} \quad (4)$$

$$\mu = \sqrt{\sum_{j=1}^{m} \frac{1}{\frac{1}{m}\sum_{i=1}^{m} a_{ij}^{-}}} \quad (5)$$

where λ and μ represent correction coefficients. If $\lambda \leq 1$ and $\mu \geq 1$, then the matrix is considered consistent. However, if the values of these coefficients do not meet the criteria, it indicates poor consistency in the judgment matrix, and it needs to be reconstructed.

(4) Weight calculation

Various methods, such as the iterative method and random simulation method [28], can be used to calculate the weights of the interval judgment matrix. In this study, the eigenvalue method is selected, and the weight vector of the interval number is obtained by [27]:

$$w_i = [\lambda X_i^-, \mu X_i^+] \quad (6)$$

The calculated weight is an interval, which is then converted using the following formula:

$$SW_i = \frac{1}{2}(w_1, w_2, \cdots w_m) = \frac{1}{2}(\lambda X_i^- + \mu X_i^+) \quad (7)$$

where SW_i represents the subjective weight of factor i.

2.2. Coefficient of Variation

The CV method [29] is an objective weighting method. It assigns more weight to indicators with a larger gap between the actual measured value and the target value, and less weight is given to indicators with smaller gaps. This method helps eliminate the influence of different dimensions on weights and provides an objective weighting method [30]. The steps involved are as follows:

(1) Normalized data

The indicators are divided into positive and negative indicators and dimensional differences are eliminated as follows [29]:

$$X_{ij} = \frac{x_{ij} - \min(x_{ij})}{\max(x_{ij}) - \min(x_{ij})} \quad (8)$$

$$X_{ij} = \frac{\max(x_{ij}) - x_{ij}}{\max(x_{ij}) - \min(x_{ij})} \quad (9)$$

where $\min(x_{ij})$ and $\max(x_{ij})$ represent the minimum and maximum values, respectively. x_{ij} represents the measured value.

(2) Calculation of the mean value and standard deviation

They are expressed as [29]:

$$\begin{cases} \overline{x_j} = \frac{1}{n}\sum_{i=1}^{n} x_{ij} \\ S_j = \sqrt{\frac{\sum_{i=1}^{n}(x_{ij} - \overline{x_{ij}})^2}{n}} \end{cases} \quad (10)$$

where S_j and $\overline{x}_j$ are the standard deviation and mean value, respectively.

(3) Calculation of coefficient of variation and weight

They are obtained by [29]:

$$V_j = \frac{S_j}{\overline{x_j}} \quad (11)$$

$$OW_j = \frac{V_j}{\sum\limits_{j=1}^{n} V_j} \quad j = 1, 2, \cdots, n \quad (12)$$

The symbols used here as defined similarly as above, where OW_j represents the subjective weight of factor j.

2.3. Game Theory

In this study, the basic idea of game theory [31] is introduced to combine different weights. The aim is to minimize the deviation between the weights and obtain the optimal comprehensive weight. The steps involved are as follows:

(1) Set R different weight methods to assign weight to the indicators. In this study, R = 2. A linear combination of weight CW is defined by [31]:

$$CW = \alpha_1 w_1^T + \alpha_2 w_2^T \quad (\alpha_{1,2} > 0, \, \alpha_1 + \alpha_2 = 1) \quad (13)$$

where α_1 and α_2 represent the correction factors.

(2) The aggregation model of game theory is introduced to minimize the deviation between W and Wi. The objective function is expressed as [32]:

$$\min \left\| \sum_{l=1}^{2} \alpha_l w_l^T - w_z \right\|_2 \quad (z = 1, 2) \quad (14)$$

In accordance with the differential property of the matrix, the optimal condition equation of the first derivative in Equation (14) is derived as [32]

$$\begin{bmatrix} w_1 \cdot w_1^T & w_1 \cdot w_2^T \\ w_2 \cdot w_1^T & w_2 \cdot w_2^T \end{bmatrix} \times \begin{bmatrix} \alpha_1 \\ \alpha_2 \end{bmatrix} = \begin{bmatrix} w_1 \cdot w_1^T \\ w_2 \cdot w_2^T \end{bmatrix} \quad (15)$$

where the symbols used here are defined similarly as above.

(3) Normalization of the optimization combination coefficient obtained from Equation (15) [33]:

$$\alpha_z^* = \frac{|\alpha_z|}{\sum\limits_{z=1}^{2} |\alpha_z|} \quad (16)$$

where α_1^* and α_2^* represent the correction coefficient after normalization.

(4) Calculation of the comprehensive weight CW [33]:

$$CW = \alpha_1^* w_1^T + \alpha_2^* w_2^T \quad (17)$$

where $w_1 = SW$ and $w_2 = OW$ represent the objective and subjective weights obtained from the IAHP and CV methods, respectively.

2.4. Improved Fuzzy Comprehensive Evaluation Method

The FCEM is a comprehensive analysis method that combines qualitative and quantitative analysis [34]. It involves determining the factors and evaluation sets, obtaining the weights for each evaluation index, establishing the membership function, constructing the fuzzy evaluation matrix, and ultimately determining the evaluation results through various logical operations and relevant criteria. The method follows a step-by-step process, starting from the bottom and progressing to the top level, to obtain the final comprehensive evaluation result [35]. The steps involved are as follows:

(1) Establishment of the factor set

It refers to the collection of various influencing factors. In this study, five evaluation factors are used, which can be expressed as:

$$F = [F_1, F_2, F_3, F_4, F_5] \tag{18}$$

where F represents the influencing factor.

(2) Establishment of the evaluation set

In this study, the evaluation set is the grades of the surrounding rock, which are divided into five categories. It is expressed as:

$$E = [E_1, E_2, E_3, E_4, E_5] \tag{19}$$

where E represents the surrounding grade from I to V.

(3) Determination of the degree of membership function

Currently, two approaches are mainly used to determine the membership degree. The first approach involves consulting an expert to determine the attribution of a subject's rating and to determine the percentage of the subject's rating in a particular category. The second approach involves determining the range of indicators in different hierarchies, constructing a membership function based on it, and using the data to solve the membership degree. Considering the fuzziness of adjacent classification boundaries and the subjectivity and uncertainty of decision-making, this study addresses the problem by constructing trapezoidal and triangular membership functions. The membership function of five different indexes is constructed under five grades using the measured values and the average boundary values of different grades. The membership function of different levels is defined as follows:

$$f_j(c_5) = \begin{cases} 1 & x_j \leq u_5 \\ \dfrac{u_5 - x_j}{u_5 - u_4} & u_4 < x_j \leq u_5 \\ 0 & x_j > u_4 \end{cases} \tag{20}$$

$$f_j(c_i) = \begin{cases} 0 & x_j \leq u_{i+1} \\ \dfrac{x_j - u_{i+1}}{u_i - u_{i+1}} & u_{i+1} < x_j \leq u_i \\ \dfrac{u_{i-1} - x_j}{u_{i-1} - u_i} & u_i < x_j \leq u_{i-1} \\ 0 & x > u_{i-1} \end{cases} \tag{21}$$

$$f_j(c_1) = \begin{cases} 0 & x_j \leq u_2 \\ \dfrac{x_j - u_2}{u_1 - u_2} & u_2 < x_j \leq u_1 \\ 1 & x_j > u_1 \end{cases} \tag{22}$$

where c represents the level of the surrounding rock stability. And $f_j(c_i)$ represents the membership function of the j-th factor under the i-th level (Figure 1). Here, i and j are equal to 1, 2, 3, 4, and 5. x_j represents the measured value of the j-th factor and u_i denotes the average of the boundary values of each grade. Each indicator at different levels is quantified into a categorical range. Once the classification criteria for different levels are determined, u_i can be determined. For example, factor I_1 u_5 represents the mean value of the boundary values under grade V. The upper and lower limit of the boundary value can be found in Table 3. In Table 3, the upper and lower limit of the boundary value of level V for factor I_1 RQD is 0–25 and u_5 is equal to 12.5 when calculating the membership degree of index 1 under level V. Its value varies on the basis of the boundary values of different grade classifications. Other calculations of u_i follow a similar procedure.

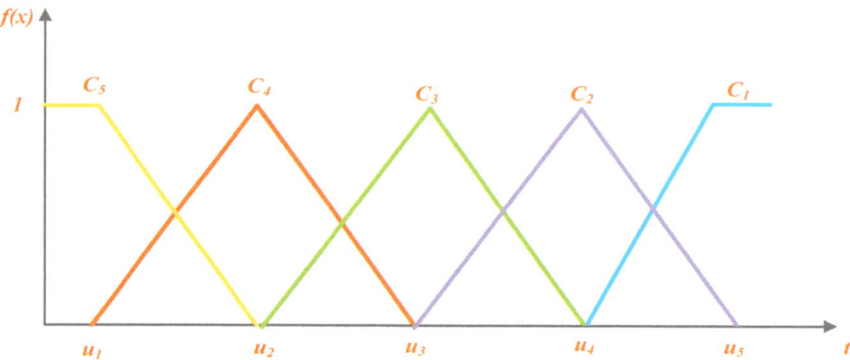

Figure 1. Membership function.

(4) Construction of the fuzzy comprehensive judgment matrix R

Once the membership function is determined, the membership degree can be obtained based on the measured value. The value is between 0 and 1, and it helps eliminate the dimensional influence of different indicators in the comprehensive evaluation. These values form a fuzzy comprehensive judgment matrix R, as expressed as [36]:

$$R_i = \begin{bmatrix} f_1(c_1) & \cdots & f_1(c_5) \\ \vdots & \vdots & \vdots \\ f_5(c_1) & \cdots & f_5(c_5) \end{bmatrix} \quad (23)$$

where R_i represents a fuzzy comprehensive judgment matrix.

(5) Comprehensive evaluation

The evaluation sets of the surrounding rock B are obtained on the basis of the weight set of evaluation indicators CW and the fuzzy evaluation matrix. The process is shown as follows [36]:

$$B_i = CW_i \cdot R_i = (w_1, w_2, \cdots w_i) \cdot \begin{pmatrix} R_1 \\ R_2 \\ \vdots \\ R_i \end{pmatrix} = (B_1, \cdots B_i) \quad (24)$$

where CW_i represents the comprehensive weight, and i = 1, 2, 3, 4, 5.

The traditional criterion of maximum membership degree will sometimes fail, resulting in unreasonable results. Therefore, this study proposes an improvement by using the confidence identification criterion to obtain the stability of the surrounding rock. It is expressed as:

$$C_k = \min\left\{k : \sum_{l=1}^{k} \mu_{xl} \geq \lambda, 1 \leq k \leq 5\right\} C_1 > C_2 > \cdots > C_5 \quad (25)$$

$$C_k = \max\left\{k : \sum_{l=5}^{k} \mu_{xl} \geq \lambda, 1 \leq k \leq 5\right\} C_1 < C_2 < \cdots < C_5 \quad (26)$$

where k = 1, 2, ... , 5 and $\lambda \in [0.5, 0.7]$.

3. Surrounding Rock Stability Evaluation System

3.1. Selection and Principle of Evaluation Indexes

The selection of assessment factors is important for obtaining accurate classification results [37]. Therefore, some principles should be observed:

(1) Comprehensiveness and independence

The evaluation indicators should comprehensively reflect the factors affecting the stability of surrounding rock while selecting significant, largely independent, and representative indicators. This simplifies and enhances the effectiveness of the calculation.

(2) Feasibility

Considering the numerous and complex monitoring and experimental data, the selected evaluation indicators should be practical, operable, and easy to investigate, collect, or measure. This ensures smooth progress in the evaluation process.

(3) Scientificity and reliability

As the purpose of classifying surrounding rock is to reduce the occurrence of risk accidents, ensuring the scientific reliability of the evaluation indicators is essential.

According to the previous research [38], and considering the specific project situation of the project, five factors are selected in accordance with the aforementioned principles [39]. The rock quality designation (RQD), uniaxial compressive strength (R_w), integrality coefficient of the rock mass (K_V), strength coefficient of the structural surface (K_f), and groundwater seepage (W) were selected as evaluation indicators for the classification system. A brief introduction is as follows:

1. Rock quality designation (I_1)

The RQD is the ratio of the cumulative length of intact columnar core samples greater than 10 cm per feed to the feed of each drill return (expressed as a percentage). RQD reflects the degree of rock integrity and is widely used in many rock stability evaluation methods, such as the RMR method and Q method, as expressed by Equation (27).

$$RQD = (\frac{\text{Cumulative core length over 10 cm}}{\text{Borehole length}}) \times 100\% \tag{27}$$

2. Uniaxial compressive strength (I_2)

It is an important parameter that reflects the mechanical properties of rock. This index has been used as an evaluation index by the Q method and the RMR method, and other methods, so it is used for the study of the classification of the surrounding rock in this paper. It is shown as follows:

$$R = \frac{P}{A} \tag{28}$$

where P and A represent the applied load and cross-sectional area of the sample, respectively.

3. Integrality coefficient of rock mass (I_3)

It is a quantitative physical indicator used to assess rock integrity and is widely used for classifying engineering rock masses. It is defined as:

$$K_v = \left(\frac{V_{pm}}{V_{pr}}\right)^2 \tag{29}$$

where V_{pr} and V_{pm} represent the p-wave velocities of the rock and rock mass (m/s), respectively.

4. Strength coefficient of structural surface (I_4)

Various forms of structural faces are observed in a rock mass, and the integrity of these structural faces is assessed on the basis of a combination of characteristics that can affect the stability of the surrounding rock.

5. Groundwater seepage (I_5)

Groundwater can cause damage to the properties of rock, and its presence or absence differs between dry and water-rich environments [40]. Therefore, understanding the state of groundwater is essential for analyzing the surrounding rock stability.

3.2. Classification of Rock Stability

This study defines the surrounding rock stability according to pertinent literature and other methods (Table 2) in order to achieve a more precise categorization [41–43].

Table 2. Surrounding rock stability classification of other methods.

Number	Method	Number of Rock Grade
1	Q method	9
2	BQ method	5
3	RMR method	5
4	HC method	5
5	Standard for Engineering Classification of Rock Mass	5
6	Code for Investigation of Geotechnical Engineering	6
7	Code for Design of Road Tunnel	6
8	New Austrian Tunneling Method	5

Various classification methods, as listed in Table 2, divide rock stability into five grades, although six grades or nine grades are also used. To ensure comparability with other methods, this study chooses to classify rock stability into five classes: I, I, II, IV, and V.

3.3. Evaluation System

The surrounding rock stability is classified into five grades, ranging from grade I (excellent rock quality) to grade V (very poor rock quality). Each evaluation index is categorized on the basis of its impact on surrounding rock stability in accordance with different grades [44] (Table 3).

Table 3. Classification criteria for various indicators of surrounding rock stability.

Level	RQD/%	R_w/Mpa	K_v	K_f	w/L/min × 10 m
I	100–90	200–120	1.00–0.75	1.0–0.8	0–5
II	90–75	120–60	0.75–0.45	0.8–0.6	5–10
III	75–50	60–30	0.45–0.3	0.6–0.4	10–25
IV	50–25	30–15	0.3–0.2	0.4–0.2	25–125
V	25–0	15–0	0.2–0	0.2–0.0	125–300

Based on the above studies, an evaluation system was constructed. It consists of two layers: the first layer represents the stability of the surrounding rock (target layer), and the second layer consists of five indicators (indicator layer).

4. Engineering Case Analysis

4.1. Engineering Background

The Guangzhou Pumped Storage Power Station is a major energy project in South China. The reservoir's normal storage level of the reservoir is 816.80 m, with a maximum dam height of 68 m and a total reservoir capacity of 24 million km^3. The water diversion and power generation system's pipeline has a total length of approximately 4407 m. The underground plant's dimensions are 152 m × 22 m × 46 m, and the vault elevation is approximately 239.9 m. Six samples of underground caverns in different parts of the study area were selected (Figure 2).

4.2. Subjective Weights Analysis

Weight seriously affects the accuracy of the results. In this study, IAHP is used to obtain the subjective weights. The procedure is as follows: an expert was invited to assess the interval number of each two indexes through the 1–9 scale to form an interval number evaluation matrix A (Table 4).

Table 4. Interval number matrix of five factors.

Factor	I_1	I_2	I_3	I_4	I_5
I_1	[1, 1]	[1/4, 1/2]	[1/5, 1/3]	[1/5, 1/2]	[4, 3]
I_2	[2, 4]	[1, 1]	[3, 5]	[1/5, 1/2]	[1/6, 1/5]
I_3	[3, 5]	[1/5, 1/3]	[1, 1]	[1/3 1/2]	[1/6 1/4]
I_4	[2, 5]	[3, 5]	[2, 3]	[1, 1]	[1/4, 1/3]
I_5	[1/4, 1/3]	[5, 6]	[4, 5]	[3, 4]	[1, 1]

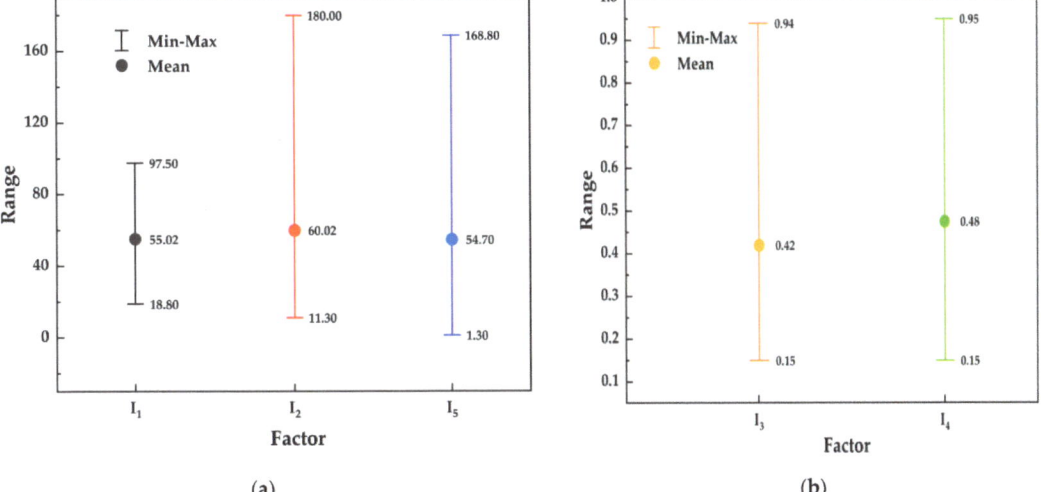

Figure 2. Surrounding rock data: (a) I_1, I_2, I_5; (b) I_3, I_4.

For example, the interval number of I_1 to I_3 is [3, 5], which indicates that the expert considers the importance of the two indicators to range between moderately important and strongly important. The interpretation of other interval numbers follows a similar pattern.

The contrast matrix A can be divided into two independent matrices A^- and A^+. After the judgment matrix is constructed, the weight vector can be calculated. The weight vectors X^- and X^+ for each matrix using the eigenvalue method through Equations (2) and (3) were calculated, resulting in $[0.085, 0.142, 0.110, 0.307, 0.356]^T$ and $[0.150, 0.172, 0.111, 0.246, 0.321]^T$, respectively.

Correction coefficients λ and μ for A^- and A^+ can be obtained using Equations (4) and (5). In this case, $\lambda = 0.99 < 1$ and $\mu = 1.014 > 1$, indicating that the weight calculation is qualified by the consistency test. And the subjective weight of each factor can be obtained using Equation (7), as expressed in Table 5.

After calculation, the subjective weight of each index is $[0.117, 0.157, 0.110, 0.277, 0.339]^T$. The weights are sorted as follows: $I_5 > I_4 > I_2 > I_1 > I_3$. It means that the surrounding rock stability is most significantly influenced by groundwater.

Table 5. Results of subjective weight.

Weight	I_1	I_2	I_3	I_4	I_5
A^-	0.085	0.142	0.110	0.307	0.356
A^+	0.150	0.172	0.111	0.246	0.321
SW	0.117	0.157	0.110	0.277	0.339

4.3. Objective Weights Analysis

Using six samples of surrounding data in the study area, the OW of each index (Table 6) is obtained by Equations (8)–(12).

Table 6. Objective weight of each index.

Factor	Mean Value	Standard Deviation	Coefficient of Variation	OW (%)
I_1	55.017	29.427	0.535	13.103
I_2	60.017	64.983	1.083	26.526
I_3	0.42	0.296	0.705	17.276
I_4	0.475	0.295	0.62	15.191
I_5	54.7	62.304	1.139	27.904

After calculation, the objective weight of each index is $[0.131, 0.265, 0.173, 0.152, 0.279]^T$. The weights are sorted as follows: $I_5 > I_2 > I_3 > I_4 > I_1$. This indicates that groundwater has the greatest influence on the surrounding rock stability based on the measured data.

4.4. Comprehensive Weights Analysis

After calculating SW and CW, the comprehensive weight can be obtained. α_1 and α_2 are obtained using Equation (15) in Python, resulting in $\alpha_1 = 0.83$, $\alpha_2 = 0.17$, and $\alpha_1 + \alpha_2 = 1$. The calculation is correct. The comprehensive weight is obtained by Equations (16) and (17), resulting in $[0.120, 0.175, 0.121, 0.255, 0.329]^T$.

The weights are sorted as follows: $I_5 > I_4 > I_2 > I_3 > I_1$. This indicates that groundwater has the greatest influence on the surrounding rock stability based on the opinion of experts and the data in the study area. The weights are compared in Figure 3 to better visualize the differences between SW, OW, and CW.

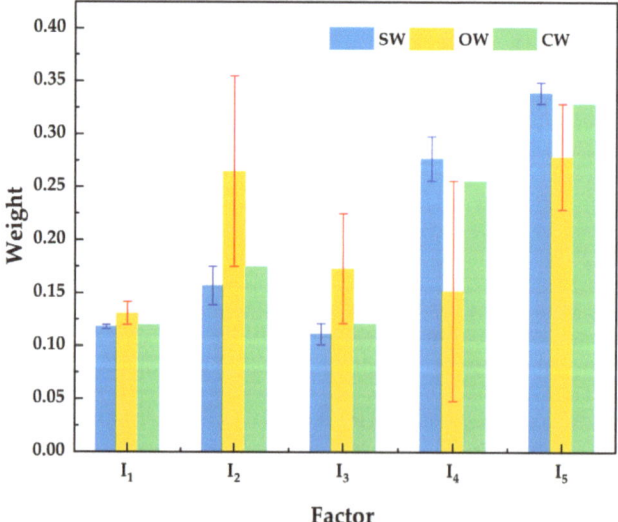

Figure 3. Comparison of different weights.

Analysis of weight results shows that the determination of subjective weights depends on the knowledge of experts, which is highly subjective and arbitrary. The determination of objective weights depends on field-measured data or monitoring data, which is highly objective but lacks human participation and may not fully reflect the actual project situation. Both subjective and objective weights have their shortcomings. Therefore, integrating the characteristics of both and conducting comprehensive empowerment is necessary to reflect experts' subjective judgment and the objective importance of parameters.

In this study, comprehensive weights are obtained by integrating the SW and OW calculated using IAHP and CV through game theory, resulting in a more reasonable and accurate weight distribution that aligns with the actual situation.

4.5. Comprehensive Fuzzy Evaluation Analysis

In this section, the index and evaluation set, along with the membership functions and evaluation results, are calculated. The membership function serves to transform the index set into the evaluation set, assigning a membership degree between 0 and 1. A higher membership degree indicates a stronger association of the index with a certain level, whereas a lower degree indicates a weaker association [45].

In this study, trapezoidal and trigonometric membership functions (Figure 4) are used to determine the membership degrees.

After determining the membership degree function, the membership degrees are calculated using Equations (20)–(22). The index membership degrees at different levels are obtained by inputting the measured data into the membership degree function, forming a fuzzy matrix. Only a portion of the fuzzy matrix for samples 1, 2, 3, and 5 is shown in Table 7 due to space limitations.

Table 7. Fuzzy matrix of samples 1, 2, 3, and 5.

Sample	Factor	V	IV	III	II	I
1	I_1	0	0	0	0	1
	I_2	0	0	0	0	1
	I_3	0	0	0	0	1
	I_4	0	0	0	0	1
	I_5	0	0	0	0	1
2	I_1	0	0.75	0.25	0	0
	I_2	0	0.83	0.17	0	0
	I_3	0	0.76	0.24	0	0
	I_4	0	0.75	0.25	0	0
	I_5	0	0.58	0.42	0	0
3	I_1	0	0.5	0.5	0	0
	I_2	0	0.66	0.34	0	0
	I_3	0	0.6	0.4	0	0
	I_4	0	0.5	0.5	0	0
	I_5	0	0.13	0.87	0	0
5	I_1	0.748	0.252	0	0	0
	I_2	0.75	0.25	0	0	0
	I_3	0.66	0.34	0	0	0
	I_4	0.75	0.25	0	0	0
	I_5	0.682	0.318	0	0	0

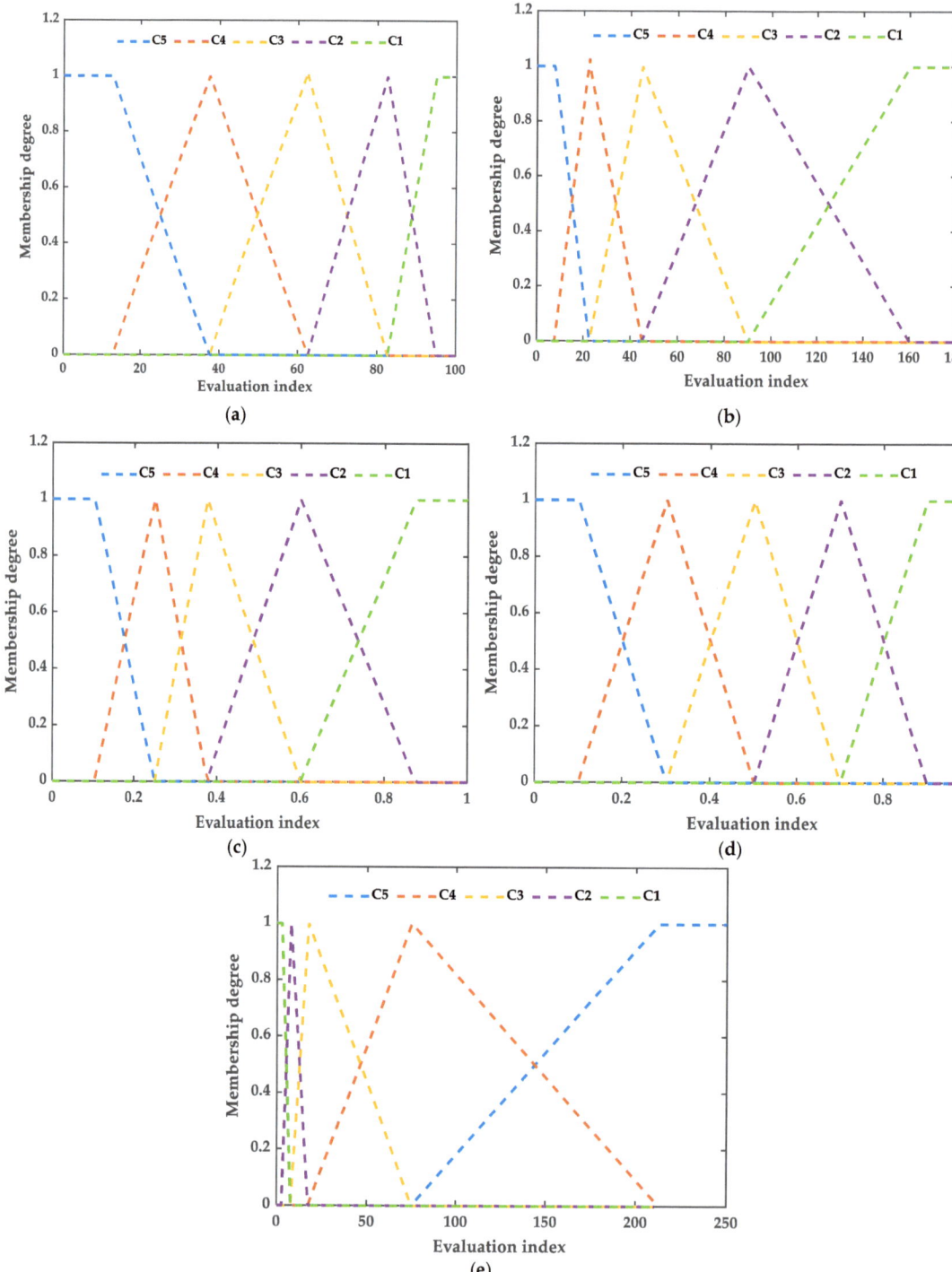

Figure 4. Membership degree of each evaluation index. (**a**) RQD; (**b**) Rw; (**c**) Kv; (**d**) Kf; (**e**) W.

The CW is $[0.120, 0.175, 0.121, 0.255, 0.329]^T$. In addition, the evaluation matrix B_i can be obtained using Equation (13). The calculations of four examples are given below:

$$B_1 = (0.120, 0.175, 0.121, 0.255, 0.329) * \begin{bmatrix} 0 & 0 & 0 & 0 & 1 \\ 0 & 0 & 0 & 0 & 1 \\ 0 & 0 & 0 & 0 & 1 \\ 0 & 0 & 0 & 0 & 1 \\ 0 & 0 & 0 & 0 & 1 \end{bmatrix} = (0, 0, 0, 0, 1)$$

$$B_2 = (0.120, 0.175, 0.121, 0.255, 0.329) * \begin{bmatrix} 0 & 0.75 & 0.25 & 0 & 0 \\ 0 & 0.83 & 0.17 & 0 & 0 \\ 0 & 0.76 & 0.24 & 0 & 0 \\ 0 & 0.75 & 0.25 & 0 & 0 \\ 0 & 0.58 & 0.42 & 0 & 0 \end{bmatrix} = (0, 0.710, 0.290, 0, 0)$$

$$B_3 = (0.120, 0.175, 0.121, 0.255, 0.329) * \begin{bmatrix} 0 & 0.50 & 0.50 & 0 & 0 \\ 0 & 0.66 & 0.34 & 0 & 0 \\ 0 & 0.60 & 0.40 & 0 & 0 \\ 0 & 0.50 & 0.50 & 0 & 0 \\ 0 & 0.13 & 0.87 & 0 & 0 \end{bmatrix} = (0, 0.418, 0.582, 0, 0)$$

$$B_5 = (0.120, 0.175, 0.121, 0.255, 0.329) * \begin{bmatrix} 0.748 & 0.252 & 0 & 0 \\ 0.750 & 0.250 & 0 & 0 \\ 0.660 & 0.340 & 0 & 0 \\ 0.750 & 0.250 & 0 & 0 \\ 0.682 & 0.318 & 0 & 0 \end{bmatrix} = (0.716, 0.284, 0, 0, 0)$$

The calculation of other Bi values follows a similar approach.

5. Results and Discussion

The evaluation results (Table 8 and Figure 5) are obtained using Equations (25) and (26).

Table 8 and Figure 5 show that the rock stability grades for the samples are I, IV, III, IV, V, and II, respectively. The selection of samples covers a range of surrounding rock stability grades ranging from I to V, indicating that each sample is representative, and the correct determination of multiple samples enhances the reasonability.

Table 8. Rock stability grade of six samples.

Sample	V	IV	III	II	I	Results
1	0	0	0	0	1	I
2	0	0.710	0.290	0	0	IV
3	0	0.418	0.582	0	0	III
4	0	1	0	0	0	IV
5	0.716	0.284	0	0	0	V
6	0	0	0	1	0	II

The rock stability grades are determined using the confidence criterion λ of 0.55. For sample 2, the sum of the membership degrees (0 + 0 + 0.290 + 0.710) is 1, which is greater than 0.55. Given that k = 4, the rock stability grade of sample 2 is determined to be IV. For sample 3, the sum of the membership degrees (0 + 0 + 0.582) is greater than 0.55, and k = 3, so the rock stability grade of sample 2 is III. For sample 5, the sum of the membership degrees (0 + 0 + 0 + 0.284 + 0.716) is 1, which is greater than 0.55. Given that k = 5, the rock stability grade of sample 5 is V. The surrounding rock stability grades for the other sections can be obtained in a similar manner. Samples 1 and 6 are determined to be I and II, respectively, indicating good quality of the surrounding rock with no need for additional measures. Samples 2, 3, 4, and 5 are determined to be IV, III, IV, and V, respectively, indicating poor quality. Reinforcement measures, such as bolt support, should be taken.

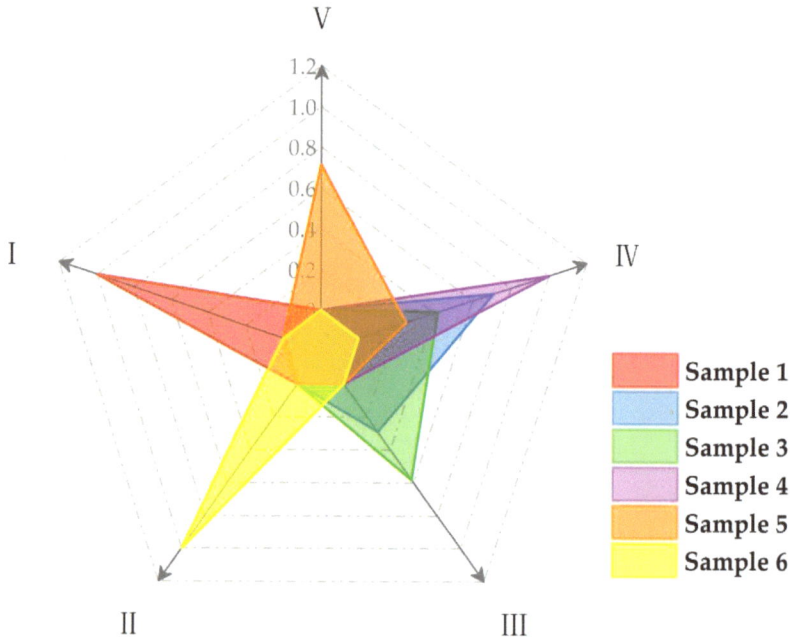

Figure 5. Results of each sample.

The relationship between the weight and results of some samples is analyzed using single-factor sensitivity. The weights of each indicator are adjusted by ±5%, ±10%, and ±20% to study their impact on rock stability. Taking sample 2 as an example, the stability of sample 2 show remains the same, that is, grade III, when the weight of factor I5 is reduced by 5%. When the weight is reduced by 10% and 20%, the stability grade is from III to IV. This shows that factor I5 has a greater influence on the stability of the surrounding rock compared with the other indexes. Similar analyses can be performed for other samples.

The results obtained using the proposed method are compared with the uncertainty measure method (UM) [46] and the TOPSIS method [47] to verify its validity and reliability. The comparison results are presented in Table 9 and Figure 6.

Table 9. Comparison of different methods.

Sample	Proposed Model	Actual Level	Uncertainty Measure Method	TOPSIS Method
1	I	I	II	I
2	IV	IV	IV	III
3	III	III	II	III
4	IV	IV	IV	IV
5	V	V	IV	IV
6	II	II	II	II

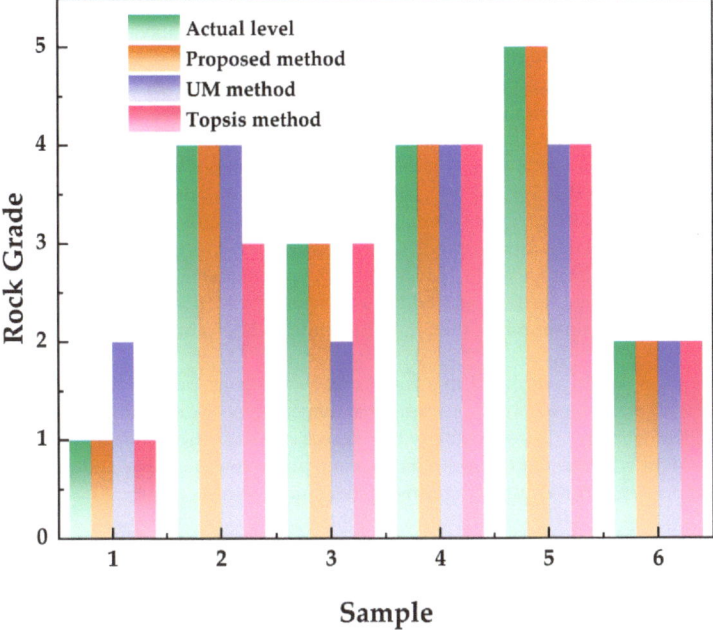

Figure 6. Comparison of results from different methods.

Figure 6 shows that the results obtained by different methods differ for different samples. The UM method yields results that match the actual levels for samples 2, 4, and 6, and the TOPSIS method's results match the actual levels for samples 1, 3, 4, and 6. The TOPSIS method calculates the closeness degree to determine the surrounding rock stability, and the result may fall between two grades, making it difficult to obtain an accurate result. The uncertainty measure method determines the stability using attribute measure values, which involves constructing a nonlinear attribute measure function that can be complicated and prone to large calculation errors. The proposed method is simple to calculate and provides accurate and quick results for surrounding rock stability, making it suitable for practical engineering. Field investigations have confirmed that the results of six samples agree with the actual situation. Therefore, the proposed method demonstrates higher precision, and its application to practical projects is feasible compared with the UM method and TOPSIS method.

Although the method presented in this study has been successfully applied in practical projects, it is worth noting that it still has some shortcomings and limitations:

(1) The number of selected sections in the study area is relatively small. Selecting a large number of sections for analysis is recommended to further validate the proposed model;
(2) The use of three different methods to calculate weights has improved the robustness of the weights. However, the subjective influence is difficult to avoid when constructing a judgment matrix in the IAHP.

In future research, more in-depth research will be conducted to address these limitations

6. Conclusions

In this study, an improved FCEM is proposed to evaluate the stability of surrounding rock and provide guidance for safety control in practical engineering. Some conclusions are as follows:

(1) On the basis of the analysis of the actual situation and previous studies, five evaluation indicators are selected: the rock quality designation (RQD), uniaxial compressive strength (R_w), integrality coefficient of the rock mass (K_V), strength coefficient of the structural surface (K_f), and groundwater seepage (W). These indicators form the evaluation system for surrounding rock stability, which is categorized into five grades on the basis of the varying influence of each factor on the stability;

(2) The comprehensive weights are determined using a combination of subjective weights through the IAHP and objective weights through CV analysis. The application of game theory helps in obtaining more reasonable and accurate weight distributions for the indicators. Subsequently, an improved FCEM is established, incorporating trapezoidal and triangular membership degree functions to determine the membership degree of each index at different levels. The traditional identification criteria of the model are improved, and the surrounding rock stability grade is determined using confidence criteria;

(3) The proposed model is applied to six sections in an actual project. Comparative analysis with other methods demonstrates that the model provides more accurate and efficient evaluations of the rock stability in different sections. The results of the model are consistent with the field investigations, confirming its rationality and practical value for underground engineering construction and design.

Author Contributions: Conceptualization, X.M.; Methodology, X.M.; Formal analysis, M.W. and R.Z.; Investigation, F.W. and R.Z.; Writing—original draft preparation, X.M. and A.H.; Writing—review and editing, X.M. and A.H. All authors have read and agreed to the published version of the manuscript.

Funding: This study received funding from the Talent Introduction Key Projects of Xihua University (Grant No. Z17112), Graduate Education Teaching Reform and Practice Key Project of Xihua University (Grant No. TJG202303), the Undergraduate Education Reform Program of Xihua University (Grant No. xjjg2019066), and the Natural Science Foundation of Sichuan Province (Grant No. 2022NSFSC1009).

Institutional Review Board Statement: Not applicable.

Informed Consent Statement: Not applicable.

Data Availability Statement: Not applicable.

Acknowledgments: The authors gratefully appreciate the support from Xihua University. The authors would like to express appreciation to the reviewers who helped to improve the quality of the paper.

Conflicts of Interest: The authors declare no conflict of interest.

Nomenclature

Symbol	Description
A	Interval Judgment matrix
a	Interval number
X	Weight vector
λ	Consistency test coefficient
μ	Consistency test coefficient
S	Standard deviation
V	Variation coefficient
x	Measured value
α	Correction coefficient of weight
F	Factor set
E	Evaluation set
f	Membership function
u	Boundary values of different grades

	R	Fuzzy comprehensive judgment matrix
	B	Fuzzy comprehensive result
	C	Surrounding rock stability grade

References

1. Zhao, J.-W.; Peng, F.-L.; Wang, T.-Q.; Zhang, X.-Y.; Jiang, B.-N. Advances in Master Planning of Urban Underground Space (UUS) in China. *Tunn. Undergr. Space Technol.* **2016**, *55*, 290–307. [CrossRef]
2. Mahdevari, S.; Shahriar, K.; Sharifzadeh, M.; Tannant, D.D. Stability Prediction of Gate Roadways in Longwall Mining Using Artificial Neural Networks. *Neural Comput. Appl.* **2016**, *28*, 3537–3555. [CrossRef]
3. Idris, M.A.; Nordlund, E.; Saiang, D. Comparison of Different Probabilistic Methods for Analyzing Stability of Underground Rock Excavations. *Electron. J. Geotech. Eng.* **2016**, *21*, 6555–6585.
4. Feng, X.-T.; Zhou, Y.-Y.; Jiang, Q. Rock Mechanics Contributions to Recent Hydroelectric Developments in China. *J. Rock Mech. Geotech. Eng.* **2019**, *11*, 511–526. [CrossRef]
5. Zhang, J.; Shi, K.; Majiti, H.; Shan, H.; Fu, T.; Shi, R.; Lu, Z. Study on the Classification and Identification Methods of Surrounding Rock Excavatability Based on the Rock-Breaking Performance of Tunnel Boring Machines. *Appl. Sci.* **2023**, *13*, 7060. [CrossRef]
6. Xiao, P.; Liu, X.; Zhao, B. Experimental Study on Gas Adsorption Characteristics of Coals under Different Protodyakonov's Coefficient. *Energy Rep.* **2022**, *8*, 10614–10623. [CrossRef]
7. Deere, D.U.; Hendron, A.J.; Patton, F.D.; Cording, E.J. Design Of Surface And Near-Surface Construction in Rock. In *ARMA US Rock Mechanics/Geomechanics Symposium*; ARMA: Tampa, FL, USA, 1966; p. ARMA-66-0237.
8. Bieniawski, Z.T. Engineering Classification of Jointed Rock Masses. *Civ. Eng. Siviele Ing.* **1973**, *15*, 335–344. [CrossRef]
9. Barton, N.; Lien, R.; Lunde, J.J.R.M. Engineering Classification of Rock Masses for the Design of Tunnel Support. *Rock Mech.* **1974**, *6*, 189–236. [CrossRef]
10. Wu, L.; Li, S.; Zhang, M.; Zhang, L. A New Method for Classifying Rock Mass Quality Based on MCS and TOPSIS. *Environ. Earth Sci.* **2019**, *78*, 199. [CrossRef]
11. Wang, Y.; Zhao, N.; Jing, H.; Meng, B.; Yin, X. A Novel Model of the Ideal Point Method Coupled with Objective and Subjective Weighting Method for Evaluation of Surrounding Rock Stability. *Math. Probl. Eng.* **2016**, *2016*, 8935156. [CrossRef]
12. Ren, Y.; Li, T.; Xiong, G.; Lin, Z. New Surrounding Rock Classification Method for High Geostress Tunnels and its Applications. *J. Eng. Geol.* **2012**, *20*, 66–73.
13. Liang, H.R.; Wang, Y.D.; Peng, H.; Liu, J.F.; Yan, X. Classification of Soft Surrounding Rock of Tunnel Based on Normal Cloud Theory. *J. Chongqing Jiaotong Univ.* **2021**, *40*, 82–87.
14. Huang, D.; Li, W.; Chang, X.; Tan, Y. Key Factors Identification and Risk Assessment for the Stability of Deep Surrounding Rock in Coal Roadway. *Int. J. Environ. Res. Public Heal.* **2019**, *16*, 2802. [CrossRef] [PubMed]
15. Liang, M.; Fu, C.; Xiao, B.; Luo, L.; Wang, Z. A Fractal Study for the Effective Electrolyte Diffusion through Charged Porous Media. *Int. J. Heat Mass Transf.* **2019**, *137*, 365–371. [CrossRef]
16. Liang, M.; Liu, Y.; Xiao, B.; Yang, S.; Wang, Z.; Han, H. An Analytical Model for the Transverse Permeability of Gas Diffusion Layer with Electrical Double Layer Effects in Proton Exchange Membrane Fuel Cells. *Int. J. Hydrog. Energy* **2018**, *43*, 17880–17888. [CrossRef]
17. Long, G.; Liu, Y.; Xu, W.; Zhou, P.; Zhou, J.; Xu, G.; Xiao, B. Analysis of Crack Problems in Multilayered Elastic Medium by a Consecutive Stiffness Method. *Mathematics* **2022**, *10*, 4403. [CrossRef]
18. Santos, A.; Lana, M.; Pereira, T. Evaluation of Machine Learning Methods for Rock Mass Classification. *Neural Comput. Appl.* **2022**, *34*, 4633–4642. [CrossRef]
19. Liu, K.; Liu, B.; Fang, Y. An Intelligent Model Based on Statistical Learning Theory for Engineering Rock Mass Classification. *Bull. Eng. Geol. Environ.* **2019**, *78*, 4533–4548. [CrossRef]
20. Ding, Y.; Zhang, W.; Yu, L.; Lu, K. The Accuracy and Efficiency of GA and PSO Optimization Schemes on Estimating Reaction Kinetic Parameters of Biomass Pyrolysis. *Energy* **2019**, *176*, 582–588. [CrossRef]
21. Xu, Z.H.; Li, S.C.; Li, L.P.; Hou, J.G.; Sui, B.; Shi, S.S. Risk Assessment of Water or Mud Inrush of Karst Tunnels Based on Analytic Hierarchy. *Process Rock Soil Mech.* **2011**, *32*, 1757–1766.
22. Saaty, T.; Tran, L. On the Invalidity of Fuzzifying Numerical Judgments in the Analytic Hierarchy Process. *Math. Comput. Model.* **2007**, *46*, 962–975. [CrossRef]
23. Sun, J.; Han, Y.; Li, Y.; Zhang, P.; Liu, L.; Cai, Y.; Li, M.; Wang, H. Construction of a Near-Natural Estuarine Wetland Evaluation Index System Based on Analytical Hierarchy Process and Its Application. *Water* **2021**, *13*, 2116. [CrossRef]
24. Ouma, Y.O.; Tateishi, R. Urban Flood Vulnerability and Risk Mapping Using Integrated Multi-Parametric AHP and GIS: Methodological Overview and Case Study Assessment. *Water* **2014**, *6*, 1515–1545. [CrossRef]
25. Zhang, Y.; Zhang, F.; Zhu, H.; Guo, P. An Optimization-Evaluation Agricultural Water Planning Approach Based on Interval Linear Fractional Bi-Level Programming and IAHP-TOPSIS. *Water* **2019**, *11*, 1094. [CrossRef]
26. Yang, Y.; Chen, G.; Wang, D. A Security Risk Assessment Method Based on Improved FTA-IAHP for Train Position System. *Electronics* **2022**, *11*, 2863. [CrossRef]
27. Huang, R.; Tian, Z.; Lv, Y. Research on Consistency of Reciprocal Judgment Matrix of Interval Rough Numbers. *Fuzzy Syst. Math.* **2019**, *33*, 124–133.

28. Yao, J. *Research on Risk Assessment of CTCS-3 Train Control System*; Lanzhou Jiaotong University: Lanzhou, China, 2020.
29. Zang, Z.; Huang, X.; Zhang, Q.; Jiang, C.; Wang, T.; Shang, J.; He, C.; Wan, F. Evaluation of the Effect of Ultrasonic Pretreatment on Vacuum Far-Infrared Drying Characteristics and Quality of Angelica Sinensis Based on Entropy Weight-Coefficient of Variation Method. *J. Food Sci.* **2023**, *88*, 1905–1923. [CrossRef]
30. Zhang, L.; Zhang, X.; Wu, J.; Zhao, D.; Fu, H. Rockburst Prediction Model Based on Comprehensive Weight and Extension Methods and Its Engineering Application. *Bull. Eng. Geol. Environ.* **2020**, *79*, 4891–4903. [CrossRef]
31. Wu, Y.; Deng, Z.; Tao, Y.; Wang, L.; Liu, F.; Zhou, J. Site Selection Decision Framework for Photovoltaic Hydrogen Production Project Using BWM-CRITIC-MABAC: A Case Study in Zhangjiakou. *J. Clean. Prod.* **2021**, *324*, 129233. [CrossRef]
32. Sun, L.; Liu, Y.; Zhang, B.; Shang, Y.; Yuan, H.; Ma, Z. An Integrated Decision-Making Model for Transformer Condition Assessment Using Game Theory and Modified Evidence Combination Extended by D Numbers. *Energies* **2016**, *9*, 697. [CrossRef]
33. Quan, H.; Li, S.; Wei, H.; Hu, J. Personalized Product Evaluation Based on GRA-TOPSIS and Kansei Engineering. *Symmetry* **2019**, *11*, 867. [CrossRef]
34. Li, J.; Deng, C.C.C.; Xu, J.; Ma, Z.; Shuai, P.; Zhang, L. Safety Risk Assessment and Management of Panzhihua Open Pit (OP)-Underground (UG) Iron Mine Based on AHP-FCE, Sichuan Province, China. *Sustainability* **2023**, *15*, 4497. [CrossRef]
35. Shi, S.; Li, S.; Li, L.; Zhou, Z.; Wang, J. Advance Optimized Classification and Application of Surrounding Rock Based on Fuzzy Analytic Hierarchy Process and Tunnel Seismic Prediction. *Autom. Constr.* **2014**, *37*, 217–222. [CrossRef]
36. Cao, J.; He, B.; Qu, N.; Zhang, J.; Liu, C.; Liu, Y.; Chen, C.-L. Benefits Evaluation Method of an Integrated Energy System Based on a Fuzzy Comprehensive Evaluation Method. *Symmetry* **2023**, *15*, 84. [CrossRef]
37. Wang, M.; Xu, X.; Li, J.; Jin, J.; Shen, F. A Novel Model of Set Pair Analysis Coupled with Extenics for Evaluation of Surrounding Rock Stability. *Math. Probl. Eng.* **2015**, *2015*, 892549. [CrossRef]
38. Ma, J.; Li, T.; Li, X.; Zhou, S.; Ma, C.; Wei, D.; Dai, K. A Probability Prediction Method for the Classification of Surrounding Rock Quality of Tunnels with Incomplete Data Using Bayesian Networks. *Sci. Rep.* **2022**, *12*, 19846. [CrossRef]
39. Xue, Y.; Li, Z.; Qiu, D.; Zhang, L.; Zhao, Y.; Zhang, X.; Zhou, B. Classification Model for Surrounding Rock Based on the PCA-Ideal Point Method: An Engineering Application. *Bull. Eng. Geol. Environ.* **2019**, *78*, 3627–3635. [CrossRef]
40. Wu, Y.; Qiao, W.; Li, Y.; Jiao, Y.; Zhang, S.; Zhang, Z.; Liu, H. Application of Computer Method in Solving Complex Engineering Technical Problems. *IEEE Access* **2021**, *9*, 60891–60912. [CrossRef]
41. *GB/T 50218-94*; National Standard of the People's Republic of China. Standard for Engineering Classification of Rock Masses. China Building Industry Press: Beijing, China, 1995.
42. *JTG D70-2004*; Industrial Standard of the People's Republic of China. Code for Design of Road Tunnel. China Communications Press: Beijing, China, 2004.
43. *GB 50021-2001*; National Standard of the People's Republic of China. Code for Investigation of Geotechnical Engineering. China Building Industry Press: Beijing, China, 2002.
44. Wu, S.; Yang, S.; Du, X. A Model for Evaluation of Surrounding Rock Stability Based on D-S Evidence Theory and Error Eliminating Theory. *Bull. Eng. Geol. Environ.* **2021**, *80*, 2237–2248. [CrossRef]
45. He, S.; Song, D.; Mitri, H.; He, X.; Chen, J.; Li, Z.; Xue, Y.; Chen, T. Integrated Rockburst Early Warning Model Based on Fuzzy Comprehensive Evaluation Method. *Int. J. Rock Mech. Min. Sci.* **2021**, *142*, 104767. [CrossRef]
46. He, H.; Yan, Y.; Qu, C.; Fan, Y. Study and Application on Stability Classification of Tunnel Surrounding Rock Based on Uncertainty Measure Theory. *Math. Probl. Eng.* **2014**, *2014*, 626527. [CrossRef]
47. Gu, X.-B.; Ma, Y.; Wu, Q.-H.; Liu, Y.-B. The Application of Intuitionistic Fuzzy Set-TOPSIS Model on the Level Assessment of the Surrounding Rocks. *Shock. Vib.* **2022**, *2022*, 4263276. [CrossRef]

Disclaimer/Publisher's Note: The statements, opinions and data contained in all publications are solely those of the individual author(s) and contributor(s) and not of MDPI and/or the editor(s). MDPI and/or the editor(s) disclaim responsibility for any injury to people or property resulting from any ideas, methods, instructions or products referred to in the content.

Article

Prediction of Rockburst Propensity Based on Intuitionistic Fuzzy Set—Multisource Combined Weights—Improved Attribute Measurement Model

Janhong Chen, Yakun Zhao, Zhe Liu, Shan Yang and Zhiyong Zhou *

School of Resources and Safety Engineering, Central South University, Changsha 410083, China
* Correspondence: csuzzy@csu.edu.cn

Abstract: A rockburst is a geological disaster that occurs in resource development or engineering construction. In order to reduce the harm caused by rockburst, this paper proposes a prediction study of rockburst propensity based on the intuitionistic fuzzy set-multisource combined weights-improved attribute measurement model. From the perspective of rock mechanics, the uniaxial compressive strength σ_c, tensile stress σ_t, shear stress σ_θ, compression/tension ratio σ_c/σ_t, shear/compression ratio σ_θ/σ_c, and elastic deformation coefficient W_{et} were selected as the indicators for predicting the propensity of rockburst, and the corresponding attribute classification set was established. Constructing a model framework based on an intuitionistic fuzzy set–improved attribute measurement includes transforming the vagueness of rockburst indicators with an intuitionistic fuzzy set and controlling the uncertainty in the results of the attribute measurements, as well as improving the accuracy of the model using the Euclidean distance method to improve the attribute identification method. To further transform the vagueness of rockburst indicators, the multisource system for combined weights of rockburst propensity indicators was constructed using the minimum entropy combined weighting method, the game theory combined weighting method, and the multiplicative synthetic normalization combined weighting method integrated with intuitionistic fuzzy sets, and the single-valued data of the indicators were changed into intervalized data on the basis of subjective weights based on the analytic hierarchy process and objective weights, further based on the coefficient of variation method. Choosing 30 groups of typical rockburst cases, the indicator weights and propensity prediction results were calculated and analyzed through this paper's model. Firstly, comparing the prediction results of this paper's model with the results of the other three single-combination weighting models for attribute measurement, the accuracy of the prediction results of this paper's model is 86.7%, which is higher than that of the other model results that were the least in addition to the number of uncertain cases, indicating that the uncertainty of attribute measurement has been effectively dealt with; secondly, the rationality of the multiple sources system for combined weights is verified, and the vagueness of the indicators is controlled.

Keywords: intuitionistic fuzzy set; multisource combined weights; attribute measures; prediction of rockburst propensity; indicator vagueness

MSC: 28E99

1. Introduction

A rockburst is a geological hazard that occurs in resource development or engineering construction, manifesting itself as a sudden destabilization of the rock body and an explosive ejection of the rock mass [1–3]. With human activities continuing to move into the deep part of the earth, the high geostress, high osmotic pressure, and other factors caused by the high depth of burial will make rockburst accidents more frequent and more intense, which will further cause irreparable damage to personnel, equipment, etc. [4,5].

Many countries around the world have suffered from rockburst hazards during deep earth operations, such as China [6], Pakistan [7], Australia [8], Germany [9], South Africa [10], the United States [11], Canada [12], and so on. In fact, the places where rockbursts occur have not only been mining ore mines; civilian underground projects such as subways, tunnels, and water conservancy facilities are also deeply affected [13]. In general, rockburst has become a worldwide difficulty in rock science. If it is possible to more accurately predict the propensity of a rockburst occurring in the construction area, a greater degree of loss can be avoided, and for the construction method, explosive area exploration and protection work will also provide more effective theoretical support.

The mechanism of rockburst is still the focus of interest for experts and scholars in the field. With the passage of time, the study of the causation mechanism of rockbursts, the rules of development, the judgments, and the prediction model are also deepening, and more and more research results make the real situation of a rockburst more and more clear [14,15]. Generally speaking, the occurrence of rockbursts is mainly explained from an energy point of view, in which the energy accumulated in the rock loses its original homeostasis under the condition of external perturbation, causing destructive phenomena in the process of energy release [16]. The prediction of the rockburst propensity is essential to determine the degree to which the possibility of rockbursts occurs in that region. The research on rockburst prediction has gone through a single-factor stage, a multi-factor stage, and an artificial intelligence method stage in the development process, and the research methods used are becoming more and more comprehensive and scientific. A single-factor approach is used in the early stages of rockburst research. This stage is mainly through a relatively single indicator for rockburst criteria research, including the cookie criterion [17], Russenes criterion [18], Turchaninov criterion [19], Hoek criterion [20], Kidybinski criterion [21], etc. The focus of the consideration was only a single rock mechanics indicator (such as shear/compression ratio σ_θ/σ_c) or elastic energy indicator (such as elastic deformation coefficient W_{et}). With the deepening of the study, it has been found that the occurrence of rockbursts is the result of the combined effect of many factors, and a single indicator criterion does not guarantee the accuracy of the prediction results. In this context, the multi-factor approach should replace the single-factor approach and become the mainstream of rockburst research [18,22,23]. Under the multi-factor approach, studies to predict rockburst propensity are mainly carried out using physical experimental methods or mathematical evaluation methods. In physical experimental studies, Lu et al. [24] used similar rock materials for physical experiments to simulate the transmission characteristics of stress waves in rock and the process of rockburst occurrence. Fakhimi et al. [25] simulated and studied the strain rupture of rock in the laboratory by designing a steel beam device connected to a compression loading machine. For the mathematical evaluation of rockbursts, Wang et al. [18] proposed a fuzzy mathematical comprehensive evaluation method to predict the rockburst with the shear/compression ratio σ_θ/σ_c, compression/tension ratio σ_c/σ_t, and elastic deformation coefficient W_{et} as the main controlling factors. Zhang et al. [26] selected some evaluation indicators based on the existing rockburst criterion, established a rockburst prediction model through rough set theory and extension theory, and then predicted and evaluated the rockburst in the case of the Jiangbian Power Station in Sichuan, China. Zhou et al. [27] investigated the destructiveness of a specific area before stress blasting, in which they evaluated it through a combination model based on the unconfirmed measures and entropy coefficients as well as eight selected indicators. Liu et al. [28] studied rockburst classification prediction through the method based on the cloud model and attribute weighting, and they verified the feasibility with the results from 164 sets of rockburst examples. Yin et al. [29] established a classification prediction model for rockburst based on the combined weighting and attribute interval identification, after which they verified the feasibility and applicability of the model through 12 sets of data calculations of rockburst cases and the optimization of average coefficients. Zhou et al. [30] analyzed the damage characteristics and key factors of rockburst in deep-buried tunnels under typical high geostress conditions and established a prediction model of rockburst in tunnels by combining the theory of unconfirmed measurements and the improved combined weighting method with the distance function, which verified its applicability through the engineering application of the model in tunnels. Hu et al. [31], aimed at improving the accuracy of rockburst prediction, optimized the theory of unconfirmed measurements using a normal cloud model, under which the accuracy of predicting rockburst was significantly higher than that of the traditional unconfirmed measurement model. Since computer technology has been widely used in the field of rock mechanics, intelligent algorithms and big data for predicting rockburst have become the future direction [32], and algorithms such as artificial neural networks and their derivatives [33–35], Bayesian networks [36,37], support vector machines [38,39], particle swarm optimization [38,40], and decision trees [41,42] have been introduced to improve the accuracy of the prediction results. In general, the current method of predicting rockburst propensity is usually based on the results of the integrated ranking of indicators, so the focus is on selecting the type of indicators, a reasonable weighting method, and modeling algorithms that fit the characteristics of rockburst data. The actual engineering situation in the field is often complex and variable, and the rockburst indicator data often have significant vagueness [4], so there are specific requirements for the predictive modeling algorithms used.

In order to adapt to the vagueness of the indicators for rockburst propensity and distinguish the attribute classification, this paper proposes a model based on intuitionistic fuzzy sets, multisource combined weights, and improved attribute measurements and studies the prediction of rockburst propensity. Building a model framework based on intuitionistic fuzzy set–attribute measure, the rockburst propensity indicator is transformed into an intervalized number field through the intuitionistic fuzzy set, and the indicator value is transformed to control the vagueness. Using the Euclidean distance method to improve the model recognition method of the attribute measure theory, which avoids artificial parameters affecting the accuracy of the prediction results. The mechanism of rockburst is analyzed and combined with actual case data, indicators of rockburst propensity are selected from the viewpoint of rock mechanics, and the relationship of the number field between the ranges of rock burst indicators are established, and the attribute classification is set. Based on the subjective weights obtained with the analytic hierarchy process and objective weights obtained with the coefficient of variation method, combined weights obtained with minimum entropy combined weighting, game theory combined weighting, and multiplicative synthesis normalization combined weighting are used to construct the multisource system for combined weights of rockburst propensity indicators, avoiding the weight bias, to the greatest extent, caused by different focuses of the weighting and converting single-valued indicators into intervalized values using intuitionistic fuzzy sets to expand the effective range of the indicators and further control the vagueness. Finally, the model prediction results for 30 sets of rockburst case data are calculated and compared with the prediction results of the other three attribute measurement models that use single combined weighting to verify the accuracy of the model proposed in this paper.

2. Theoretical Overview
2.1. Intuitionistic Fuzzy Set Theory

Intuitionistic fuzzy set theory was proposed by Atanassov in 1983 [43–45] by expanding the space of fuzzy sets to three dimensions through the three characteristic values of the degree of affiliation, non-affiliation, and hesitation to better control the vagueness of the problem to be solved [46–48].

Assuming that the set $A = \{x_i | i = 1, \ldots, w\}$ is a defined domain and non-empty, then the intuitionistic fuzzy set X of A is defined as:

$$X = \{|x_i, e(x_i), f(x_i)|x_i \in A\} \tag{1}$$

where $e(x_i)$ and $f(x_i)$ are the degree of affiliation and non-affiliation of x_i to the set X, respectively, and additionally, $g(x_i)$ is introduced to denote the degree of hesitation, which is satisfied as follows:

$$\begin{cases} 0 \leq e(x_i) + f(x_i) \leq 1 \\ e(x_i) \in [0,1]; f(x_i) \in [0,1] \\ g(x_i) = 1 - [e(x_i) + f(x_i)] \end{cases} \quad (2)$$

If there are two intuitionistic fuzzy sets X_1 and X_2, when sum and product operations are required, the equation are as follows:

$$\begin{cases} X_1 \bullet X_2 = \langle e_1(x_{1i}) \times e_2(x_{2i}), f_1(x_{1i}) + f_2(x_{2i}) - f_1(x_{1i}) \times f_2(x_{2i}) \rangle \\ X_1 + X_2 = \langle e_1(x_{1i}) + e_2(x_{2i}) - e_1(x_{1i}) \times e_2(x_{2i}), f_1(x_{1i}) \times f_2(x_{2i}) \rangle \end{cases} \quad (3)$$

where e_1 denotes the degree of affiliation for x_{1i} to X_1, e_2 denotes the degree of affiliation for x_{2i} to X_2, f_1 denotes the degree of non-affiliation for x_{1i} to X_1, and f_2 denotes the degree of non-affiliation for x_{2i} to X_2.

2.2. Attribute Measurement Theory

Attribute measurement theory, also known as attribute identification, is used to describe the measurement relationship between qualitative problems and attribute classes, which consists of three main components: single-indicator attribute measurement, composite attribute measurement, and attribute identification [49–51].

Assuming that the object to be evaluated $A = \{x_i | i = 1, 2, \ldots, w\}$ has a set of attribute classes $C = \{C_k | k = 1, 2, \ldots, n\}$, $C_1, C_2, \ldots C_n$ are different attribute intervals of the set C, and there are m indicators $I = \{I_j | j = 1, \ldots, m\}$ that characterize the attributes. When the indicator is $I_j \in C_k, 1 \leq k \leq n$, the probability of belonging to class C_k is u_{jk}, the attribute classification of the indicator is shown as Equation (4), and a_{jk} denotes the boundaries of the values of the class, which are usually $a_{j0} > a_{j1} > \ldots > a_{jk}$ or $a_{j0} < a_{j1} < \ldots < a_{jk}$.

$$\begin{pmatrix} & C_1 & C_2 & \cdots & C_n \\ I_1 & a_{10} \sim a_{11} & a_{11} \sim a_{12} & \cdots & a_{1(n-1)} \sim a_{1n} \\ I_2 & a_{20} \sim a_{21} & a_{21} \sim a_{22} & \cdots & a_{2(n-1)} \sim a_{2n} \\ \vdots & \vdots & \vdots & \vdots & \vdots \\ I_m & a_{m0} \sim a_{m1} & a_{m1} \sim a_{m2} & \cdots & a_{m(n-1)} \sim a_{mn} \end{pmatrix} \quad (4)$$

Assuming a median value of b_{jk} for attribute class C_k and a median value of d_{jk} for the measure, the equation is calculated as follows:

$$\begin{cases} b_{jk} = \frac{(a_{jk-1} + a_{jk})}{2} \\ d_{jk} = \min\left\{ \left| \frac{a_{jk-1} - a_{jk}}{2} \right|, \left| \frac{a_{jk} - a_{jk+1}}{2} \right| \right\} \\ k = 1, 2, \ldots, n-1 \end{cases} \quad (5)$$

where a_{jk-1} and a_{jk} denote the boundary values of C_k.

When there is a scheme x_i in set A that has a value of l_j for an indicator I_j and $a_{j0} < a_{j1} < \ldots < a_{jk}$, the single-indicator attribute measurement equation $u_{jk}(l_j)$ is expressed as follows:

$$u_{j1}(l_j) = \begin{cases} 1 & l_j < (a_{j1} - d_{j1}) \\ \frac{(a_{j1} + d_{j1} - l_j)}{2d_{j1}} & (a_{j1} - d_{j1}) \leq l_j \leq (a_{j1} + d_{j1}) \\ 0 & l_j > (a_{j1} + d_{j1}) \end{cases} \quad (6)$$

$$u_{jk}(l_j) \begin{cases} 0 & l_j < (a_{j(k-1)} - d_{j(k-1)}) \\ \frac{(l_j - a_{j(k-1)} + d_{j(k-1)})}{2d_{j(k-1)}} & (a_{j(k-1)} - d_{j(k-1)}) \le l_j \le (a_{j(k-1)} + d_{j(k-1)}) \\ 1 & (a_{j(k-1)} + d_{j(k-1)}) < l_j < (a_{jk} - d_{jk}) \\ \frac{(a_{jk} + d_{jk} - l_j)}{2d_{jk}} & (a_{jk} - d_{jk}) \le l_j \le (a_{jk} + d_{jk}) \\ 0 & l_j > (a_{jk} + d_{jk}) \end{cases} \quad (7)$$

$$u_{jn}(l_j) \begin{cases} 0 & l_j < (a_{j(n-1)} - d_{j(n-1)}) \\ \frac{(l_j - a_{j(n-1)} + d_{j(n-1)})}{2d_{j(n-1)}} & (a_{j(n-1)} - d_{j(n-1)}) \le l_j \le (a_{j(n-1)} + d_{j(n-1)}) \\ 1 & l_j > (a_{j(n-1)} + d_{j(n-1)}) \end{cases} \quad (8)$$

where d_{jk} denotes the median value of the measure for C_k, $a_{j(k-1)}$ denotes the value of the left boundary for indicator I_j about C_k, and a_{jk} denotes the value of the right boundary for indicator I_j about C_k.

When $a_{j0} > a_{j1} > \ldots > a_{jk}$, the equation for the single-indicator attribute measurement function $u_{jk}(l_j)$ is as follows:

$$u_{j1}(l_j) \begin{cases} 0 & l_j < (a_{j1} - d_{j1}) \\ \frac{(l_j - a_{j1} + d_{j1})}{2d_{j1}} & (a_{j1} - d_{j1}) \le l_j \le (a_{j1} + d_{j1}) \\ 1 & l_j > (a_{j1} + d_{j1}) \end{cases} \quad (9)$$

$$u_{jk}(l_j) \begin{cases} 0 & l_j < (a_{jk} - d_{jk}) \\ \frac{(l_j - a_{jk} + d_{jk})}{2d_{jk}} & (a_{jk} - d_{jk}) \le l_j \le (a_{jk} + d_{jk}) \\ 1 & (a_{jk} + d_{jk}) < l_j < (a_{j(k-1)} - d_{j(k-1)}) \\ \frac{(a_{j(k-1)} + d_{j(k-1)} - l_j)}{2d_{j(k-1)}} & (a_{j(k-1)} - d_{j(k-1)}) \le l_j \le (a_{j(k-1)} + d_{j(k-1)}) \\ 0 & l_j > (a_{j(k-1)} + d_{j(k-1)}) \end{cases} \quad (10)$$

$$u_{jn}(l_j) \begin{cases} 1 & l_j < (a_{j(n-1)} - d_{j(n-1)}) \\ \frac{(a_{j(n-1)} + d_{j(n-1)} - l_j)}{2d_{j(n-1)}} & (a_{j(n-1)} - d_{j(n-1)}) \le l_j \le (a_{j(n-1)} + d_{j(n-1)}) \\ 0 & l_j > (a_{j(n-1)} + d_{j(n-1)}) \end{cases} \quad (11)$$

After obtaining the attribute measure values from Equations (6)–(11) for indicator I_j corresponding to classification interval C_k, they have been integrated into a matrix U of single-indicator attribute measures as follows:

$$U = \begin{pmatrix} & C_1 & C_2 & \cdots & C_n \\ I_1 & u_{11} & u_{12} & \cdots & u_{1n} \\ I_2 & u_{21} & u_{22} & \cdots & u_{2n} \\ \vdots & \vdots & \vdots & \vdots & \vdots \\ I_m & u_{m1} & u_{m2} & \cdots & u_{mn} \end{pmatrix} \quad (12)$$

3. Research Methodology

3.1. Model Framework Based on Intuitionistic Fuzzy Set–Improved Attribute Measures

3.1.1. Constructing a Matrix of Intuitionistic Fuzzy Sets for Attribute Measurement

1. Matrix of Intuitionistic Fuzzy Sets for Single-Indicator Attribute Measurement

From the concept of attribute measurement, the essence of the attribute measurement function is to characterize the degree of affiliation in a certain classification interval, so $u_{jk}(I_j)$ is $e(x_i)$ in intuitionistic fuzzy set theory. In the concept of intuitionistic fuzzy set theory, the single-indicator attribute measurement value of the set $A = \{x_i | i = 1, \ldots, w\}$ with respect to the attribute classification set $C = \{C_k | k = 1, 2, \ldots, n\}$ is denoted as an intuitionistic fuzzy set matrix of $B = \langle x_i, u_{ik}, f_{ik} \rangle$. When the problem to be evaluated is quantitative, the degree of hesitation as $g_{ik} = 0$ and then $f_{ik} = 1 - u_{ik}$ is considered, and the matrix B is simplified to $B = \langle u_{ik}, f_{ik} \rangle = \langle u_{ik}, (1 - u_{ik}) \rangle$, specifically as follows:

$$B = \begin{pmatrix} & C_1 & C_2 & \cdots & C_n \\ I_1 & \langle u_{11}, (1-u_{11}) \rangle & \langle u_{12}, (1-u_{12}) \rangle & \cdots & \langle u_{1n}, (1-u_{1n}) \rangle \\ I_2 & \langle u_{21}, (1-u_{21}) \rangle & \langle u_{22}, (1-u_{22}) \rangle & \cdots & \langle u_{2n}, (1-u_{2n}) \rangle \\ \vdots & \vdots & \vdots & \vdots & \vdots \\ I_m & \langle u_{m1}, (1-u_{m1}) \rangle & \langle u_{m2}, (1-u_{m2}) \rangle & \cdots & \langle u_{mn}, (1-u_{mn}) \rangle \end{pmatrix} \quad (13)$$

2. Matrix of Intuitionistic Fuzzy Sets for Weighted Attribute Measurement

On the basis of the matrix of intuitionistic fuzzy sets for single-indicator attribute measures, the expression form of the intuitionistic fuzzy set matrix for weighted attribute measures is further studied. In the concept of attribute measurement theory, the value h_k of the weighted attribute measure corresponding to each class is calculated using the sum of the product between the indicator weights Q_j and the single-indicator attribute measure u_{jk}. The equation is as follows:

$$h_k = Q_j u_{jk} \quad (14)$$

where Q_j denotes the weight value of indicator I_j, and u_{jk} denotes the measurement value of indicator I_j about C_k.

The matrix of intuitionistic fuzzy sets for weighted attribute measures is consistent with the computational mode of Equation (14), but the indicator weights should also be in the form of intuitionistic fuzzy sets, on the one hand, in order to fit the matrix calculation and, on the other hand, to also transform the vagueness of the indicator with intuitionistic fuzzy sets. The intuitionistic fuzzy set form of the indicator is denoted as $W_j = \langle q_{mj}, \tau_{mj} \rangle$, where q_{mj} and τ_{mj} denote the degree of affiliation and non-affiliation of the indicator, respectively, and the properties are consistent with Equation (2). According to the product calculation principle of Equation (3), the matrix h_i of the intuitionistic fuzzy set of weighted attribute measures is calculated using Equation (13) and W_j, which leads to the equation of h_{ik} as shown in Equation (15) and the form of matrix h_i as shown in Equation (16):

$$h_{ik} = W_j \bullet B = \langle \overline{u_{ik}}, \overline{f_{ik}} \rangle = \langle u_{ik} q_{mj}, (f_{ik} + \tau_{mj} - f_{ik} \tau_{mj}) \rangle \quad (15)$$

where q_{mj} and τ_{mj} denote the degree of affiliation and non-affiliation for the indicator I_j, respectively; u_{ik} and f_{ik} denote the degree of affiliation and non-affiliation of the attribute measure for indicator I_j, respectively.

$$h_i = \begin{pmatrix} & C_1 & C_2 & \cdots & C_n \\ I_1 & h_{11} & h_{12} & \cdots & h_{1n} \\ I_2 & h_{21} & h_{22} & \cdots & h_{2n} \\ \vdots & \vdots & \vdots & \vdots & \vdots \\ I_m & h_{m1} & h_{m2} & \cdots & h_{mn} \end{pmatrix} \quad (16)$$

3.1.2. Calculating the Value of the Composite Attribute Measure and Improving Attribute Identification

1. Calculating the value of the composite attribute measure

According to Equation (15), it is known that the values of weighted attribute measures of any scheme x_i in set $A = \{x_i | i = 1, \ldots, w\}$ with respect to class C_k are vectors of intuitionistic fuzzy sets [52], so the calculation of the composite attribute measures for this scheme follows the principle of sum calculation in Equation (3), and the vector equation H_k and numerical calculation equation δ_k are as follows:

$$\begin{cases} H_k = \sum_{j=1}^{m} h_{jk} \\ \delta_k = \overline{u_{ik}} - \overline{f_{ik}} \end{cases} \quad (17)$$

where $j = 1, 2, \ldots, m$ and $i = 1, 2, \ldots, w$.

2. Improving attribute recognition methods

For the identification of attribute measures, methods such as numerical comparisons or confidence criteria are usually used, and the identification accuracy is largely dependent on the data set via artificial means [22,29]. The Euclidean distance method is used in this paper for the identification of composite attribute measures, establishing the set of classes as the origin for distance measurement, and carrying out the independent identification of each class separately to improve accuracy. The identification equation based on the Euclidean distance method is as follows:

$$\begin{cases} R_{i1} = \sqrt{(\delta_{i1} - 1)^2 + (\delta_{i2} - 0)^2 + \cdots + (\delta_{in} - 0)^2} \\ R_{i2} = \sqrt{(\delta_{i1} - 0)^2 + (\delta_{i2} - 1)^2 + \cdots + (\delta_{in} - 0)^2} \\ \vdots \\ R_{in} = \sqrt{(\delta_{i1} - 0)^2 + (\delta_{i2} - 0)^2 + \cdots + (\delta_{in} - 1)^2} \end{cases} \quad (18)$$

R_{in} denotes the "distance" between the value of the composite measure for the case and the set of attribute classes, and the smaller the value is, the more it belongs to the class.

3.2. The Method of Indicator Weighting Based on Intuitionistic Fuzzy Set–Multisource Combined Weights

3.2.1. Single-Weighting Method

Subjective weighting method: the analytic hierarchy process (AHP). The analytic hierarchy process is a subjective weighting method proposed by Saaty that has been more widely used in the field of analyzing and evaluating indicator weights [53,54]. When there are no data on the objective factors and the importance of the indicators cannot be quantified, the indicator weights are obtained through empirical judgment by the decision maker. For the AHP method, selecting the appropriate scale is an important guarantee for the reasonableness of the judgment matrix, usually choosing a 1–9 scale, and the index RI of the average random consistency test is also a necessary correction parameter. The contents of the AHP method are building a hierarchical model; constructing a judgment matrix; consistency testing of the judgment matrix and hierarchical single ranking; and hierarchical total ranking. The calculation formula for the consistency index CI is as follows:

$$CI = \frac{\lambda_{\max} - n}{n - 1} \quad (19)$$

where $\lambda_{\max}$ is the largest characteristic value of the judgment matrix, and n is the order of the judgment matrix.

The calculation formula for the random consistency ratio CR is as follows:

$$CR = \frac{CI}{RI} \tag{20}$$

where the value of RI is determined on the 1–9 scale.

Objective weighting method: coefficient of variation method (CVM). The principle of the coefficient of variation method is to determine the value of weights according to the degree of variation for an indicator; if the degree of variation for an indicator is higher, it means that each object to be evaluated has a higher degree of differentiation in the field of that indicator and that the weight of that indicator should be higher, and vice versa, it is the same. This method is an objective weighting method, and important parameters include the variation coefficient, coefficient of standard deviation, etc. [55,56]. The specific steps of the calculation are as follows:

Step 1: Calculating the average value $\overline{x}_j$ and standard deviation S_j of the indicator

$$\overline{x}_j = \frac{1}{n}\sum_{i=1}^{n} x_{ij} \tag{21}$$

$$S_j = \sqrt{\frac{1}{n}\sum_{i=1}^{n}(x_{ij} - \overline{x}_j)^2} \tag{22}$$

where $i = 1, 2, \ldots, n, j = 1, 2, \ldots, m$.

Step 2: Calculating the coefficient of variation V_j for the indicator

$$V_j = \frac{S_j}{\overline{x}_j} \tag{23}$$

where $j = 1, 2, \ldots, m$.

Step 3: Normalizing the coefficient of variation and calculating indicator weights ω_j

$$\omega_j = \frac{V_j}{\sum_{j=1}^{m} V_j} \tag{24}$$

where $j = 1, 2, \ldots, m$.

From that, the weight vector $\omega_j^T = [\omega_1, \omega_2, \ldots, \omega_m]^T$ can be obtained.

3.2.2. Multisource System for Combined Weights

The combination of subjective and objective weights to replace the single weight can eliminate the one-sidedness and bias of the single-weight method to a certain extent. There are many methods and different principles of combined weighting, and different combined weighting methods have different focuses, so it is difficult to guarantee that one combined weighting method can guarantee the reasonableness of the weights. Therefore, three widely used combined weighting methods are selected in this paper to construct a multisource system for combined weights.

1. Combined weighting method based on minimum entropy

Assuming that the weight of the AHP is α_j and the weight of the CVM is β_j, according to the principle of minimum entropy [57], the equation for the combined weight ω_{aj} is as follows:

$$\begin{cases} \min f = \sum_{j=1}^{m} \omega_{aj}(\ln \omega_{aj} - \ln \alpha_j) + \sum_{j=1}^{m} \omega_{aj}(\ln \omega_{aj} - \ln \beta_j) \quad j = 1, 2, \ldots, m \\ \sum_{j=1}^{m} \omega_{aj} = 1 \quad \omega_j > 0 \end{cases} \tag{25}$$

In order to obtain the distribution when the information entropy is extremely large, the Undetermined Lagrange Multipliers Algorithm [58] is used to solve Equation (25), which can be obtained as the following expression for w_{aj}:

$$w_{aj} = \frac{\sqrt{\alpha_j \beta_j}}{\sum_{j=1}^{m} \sqrt{\alpha_j \beta_j}} \qquad (26)$$

2. Combined weighting method based on game theory

Using a combined weighting method based on game theory, it is possible to optimize a combination for multiple methods of determining weights [59,60].

Step 1: Assuming that the weights of m indicators are calculated using more than one method and that the weights can be formed into a set $w_j = \{w_{j1}, w_{j2}, \ldots, w_{jm}\}$, the linear combination of the weight vectors is as follows:

$$\omega = \sum_{j=1}^{m} \pi_j \omega_j^T \qquad (27)$$

where ω_j^T is the underlying weight vector, π_j is a coefficient of a linear combination for different weighting methods, and $\sum_{j=1}^{m} \pi_j = 1$.

Step 2: The coefficient of the linear combination is optimized to achieve a minimal deviation between the possible weights and the basic weights of ω_j. The equation is calculated as follows:

$$\min \left\| \sum_{j=1}^{m} \pi_j \omega_j^T - \omega_t^T \right\|_2 \qquad (28)$$

where $j = 1, 2, \ldots, m$, $t = 1, 2, \ldots, m$.

According to the properties of matrix differentials, the optimal first-order derivative of the above equation is:

$$\begin{bmatrix} \omega_1 \omega_1^T & \cdots & \omega_1 \omega_m^T \\ \vdots & \ddots & \vdots \\ \omega_m \omega_1^T & \cdots & \omega_m \omega_m^T \end{bmatrix} \begin{bmatrix} \pi_1 \\ \vdots \\ \pi_m \end{bmatrix} = \begin{bmatrix} \omega_1 \omega_1^T \\ \vdots \\ \omega_m \omega_m^T \end{bmatrix} \qquad (29)$$

$\pi_j = \{\pi_1, \pi_2, \ldots, \pi_m\}$ is calculated from the above equation, and π_j is normalized:

$$\pi_j^* = \frac{\pi_j}{\sum_{j=1}^{m} \pi_j} \qquad (30)$$

Step 3: The combined weights are calculated using the following equation:

$$\omega_{bj} = \sum_{j=1}^{m} \pi_j^* \omega_j^T \qquad (31)$$

3. Combined weighting method based on multiplicative synthetic normalization

Multiplicative synthetic normalization is used to normalize the product of two weight multiplications [61] with the following equation:

$$\omega_{cj} = \frac{\alpha_j \beta_j}{\sum_{j=1}^{m} \alpha_j \beta_j} \qquad (32)$$

where α_j denotes the AHP weights, β_j denotes the CVM weights, and $j = 1, 2, \ldots, m$.

By constructing a multisource system for combined weights, on the one hand, three combined weights are used to replace one single weight or one single combined weight, and on the other hand, the range of indicator weights is expanded, and the vagueness of the indicators is upgraded in dimensions, so that further processing can be carried out using the method of intuitionistic fuzzy sets.

3.2.3. Transformation of Multisource Combined Weights Based on Intuitionistic Fuzzy Sets

The multisource system for combined weights constructed in Section 3.2.2 shows that the weights of indicator I_j are transformed into combined weights ω_{aj}, ω_{bj}, and ω_{cj}. The weights of the indicators are fuzzified according to the intuitionistic fuzzy set to $\omega_j = \langle q_j, \tau_j \rangle$, where q_j and τ_j characterize the degree of importance and the degree of unimportance, respectively, which satisfies $0 \leq q_j + \tau_j \leq 1$ [47].

Assuming that there is a relationship, $\omega_{aj} < \omega_{bj} < \omega_{cj}$, between the three combined weights of indicator I_j, the importance of the weights is ranged as $\omega_{aj} \sim \omega_{cj}$, the unimportance as $(1 - \omega_{cj}) \sim (1 - \omega_{aj})$, and the vector form of the intuitionistic fuzzy set for the weights is denoted as $\langle \omega_{aj}, (1 - \omega_{cj}) \rangle$. It can be noted that the numerical sum of the importance and unimportance of the weights does not necessarily have to be 1. This is because of the superimposed vagueness of the three data sources under the multisource system for combined weights, and the values of the indicators are intervalized into a range of number fields, which are no longer explicitly quantitative data, so that the degree of hesitation exists and is numerically equal to the length of the interval for taking values.

4. Prediction of Rockburst Propensity

4.1. Workflows

The research content of this paper is to predict the degree of the propensity for rockburst occurrence through the composite model using intuitionistic fuzzy sets, multisource combined weights, and improved attribute measures. The research content of this paper is to predict the degree of the propensity for rockburst occurrence through the composite model using an intuitionistic fuzzy set–multisource combined assignment–improved attribute measure. By sorting out the modeling process in Sections 2 and 3 and combining the characteristics of rockburst, a schematic diagram of work is listed as shown in Figure 1, and the overall process of the prediction work includes the following five parts:

(1) Studying the phenomenon and mechanism of the rock burst, reasonably selecting the indicators that characterize the rockburst propensity, and analyzing the measurement connection and correspondence of numerical domains between the rockburst indicators and the propensity classification from the viewpoint of the attribute classification set;

(2) Choosing a typical case of the rockburst as the data source of this paper, according to the relationship of the numerical domain between rockburst propensity and classification, calculating the value of the single-indicator attribute measure for rockburst propensity, and establishing the matrix of the intuitionistic fuzzy set for the single-indicator attribute measure based on the case data;

(3) According to the case data of rockbursts, the subjective weight of the hierarchical analysis method and the objective weight of the coefficient of variation method for indicators are calculated, based on which the multisource system for combined weights is constructed, and considering the deficiencies of the single weight method and one combined weight method, the combined weight based on the minimum entropy, game theory, and multiplication synthetic normalization, respectively, is used as the data source to range the indicator weights, and the analysis and transformation of the vagueness based on the intuitionistic fuzzy set are carried out;

(4) Combining the matrix of intuitionistic fuzzy sets for single-indicator attribute measures about rockburst propensity and the vector of intuitionistic fuzzy sets for multisource combined weights of rockburst indicators, the matrix of intuitionistic fuzzy sets for weighted attribute measures is calculated;

(5) Calculating the composite attribute measure of rockburst propensity, improving the attribute identification mode using the Euclidean distance method, and finally determining the propensity classification of rockburst cases.

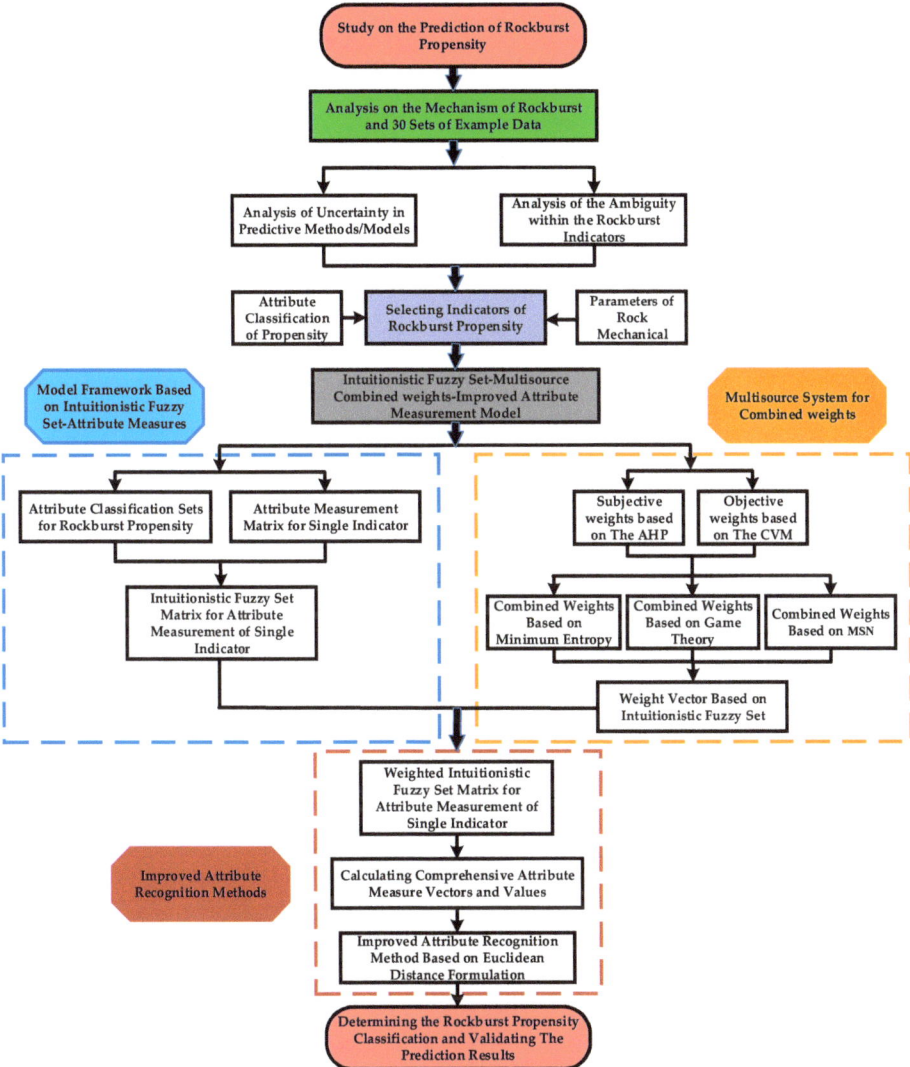

Figure 1. A model process for predicting rockburst propensity.

4.2. Applied Research on the Model

4.2.1. Single-Weighting Method

1. Selecting indicators of rockburst propensity

Generally speaking, the selection of rockburst indicators requires a comprehensive consideration of stress conditions and physical parameters of the rock [22,52]. In the process of in-depth study, it can be found that due to the differences in normative standards, testing methods, such as integrity coefficients K_v and other rock physical property parameters may not be able to truly reflect the quality of the rock body to some extent, and many scholars who only use mechanical indicators have also obtained good prediction results [39,62]. Therefore, this paper focuses on the mechanical properties of the rock to study the prediction of rockburst propensity, selecting the uniaxial compressive strength σ_c, tensile stress σ_t, shear stress σ_θ, rock compression tension ratio σ_c/σ_t, rock shear compression ratio σ_θ/σ_c, and elastic deformation coefficient W_{et} as the rockburst indicators based on the three-axis force situation.

2. Determining classification of rockburst propensity

According to the selected indicators of rockburst propensity, in order to fit the calculation requirements of attribute measurement theory, through studying and sorting out the existing literature [51,52], the classes and corresponding numerical domains of the uniaxial compressive strength σ_c, compressive tensile ratio σ_c/σ_t, shear compression ratio σ_θ/σ_c, and the elastic deformation coefficient W_{et} can be obtained, and the attribute classification of tensile stress σ_t and shear stress σ_θ can be deduced on the basis of the calculation, as shown in Table 1.

Table 1. Classification of rockburst propensity and the corresponding numerical domains.

Classification	Propensity	σ_c	σ_t	σ_θ	σ_c/σ_t	σ_θ/σ_c	W_{et}
I	None	<80	<2	<24	>40	<0.3	<2
II	Slight	80~120	2~4.5	24~60	26.7~40	0.3~0.5	2~3.5
III	Medium	120~180	4.5~12.4	60~126	14.5~26.7	0.5~0.7	3.5~5
IV	Strong	>180	>12.4	>126	<14.5	>0.7	>5

4.2.2. Calculating the Rockburst Cases

In order to verify the accuracy of predicting rockburst propensity with an intuitionistic fuzzy set–multisource combined weights–attribute measure model, 30 groups of classical rockburst cases worldwide were selected in this study [1,3,52], and the indicator data of each case is shown in detail in Table 2, with the data of rockburst case 1 as an example for the model validation.

Table 2. 30 sets of data for rockburst cases.

Sample	Actual Data for Rockburst Indicators					
	σ_c	σ_t	σ_θ	σ_c/σ_t	σ_θ/σ_c	W_{et}
1	148.400	8.480	66.780	17.500	0.450	5.100
2	132.100	6.321	51.519	20.900	0.390	4.600
3	107.500	2.622	21.500	41.000	0.200	1.700
4	106.320	2.919	23.390	36.420	0.220	1.750
5	165.000	9.429	62.700	17.500	0.380	4.500
6	116.780	3.928	43.209	29.730	0.370	3.520
7	170.000	11.333	90.100	15.000	0.530	6.500
8	181.000	8.341	76.020	21.700	0.420	4.500
9	180.000	8.295	70.200	21.700	0.390	5.000
10	140.000	5.204	61.600	26.900	0.440	5.500
11	120.000	6.486	97.200	18.500	0.810	3.800
12	220.100	7.486	90.241	29.400	0.410	7.300
13	148.520	6.660	98.023	22.300	0.660	3.230
14	178.000	5.705	19.580	31.200	0.110	3.700
15	109.330	3.336	45.919	32.770	0.420	2.970
16	156.730	7.786	76.798	20.130	0.490	3.820
17	100.320	3.487	38.122	28.770	0.380	3.020
18	142.200	5.167	102.384	27.520	0.720	4.300
19	97.600	6.297	40.992	15.500	0.420	3.200
20	100.200	3.327	58.116	30.120	0.580	4.500

Table 2. Cont.

Sample	Actual Data for Rockburst Indicators					
	σ_c	σ_t	σ_θ	σ_c/σ_t	σ_θ/σ_c	W_{et}
21	167.200	12.667	110.352	13.200	0.660	6.800
22	146.750	7.584	90.985	19.350	0.620	4.500
23	107.750	3.454	61.418	31.200	0.570	3.150
24	146.720	7.825	86.565	18.750	0.590	4.200
25	162.700	5.478	118.771	29.700	0.730	3.820
26	105.700	2.830	39.109	37.350	0.370	3.080
27	215.000	8.958	64.500	24.000	0.300	6.600
28	185.000	7.676	68.450	24.100	0.370	5.000
29	153.000	6.923	58.140	22.100	0.380	5.100
30	173.000	7.972	72.660	21.700	0.420	5.200

1. Matrix of intuitionistic fuzzy sets for rockburst single-indicator

From Equation (4) and Table 1, the matrix of attribute classification for rockburst propensity indicators can be listed as follows:

$$C = \begin{pmatrix} & I & II & III & IV \\ \sigma_c & <80 & 80\sim120 & 120\sim180 & >180 \\ \sigma_t & <2 & 2\sim4.5 & 4.5\sim12.4 & >12.4 \\ \sigma_\theta & <24 & 24\sim60 & 60\sim126 & >126 \\ \frac{\sigma_c}{\sigma_t} & >40 & 40\sim26.7 & 26.7\sim14.5 & <14.5 \\ \frac{\sigma_\theta}{\sigma_c} & <0.3 & 0.3\sim0.5 & 0.5\sim0.7 & >0.7 \\ W_{et} & <2 & 2\sim3.5 & 3.5\sim5 & >5 \end{pmatrix} \quad (33)$$

According to Equations (6)–(11) and (33), the matrix U_1 of single-indicator attribute measures for the sample are listed as follows:

$$U_1 = \begin{bmatrix} & I & II & III & IV \\ \sigma_c & 0 & 0 & 1 & 0 \\ \sigma_t & 0 & 0 & 1 & 0 \\ \sigma_\theta & 0 & 0.2175 & 0.7825 & 0 \\ \frac{\sigma_c}{\sigma_t} & 0 & 0 & 0.8 & 0.2 \\ \frac{\sigma_\theta}{\sigma_c} & 0 & 0.75 & 0.25 & 0 \\ W_{et} & 0 & 0 & 0.4333 & 0.5667 \end{bmatrix} \quad (34)$$

From Equation (3), (13), and (34), the matrix B_1 of intuitionistic fuzzy sets for single-indicator attribute measures can be obtained as follows:

$$B_1 = \begin{bmatrix} & I & II & III & IV \\ \sigma_c & \langle 0,1 \rangle & \langle 0,1 \rangle & \langle 1,0 \rangle & \langle 0,1 \rangle \\ \sigma_t & \langle 0,1 \rangle & \langle 0,1 \rangle & \langle 1,0 \rangle & \langle 0,1 \rangle \\ \sigma_\theta & \langle 0,1 \rangle & \langle 0.2175, 0.7825 \rangle & \langle 0.7825, 0.2175 \rangle & \langle 0,1 \rangle \\ \frac{\sigma_c}{\sigma_t} & \langle 0,1 \rangle & \langle 0,1 \rangle & \langle 0.8, 0.2 \rangle & \langle 0.2, 0.8 \rangle \\ \frac{\sigma_\theta}{\sigma_c} & \langle 0,1 \rangle & \langle 0.75, 0.25 \rangle & \langle 0.25, 0.75 \rangle & \langle 0,1 \rangle \\ W_{et} & \langle 0,1 \rangle & \langle 0,1 \rangle & \langle 0.4333, 0.5667 \rangle & \langle 0.5667, 0.4333 \rangle \end{bmatrix} \quad (35)$$

2. Calculating multisource combined weights of rockbursts

According to the description in Section 3.2.1, the subjective weights of the AHP method and the objective weights of the CVM for rockburst case 1 can be obtained as shown in Table 3.

Table 3. Values of subjective and objective weights.

Indicators	AHP	CVM
σ_c	0.121	0.159
σ_t	0.127	0.142
σ_θ	0.139	0.174
σ_c/σ_t	0.243	0.208
σ_θ/σ_c	0.221	0.159
W_{et}	0.148	0.158

Based on the AHP weights and CVM weights, and according to the calculation method in Section 3.2.2, the minimum entropy combined weights, game theory combined weights, and multiplicative synthetic normalization weights of the indicators are obtained, as shown in Table 4, so as to construct the multisource system combined weights of rockburst propensity.

Table 4. Values of the three combined weights.

Indicators	Minimum Entropy	Game Theory	Multiplicative Synthetic Normalization
σ_c	0.140	0.115	0.113
σ_t	0.135	0.125	0.105
σ_θ	0.157	0.133	0.142
σ_c/σ_t	0.227	0.249	0.296
σ_θ/σ_c	0.189	0.232	0.206
W_{et}	0.154	0.146	0.137

According to the multisource combined weights of rockburst indicators, combined with the description in Section 3.2.3, the indicator system is converted into the form of intuitionistic fuzzy sets, as shown in Table 5, and the vector ω_1 is obtained, as shown in Figure 2.

Table 5. The form of intuitionistic fuzzy sets for multisource combined weights.

Indicators	Degree of Importance	Degree of Unimportance	Vectors of Intuitive Fuzzy Sets
σ_c	0.113~0.140	0.860~0.887	<0.113, 0.860>
σ_t	0.105~0.135	0.865~0.895	<0.105, 0.865>
σ_θ	0.133~0.157	0.843~0.867	<0.133, 0.843>
σ_c/σ_t	0.227~0.296	0.704~0.773	<0.227, 0.704>
σ_θ/σ_c	0.189~0.232	0.768~0.811	<0.189, 0.768>
W_{et}	0.137~0.154	0.846~0.863	<0.137, 0.846>

3. Intuitionistic fuzzy matrices and numerical computation of composite measures for rockbursts

According to the intuitionistic fuzzy vector ω_1 of the rockburst indicators, Equations (15) and (35), it is possible to obtain the matrix h_1 of weighted intuitionistic fuzzy sets as follows:

$$h_1 = \begin{bmatrix} & I & II & III & IV \\ \sigma_c & \langle 0,1 \rangle & \langle 0,1 \rangle & \langle 0.113, 0.86 \rangle & \langle 0,1 \rangle \\ \sigma_t & \langle 0,1 \rangle & \langle 0,1 \rangle & \langle 0.105, 0.865 \rangle & \langle 0,1 \rangle \\ \sigma_\theta & \langle 0,1 \rangle & \langle 0.0289, 0.9659 \rangle & \langle 0.1041, 0.8771 \rangle & \langle 0,1 \rangle \\ \frac{\sigma_c}{\sigma_t} & \langle 0,1 \rangle & \langle 0,1 \rangle & \langle 0.1816, 0.7632 \rangle & \langle 0.0454, 0.9408 \rangle \\ \frac{\sigma_\theta}{\sigma_c} & \langle 0,1 \rangle & \langle 0.1418, 0.826 \rangle & \langle 0.0473, 0.942 \rangle & \langle 0,1 \rangle \\ W_{et} & \langle 0,1 \rangle & \langle 0,1 \rangle & \langle 0.0594, 0.9333 \rangle & \langle 0.0776, 0.9127 \rangle \end{bmatrix} \quad (36)$$

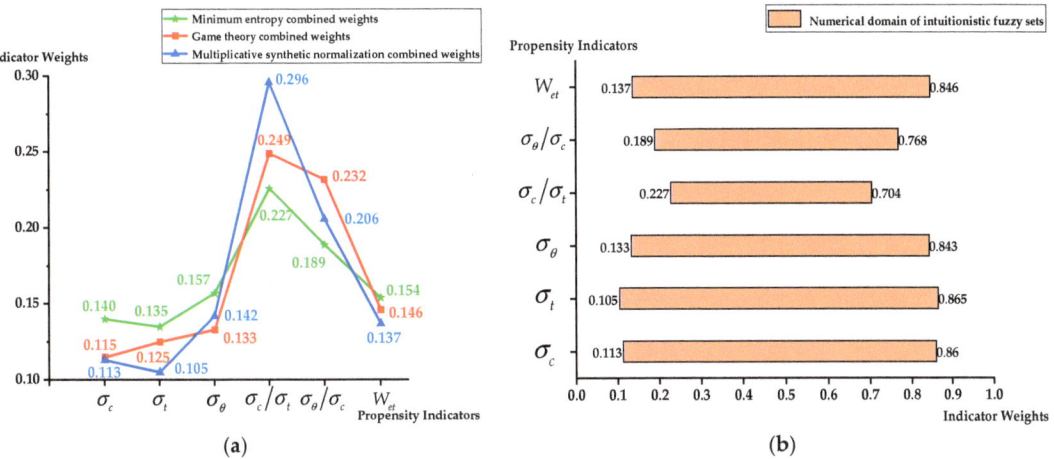

Figure 2. Values and distribution of indicator weights. (**a**) Values and distribution of combined weights; (**b**) numerical domains of intuitionistic fuzzy sets for combined weights.

From Equation (17), the intuitionistic fuzzy set vectors and values of the composite attribute measure for rock burst propensity are shown below:

$$\begin{cases} H_{11} = \langle 0, 1 \rangle \\ H_{12} = \langle 0.1666, 0.7978 \rangle \\ H_{13} = \langle 0.4783, 0.4378 \rangle \\ H_{14} = \langle 0.1195, 0.8587 \rangle \end{cases} \quad (37)$$

$$\begin{cases} \delta_{11} = 0 - 1 = -1 \\ \delta_{12} = 0.1666 - 0.7978 = -0.6312 \\ \delta_{13} = 0.4783 - 0.4378 = 0.0405 \\ \delta_{14} = 0.1195 - 0.8587 = -0.7392 \end{cases} \quad (38)$$

4. Determining the classification of rockbursts

According to Equation (4), Table 1, and Section 3.1.2, the set C_1 of attribute classification for rockburst propensity in case 1 is defined as follows:

$$C_1 \begin{cases} C_{11} = [1, 0, 0, 0] \\ C_{12} = [0, 1, 0, 0] \\ C_{13} = [0, 0, 1, 0] \\ C_{14} = [0, 0, 0, 1] \end{cases} \quad (39)$$

Then, the Euclidean distances of the composite attribute measures for each class of case 1 with respect to the corresponding classification are calculated as shown below:

$$\begin{cases} R_{11} = \sqrt{(-1-1)^2 + (-0.6312-0)^2 + (0.0405-0)^2 + (-0.7392-0)^2} = 2.2241 \\ R_{12} = \sqrt{(-1-0)^2 + (-0.6312-1)^2 + (0.0405-0)^2 + (-0.7392-0)^2} = 2.0516 \\ R_{13} = \sqrt{(-1-0)^2 + (-0.6312-0)^2 + (0.0405-1)^2 + (-0.7392-0)^2} = 1.6928 \\ R_{14} = \sqrt{(-1-0)^2 + (-0.6312-0)^2 + (0.0405-0)^2 + (-0.7392-1)^2} = 2.1035 \end{cases} \quad (40)$$

Comparing the distances of case 1 to the subsets in the attribute class set, it can be concluded that $R_{13} < R_{12} < R_{14} < R_{11}$, and therefore the composite attribute measure, is closest to class III and is able to predict the propensity to rockburst occurrence class of III for case 1.

4.3. Analysis of The Results

4.3.1. Analysis of the Results Calculated using the Model

According to the calculation steps of case 1, the remaining 29 sets of rockburst case data are calculated based on the model in this paper. Summarizing the results of rockburst propensity with this paper's model, they are compared with the results of the minimum entropy–attribute measure model, the game theory–attribute measure model, and the multiplicative synthetic normalization–attribute measure model, respectively, and at the same time, they are verified with the data of the actual rockburst propensity class. The comparisons are shown in Table 6.

Table 6. Comparison of 30 sets of prediction results for rockburst propensity.

		Predicted Result (Rockburst Susceptibility Classification)			
Sample	Actual Class	Intuitionistic Fuzzy Sets—Multisource Combined Weights—Attribute Measures (IMAM)	Minimum Entropy–Attribute Measures (MEAM)	Game Theory–Attribute Measures (GTAM)	Multiplicative Synthetic Normalization–Attribute Measures (MSNAM)
1	III	III	III	III	III
2	III	III	III	III	III
3	I	I	I	I	I
4	I	* II	* II	* II	* II
5	II	* III	* III	* III	* III
6	II	II	II	II	II
7	III	III	III	III	III
8	III	III	III	III	III
9	III	III	III	III	III
10	III	III	III	III	Δ II~III
11	III	III	III	III	III
12	II	II	Δ II~III	Δ II~III	Δ II~III
13	III	III	III	III	III
14	I	* II	* II~III	Δ I~II	* II
15	II	II	II	II	II
16	III	III	III	III	III
17	II	II	II	II	II
18	III	III	III	III	III
19	II	II	II	II	II
20	II	II	II	II	II
21	IV	Δ III~IV	Δ III~IV	Δ III~IV	Δ III~IV
22	III	III	III	III	III
23	II	II	II	II	II
24	III	III	III	III	III
25	III	III	III	III	III
26	II	II	II	II	II
27	III	III	Δ III~IV	III	III
28	III	III	III	III	III
29	III	III	III	III	III
30	III	III	III	III	III

In the table, * indicates a misjudgement, and Δ indicates an uncertain judgement.

Comparisons of the actual propensity of the selected rockburst cases and summaries of the number of cases where the results for each model in the table are accurate, uncertain, or misjudged are shown in Table 7, and the drawing of the comparison is shown in Figure 3.

Table 7. Summary and comparison of results.

Sample	Intuitionistic Fuzzy Set—Multisource Combined Weights—Attribute Measures	Minimum Entropy–Attribute Measures	Game Theory–Attribute Measures	Multiplicative Synthetic Normalization–Attribute Measures
Accurate	26	24	25	24
Uncertain	1	3	3	3
Misjudged	3	3	2	3
Accuracy	86.7%	80%	83.3%	80%

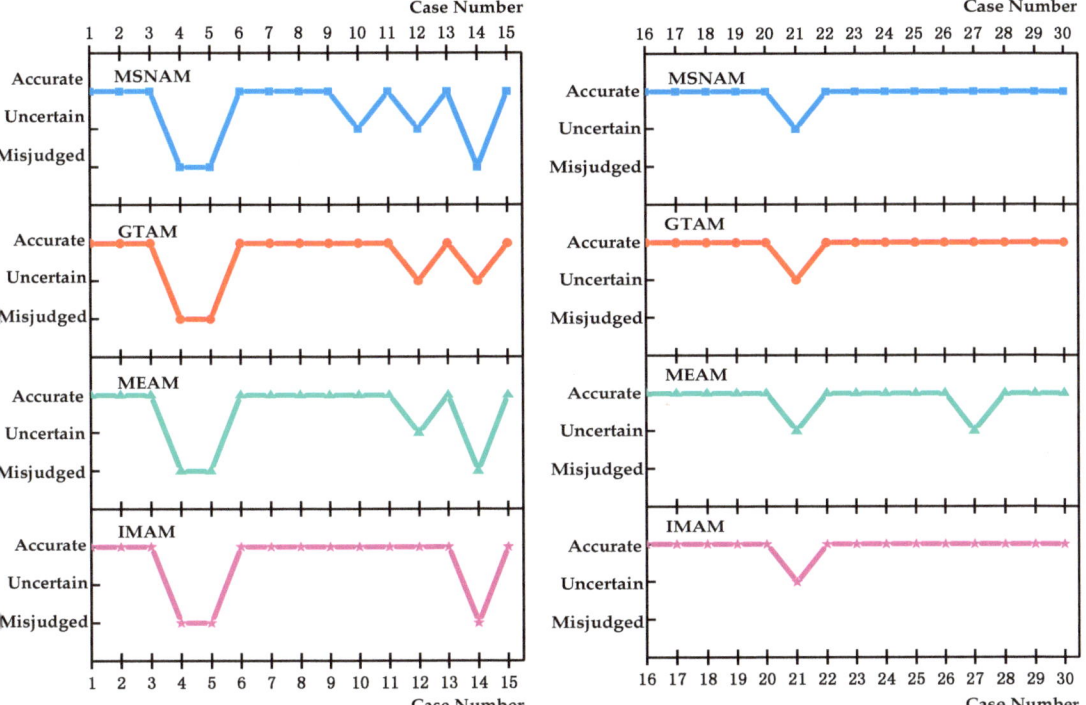

Figure 3. Comparison between prediction results of models.

By analyzing the results, it can be found that:

(1) In terms of accuracy, the results of the intuitionistic fuzzy set–multisource combined weights–attribute measurement model proposed in this paper are better than the other three combined models, which makes this paper's model more practical in practical applications;

(2) In the structure of models with single combined weighting, the model with the highest accuracy rate is the game theory–attribute measurement model. It can be further determined that among the three single combined weighting methods, the indicator weights of game theory are more reasonable;

(3) Comparing the results of the other three models, the number of uncertain cases in the results for the model proposed in this paper is the least, and the main reason is that the vagueness of the rockburst data is effectively controlled through the intuitionistic fuzzy set, which makes it tend to the corresponding attribute set to a certain degree.

4.3.2. Analysis of the Weights of Indicators

Analyzing Tables 3–5 and Figure 2, it can be found that the values of rockburst propensity indicators obtained through different weighting methods have large differences in the distribution, so it is necessary to further deepen the study of the rationality of the indicators by drawing the value distribution of multisource combined weights and the comparison chart as shown in Figures 4 and 5:

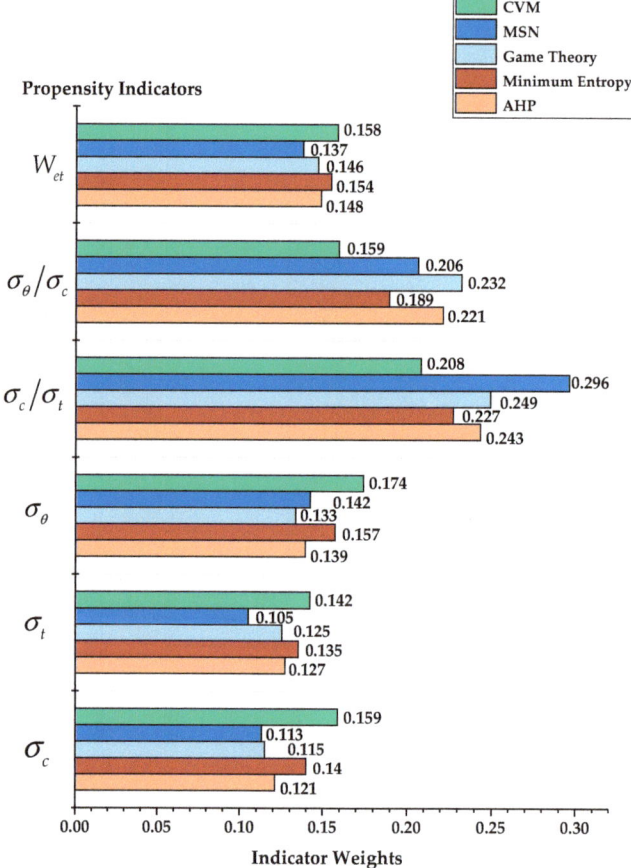

Figure 4. Distribution of indicator weights.

(1) The principles of the subjective weighting method and the objective weighting method are not the same, which leads to a significant difference in the values of the indicators. In the model calculation, if a single weighting method is used, the prediction results will have a large bias. Compared with the single-weight method, the combined weighing method is more reasonable and can balance the subjective and objective weights, thus making the indicator weights numerically more average and reasonable;

(2) Due to the differences in the weighting mechanism and the adopted algorithm, different combined weighting methods will have different focuses. As can be seen from Figures 4 and 5, under the conditions of the indicators in this paper, the game theory combined weights are numerically closer to the AHP method weights, while the minimum entropy combined weights are closer to the CVM weights, which can be deduced from the fact that even though it is the combined weighting method, only one method cannot comprehensively reflect the real situation of the indicators;

(3) Using the intuitionistic fuzzy set method to defuzzify the multisource combined weights, the indicator weights are generalized from specific numbers to a range of numerical intervals, which combines the advantages of the three combined weighting methods and expands the numerical domain of the model's prediction results. From the results, the indicator vagueness is controlled to a certain extent, and the prediction results of the model in this paper are better than those of the other combined weights models listed.

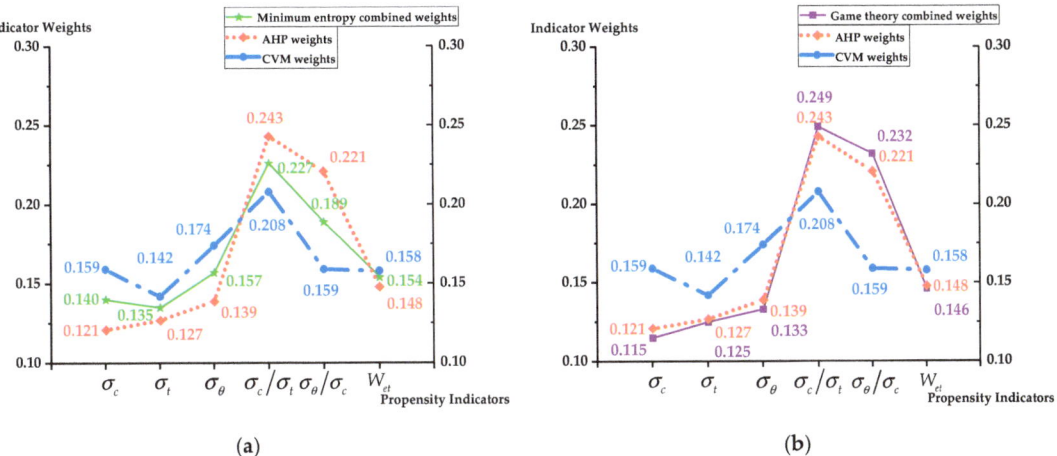

Figure 5. Trends in indicator values. (**a**) Trends in combined weights of minimum entropy; (**b**) trends in combined weights of game theory.

5. Conclusions

The conclusions are as follows:

(1) Using the intuitionistic fuzzy set–attribute measure model for predicting the propensity of rockburst, the vagueness of the indicator data is transformed into the intervalisation of the numerical domain, which controls the uncertainty of the prediction results to a certain extent; through calculating the "degree of measurement" between the case data and attribute classification set, it makes the evaluation of the scheme and the classification evaluation become a unified whole. The Euclidean distance method is used to improve the attribute identification of the model, and it is based on the perspective of the "distance" between the values of composite attribute measure and the attribute classification set, which avoids the influence of the objectivity that is affected by the artificial parameter setting, and the accuracy of attribute identification in the model is improved;

(2) Through the study of rockburst cases and mechanisms, from the perspective of rock mechanics, six indicators were selected to characterize the propensity of rockbursts: the uniaxial compressive strength σ_c, tensile stress σ_t, shear stress σ_θ, compression/tension ratio σ_c/σ_t, shear/compression ratio σ_θ/σ_c, and elastic deformation coefficient W_{et}. Based on the selected indicators of the rock burst propensity, the attribute classification set and range of the numerical domains for the corresponding classification are determined so that the indicators are internalized as the basis of the model and the standard of the calculations;

(3) Based on the subjective weights of AHP and objective weights of CVM, the multisource system for combined weights for rockburst propensity indicators is constructed with minimum entropy combined weights, game theory combined weights, and multiplicative synthetic normalization combined weights, and with the help of intuitionistic fuzzy sets, the single-valued indicators are transformed into interval values, which further transforms the vagueness while expanding the range of reasonable numerical domains for the indicators, taking into account and balancing the experts' experience and data information of the rock burst indicators;

(4) Selecting 30 sets of typical rockburst cases in the world, the prediction results for rockburst propensity of the intuitionistic fuzzy set–multisource combined weights-attribute measure model are compared with those of the other three single combined weighting methods with the attribute measure model, and it is verified that the model proposed in this paper is better than the other three models in improving the accuracy and controlling the vagueness of the indicators.

Author Contributions: Conceptualization, J.C.; methodology, Y.Z.; data curation, J.C. and Y.Z.; formal analysis, Y.Z. and S.Y.; validation, J.C. and Z.Z.; resources, J.C. and Z.Z.; writing—original draft preparation, Y.Z. and Z.L.; writing—review and editing, Y.Z. and Z.L.; project administration, Z.Z. and J.C. All authors have read and agreed to the published version of the manuscript.

Funding: This research was funded by the National Natural Science Foundation Project of China under Grant No. 52274163.

Institutional Review Board Statement: Not applicable.

Informed Consent Statement: Not applicable.

Data Availability Statement: Data are contained within the article.

Acknowledgments: The authors would like to express their thanks to the National Natural Science Foundation.

Conflicts of Interest: The authors declare no conflict of interest.

References

1. Xue, Y.; Li, Z.; Li, S.; Qiu, D.; Tao, Y.; Wang, L.; Yang, W.; Zhang, K. Prediction of rock burst in underground caverns based on rough set and extensible comprehensive evaluation. *Bull. Eng. Geol. Environ.* **2019**, *78*, 417–429. [CrossRef]
2. Zhao, W.; Qin, C.; Xiao, Z.; Chen, W. Characteristics and contributing factors of major coal bursts in longwall mines. *Energy Sci. Eng.* **2022**, *10*, 1314–1327. [CrossRef]
3. Wang, Y.; Xu, Q.; Chai, H.; Liu, L.; Xia, Y.; Wang, X. Rock burst prediction in deep shaft based on RBF-AR model. *J. Jilin Univ.* **2013**, *43*, 1943–1949. (In Chinese) [CrossRef]
4. Xue, Y.; Bai, C.; Qiu, D.; Kong, F.; Li, Z. Predicting rockburst with database using particle swarm optimization and extreme learning machine. *Tunn. Undergr. Space Technol.* **2020**, *98*, 103287. [CrossRef]
5. Liu, Z.X.; Han, K.W.; Yang, S.; Liu, Y.X. Fractal evolution mechanism of rock fracture in undersea metal mining. *J. Cent. South Univ.* **2020**, *27*, 1320–1333. [CrossRef]
6. Zhou, J.; Li, X.; Mitri, H.S. Classification of rockburst in underground projects: Comparison of ten supervised learning methods. *J. Comput. Civ. Eng.* **2016**, *30*, 04016003. [CrossRef]
7. Feng, G.L.; Feng, X.T.; Xiao, Y.X.; Yao, Z.B.; Hu, L.; Niu, W.J.; Li, T. Characteristic microseismicity during the development process of intermittent rockburst in a deep railway tunnel. *Int. J. Rock Mech. Min. Sci.* **2019**, *124*, 104135. [CrossRef]
8. Yang, Z.G.; Wang, P.F. Reinforced support of drift with rockburst in deep mine. *Nonferrous Met.* **2017**, *69*, 91–94. (In Chinese)
9. Gong, F.Q.; Pan, J.F.; Jiang, Q. The difference analysis of rock burst and coal burst and key mechanisms of deep engineering geological hazards. *J. Eng. Geol.* **2021**, *29*, 933–961. (In Chinese)
10. Lee, S.M.; Park, B.S.; Lee, S.W. Analysis of rockbursts that have occurred in a waterway tunnel in Korea. *Int. J. Rock Mech. Min. Sci.* **2004**, *41* (Suppl. 1), 911–916. [CrossRef]
11. Liu, C.L. Microearthquake acrivity associated with underground coal-mining in Buchanan County, Virginia, U.S.A. *Recent Dev. World Seismol.* **1995**, *10*, 33.
12. Ma, S.; Wang, L.; Zhang, M.; Li, G. Study on Blasting Hazard in Canada. *Chin. J. Geol. Hazard Control.* **1998**, *3*, 107–112.
13. Yang, B.; He, M.; Zhang, Z.; Zhu, J.; Chen, Y. A New Criterion of Strain Rockburst in Consideration of the Plastic Zone of Tunnel Surrounding Rock. *Rock Mech. Rock Eng.* **2022**, *55*, 1777–1789. [CrossRef]
14. Gong, F.; Wang, Y.; Luo, S. Rockburst proneness criteria for rock materials: Review and new insights. *J. Cent. South Univ. Technol.* **2020**, *27*, 2793–2821. [CrossRef]
15. Ouyang, L.; Zhang, R.-J.; Liu, Y.-R.; Huang, Q.-S.; Li, J.-H.; Pang, Z.-Y. Review on Rockburst Prevention Techniques and Typical Applications in Deep Tunnels. *J. Yangtze River Sci. Res. Inst.* **2022**, *39*, 161. (In Chinese)
16. Cai, W.; Bai, X.; Si, G.; Cao, W.; Gong, S.; Dou, L. A Monitoring Investigation into Rock Burst Mechanism Based on the Coupled Theory of Static and Dynamic Stresses. *Rock Mech. Rock Eng.* **2020**, *53*, 5451–5471. [CrossRef]
17. Cook, N.G.W.; Hoek, E.; Pretorius, J.P.; Ortlepp, W.D.; Salamon, M.D.G. Rock mechanics applied to study of rockbursts. *J. S. Afr. Inst. Min. Metall.* **1966**, *66*, 436.
18. Wang, Y.H.; Li, W.D.; Li, Q.G.; Xu, Y.; Tan, G.H. Method of fuzzy comprehensive evaluations for rockburst prediction. *J. Rock Mech. Eng.* **1998**, *5*, 15–23. (In Chinese)

1. Turchaninov, I.A.; Markov, G.A.; Gzovsky, M.V.; Kazikayev, D.M.; Frenze, U.K.; Batugin, S.A.; Chabdarova, U.I. State of stress in the upper part of the Earth's crust based on direct measurements in mines and on tectonophysical and seismological studies. *Phys. Earth Planet. Inter.* **1972**, *6*, 229–234. [CrossRef]
2. Zhu, H.H.; Zhang, Q.; Zhang, L.Y. Review of research progresses and applications of Hoek-Brown strength criterion. *Chin. J. Rock Mech. Eng.* **2013**, *32*, 1945–1963. (In Chinese)
3. Kidybiński, A. Bursting liability indices of coal. *Int. J. Rock Mech. Min. Sci. Geomech. Abstr.* **1981**, *18*, 295–304. [CrossRef]
4. Zhao, Y.; Chen, J.; Yang, S.; Liu, Z. Game Theory and an Improved Maximum Entropy-Attribute Measure Interval Model for Predicting Rockburst Intensity. *Mathematics* **2022**, *10*, 2551. [CrossRef]
5. Chen, X.; Sun, J.; Zhang, J.; Chen, Q. Judgment indexes and classification criteria of rock-burst with the extension judgment method. *China Civ. Eng. J.* **2009**, *42*, 82–88. (In Chinese)
6. Lu, A.; Mao, X.; Liu, H. Physical simulation of rock burst induced by stress waves. *J. China Univ. Min. Technol.* **2008**, *18*, 401–405. [CrossRef]
7. Fakhimi, A.; Hosseini, O.; Theodore, R. Physical and numerical study of strain burst of mine pillars. *Comput. Geotech.* **2016**, *74*, 36–44. [CrossRef]
8. Zhang, L.W.; Zhang, D.Y.; Qiu, D.H. Application of extension evaluation method in rockburst prediction based on rough set theory. *J. China Coal Soc.* **2010**, *35*, 1461–1465. (In Chinese) [CrossRef]
9. Zhou, J.; Chen, C.; Du, K.; Jahed Armaghani, D.; Li, C. A new hybrid model of information entropy and unascertained measurement with different membership functions for evaluating destressability in burst-prone underground mines. *Eng. Comput.* **2022**, *38* (Suppl. 1), 381–399. [CrossRef]
10. Liu, Z.; Shao, J.; Xu, W.; Meng, Y. Prediction of rock burst classification using the technique of cloud models with attribution weight. *Nat. Hazards* **2013**, *68*, 549–568. [CrossRef]
11. Yin, X.; Liu, Q.; Wang, X.; Huang, X. Prediction model of rockburst intensity classification based on combined weighting and attribute interval recognition theory. *J. China Coal Soc.* **2020**, *45*, 3772–3780. (In Chinese) [CrossRef]
12. Zhou, H.; Liao, X.; Chen, S.; Feng, T.; Wang, Z. Rockburst Risk Assessment of Deep Lying Tunnels Based on Combination Weight and Unascertained Measure Theory: A Case Study of Sangzhuling Tunnel on Sichuan-Tibet Traffic Corridor. *Earth Sci.* **2022**, *47*, 2130–2148. [CrossRef]
13. Hu, X.; Huang, L.; Chen, J.; Li, X.; Zhang, H. Rockburst prediction based on optimization of unascertained measure theory with normal cloud. *Complex Intell. Syst.* **2023**. [CrossRef]
14. Li, P.X.; Cheng, B.R.; Zhou, Y.Y. Research progress of rockburst prediction and early warning in hard rock underground engineering. *J. China Coal Soc.* **2019**, *44*, 447–465. (In Chinese)
15. Kai, Z.; Ke, Z.; Kun, L.I. Prediction model of rockburst grade based on PCA-neural network. *China Saf. Sci. J.* **2021**, *31*, 96. (In Chinese)
16. Chen, D.F.; Feng, X.T.; Yang, C.X.; Chen, B.R.; Qiu, S.L.; Xu, D.P. Neural network estimation of rockburst damage severity based on engineering cases. In Proceedings of the ISRM SINOROCK, ISRM, Shanghai, China, 18–20 June 2013.
17. Yang, X.B.; Pei, Y.Y.; Cheng, H.M.; Hou, X.; Lu, J. Prediction method of rockburst intensity grade based on SOFM neural network model. *Chin. J. Rock Mech. Eng.* **2021**, *40*, 2708–2715. (In Chinese)
18. e Sousa, L.R.; Miranda, T.; e Sousa, R.L.; Tinoco, J. The use of data mining techniques in rockburst risk assessment. *Engineering* **2017**, *3*, 552–558. [CrossRef]
19. Li, T.; Ma, C.; Zhu, M.; Meng, L.; Chen, G. Geomechanical types and mechanical analyses of rockbursts. *Eng. Geol.* **2017**, *222*, 72–83. [CrossRef]
20. Zhou, J.; Li, X.; Shi, X. Long-term prediction model of rockburst in underground openings using heuristic algorithms and support vector machines. *Saf. Sci.* **2012**, *50*, 629–644. [CrossRef]
21. Zhou, J.; Li, X.; Mitri, H.S. Evaluation method of rockburst: State-of-the-art literature review. *Tunn. Undergr. Space Technol.* **2018**, *81*, 632–659. [CrossRef]
22. Tran, Q.-H.; Bui, X.-N.; Nguyen, H. Classifying rockburst in deep underground mines using a robust hybrid computational model based on gene expression programming and particle swarm optimization. *J. Civ. Environ. Eng.* **2023**, *45*, 21–38. [CrossRef]
23. Shirani Faradonbeh, R.; Taheri, A. Long-term prediction of rockburst hazard in deep underground openings using three robust data mining techniques. *Eng. Comput.* **2019**, *35*, 659–675. [CrossRef]
24. Chen, S.; Wu, A.; Wang, Y.; Xu, M. Prediction of rockburst intensity based on decision tree model. *J. Wuhan Univ. Sci. Technol.* **2016**, *39*, 195–199.
25. Atanassov, K.T. Intuitionistic Fuzzy Sets, VII ITKR Session, Sofia, 20-23 June 1983 (Deposed in Centr. Sci.-Techn. Library of the Bulg. Acad. of Sci., 1697/84) (in Bulgarian). *Int. J. Bioautom.* **2016**, *20*, S1–S6.
26. Atanassov, K.T. Intuitionistic Fuzzy Sets. In *Intuitionistic Fuzzy Sets. Studies in Fuzziness and Soft Computing*; Physica: Heidelberg, Germany, 1999; Volume 35. [CrossRef]
27. Hussain, A.; Mahmood, T.; Smarandache, F.; Ashraf, S. TOPSIS approach for MCGDM based on intuitionistic fuzzy rough Dombi aggregation operations. *Comput. Appl. Math.* **2023**, *42*, 176. [CrossRef]
28. Li, Y.; Li, T.; Zhao, Q. Remote sensing image intuitionistic fuzzy set segmentation method. *Acta Geod. Cartogr. Sin.* **2023**, *52*, 405. (In Chinese)

47. Wu, S.; Zhou, Z.; Chen, J.; Zheng, R. Evaluation of rock mass quality based on intuitionistic fuzzy set TOPSIS in open-pit min *J. Cent. South Univ. (Sci. Technol.)* **2016**, *47*, 2463–2468. (In Chinese)
48. Li, T. Based on Intuitionistic Fuzzy Sets Research on Segmentation Algorithm of Remote Sensing Image. Master's Thesis, Liaonin Technical University, Fuxin, China, 2022. (In Chinese) [CrossRef]
49. Xu, Z.; Cai, N.; Li, X.; Xian, M.; Dong, T. Risk assessment of loess tunnel collapse during construction based on an attribu recognition model. *Bull. Eng. Geol. Environ.* **2021**, *80*, 6205–6220. [CrossRef]
50. Zhou, Z.; Zhang, K.; Zhang, H.; Chen, S.; Gan, H. Risk assessment of surface subsidence in karst tunnels under attribu recognition theory. *China Saf. Sci. J.* **2022**, *32*, 105. (In Chinese)
51. Wang, L.; Pei, A.; Peng, P. Attribute Synthetic Evaluation Model for Rockburst Disaster Prediction in Underground Engineerin *Sci. Technol. Rev.* **2014**, *32*, 22–26.
52. Wu, S.; Yang, S.; Huo, L. Prediction of rock burst intensity based on unascertained measure-intuitionistic fuzzy set. *Chin. J. Ro Mech. Eng.* **2020**, *39*, 2930–2939. (In Chinese)
53. Saaty, T.L.; Kearns, K.P. The analytic hierarchy process. In *Analytical Planning: The Organization of System*; Pergamon Pres Oxford, UK, 1985.
54. Naddeo, V.; Belgiorno, V.; Zarra, T.; Scannapieco, D. Dynamic and embedded evaluation procedure for strategic environment assessment. *Land Use Policy* **2012**, *31*, 605–612. [CrossRef]
55. Li, Z.; Xiang, J.; Sheng, T.; Xiao, B. G1-variation-coefficient-KL based TOPSIS radar jamming effectiveness evaluation. *J. Beijin Univ. Aeron Astron.* **2021**, *47*, 2571–2578. (In Chinese)
56. Li, Y.; Li, F.; Wang, S.; Shang, Q. Credit Evaluation of Electricity Sales Companies Based on Improved Coefficient of Variatic Method and BP Neural Network. *Power Syst. Technol.* **2022**, *46*, 4228–4237. [CrossRef]
57. Cao, M.; Fang, Q.-C. Research on green degree evaluation model of prefabricated buildings based on combination weighting an attribute recognition model. *J. Saf. Environ.* **2022**, *22*, 2166–2175. (In Chinese) [CrossRef]
58. Feng, L.-H.; Li, F.-Q. Analysis of Disaster Loss Based on Maximum Entropy Principle. *J. Math. Pract. Theory* **2005**, *8*, 73–77.
59. Zhao, R.; Neighbour, G.; McGuire, M.; Deutz, P. A software based simulation for cleaner production: A game betwee manufacturers and government. *J. Loss Prev. Process Ind.* **2013**, *26*, 59–67. [CrossRef]
60. Wang, S.; Fei, L.; Lei, Y.; Tian, W. Two Kinds of Comprehensive Weight Combination Method Applied to Irrigation District Evaluation. *J. Xi'an Univ. Technol.* **2009**, *25*, 207–211. (In Chinese) [CrossRef]
61. Li, K.G.; Li, M.L.; Qin, Q.C. Research on evaluation method of rock burst tendency based on improved comprehensive weightin *Chin. J. Rock Mech. Eng.* **2020**, *39*, 2751–2762. (In Chinese)
62. Duan, S.; Xu, X. Discussion of problems in calculation and application of rock mass integrity coefficient. *J. Eng. Geol.* **201** *21*, 548–553. (In Chinese)

Disclaimer/Publisher's Note: The statements, opinions and data contained in all publications are solely those of the individu author(s) and contributor(s) and not of MDPI and/or the editor(s). MDPI and/or the editor(s) disclaim responsibility for any injury people or property resulting from any ideas, methods, instructions or products referred to in the content.

Article

Numerical Simulation of Failure Modes in Irregular Columnar Jointed Rock Masses under Dynamic Loading

Yingjie Xia [1,2,3], Bingchen Liu [2,3], Tianjiao Li [2,3,*], Danchen Zhao [2,3], Ning Liu [4], Chun'an Tang [2,3] and Jun Chen [4]

[1] State Key Laboratory of Geomechanics and Geotechnical Engineering, Institute of Rock and Soil Mechanics, Chinese Academy of Sciences, Wuhan 430071, China; xiayingjie@dlut.edu.cn
[2] State Key Laboratory of Coastal and Offshore Engineering, Dalian University of Technology, Dalian 116024, China
[3] School of Civil Engineering, Dalian University of Technology, Dalian 116024, China
[4] Power China Huadong Engineering Corporation, Hangzhou 310014, China
* Correspondence: tianjiaoli@dlut.edu.cn; Tel.: +86-158-4062-1813

Abstract: The mechanical properties and failure characteristics of columnar jointed rock mass (CJRM) are significantly influenced by its irregular structure. Current research on CJRMs is mainly under static loading, which cannot meet the actual needs of engineering. This paper adopts the finite element method (FEM) to carry out numerical simulation tests on irregular CJRMs with different dip angles under different dynamic stress wave loadings. The dynamic failure modes of irregular CJRMs and the influence law of related stress wave parameters are obtained. The results show that when the column dip angle α is 0°, the tensile-compressive-shear failure occurs in the CJRMs; when α is 30°, the CJRMs undergo tensile failure and a small amount of compressive shear failure, and an obvious crack-free area appears in the middle of the rock mass; when α is 60°, tensile failure is dominant and compressive shear failure is minimal and no crack area disappears; and when α is 90°, the rock mass undergoes complete tensile failure. In addition, in terms of the change law of stress wave parameters, the increase in peak amplitude will increase the number of cracks, promote the development of cracks, and increase the proportion of compression-shear failure units for low-angle rock mass. The changes in the loading and decay rate only affect the degree of crack development in the CJRMs, but do not increase the number of cracks. Meanwhile, the simulation results show that the crack expansion velocity of the CJRMs increases with the increase in dip angle, and the CJRMs with dip angle $\alpha = 60°$ are the most vulnerable to failure. The influence of the loading and decay rate on the rock mass failure is different with the change in dip angle. The results of the study provide references for related rock engineering.

Keywords: columnar jointed rock mass; numerical simulation; rock failure process analysis; dynamic loading; rock damage

MSC: 74S05

1. Introduction

As a unique geological structure of basalt, the columnar joint is a primary tensile fracture structure [1–4]. Many scholars believe that it is formed by cooling condensation and contraction of unexposed magma after volcanic eruption [5–7]. Due to the difference in magma cooling time, the cross-section of CJRMs shows a variety of irregular polygons, such as quadrilaterals, pentagons, and hexagons [8,9]. Meanwhile, compared with other rock masses because of the unique structure and formation mode, CJRMs exhibit complex discontinuity, non-uniformity, and strong anisotropy [10], which bring difficulties and challenges to some large-scale geotechnical hydropower, mining tunnel basting excavation projects [11].

With the construction of large hydropower stations, such as Tongjiezi, Xiluodu, and Baihetan, a large area of CJRMs were exposed and revealed as engineering rock masses, as in Figure 1, and related geotechnical engineering problems have followed, among which the stability of hydropower stations during blasting excavation is a great challenge [12–15]. The research methods of CJRMs mainly include mechanical tests, theoretical analysis, and numerical simulation [16–20]. Field tests and prototype observation are important means to study the mechanical properties of rock mass and are also the main basis for theoretical analysis. Jiang et al. [21] and Xia et al. [22] elucidated the anisotropy of columnar jointed basalts by in situ P-wave test. Fan et al. [23] and Shi et al. [24] have comprehensively clarified the mechanical properties, deformation characteristics, and failure modes of columnar jointed basalts under different boundary conditions via in situ tests and field monitoring. Laboratory tests are generally divided into rock tests and model tests, which overcome problems of high cost, low efficiency, and high data discreteness in field tests [25–28]. Jiang et al. [29–31] explained the influence of cracks on rock mass failure mode and joint concavity on anisotropy via laboratory tests. Based on theoretical analysis, Sonmez et al. [18] proposed a new method for the anisotropy classification of jointed rock mass. In addition, natural columnar joints have different joint dip angles. Jin et al. [11] and Xiao et al. [32] analyzed the relationship between joint dip angles and rock mass strength and deformation modulus via laboratory tests. At the same time, with the development of rock mechanics, numerical simulation is widely used in all aspects of rock mechanics properties [33]. Liu et al. [19] systematically elaborated on the size-dependence of jointed basalts and discussed the different failure modes of basalts at different scales.

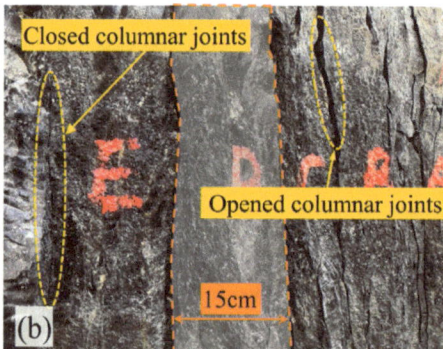
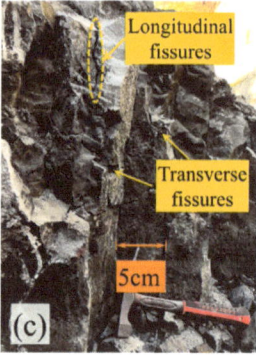

Figure 1. Structural characteristics of CJRMs: (**a**) left bank of Baihetan hydropower station; (**b**) columnar joints; (**c**) fissures.

However, the above studies on CJRMs considered the rock masses under static load, while the rock masses are often subjected to impact loads such as earthquakes and blasting in engineering [34], leading to catastrophic damage. Therefore, one of the practical problems in engineering is to study the mechanical behavior of rock under dynamic loadings. In the laboratory, the Split Hopkinson Pressure Bar system (SHPB) is usually used for dynamic loading analysis of rock samples to analyze the dynamic hazards of rock in engineering [35–38]. Chang et al. [39] analyzed the effect of loading rate on the dynamic fracture behavior of laminated micrite. Pei et al. [40] analyzed the dynamic tensile response of sandstone under different loading rates. Li et al. [41] pointed out that dynamic loading produces tensile failure under low-axial static pressure. Gong et al. [42] systematically studied the influence of strain rate on the dynamic strength of sandstone. Moreover, for jointed rocks, the interaction between stress waves and joints and cracks becomes the focus of rock dynamics research [43,44]. Huang et al. [45] learned by impact loading tests that the energy propagation coefficient decreases with the increase in joint inclination angle. Wang et al. [46] pointed out that the rock dynamic stress–strain curve can be divided into four stages: elastic, plastic, crack unsteady propagation, and post-failure, and proposed the damage weight theory of joint position. Li et al. [47] systematically studied the transmission and reflection law of stress waves traversing a single fractal joint. Meanwhile, numerical simulations are also widely used to study the dynamic mechanical properties of rocks. Wang et al. [48] studied the dynamic fracture propagation process of jointed rock masses under explosion loading by LS-DYNA and UEDC. Zhang et al. [49] modified the dynamic tensile model by using the improved DDA method. RFPA is also used to study the dynamic mechanical behavior of rocks [50]. Islam and Shaw [51] simulated crack initiation and propagation under dynamic load and proposed a new numerical method in good agreement with experimental results. And Yilmaz et al. [52] used FLAC3D to study the mechanical behavior of two different rock masses under blasting loads and applied the Mohr–Coulomb criterion to evaluate the damage of rock mass. Qian et al. [53] performed dynamic simulations on fractured rock mass with different angles and pointed out that crack dip angle has a huge influence on the fracture expansion and failure mode of rock masses. At the same time, jointed rock shows different mechanical properties and failure modes under different dip angles, so it is very important to explore the influence of dip angle on jointed rock. In addition, the dynamic constitutive models of jointed rock were studied extensively. Liu et al. [54] proposed a dynamic damage constitutive model, coupling the macroscopic and mesoscopic flaws, and pointed out that the peak strength of rock masses gradually decreases and tends to be stable when the number of joints increases. At the same time, based on the influence of joints on stress waves and the dynamic characteristics of the jointed rock mass, the dynamic damage model [55] and equivalent continuous medium model [56,57] of jointed rock mass are also proposed.

Moreover, stress wave parameters are rarely involved in the research of rock mechanical behavior and failure mode under dynamic conditions. Some scholars have analyzed the effect of a single parameter on rock mechanical behavior using relevant experiments, such as the influence of loading rate on the dynamic fracture behavior of rocks [58,59] and the influence of loading rate and peak amplitude on the dynamic evolution of fractures [60]. However, the studies did not take into account the interaction of multiple parameters, lacking a comprehensive analysis of waveform parameters on the dynamic mechanical properties of rock masses.

In this paper, CT scanning, Weibull distribution [61], and the finite element method (FEM) are used to establish numerical models of columnar jointed rock mass based on 3D printed samples of irregular columnar jointed rock mass with different angles established by Xia et al. [62]. By conducting numerical simulation under different dynamic loading conditions, the effects of peak value, loading rate, decay rate, and column dip angle on dynamic mechanical characteristics and failure mode of CJRMs are analyzed. Subsequently, the influences of dip angle and dynamic loading conditions on the mechanical properties of CJRMs are summarized. The results of this study can provide references for the dynamic stability analysis of CJRM engineering and the design and construction of geotechnical projects.

2. Methods

The dynamic mechanical behavior of CJRMs is a three-dimensional problem with a complex rock matrix and involves a failure process and crack development. Therefore, the dynamic numerical simulation of rock mass should meet the following requirements: (1) it should accurately reflect the complex structure of rock mass; and (2) it should be able to simulate the entire dynamic failure process of rock mass. In this study, a finite element method (FEM) based simulator RFPA^{3D}-CT (V1.0) developed by Mechsoft Technology(Dalian), considering Weibull distribution and equivalent continuous damage mechanics, was used to simulate the damage evolution process of CJRMs under dynamic loading.

In the numerical model, elastic damage mechanics are used to describe the mesomechanical properties of rock. Figure 2 shows the constitutive relationship of an element under uniaxial stress [63], where f_c and f_t indicate the uniaxial compressive and tensile strength of the element and f_{cr} and f_{tr} represent the residual strength of an element after phase transformation.

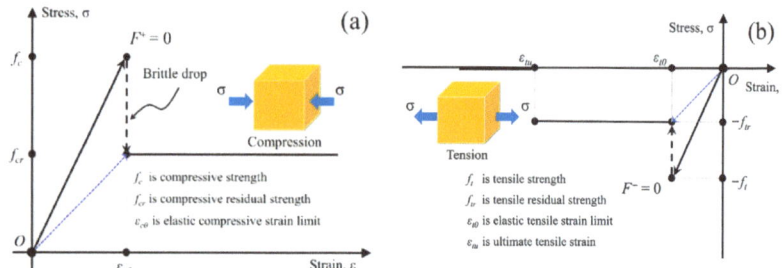

Figure 2. Constitutive relation of rock under uniaxial stress: (**a**) uniaxial compression; (**b**) uniaxial tension [63].

When the stress of the meso-element reaches the tensile strength, the element will have tensile damage, and the damage variable should meet the following requirements:

$$D = \begin{cases} 0, (\bar{\varepsilon} \geq \varepsilon_{t0}) \\ 1 - \frac{\lambda \varepsilon_{t0}}{\varepsilon}, (\varepsilon_{t0} \geq \bar{\varepsilon} \geq \varepsilon_{tu}) \\ 1, (\bar{\varepsilon} \leq \varepsilon_{tu}) \end{cases} \quad (1)$$

where λ is the residual strength coefficient of the element; and $\bar{\varepsilon}$, ε_{t0}, and ε_{tu} are the equivalent strain, elastic tensile strain, and ultimate tensile strain, respectively. When the tensile strain exceeds the ultimate tensile strain, the meso-element completely fails. In the three-dimensional state, the equivalent strain $\bar{\varepsilon}$ is usually used to replace the tensile strain ε:

$$\bar{\varepsilon} = -\sqrt{\langle -\varepsilon_1 \rangle^2 + \langle -\varepsilon_2 \rangle^2 + \langle -\varepsilon_3 \rangle^2} \quad (2)$$

Among them, ε_1, ε_2, ε_3 are the three principal strains of the element, and $\langle \rangle$ is operated as in Equation (3).

$$\langle x \rangle = \begin{cases} x, & x \geq 0 \\ 0, & x < 0 \end{cases} \quad (3)$$

When the stress value of the element meets the compression/shear criterion of Equation (4), the element can be considered to have compression/shear failure. In this case, the damage variable of the element can be expressed in accordance with Equation (5).

$$\frac{1 + \sin \varphi}{1 - \sin \varphi} \sigma_1 - \sigma_3 \geq \sigma_c \quad (4)$$

$$D = \begin{cases} 0, & \varepsilon < \varepsilon_c \\ 1 - \frac{\lambda \varepsilon_c}{\varepsilon}, & \varepsilon \geq \varepsilon_c \end{cases} \quad (5)$$

To realistically reflect the heterogeneity of rock materials, the mechanical properties of meso-elements, such as elastic modulus and strength, are assumed to meet Weibull distribution [61]:

$$\varphi(\alpha) = \frac{m}{\alpha_0} \cdot \left(\frac{a}{\alpha_0}\right)^{m-1} \cdot e^{-\left(\frac{a}{\alpha_0}\right)^m} \quad (6)$$

where α is the mechanical property parameter of rock element; α_0 is the mean value of physical properties; m is the homogeneity index; and $\varphi(\alpha)$ is the statistical distribution density of the mechanical properties, where the larger m is, the more uniform the material inside the rock is.

In the process of the dynamic finite element calculation, the space is discretized according to the Hamilton variational principle, and the dynamic equation is obtained as follows:

$$M\ddot{u} + C\dot{u} + Ku = Q \tag{7}$$

$\ddot{u}$, $\dot{u}$, and u represent acceleration, velocity, and displacement vectors, respectively; M, C, and K are the mass, damping, and stiffness matrices of the system, respectively. Q is the Force.

The numerical method was validated by many researchers [64–68].

3. Numerical Modeling and Parameter Calibration

In order to study the dynamic mechanical characteristics and failure modes of irregular CJRM samples under different dynamic loading conditions, four numerical models of rock mass with 0°, 30°, 60° and 90° in dip angle were established. According to the reconstruction of CJRMs and the establishment of numerical models [62,69,70], parameters of the numerical model are validated by the static loading experimental results first, and the dynamic mechanical characteristics and failure modes of the CJRM samples under different dynamic loading schemes are studied.

3.1. Establishment of the Numerical Simulation Model

According to the model-building method proposed by Xia et al. [71,72] and Zhao et al. [69], the digital models of irregular CJRMs with four different dip angles were established using a certain number of slices. The corresponding numerical models of CRJMs were built in numerical software, as shown in Figure 3a. The precision of meshing greatly affects the time of numerical calculation, the process of crack propagation, and the accuracy of the calculation. A numerical model of CJRM of 100 mm × 100 mm × 200 mm was established, and the mesh size is 1 mm, as shown in Figure 3c, to increase calculation efficiency and ensure the accuracy of the calculation. Considering that the stress loading area will change slightly when the boundary elements damage or fail. Therefore, in order to ensure uniform stress and long duration, high-strength ends are set on both sides of the numerical model, as shown in Figure 3b.

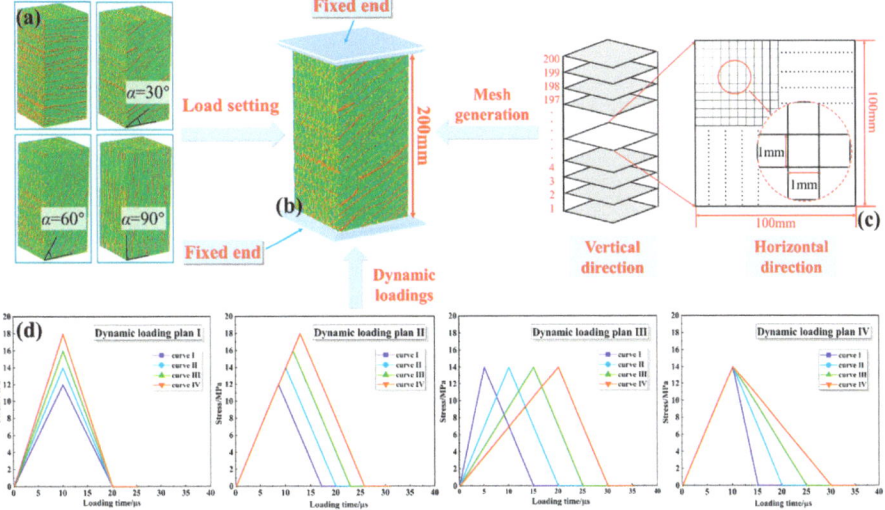

Figure 3. Numerical model under dynamic loading: (**a**) numerical model of the CJRMs; (**b**) load settings; (**c**) mesh generation; (**d**) loading plans.

3.2. Calibration of Numerical Model Parameters

The calibration of mechanical parameters is a prerequisite for accurate numerical simulation results. In this model, the parameters of rock and columnar joints are mainly calibrated. The rock mechanical parameters are obtained directly via physical tests, and those of the columnar joints are determined indirectly because of their complex structure. In parameter calibration, core drilling and freezing sampling of CJRM were carried out. The sample size should meet the requirements of the International Society for Rock Mechanics (ISRM) [73]. In the uniaxial compression test, the size of the sample is 50 mm in diameter and 100 mm in height, while in the shear test, it is 50 mm in height. CT scanning and laboratory physical tests were conducted on the CJRMs, as shown in Figure 4, to obtain the sample sections, stress–strain curves, and failure modes. The geometry of the numerical model was consistent with the physical sample. In the simulation, columnar joints are treated as elements with relatively weak elastic modulus and low strength, and their mechanical parameters are determined by the indirect method in reference [72]. The mechanical parameters of the rock matrix and joint were obtained by comparing the results of the numerical simulations and the laboratory tests with the trial-and-error method. The stress–strain curve and shear stress-displacement curves obtained from the simulations were compared with those obtained from the laboratory uniaxial compression test and shear tests. The parameters were adjusted continuously until the curves matched. The numerical mechanical parameters after calibration are shown in Table 1.

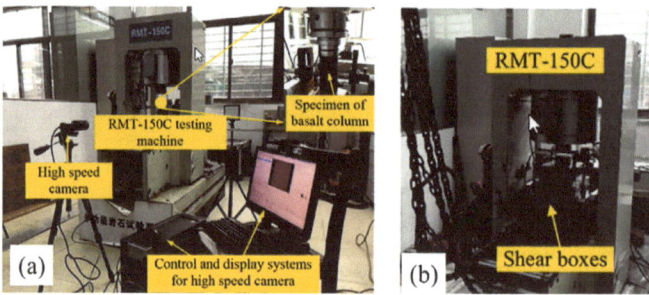

Figure 4. Physical laboratory experiments: (**a**) uniaxial compression test system; (**b**) columnar joint shear test [22].

Table 1. Mechanical parameters in numerical simulation.

Materials	Elastic Modulus/GPa	Compressive Strength/MPa	Poisson's Ratio	Density (g/cm^3)	Fraction Angle/°	C-T Ratio *
Rock	50	300	0.25	2.58	30	10
Joint	10	30	0.35	2.58	15	20
Fixed end	50	30,000	0.25	2.58	30	10

* C-T ratio is the ratio of compression strength to tensile strength.

3.3. Dynamic Loading Parameter Setting

Nowadays, the typical triangular distributed load model and exponential distributed load model are adopted in the analysis of explosion-induced stress waves. Because of the simple form of triangular load distribution and the accurate expression of the basic characteristics of an explosion, it is widely used in practical applications. In this paper, triangular stress waves are also used to simulate an explosion applied on CJRM. Meanwhile, in order to study the influence of stress wave parameters on mechanical properties and failure modes of the CJRM under dynamic loading, the CJRM is subjected to different peak amplitudes with different loading/decay rates (loading plan I), different peak amplitudes with the same loading/decay rate (loading plan II), different loading rates with the same decay rate (loading plan III), and different decay rates with the same loading rate (loading plan IV), for a total of 16 stress waves with different waveforms, as shown in Figure 3d. In loading plan I, the peak amplitude of 12 MPa, 14 MPa, 16 MPa, and 18 MPa was finally selected after preliminary trial calculation to prevent the rock mass from being damaged in advance due to excessive peak value. The loading rate to reach the peak amplitude is 5 μs, 10 μs, 15 μs, and 20 μs, and the influence of high and low rates on the failure mode of rock mass was studied, as well as the decay rate. The effects of stress waveform parameters (peak amplitude, loading rate, and decay rate) on the dynamic mechanical properties and failure modes of CJRMs are comprehensively compared. For the accuracy and efficiency of the calculation, the dynamic time step is set as 0.5 μs.

4. Numerical Simulation Results

4.1. Dynamic Failure Mode and Acoustic Emission Characteristics

Figure 5 shows the failure modes of numerical models with different dip angles α at the peak value of 12 MPa. In the Acoustic Emission (AE), blue dots are the tensile failure events, and red dots are the compression-shear failure events. Figure 6 shows the single-step AE energy curves of models with different dip angles α at the peak value of 12 MPa. The yellow, green and blue backgrounds in the figure mark foreshock, mainshock and aftershock, respectively.

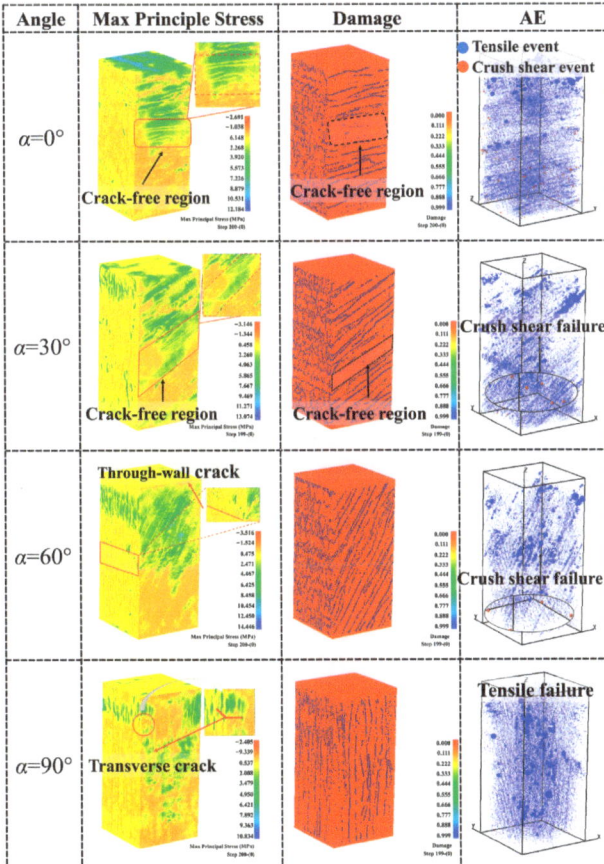

Figure 5. Numerical results of models with different column dip angles α at the peak amplitude of 12 MPa.

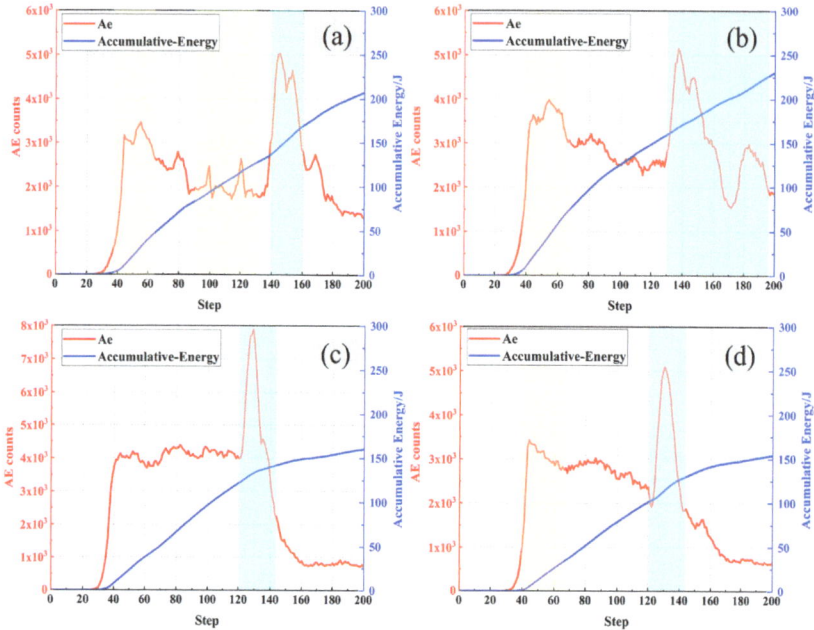

Figure 6. Single-step AE energy curves of models with different column dip angles α at the peak amplitude of 12 MPa: (**a**) $\alpha = 0°$; (**b**) $\alpha = 30°$; (**c**) $\alpha = 60°$; (**d**) $\alpha = 90°$.

For $\alpha = 0°$, when the stress wave begins to transfer, the crack sprouts at the bottom and develops upward gradually with a certain lag phenomenon compared to the stress propagation. Then, the upper part generates cracks and gradually transmits downward. At the same time, the cracks at the lateral joints develop further along the joints, forming through-cracks. At this dip angle, the compression-shear cracks are first generated, and then the tensile cracks initiate and propagate. The failure elements are distributed parallel to the joint surface, and there is a tensile AE events aggregation area at the axial top. The AE energy is manifested as a multi-modal "foreshock—mainshock—aftershock" [74]. When $\alpha = 30°$, the crack development mode is similar to 0°. The region without through-wall cracks in the middle of the model decreases, and the crack germination rate is faster. At this angle, the tensile cracks are produced first. In terms of failure type, tensile failures are distributed in the main position, except for a small number of compression-shear failures, which are distributed in the bottom and middle of the rock mass. The AE energy is a multi-model "foreshock—aftershock". At $\alpha = 60°$, the cracks germinate in the lower left corner of the numerical model and gradually develop upward to the right along the joint surface. It extends to the top, and an obvious through-wall crack appears in the middle of the rock mass. Tensile failures occupy the entire model, and few compression-shear failures are distributed at the bottom of the rock mass. The AE energy shows a unimodal "aftershock". When $\alpha = 90°$, the crack germination rate is consistent with the stress propagation rate. The cracks are generated from the bottom of the rock mass and expand along the joint surface, forming vertical tensile cracks along the joint direction. The failure mode of meso elements is all tensile failure. The stress on the top side column exceeds the tensile strength, resulting in an obvious transverse tensile crack. The AE energy appears as a bimodal "foreshock—aftershock".

Figure 7 is the picture of stress and crack evolution of the $\alpha = 30°$ model during a loading time of 20 μs and the peak stresses of 12 MPa, 14 MPa, 16 MPa, and 18 MPa, respectively. Vertically, the propagation velocity of vertical cracks under different peak stresses is much higher than that along the joint direction, and the joint direction cracks show a certain hysteresis phenomenon. Horizontally, the stress distribution in the initial loading stage is basically the same. The stress distribution under different peak stress varies in the late loading stage. When the peak stress is small, the number of failure cracks is small and mainly distributed at the top of the rock mass. With the increase in peak stress, the number of cracks increases, and they are distributed in the top, middle, and bottom of the rock mass. In addition, for the 200 steps, the crack development degree generally increases with the increase in peak stress. Therefore, the crack development is affected by the peak stress, loading rate, and decay rate.

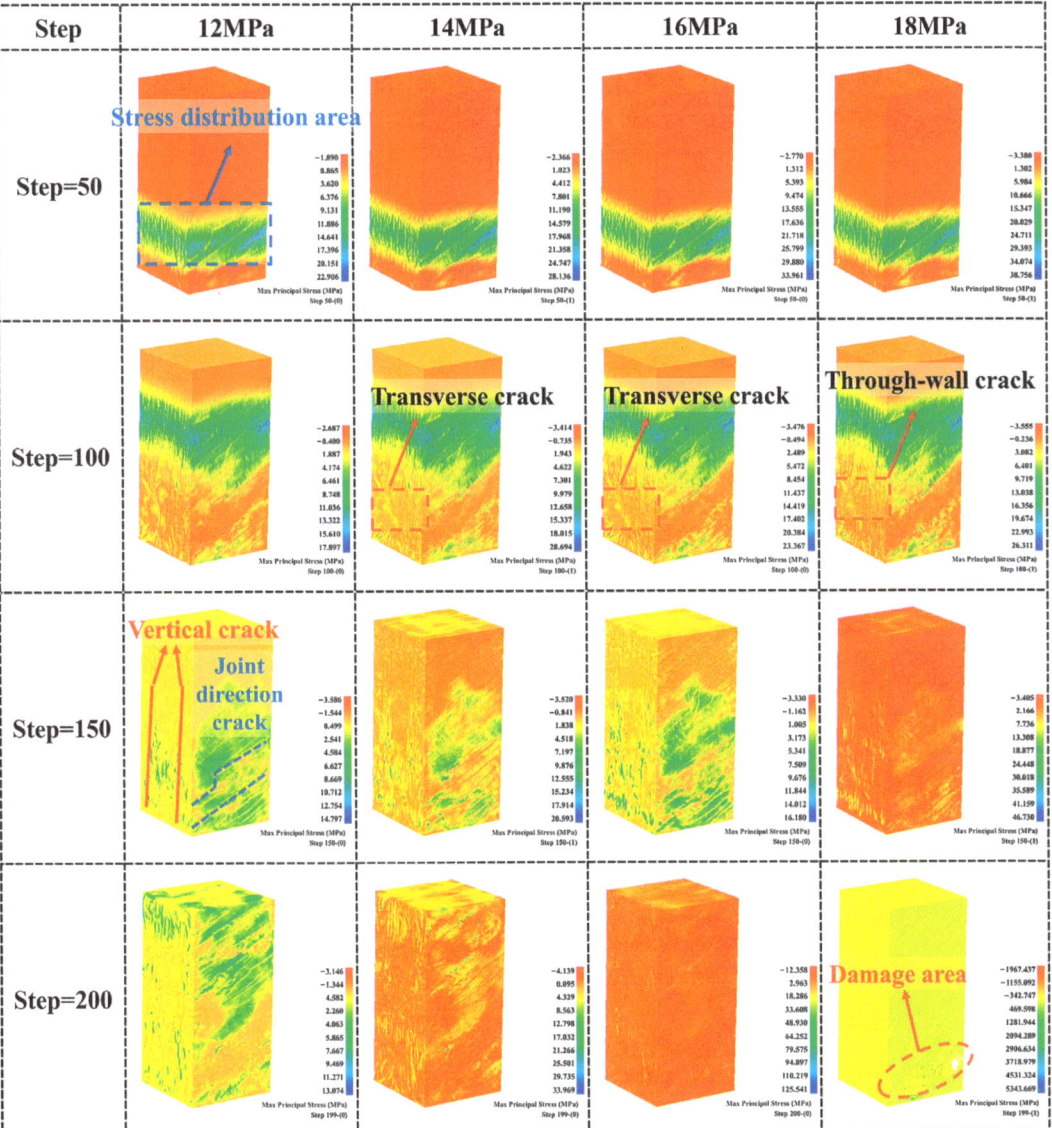

Figure 7. Numerical results of the CJRM with $\alpha = 30°$ under loading plan I.

The stress nephogram of CJRMs under the loading plan I is shown in Figure 8. When α = 0°, the penetrating cracks are concentrated in the top and bottom of the rock mass, and the area without cracks is larger. The through-wall cracks are formed at the position of the joints. The maximum principal stress in rock mass increases with the increase in peak stress. When α = 60°, the fractured volume increases first and then decreases with the increase in peak stress, and the failure moment of rock mass is advanced. The penetrating cracks mainly concentrate in the middle of the rock mass. There is no through-wall crack at the bottom and no obvious crack-free region. When α = 90°, the cracks mainly occur at the vertical joints, and the transverse crack occurs at the top and gradually develops into a through-wall crack. The cracks are tensile cracks, and there is no obvious crack-free region on the surface of the rock mass.

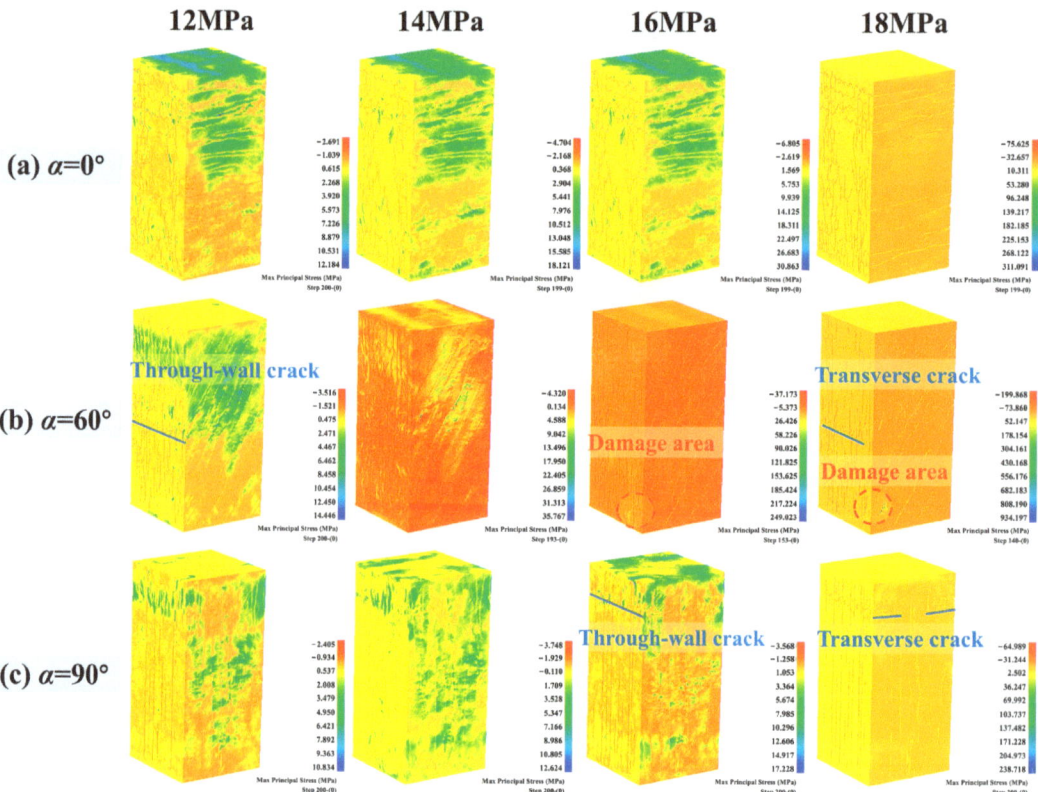

Figure 8. Stress nephogram of the CJRMs under the loading plan I: (**a**) α = 0°; (**b**) α = 60°; (**c**) α = 90°.

Figure 9 shows the AE event image of the loading plan I. The AE events are concentrated at the top of the rock mass and parallel to the joints. In particular, some accumulation area of tensile failure of α = 90° rock mass is perpendicular to the vertical joint. With the increase in peak stress, the distribution range and density of compression-shear failure elements increase, and the proportion of compression-shear failure increases. The energy and distribution of tensile AE events are more uniform, and the failure time is earlier. The AE cloud image of α = 60° rock mass is the most obvious, and the tensile AE events release more energy in the early stage of loading. It is also seen from Figure 10a that the number of AE events increases linearly with the increase in peak stress. In addition, rock mass with α = 60° increases most significantly.

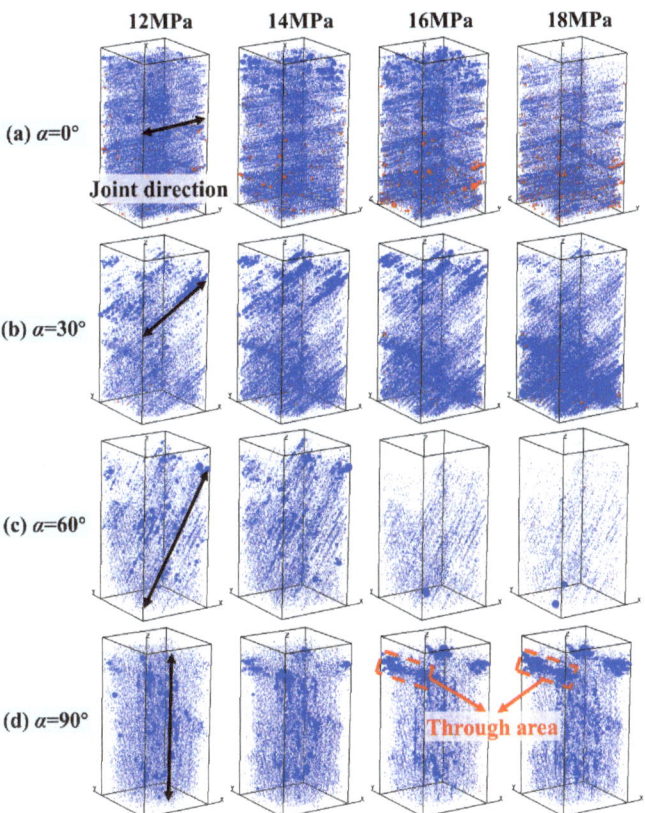

Figure 9. AE diagram of the CJRMs under the loading plan I: (**a**) α = 0°; (**b**) α = 30°; (**c**) α = 60°; (**d**) α = 90°.

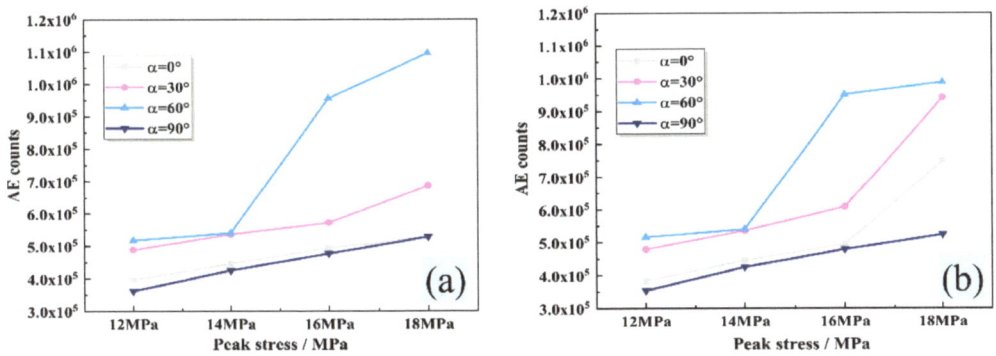

Figure 10. AE events under different peak amplitudes: (**a**) Loading plan I; (**b**) Load plan II.

4.2. Effect of Stress Peak on Failure Mode and AE of Rock Mass

Figure 11 shows the numerical simulation results of the CJRM numerical models under the condition that only the peak stress is changed. When the peak stress increases, the maximum principal stress inside the rock mass increases, and the failure time is advanced. When the peak stress is too large, the through-wall cracks cannot be formed. When α = 0°, the increase in peak stress within a certain range makes the through-wall cracks loading, mainly distributed at the top and bottom of the rock mass, and there is a crack-free area in the middle. When α = 30°, the number of lateral through-wall cracks increases with the increase in the peak stress at low peak stress. However, when the peak stress is high, the failure time of rock mass is advanced, and the lateral cracks cannot be developed completely, so the number of cracks does not change or even decrease, such as 16 MPa. When α = 60°, the cracks germinate from the bottom of the rock mass and extend upward continuously along the joints. The propagation of the crack is inhibited by the transverse penetrating crack, which is in the middle of the rock mass instead of the top. Meanwhile, the fractured volume is greatly increased. The crack propagation pattern of α = 90° rock mass is consistent with the joint direction and increases with the peak stress; the number of vertical cracks also increases, and the stress concentration area becomes smaller. The transverse crack appears at the top of the rock mass and extends to the interior of the rock mass, forming a transverse penetration crack, which is a tensile crack. In conclusion, the peak amplitude applied to rock mass can increase the number of cracks and promote the development of cracks within a certain range.

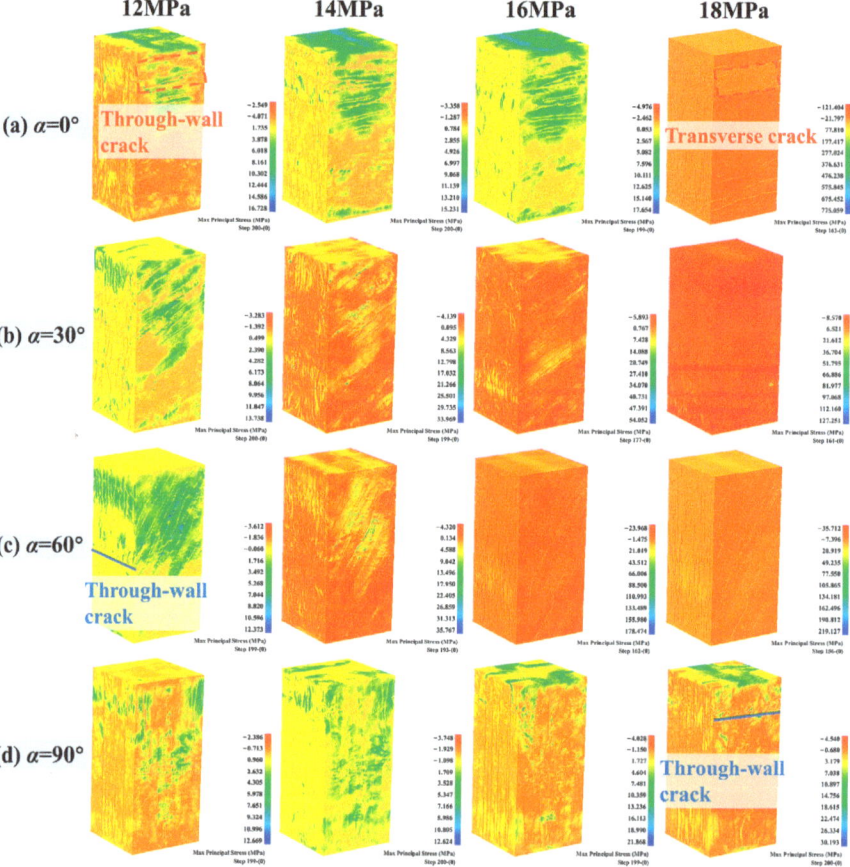

Figure 11. Stress nephogram of the CJRMs under the loading plan II: (**a**) α = 0°; (**b**) α = 30°; (**c**) α = 60°; (**d**) α = 90°.

Figure 12 shows the AE events under loading plan II. The AE concentration area is mainly located at the top of the rock mass and parallel to the joint direction. The concentration area in 90° rock mass is distributed transversely to the vertical joints. The increase in peak stress results in more uniform AE energy. At the same time, when the loading rate is constant, the increase in peak stress also promotes the occurrence of compression-shear failure, which is seen clearly in the image of the $\alpha = 30°$ model. When $\alpha = 90°$, the model presents complete tensile failure, and the accumulation area of tensile failure at the top of the rock mass develops from the failure point to the throughline and the penetration surface, as in Figure 11d, which corresponds to the stress nephogram. The AE cloud diagram illustrates that the increase in peak value is conducive to the generation of compression-shear failure and the increase in the proportion of compression-shear failure units. Meanwhile, according to Figure 10b, it can be found that the total number of AE events increases when the peak stress increases and the loading rate is constant.

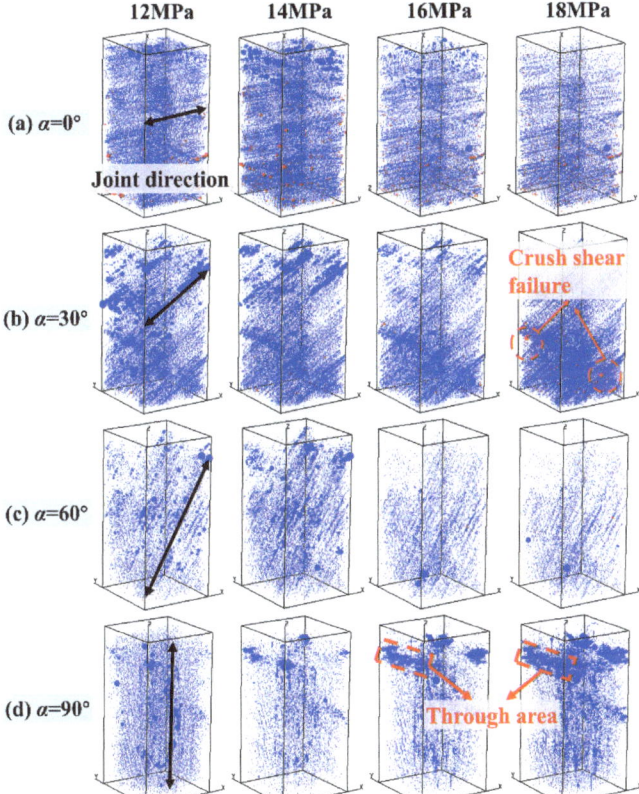

Figure 12. AE diagram of the CJRMs under the loading plan II: (**a**) $\alpha = 0°$; (**b**) $\alpha = 30°$; (**c**) $\alpha = 60°$; (**d**) $\alpha = 90°$.

4.3. Effect of Loading Rate on Failure Mode and AE of Rock Mass

In order to fully consider the effect of the loading rate on the dynamic mechanical properties and failure modes of the CJRMs, four different loading rates are designed, which are 5 µs, 10 µs, 15 µs, and 20 µs to reach the peak strength of 14 MPa. The decay rates are all 10 µs. The numerical simulation analysis of the CJRMs at four angles is carried out.

Figure 13 shows the stress nephogram of the numerical simulation results of CJRM models. The stress distribution of rock mass under dynamic load is not affected by the loading rate. The number of cracks on the surface of rock mass does not change clearly, but the length of cracks increases. At the same time, the crack-free region in the middle of

0° and 30° models do not change. The transverse crack at the top of the 90° models does not form penetrating cracks, as shown in Figure 13d. It can be seen that the change in the loading rate affects the crack length but does not affect the crack distribution. In addition, for the 60° rock mass, the failure time gradually delays as the loading rate slows down. The 30° rock mass appears to be a concentrated area of damage and failure at a high loading rate, as in Figure 13b. Therefore, the loading rate is negatively correlated with the breakout time of rock mass.

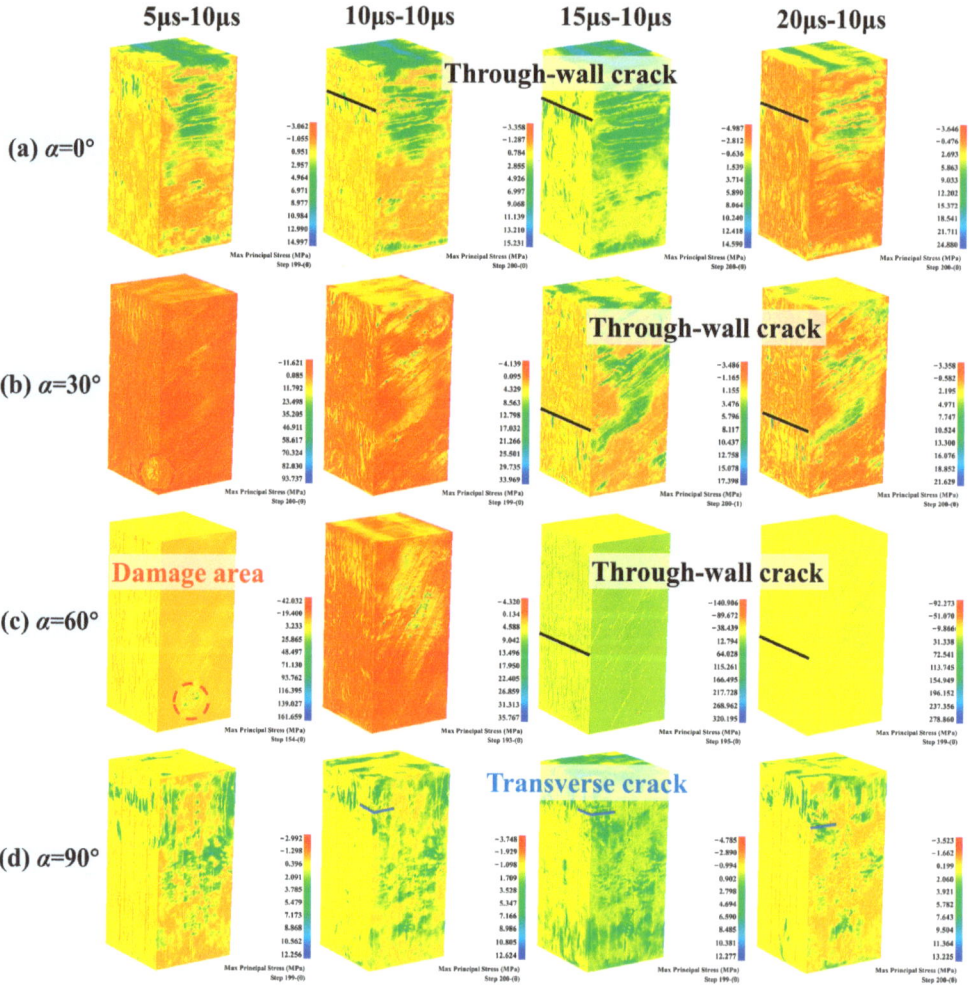

Figure 13. Stress nephogram of the CJRMs under the loading plan III: (**a**) α = 0°; (**b**) α = 30°; (**c**) α = 60°; (**d**) α = 90°.

Figure 14 shows the AE cloud image of the CJRM under loading plan III. The aggregation area of tensile AE events appears at the top of the rock mass and is distributed parallel to the joint direction, while the 90° rock mass presents vertical joint direction distribution. The slowing of the loading rate promotes the increase in compression-shear failure range and density (Figure 14a) but does not affect the location of the tensile aggregation area. In addition, a slower loading rate makes the distribution of AE more uniform and increases the total number of AE events. Figure 15 shows the curves of each step AE of the 30° rock mass under loading plan III.

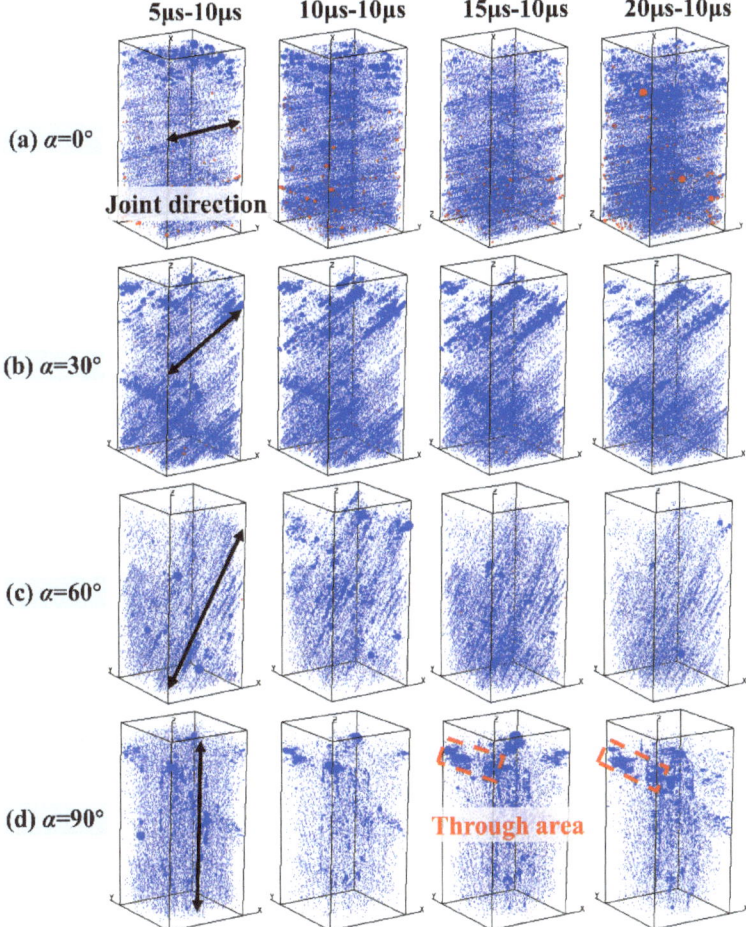

Figure 14. AE diagram of the CJRMs under the loading plan III: (**a**) $\alpha = 0°$; (**b**) $\alpha = 30°$; (**c**) $\alpha = 60°$; (**d**) $\alpha = 90°$.

According to the different responses of rock mass, the dynamic propagation process can be divided into four stages: the accelerated accumulation of AE, the propagation of stress wave to the top, the development of vertical crack to the top, and the rock mass failure stage, as shown in Figure 15a,b. At the same time, it can be observed that with the slow loading rate, the time of different stages is delayed, which explains why there are only three stages in the dynamic propagation process of rock mass in Figure 15c,d. When the loading time is 100 μs, the rock masses do not fail at a low loading rate, so the failure stage is not shown in the curve, which is consistent with the law in Figure 13. Meanwhile, in Figure 15a,b, the time of the accelerated accumulation of AE in the curve is delayed, the energy accumulation speed slows down, the energy accumulation slows down, and the total energy value increases. For the stress propagation stage, the fluctuation of single-step acoustic emission events becomes smaller, and the failure inside the rock mass becomes more uniform. However, when the vertical crack develops to the top of the rock mass, the AE events change dramatically, corresponding to the peak value in the curve. Compared with the four loading rate curves, the peak value of AE events in Figure 15a appears more rapidly and violently at a high loading rate, while the peak value of AE events gradually decreases and increases more gently as the loading rate slows down. On the whole, it can be noted that compared with Figure 15a, the number of single-step AE events in Figure 15d changes more gently, indicating that the rock mass failure is more uniform at a low loading rate, which takes longer time and accumulates more energy.

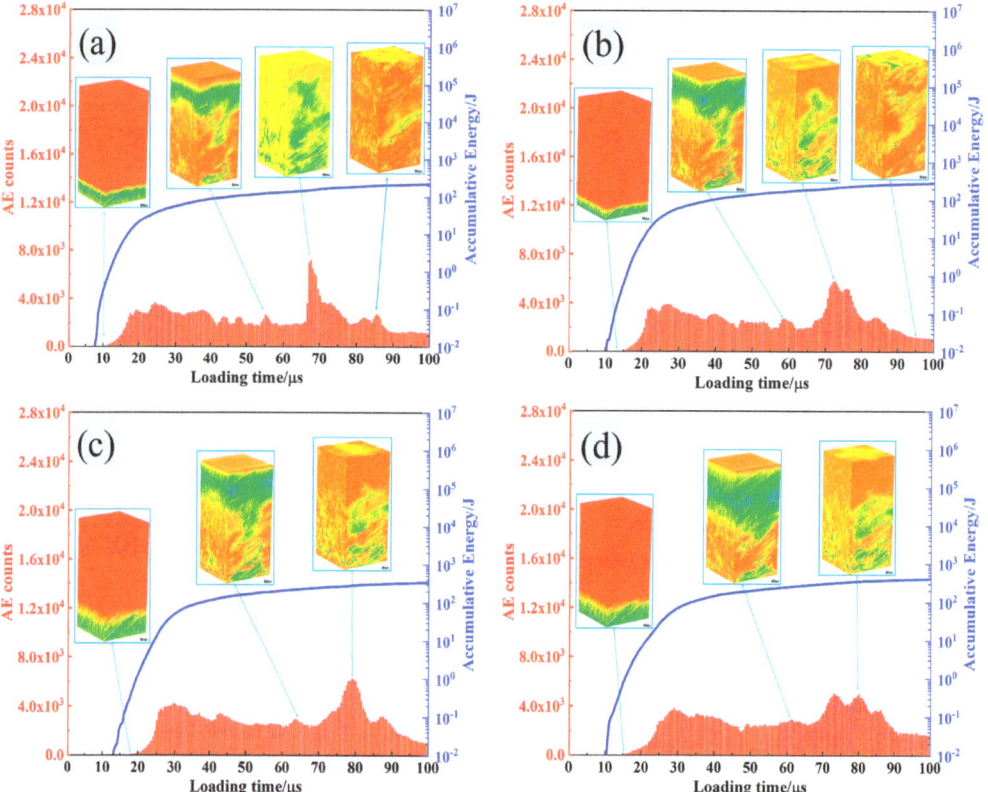

Figure 15. Single step AE and energy curves of loading plan III: (**a**) peak amplitude of 5 µs; (**b**) peak amplitude of 10 µs; (**c**) peak amplitude of 15 µs; (**d**) peak amplitude of 20 µs.

4.4. Effect of Decay Rate on Failure Mode and AE of Rock Mass

Models with four different decay rates were established to study the effect of decay rate on the dynamic mechanical properties and failure mode of the CJRMs. The descending time from the peak strength of 14 MPa to 0 MPa was 5 µs, 10 µs, 15 µs, and 20 µs, respectively, while the loading rate in the models was the same. Numerical simulation analysis was carried out for the CJRMs with four different angles.

Figure 16 shows the stress nephogram results of the CJRM models under loading plan IV. As the decay rate slows down in the 0° models, the stress concentration area inside the rock mass gradually increases, extending from the top to the middle of the rock mass. There is no significant change in the crack geometry and fractured volume of rock mass except for the model with 5 µs in descending time, where the number and development degree of cracks are suppressed, as in Figure 16a. In addition, when the decay rate becomes slower, the failure planes of 30° rock mass and 60° rock mass form earlier. Therefore, the slowing decay rate will increase the maximum stress value and advance the failure time of rock mass. High decay rates inhibit the crack development in rock mass, while low decay rates have little effect on it.

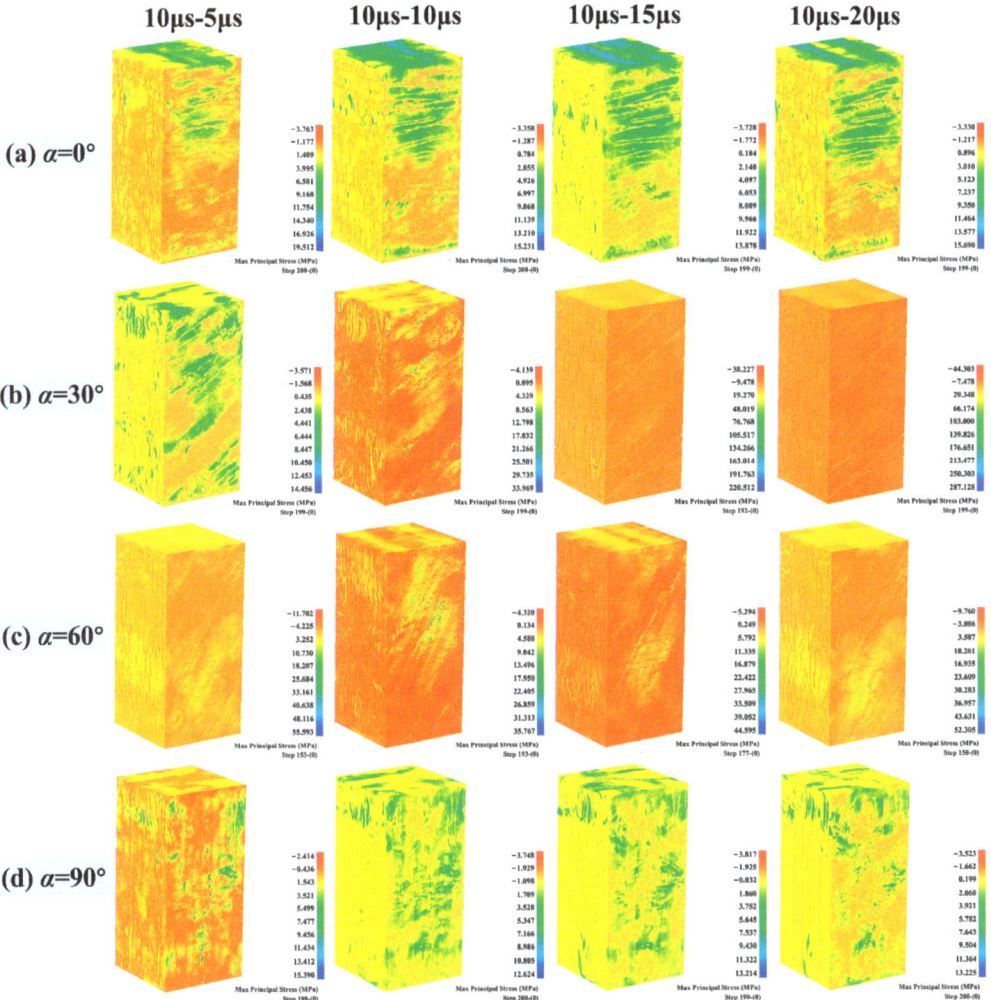

Figure 16. Stress nephogram of the CJRMs under loading plan IV: (**a**) $\alpha = 0°$; (**b**) $\alpha = 30°$; (**c**) $\alpha = 60°$; (**d**) $\alpha = 90°$.

As the decline rate slows down, the number of tensile AE events increases, as in Figure 17. For models with a dip angle of less than 90°, the accessorial events mainly concentrate at the bottom of the models. However, the distribution range of compression-shear failure elements did not change. As for Figure 16b,c, the decay rate slows down, and the rock mass breakout time is advanced so as to form a more tensile failure gathering area and transverse penetration area. Therefore, the slowing decay rate, on one hand, is conducive to reducing the generation of great AE energy; on the other hand, it will increase the compression-shear AE events inside the rock mass and accelerate the fragmentation.

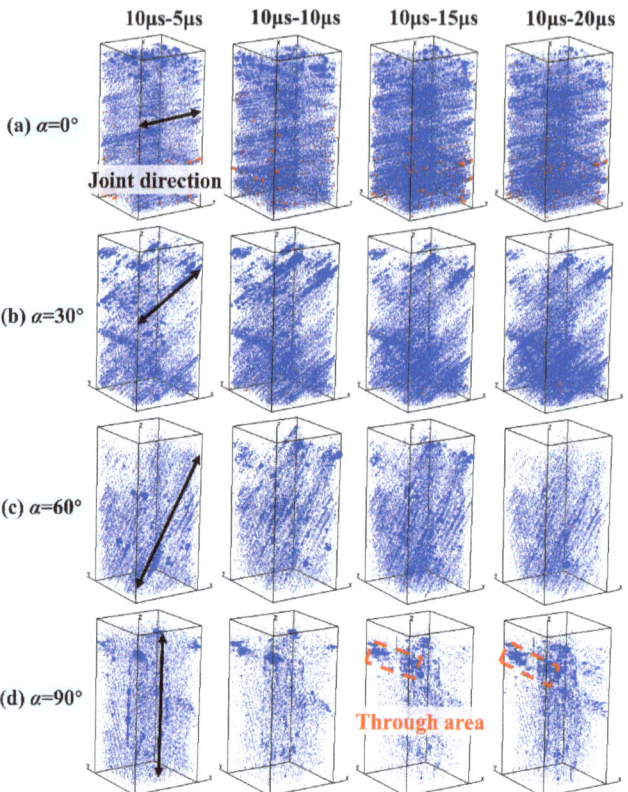

Figure 17. AE diagram of the CJRMs under the loading plan IV: (**a**) $\alpha = 0°$; (**b**) $\alpha = 30°$; (**c**) $\alpha = 60°$; (**d**) $\alpha = 90°$.

5. Discussion

The dynamic failure modes of the CJRMs in this paper are consistent with similar past studies about physical and numerical simulation tests on the dynamic loading of rock mass [42,46,75–77], which concluded that the failure mode of rock mass under dynamic loading is mainly tensile failure and the compressive shear failure of the CJRMs may be determined by the special properties of basalt columns at low angles. Pan et al. [76] studied the dynamic loading of jointed rock mass, and the results show that rock mass with a dip angle of 45-60 is more prone to failure, which is consistent with the thesis in this research that the CJRMs with a dip angle of 60 is the most prone to failure. In addition, cracks in jointed rock mass mainly develop along the joints and are dynamic [77], which is a good mirror of the crack propagation pattern studied in this paper. At the same time, the existence of joints weakens the propagation of stress waves in the rock mass [77], which also explains the reason why there is no crack area in the middle of the CJRMs with low angles.

5.1. Difference of the CJRMs under Dynamic and Static Loading

The failure modes of the CJRMs are different under different loading modes. At present, static load test studies on irregular CJRMs mainly include biaxial compression [58] and true triaxial compression tests with one free face [57]. Under biaxial compression, $\alpha = 30°$ is the most unfavorable dip angle, while under dynamic loading, $\alpha = 60°$ is the most unfavorable dip angle. The main failure modes of CJRMs under biaxial compression are tensile failure along the joint face, mixed tensile-shear failure, shear-slip failure, and disintegration failure of the intercolumnar jointed face. The failure modes of CJRMs under true triaxial compression with one free face are a split failure and shear failure of the columnar jointed structure. However, the failure mode under dynamic loading differs from static. Tensile failure is the primary failure mode, and the number of compression-shear failures decreases with the increase in dip angle. When $\alpha = 90°$, the model is a complete tensile failure.

In addition, under dynamic loading, the crack development of CJRMs will not stop immediately after the stress disappears but will continue to expand. In contrast, under static loading, the crack stops as soon as the stress or displacement is removed. In dynamic tests, the cracks initiate from the bottom of the rock mass and expand upward, as shown in Figure 18a, and the crack propagation speed along the vertical direction is much greater than that through the joints. The cracks do not develop all the way to the top of the rock mass. When the stress spreads for a period of time, new joints are generated at the top and gradually develop downward. With the propagation of stress, transverse penetrating cracks appear on the side of the rock mass and develop gradually. However, the development of joint cracks does not completely activate all the joint planes, and there is a crack-free area in the middle of the rock mass, which is caused by the different expansion rates of vertical cracks and joint cracks. Moreover, the crack-free region gradually decreases with the increase in the dip angle, as shown in Figure 18b. Under static loading, cracks in rock mass are evenly distributed along the joint direction, and no crack-free zone is observed. At the same time, when a model with $\alpha = 90°$ is under dynamic loading, transverse tensile cracks occur at the top of rock mass, which is also unique for dynamic loading conditions.

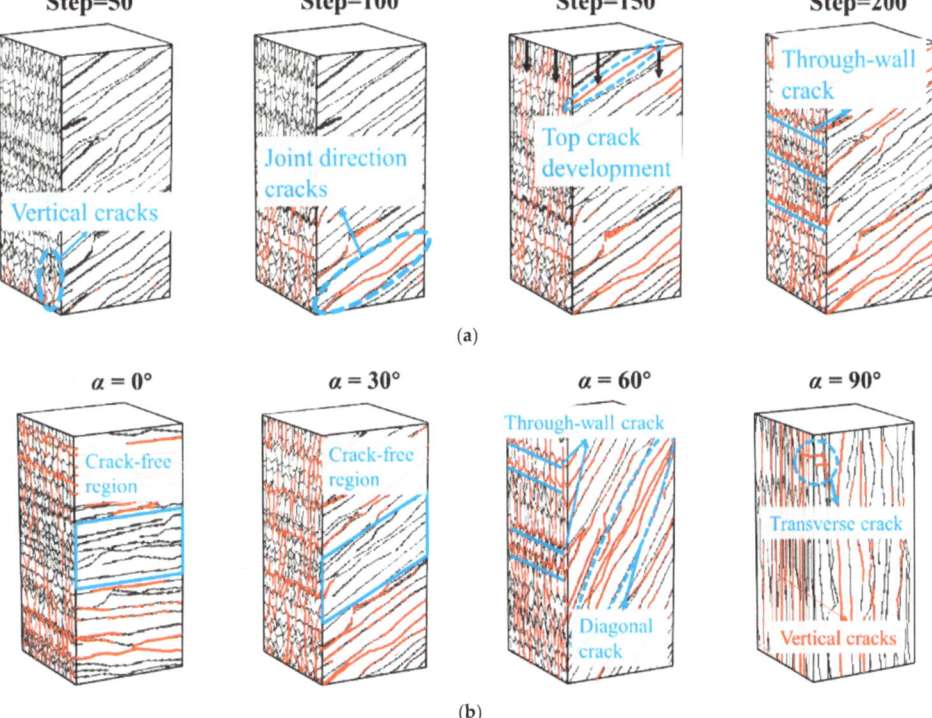

Figure 18. Sketch diagram of cracks of the CJRMs at the peak value of 12 MPa: (**a**) crack development process of $\alpha = 30°$ rock mass; (**b**) cracks in rock mass under different dip angles. Red lines represent the activated joints.

5.2. Differences in the Effects of Loading and Decay Rates

In order to eliminate the influence of loading time on the failure mode of CJRMs, the results of models under different loading rates and decay rates but the same peak amplitude (14 MPa) and wave period are compared.

By comparing Figures 13 and 16, the crack development degree in the slow loading rate model is higher, the stress distribution range is smaller, the fracture time of rock mass is delayed, and the rock mass failure is more dramatic. There are a few differences in the crack development degree caused by the slowing decay rate. The stress distribution range is large, and the time of rock breakout is gradually advanced. In addition, the maximum principal stress of rock mass generated by a high loading rate is larger than that of a high decay rate, while the tensile stress value generated by a low loading rate is smaller than that generated by a low decay rate. A high descending rate can inhibit the crack development of the CJRM. According to the comparison of AE clouds in Figures 14 and 17, a slower loading rate promotes the range and density of compression-shear failures, while the slower decay rate inhibits the range of AE events, but increases the number of compression-shear failures, and speeds up the rock mass fragmentation.

Figure 19 shows the accumulative AE events and energy curves of loading plans III and IV. When the rock mass strength is high, i.e., $\alpha = 0°$ and $90°$, the AE events and energy have an upward trend, and the gradient of loading plan III is greater than that of plan IV. Therefore, the increased AE events and energy caused by the loading rate of rock mass are higher than the decay rate. When the rock mass strength is low, i.e., $\alpha = 30°$ and $60°$, the slowing down rate will promote the rock mass fragmentation and the accumulated AE energy will be larger. Moreover, the influence of loading plan IV is greater than loading plan III, so the AE events and energy of the rock mass caused by the slowing down rate are higher than the loading rate. When $\alpha = 60°$, the AE events and energy curves of rock mass show a "U" shape. In addition, the AE energy of rock mass is higher at a high loading rate and higher at a low decay rate.

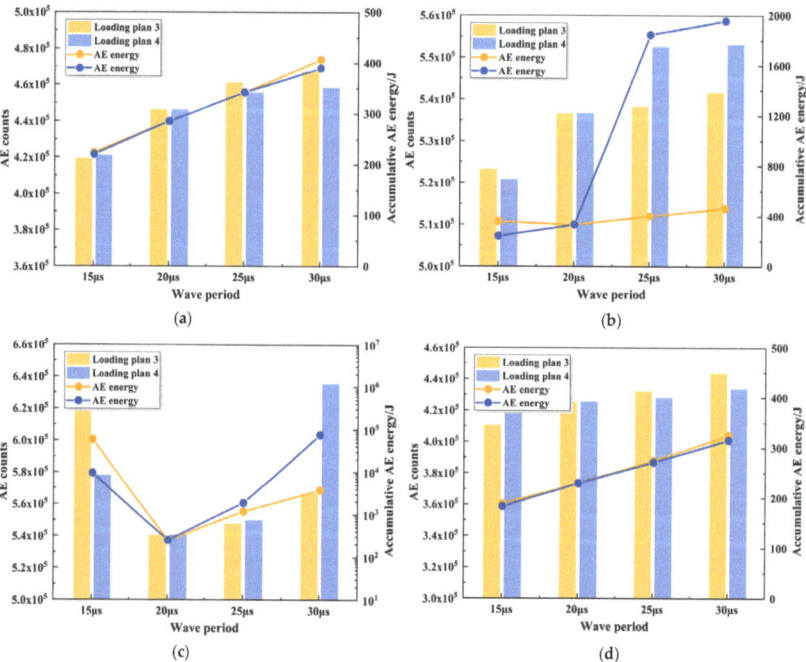

Figure 19. AE events and energy curves of models at the peak value of 14 MPa with different ascending and descending rates and the same loading period: (**a**) $\alpha = 0°$; (**b**) $\alpha = 30°$; (**c**) $\alpha = 60°$; (**d**) $\alpha = 90°$.

5.3. Influence of Dip Angle of CJRM on Failure Mode

The strength of CJRM varies with the change in dip angle. The lowest strength of rock mass is model with 60° in dip angle, followed by 30°, 0°, and the highest is 90°. Therefore, it is important to study the influence of the dip angle of CJRM on dynamic mechanical properties.

With the increase in columnar joint dip angles, the compression-shear failure distribution range and intensity decrease, and the failure mode of rock mass changes from compression-shear-tensile failure (0°) to tensile failure (90°). In addition, the dip angle of CJRM affects the initiation and propagation of cracks. The crack development velocity of rock mass with a dip angle of 0° is less than the propagation velocity of the stress wave, and there is an obvious crack-free area in the middle of the rock mass. With the increase in the dip angle, the region becomes smaller and disappears when it reaches 60°. For the 90° rock mass, the crack develops completely, forming a complete joint-oriented crack network and a penetrating crack perpendicular to the joint-oriented cracks.

The influence of joint dip angle on AE events of rock mass is explored, and AE event curves of four loading plans under different dip angles are drawn in Figure 20. With the increase in the dip angle, the total number of AE events presents an inverted "V" shape, increasing first and then decreasing, which indicates that the CJRMs with 60° joints have more AE events and are more likely to be fractured. Figure 20c shows the different dip curves of loading plans III and IV. It can be noted that the yellow and green curves at 30° and 60° in Figure 20c do not increase significantly, which is because the failure time of the rock mass with the two dip angles is close to each other in the two plans, and no obvious failure area appears. The models are in a steady state, and the intensity of the models with the two angles is close to each other, so the increase in the number of AE events is small. As for the brown curve, the slight decrease is caused by the data error induced by the advance of the rock mass breaking time and the damage evolution mechanism of RFPA for the damage and failed elements. Moreover, for the 60° rock mass, the AE event difference at different loading and decay rates is largest, which further indicates that the 60° rock mass has the lowest strength and is easily affected. In addition, taking the loading time and decay time of 10 μs as the cut-off, when $\alpha = 0°$ and 90°, the influence of a low loading rate is greater than that of a low decay rate, and the influence of a high loading rate is less than that of a high decay rate. When $\alpha = 30°$ and 60°, the influence of a low loading rate is less than that of a low decay rate, and the influence of a high loading rate is more than that of a high decay rate.

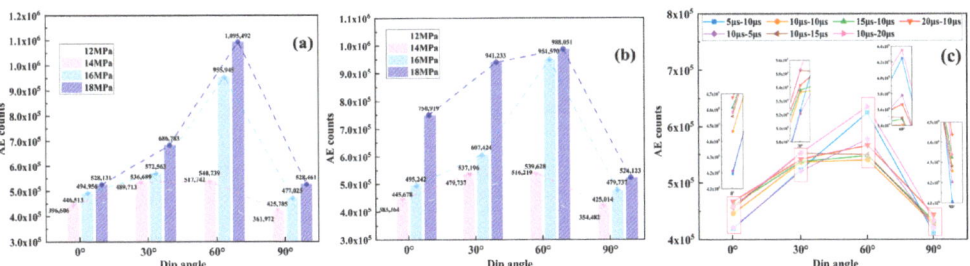

Figure 20. AE event curves of rock mass with changes in different dynamic stress wave parameters at different dip angles: (**a**) Loading plan I; (**b**) Loading plan II; (**c**) Loading plan III and loading plan IV.

6. Conclusions

In this paper, numerical models of irregular CJRMs with different dip angles of the columnar joints (0°, 30°, 60°, and 90°) are established using CT scanning technology and a FEM simulator. By applying four different dynamic loading plans on the bottom of the rock mass, the dynamic failure mode of CJRMs is analyzed, and the influence of stress wave parameters and columnar dip angle on dynamic performance is explored. The conclusions provide references for the engineering construction of underground caverns of rock mass with columnar joints, including the blasting excavation of the caverns, the stability under the earthquake, and the support setting of the caverns. The main conclusions are as follows:

1. In terms of the failure characteristics of the numerical model, the failure modes of different dip angles differ widely. When $\alpha = 0°$, the failure mode is the tension-compression-shear failure parallel to the joint plane, showing a multi-modal of "foreshock—mainshock—aftershock". When $\alpha = 30°$, the tensile failure parallel to the direction of the joint plane is the primary failure mode. A small amount of compression-shear failures is distributed at the bottom and middle of the rock mass, and the failure mode is a multi-model of "foreshock—aftershock". When $\alpha = 60°$, tensile failure takes the dominant position, there are obvious penetrating cracks in the middle of the rock mass, and a few compressive shear failures are distributed at the bottom of the rock mass. The failure mode is the unimodal "aftershock". When $\alpha = 90°$, the rock mass failures are all tensile failures, a transverse tensile crack occurs at the top of the model, and the failure mode is a bimodal "foreshock—aftershock".
2. In terms of the relationship between stress wave parameters and the failure mode, the increase in stress peak value will increase the number of cracks and promote the development of cracks within a certain range. For low-angle rock mass, it will promote the generation of compressive shear failure and increase the ratio of compressive shear failure. The slow loading rate will benefit the crack development but does not affect the crack distribution range. For 0° and 30° rock mass, the distribution range and intensity of compressive shear failure will be increased. The high descending rate inhibits crack development. The slower descending rate increases the compressive shear failure and advances the fracture time but has no obvious effect on crack development. At the same time, when the rock mass strength is high, the AE counts and energy caused by the loading rate are higher than those caused by the decay rate, but the opposite is true when the rock mass strength is low.
3. With the change in dip angle of CJRM, the crack propagation speed in rock mass increases, and the crack-free area decreases with the increase in dip angle. The number of AE events shows an inverted "V" shape, and the rock mass of 60° is the most vulnerable angle, followed by 30°, 0° and 90°. When $\alpha = 0°$ and 90°, the rock mass destruction effect caused by a low loading rate and a high decay rate is greater; and when $\alpha = 30°$ and 60°, the rock mass destruction effect caused by a high loading rate and a low decay rate is greater.

Author Contributions: Conceptualization, Y.X. and C.T.; Formal analysis, B.L. and D.Z.; Funding acquisition, Y.X. and T.L.; Investigation, Y.X. and B.L.; Methodology, Y.X. and C.T.; Project administration, Y.X.; Resources, N.L. and J.C.; Software, T.L. and C.T.; Supervision, C.T.; Validation, B.L., D.Z., and N.L.; Visualization, B.L.; Writing—original draft, Y.X. and B.L.; Writing—review and editing, Y.X. and T.L. All authors have read and agreed to the published version of the manuscript.

Funding: This research was funded by the Open Research Fund of State Key Laboratory of Geomechanics and Geotechnical Engineering, Institute of Rock and Soil Mechanics, Chinese Academy of Sciences (Grant NO. Z020011). The work presented in this paper was also supported by the National Natural Science Foundation of China (Grant Nos. 42077251, 42202305, 41807269, U1865203).

Data Availability Statement: Some or all data that support the findings of this study are available from the corresponding author upon reasonable request.

Conflicts of Interest: The authors declare no conflict of interest.

References

1. Xiao, Y.; Feng, X.; Chen, B.; Feng, G.; Yao, Z.; Hu, L. Excavation-induced microseismicity in the columnar jointed basalt of an underground hydropower station. *Int. J. Rock Mech. Min.* **2017**, *97*, 99–109.
2. Meng, Q.; Wang, H.; Xu, W.; Chen, Y. Numerical homogenization study on the effects of columnar jointed structure on the mechanical properties of rock mass. *Int. J. Rock Mech. Min.* **2019**, *124*, 104127.

Hatzor, Y.H.; Feng, X.; Li, S.; Yagoda-Biran, G.; Jiang, Q.; Hu, L. Tunnel reinforcement in columnar jointed basalts: The role of rock mass anisotropy. *Tunn. Undergr. Space Technol.* **2015**, *46*, 1–11.

Jin, C.; Yang, C.; Fang, D.; Xu, S. Study on the Failure Mechanism of Basalts with Columnar Joints in the Unloading Process on the Basis of an Experimental Cavity. *Rock Mech. Rock Eng.* **2015**, *48*, 1275–1288.

Budkewitsch, P.; Robin, P.Y. Modeling the evolution of columnar joints. *J. Volcanol. Geoth. Res.* **1994**, *59*, 219–239.

Jaeger, J.C. The cooling of irregularly shaped igneous bodies. *Am. J. Sci.* **1961**, *259*, 721–734.

Weinberger, R.; Burg, A. Reappraising columnar joints in different rock types and settings. *J. Struct. Geol.* **2019**, *125*, 185–194.

Goehring, L. Evolving fracture patterns: Columnar joints, mud cracks and polygonal terrain. *Philos. Trans. R. Soc. A* **2013**, *371*, 20120353.

Phillips, J.C.; Humphreys, M.C.S.; Daniels, K.A.; Brown, R.J.; Witham, F. The formation of columnar joints produced by cooling in basalt at Staffa, Scotland. *Bull. Volcanol.* **2013**, *75*, 715.

Cui, J.; Jiang, Q.; Feng, X.; Li, S.; Liu, J.; Chen, W.; Zhang, J.; Pei, S. Insights into statistical structural characteristics and deformation properties of columnar jointed basalts: Field investigation in the Baihetan Dam base, China. *Bull. Eng. Geol. Environ.* **2018**, *77*, 775–790.

Jin, C.; Li, S.; Liu, J. Anisotropic mechanical behaviors of columnar jointed basalt under compression. *Bull. Eng. Geol. Environ.* **2018**, *77*, 317–330.

Feng, X.; Hao, X.; Jiang, Q.; Li, S.; Hudson, J.A. Rock Cracking Indices for Improved Tunnel Support Design: A Case Study for Columnar Jointed Rock Masses. *Rock Mech. Rock Eng.* **2016**, *49*, 2115–2130.

Fan, Q.; Feng, X.; Weng, W.; Fan, Y.; Jiang, Q. Unloading performances and stabilizing practices for columnar jointed basalt: A case study of Baihetan hydropower station. *J. Rock Mech. Geotech.* **2017**, *9*, 1041–1053.

Dai, F.; Li, B.; Xu, N.; Meng, G.; Wu, J.; Fan, Y. Microseismic Monitoring of the Left Bank Slope at the Baihetan Hydropower Station, China. *Rock Mech. Rock Eng.* **2017**, *50*, 225–232.

Fan, Q.; Zhou, S.; Yang, N. Optimization design of foundation excavation for Xiluodu super-high arch dam in China. *J. Rock Mech. Geotech.* **2015**, *7*, 120–135.

Ji, H.; Zhang, J.C.; Xu, W.Y.; Wang, R.B.; Wang, H.L.; Yan, L.; Lin, Z.N. Experimental Investigation of the Anisotropic Mechanical Properties of a Columnar Jointed Rock Mass: Observations from Laboratory-Based Physical Modelling. *Rock Mech. Rock Eng.* **2017**, *50*, 1919–1931.

Smith, J.V.; Holden, L. Rock slope kinematic instability controlled by large-scale variation of basalt column orientation. *Bull. Eng. Geol. Environ.* **2021**, *80*, 239–250.

Sonmez, H.; Ercanoglu, M.; Dagdelenler, G. A novel approach to structural anisotropy classification for jointed rock masses using theoretical rock quality designation formulation adjusted to joint spacing. *J. Rock Mech. Geotech.* **2022**, *14*, 329–345.

Liu, Z.; Wang, H.; Zhang, C.; Zhou, B.; Zhou, H. Size dependences of the mechanical behaviors of basalt rock blocks with hidden joints analyzed using a hybrid DFN–FDEM model. *Eng. Fract. Mech.* **2021**, *258*, 108078.

Mu, W.; Li, L.; Yang, T.; Yu, G.; Han, Y. Numerical investigation on a grouting mechanism with slurry-rock coupling and shear displacement in a single rough fracture. *Bull. Eng. Geol. Environ.* **2019**, *78*, 6159–6177.

Jiang, Q.; Feng, X.; Hatzor, Y.H.; Hao, X.; Li, S. Mechanical anisotropy of columnar jointed basalts: An example from the Baihetan hydropower station, China. *Eng. Geol.* **2014**, *175*, 35–45. [CrossRef]

Xia, Y.; Zhang, C.; Zhou, H.; Hou, J.; Su, G.; Gao, Y.; Liu, N.; Singh, H.K. Mechanical behavior of structurally reconstructed irregular columnar jointed rock mass using 3D printing. *Eng. Geol.* **2020**, *268*, 105509. [CrossRef]

Fan, Q.; Wang, Z.; Xu, J.; Zhou, M.; Jiang, Q.; Li, G. Study on Deformation and Control Measures of Columnar Jointed Basalt for Baihetan Super-High Arch Dam Foundation. *Rock Mech. Rock Eng.* **2018**, *51*, 2569–2595. [CrossRef]

Shi, A.; Wei, Y.; Zhang, Y.; Tang, M. Study on the Strength Characteristics of Columnar Jointed Basalt with a True Triaxial Apparatus at the Baihetan Hydropower Station. *Rock Mech. Rock Eng.* **2020**, *53*, 4947–4965. [CrossRef]

Zhou, Z.; Wang, P.; Cai, X.; Cao, W. Influence of Water Content on Energy Partition and Release in Rock Failure: Impli-Cations for Water-Weakening on Rock-Burst Proneness. *Rock Mech. Rock Eng.* **2023**, *56*, 6189–6205. [CrossRef]

Zhou, Z.; Cai, X.; Li, X.; Cao, W.; Du, X. Response and energy evolution of sandstone under coupled static–dynamic compression: Insights from experimental study into deep rock engineering applications. *Rock Mech. Rock Eng.* **2020**, *53*, 1305–1331. [CrossRef]

Wang, Y.; Cao, Z.; Li, P.; Yi, X. On the fracture and energy characteristics of granite containing circular cavity under vari-able frequency-amplitude fatigue loads. *Theor. Appl. Fract. Mec.* **2023**, *125*, 103872. [CrossRef]

Wang, Y.; Yan, M.; Song, W. The effect of cyclic stress amplitude on macro-meso failure of rock under triaxial confining pressure unloading. *Fatigue Fract. Eng. M.* **2023**, *46*, 2212–2228. [CrossRef]

Jiang, Q.; Feng, X.; Fan, Y.; Zhu, X.; Hu, L.; Li, S.; Hao, X. Survey and Laboratory Study of Anisotropic Properties for Columnar Jointed Basaltic Rock Mass. *Chin. J. Rock Mech. Eng.* **2013**, *32*, 2527–2535.

Jiang, Q.; Yan, F.; Liu, C.; Shi, Y.G.; Li, L.F. New Method for Characterizing the Shear Damage of Natural Rock Joint Based on 3D Engraving and 3D Scanning. *Int. J. Geomech.* **2020**, *20*, 06019022. [CrossRef]

Jiang, Q.; Song, L.B.; Yan, F.; Liu, C.; Yang, B.; Xiong, J. Experimental Investigation of Anisotropic Wear Damage for Natural Joints under Direct Shearing Test. *Int. J. Geomech.* **2020**, *20*, 04020015. [CrossRef]

Xiao, W.; Deng, R.; Zhong, Z.; Fu, X.; Wang, C. Experimental study on the mechanical properties of simulated columnar jointed rock masses. *J. Geophys. Eng.* **2015**, *12*, 80–89. [CrossRef]

33. Cai, X.; Yuan, J.; Zhou, Z.; Pi, Z.; Tan, L.; Wang, P.; Wang, S.; Wang, S. Effects of hole shape on mechanical behavior and fracturing mechanism of rock: Implications for instability of underground openings. *Tunn. Undergr. Sp. Tech.* **2023**, *141*, 105361. [CrossRef]
34. Deng, X.F.; Chen, S.G.; Zhu, J.B.; Zhou, Y.X.; Zhao, Z.Y.; Zhao, J. UDEC–AUTODYN Hybrid Modeling of a Large-Scale Underground Explosion Test. *Rock Mech. Rock Eng.* **2015**, *48*, 737–747. [CrossRef]
35. Dai, F.; Huang, S.; Xia, K.; Tan, Z. Some Fundamental Issues in Dynamic Compression and Tension Tests of Rocks Using Split Hopkinson Pressure Bar. *Rock Mech. Rock Eng.* **2010**, *43*, 657–666. [CrossRef]
36. Wu, B.; Yao, W.; Xia, K. An Experimental Study of Dynamic Tensile Failure of Rocks Subjected to Hydrostatic Confinement. *Rock Mech. Rock Eng.* **2016**, *49*, 3855–3864. [CrossRef]
37. Fan, L.F.; Wu, Z.J.; Wan, Z.; Gao, J.W. Experimental investigation of thermal effects on dynamic behavior of granite. *Appl. Therm. Eng.* **2017**, *125*, 94–103. [CrossRef]
38. Zhu, J.; Bao, W.; Peng, Q.; Deng, X. Influence of substrate properties and interfacial roughness on static and dynamic tensile behaviour of rock-shotcrete interface from macro and micro views. *Int. J. Rock Mech. Min.* **2020**, *132*, 104350. [CrossRef]
39. Chang, X.; Zhang, X.; Qian, L.Z.; Chen, S.H.; Yu, J. Influence of bedding anisotropy on the dynamic fracture behavior of layered phyllite. *Eng. Fract. Mech.* **2022**, *260*, 108183. [CrossRef]
40. Pei, P.; Dai, F.; Liu, Y.; Wei, M. Dynamic tensile behavior of rocks under static pre-tension using the flattened Brazilian disc method. *Int. J. Rock Mech. Min.* **2020**, *126*, 104208. [CrossRef]
41. Li, D.; Xiao, P.; Han, Z.; Zhu, Q. Mechanical and failure properties of rocks with a cavity under coupled static and dynamic loads. *Eng. Fract. Mech.* **2020**, *225*, 106195. [CrossRef]
42. Gong, F.; Si, X.; Li, X.; Wang, S. Dynamic triaxial compression tests on sandstone at high strain rates and low confining pressures with split Hopkinson pressure bar. *Int. J. Rock Mech. Min.* **2019**, *113*, 211–219. [CrossRef]
43. Yang, W.; Geng, Y.; Zhou, Z.; Li, L.; Gao, C.; Wang, M.; Zhang, D. DEM numerical simulation study on fracture propagation of synchronous fracturing in a double fracture rock mass. *Geomech. Geophys. Geo-Energy Geo-Resour.* **2020**, *6*, 39. [CrossRef]
44. Huang, L. Development and new achievements of rock dynamics in China. *Rock Soil. Mech.* **2011**, *32*, 2889–2900.
45. Huang, J.; Liu, X.; Song, D.; Zhao, J.; Wang, E.; Zhang, J. Laboratory-scale investigation of response characteristics of liquid-filled rock joints with different joint inclinations under dynamic loading. *J. Rock Mech. Geotech.* **2022**, *14*, 396–406. [CrossRef]
46. Wang, F.; Cao, P.; Zhou, C.; Li, C.; Qiu, J.; Liu, Z. Dynamic compression mechanical behavior and damage model of singly-jointed samples. *Geomech. Geophys. Geo-Energy Geo-Resour.* **2020**, *6*, 71. [CrossRef]
47. Li, Y.; Xie, H.; Zhu, Z.; Feng, H.; Ye, J. Study on rules of transmission and reflection of stress wave across fractal joint. *Chin. J. Rock Mech. Eng.* **2009**, *28*, 120–129.
48. Wang, Z.L.; Konietzky, H. Modelling of blast-induced fractures in jointed rock masses. *Eng. Fract. Mech.* **2009**, *76*, 1945–1955. [CrossRef]
49. Zhang, X.; Jiao, Y.; Ma, J. Simulation of rock dynamic failure using discontinuous numerical approach. *Comput. Geotech.* **2018**, *9*, 160–166. [CrossRef]
50. Liao, Z.Y.; Zhu, J.B.; Xia, K.W.; Tang, C.A. Determination of Dynamic Compressive and Tensile Behavior of Rocks from Numerical Tests of Split Hopkinson Pressure and Tension Bars. *Rock Mech. Rock Eng.* **2016**, *49*, 3917–3934. [CrossRef]
51. Islam, M.R.I.; Shaw, A. Numerical modelling of crack initiation, propagation and branching under dynamic loading. *Eng. Fract. Mech.* **2020**, *224*, 106760. [CrossRef]
52. Yilmaz, O.; Unlu, T. Three dimensional numerical rock damage analysis under blasting load. *Tunn. Undergr. Sp. Tech.* **2013**, *38*, 266–278. [CrossRef]
53. Liu, H.Y.; Lv, S.R.; Zhang, L.M.; Yuan, X.P. A dynamic damage constitutive model for a rock mass with persistent joints. *Int. J. Rock Mech. Min.* **2015**, *75*, 132–139. [CrossRef]
54. Ning, L.; Ping, Z.; Duan, Q.W. Dynamic damage model of the rock mass medium with microjoints. *Int. J. Damage Mech.* **2003**, *1*, 163–173. [CrossRef]
55. Li, J.; Ma, G.; Zhao, J. An equivalent viscoelastic model for rock mass with parallel joints. *J. Geophys. Res.* **2010**, *115*, B03305. [CrossRef]
56. Li, J.C.; Ma, G.W. Experimental study of stress wave propagation across a filled rock joint. *Int. J. Rock Mech. Min.* **2009**, *46*, 471–478. [CrossRef]
57. Wang, Q.Z.; Yang, J.R.; Zhang, C.G.; Zhou, Y.; Li, L.; Zhu, Z.M.; Wu, L.Z. Sequential determination of dynamic initiation and propagation toughness of rock using an experimental–numerical–analytical method. *Eng. Fract. Mech.* **2015**, *141*, 78–94. [CrossRef]
58. Li, Y.; Dai, F.; Wei, M.; Du, H. Numerical investigation on dynamic fracture behavior of cracked rocks under mixed mode I/II loading. *Eng. Fract. Mech.* **2020**, *235*, 107176. [CrossRef]
59. Liang, Z.; Qian, X.; Zhang, Y.; Liao, Z. Numerical simulation of dynamic fracture properties of rocks under different static stress conditions. *J. Cent. South Univ.* **2022**, *29*, 624–644. [CrossRef]
60. Qian, X.K.; Liang, Z.Z.; Liao, Z.Y.; Wang, K. Numerical investigation of dynamic fracture in rock specimens containing pre-existing surface flaw with different dip angles. *Eng. Fract. Mech.* **2020**, *223*, 106675. [CrossRef]
61. Weibull, W. A statistical distribution function of wide applicability. *J. Appl. Mech. T Asme.* **1951**, *18*, 293–297. [CrossRef]

Xia, Y.; Liu, B.; Zhang, C.; Liu, N.; Zhou, H.; Chen, J.; Tang, C.A.; Gao, Y.; Zhao, D.; Meng, Q. Investigations of mechanical and failure properties of 3D printed columnar jointed rock mass under true triaxial compression with one free face. *Geomech. Geophys. Geo-Energy Geo-Resour.* **2022**, *8*, 26. [CrossRef]

Li, G.; Zhao, Y.; Hu, L.; Qi, S.; Tang, C. Simulation of the rock meso-fracturing process adopting local multiscale high-resolution modeling. *Int. J. Rock Mech. Min.* **2021**, *142*, 104753. [CrossRef]

Li, Y.; Jia, H. Numerical simulation and mining width design of extremely inadequate mining of Linnancang coal mine. *Coal. Min. Tech.* **2016**, *21*.

Jing, G.; Wang, Y.; Zhou, F.; Tan, Z. Numerical simulation study of water fracturing with different angle through beds holes based on RFPA^{2D}. *Coal. Min. Tech.* **2018**, *23*.

Li, T.; Li, L.; Tang, C.; Zhang, Z.; Li, M.; Zhang, L.; Li, A. A coupled hydraulic-mechanical-damage geotechnical model for simulation of fracture propagation in geological media during hydraulic fracturing. *J. Pet. Sci. Eng.* **2019**, *173*, 1390–1416. [CrossRef]

Li, T.; Tang, C.; Rutqvist, J.; Hu, M. TOUGH-RFPA: Coupled thermal-hydraulic-mechanical Rock Failure Process Analysis with application to deep geothermal wells. *Int. J. Rock Mech. Min.* **2021**, *142*, 104726. [CrossRef]

Xia, Y.; Li, L.; Tang, C.; Li, X.; Ma, S.; Li, M. A new method to evaluate rock mass brittleness based on stress–strain curves of class I. *Rock Mech. Rock Eng.* **2017**, *50*, 1123–1139. [CrossRef]

Zhao, D.; Xia, Y.; Zhang, C.; Zhou, H.; Tang, C.A.; Liu, N.; Chen, J.; Wang, P.; Wang, C. Laboratory test and numerical simulations for 3D printed irregular columnar jointed rock masses under biaxial compression. *Bull. Eng. Geol. Environ.* **2022**, *81*, 124. [CrossRef]

Zhao, D.; Xia, Y.; Zhang, C.; Tang, C.; Zhou, H.; Liu, N.; Singh, H.K.; Zhao, Z.; Chen, J.; Mu, C. Failure modes and excavation stability of large-scale columnar jointed rock masses containing interlayer shear weakness zones. *Int. J. Rock Mech. Min.* **2022**, *159*, 105222. [CrossRef]

Xia, Y.; Zhang, C.; Zhou, H.; Chen, J.; Gao, Y.; Liu, N.; Chen, P. Structural characteristics of columnar jointed basalt in drainage tunnel of Baihetan hydropower station and its influence on the behavior of P-wave anisotropy. *Eng. Geol.* **2020**, *264*, 105304. [CrossRef]

Xia, Y.; Zhang, C.; Zhou, H.; Zhang, C.; Hong, W. Mechanical anisotropy and failure characteristics of columnar jointed rock masses (CJRM) in Baihetan Hydropower Station: Structural considerations based on digital image processing technology. *Energies* **2019**, *12*, 3602. [CrossRef]

Aydin, A. ISRM Suggested method for determination of the Schmidt hammer rebound hardness: Revised version. *Int. J. Rock Mech. Min.* **2009**, *46*, 627–634. [CrossRef]

Li, H.; Li, H.; Gao, B.; Jiang, D.; Feng, J. Study of acoustic emission and mechanical characteristics of coal samples under different loading rates. *Shock Vib.* **2015**, *2015*, 458519. [CrossRef]

Luo, Y.; Wang, G.; Li, X.; Liu, T.; Mandal, A.K.; Xu, M.; Xu, K. Analysis of energy dissipation and crack evolution law of sandstone under impact load. *Int. J. Rock Mech. Min.* **2020**, *132*, 104359. [CrossRef]

Pan, B.; Wang, X.; Xu, Z.; Guo, L.; Wang, X. Experimental and numerical study of fracture behavior of rock-like material specimens with single pre-set joint under dynamic loading. *Materials* **2021**, *14*, 2690. [CrossRef]

Zeng, S.; Jiang, B.; Sun, B. Experimental study on the mechanical properties and crack propagation of jointed rock mass under impact load. *Geotech. Geol. Eng.* **2019**, *6*, 5359–5370. [CrossRef]

Disclaimer/Publisher's Note: The statements, opinions and data contained in all publications are solely those of the individual author(s) and contributor(s) and not of MDPI and/or the editor(s). MDPI and/or the editor(s) disclaim responsibility for any injury to people or property resulting from any ideas, methods, instructions or products referred to in the content.

Review

The Application of Machine Learning Techniques in Geotechnical Engineering: A Review and Comparison

Wei Shao [1], Wenhan Yue [1], Ye Zhang [2], Tianxing Zhou [2], Yutong Zhang [2], Yabin Dang [1], Haoyu Wang [1], Xianhui Feng [3,*] and Zhiming Chao [1,4,5,6,*]

[1] College of Ocean Science and Engineering, Shanghai Maritime University, Shanghai 201306, China
[2] Mentverse Ltd., 25 Cabot Square, Canary Wharf, London E14 4QZ, UK
[3] School of Civil and Resources Engineering, University of Science and Technology Beijing, Beijing 100083, China
[4] Institute of Water Sciences and Technology, Hohai University, Nanjing 211106, China
[5] Shanghai Estuarine and Coastal Science Research Center, Shanghai 201201, China
[6] Failure Mechanics and Engineering Disaster Prevention, Key Laboratory of Sichuan Province, Sichuan University, Chengdu 610065, China
* Correspondence: fengxianhui@ustb.edu.cn (X.F.); zmchao@shmtu.edu.cn (Z.C.); Tel.: +86-199-6559-5212 (Z.C.)

Abstract: With the development of data collection and storage capabilities in recent decades, abundant data have been accumulated in geotechnical engineering fields, providing opportunities for the usage of machine learning approaches. Thus, a rising number of scholars are adopting machine learning techniques to settle geotechnical issues. In this paper, the application of three popular machine learning algorithms, support vector machine (SVM), artificial neural network (ANN), and decision tree (DT), as well as other representative algorithms in geotechnical engineering, is reviewed. Meanwhile, the applicability of diverse machine learning algorithms in settling specific geotechnical engineering issues is compared. The main findings are as follows: ANN, SVM, and DT have been widely adopted to solve a variety of geotechnical engineering issues, such as the classification of soil and rock types, predicting the properties of geotechnical materials, etc. Based on the collected relevant research, the performance of random forest (RF) in sorting soil types and assessing landslide susceptibility is satisfying; SVM has high precision in classifying rock types and forecasting rock deformation; and backpropagation ANNs and Hopfield ANNs are recommended to forecast rock compressive strength and soil settlement, respectively.

Keywords: geotechnical engineering; rock; soil line

MSC: 68T01

1. Introduction

Correctly evaluating the properties of geomaterials is the key to the operation and safe construction of geotechnical engineering facilities such as landfills, foundations, dams, etc. [1–5]. Carrying out physical tests is a vital approach to determining the properties of geomaterials [6–8]. However, conducting physical tests is expensive and time-consuming, and the specific material to be adopted on engineering sites is usually selected well after the design stage; thus, there is a clear need to construct predictive models to assess the properties of geomaterials.

Since the properties of geomaterials, including rock and soil, are significantly nonlinear, the majority of the assessing models built based on traditional fitting or analytical approaches have a relatively low precision in predicting the characteristics of geomaterials [9–11]. Especially for geomaterials subjected to multiple impact factors, the traditional modeling approaches are not able to fully describe the influence of multiple factors on the nonlinear characteristics of geomaterials, causing predictive errors [12–17]. Artificial intelligence techniques can avoid the weaknesses of traditional modeling methods in describing the complicated relationships between multiple parameters effectively. Thus, a rising number of scholars have applied machine learning approaches to address a variety of geotechnical issues [18,19], such as classifying soil types [20], classifying rock types, forecasting landslide susceptibility [21], predicting rock deformation [22], forecasting soil settlement [23,24], assessing rock compressive strength [25], etc.

The algorithm is the key to machine learning modeling [26]. With the rapid progress in machine learning techniques, the number of available machine learning algorithms has risen significantly [27]. Different machine learning algorithms have diverse features which can be applied to different geotechnical issues [28,29]. For a specific geotechnical issue, different machine learning algorithms have diverse predictive performance, and selecting suitable algorithms can remarkably improve the forecasting accuracy [30]. However, to date, a summary of the applicability of different machine learning algorithms in solving certain geotechnical engineering issues has not been reported. Hence, a comprehensive summary of the existing usage of machine learning techniques in geotechnical engineering is required to contrast the forecasting accuracy of different machine algorithms in specific geotechnical areas. This is vital for the more effective utilization of machine learning methods in geotechnical engineering. The aim of this paper is to conduct an in-depth investigation and summary of the current application of machine learning techniques in geotechnical engineering. It also involves a comparative analysis of the performance of various machine learning algorithms in specific geotechnical fields. This paper can provide a comprehensive reference for professionals and researchers in the field of geotechnical engineering, allowing them to gain a better understanding of the potential and limitations of machine learning methods. Additionally, it seeks to offer guidance to engineers and researchers in selecting suitable machine learning algorithms for specific issues, ultimately enhancing the accuracy and efficiency of predictions.

In this paper, firstly, the existing research related to the usage of machine learning approaches in geotechnical engineering is summarized; after that, a comparison of the performance of diverse machine learning algorithms in solving specific geotechnical engineering issues is presented.

2. Applying Machine Learning Techniques in Geotechnical Engineering

SVM, ANN, and DT are some of the most dominant machine learning techniques used in geotechnical engineering. This is because of two reasons: firstly, the algorithms have normalized steps for their usage [31]; and secondly, the algorithms can describe the complex nonlinear relationships between multiple influence factors accurately [32]. Thus, in the following, details of the application of SVM, ANN, and DT in solving geotechnical issues, and the utilization of other machine learning algorithms, are introduced.

2.1. SVM

SVM is widely adopted in geotechnical fields [33,34]; it is able to effectively handle regression and pattern recognition problems [35]. SVM has three main strengths: (1) It is able to conduct nonlinear mappings from raw low-dimensional spaces to higher-dimensional spaces based on kernel functions, as shown in Figure 1. (2) It is able to carry out accurate forecasting based on few specimen data points. (3) Its computational cost is low [36].

Many researchers have adopted SVM to implement the classification of geotechnical materials, including rock and soil, etc. Regarding the classification of soil, Kovačević et al. [37] first used linear and non-linear SVM to classify soil types. The results indicated that non-linear SVM has higher precision in identifying kinds of soil than linear SVM. Then, Heung et al. [38] further studied the effects of kernel functions on the accuracy of soil classification by comparing the performance of four SVM models with different kernel functions, and pointed out that the SVM model with the radial basis function model has the highest accuracy. In terms of rock classification, Seng and Chen [39] first integrated a rough set into SVM to classify rock ores, and Seng pointed out that the established model has a fast operation speed and high precision. Then, Qiu et al. [40] adopted a genetic algorithm (GA) to raise the precision of SVM in classifying rock, and the outcomes demonstrate that the GA-SVM model can effectively sort the types of soil.

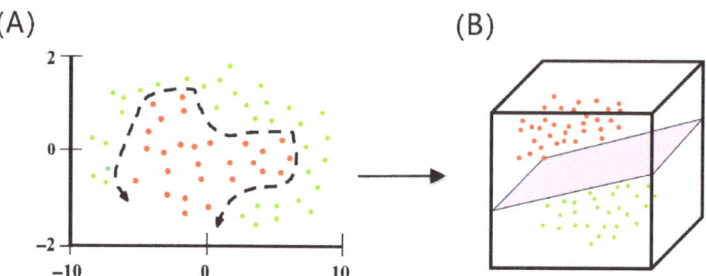

Figure 1. The mapping from low-dimensional spaces to high-dimensional spaces: (**A**) low-dimensional space; (**B**) high-dimensional space.

SVM is extensively used in analyzing landslide susceptibility. Yao et al. [41] first applied SVM techniques to predict landslide susceptibility according to landslide records. Then, Xu et al. [42] examined the efficiency of SVM-based models with various kernel functions in predicting landslide susceptibility under earthquakes. The highest forecasting accuracy was obtained from the SVM model related to the radial basis kernel function. After that, Pham et al. [43] carried out comparison research on SVM and DT in forecasting rainfall-induced landslides. The research indicates that the predictive results gained via adopting SVM are closest to the measured values. Subsequently, Pham et al. [44] further applied five different predictive methods, SVM, logistic regression, linear discrimination analysis, Bayesian network, and naïve Bayes, to evaluate the susceptibility to landslides. The results indicate that SVM has the highest predictive accuracy among the five approaches.

2.2. ANN

A large number of researchers have utilized ANNs in geotechnical engineering, which include three main models: feed-forward, feed-back, and self-organizing competition models. BPANN, Hopfield ANN, and self-organizing map network (SOM) ANN are the most representative ANN algorithms used with the corresponding fundamental models, respectively.

The majority of ANN models that are used in geotechnical engineering employ the BPANN algorithm, whose typical structure is shown in Figure 2 [45]. A BPANN model to categorize soil textures was constructed by Zhai et al. [46], and their research shows that the BPANN algorithm has lower predictive accuracy if the data specimens are limited. Then, Wang et al. [47] established a BPANN model to assess the settlements of a soil embankment by integrating the momentum method and the self-adaptive learning rate. After that, Saito et al. [48] used BPANN to establish landslide susceptibility maps. The outcomes indicate that BPANN is a powerful tool in evaluating landslide susceptibility. Subsequently, Samui and Sitharam [49] developed BPANN models to evaluate the liquefaction susceptibilities of soil after an earthquake. Afterward, BPANN was utilized by Ardakani and Kohestani [50] to forecast the liquefaction potential of soil under dynamic loading based on cone penetration test results. In the same year, Brungard et al. [51] used the BPANN technique to determine the types of soil and map the distribution of different types of soil. Cooner et al. [52] adopted machine learning techniques such as BPANN, SVM with a radial basis kernel function, and random forest (RF) for detecting the damages caused by the Haiti Earthquake. The study indicates that machine learning algorithms can be applied to assess earthquake damage.

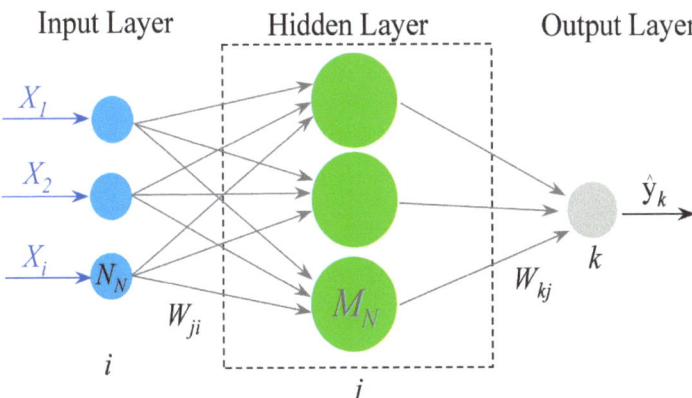

Figure 2. The typical structure of BPANN.

Hopfield ANN is a symmetrical single-layer full-feedback neural network. It can be classified into the discrete Hopfield neural network (DHNN) and continuous Hopfield neural network (CHNN) according to different activation functions. Most of the usage related to Hopfield ANN in geotechnical engineering adopts the DHNN [53]. The DHNN has two main strengths: (1) it has favorable stability, and (2) it has a limited number of balancing points. Ambrožič and Turk [54] first applied the DHNN to foretell soil settlement, and the investigation demonstrated that the model can obtain satisfactory predictions. Then, Tiryaki [55] applied the DHNN to evaluate rock cuttability, and the predictive outcomes were verified by experiment results. After that, Yao et al. [56] proposed a DHNN model to predict the deformation of rock. Subsequently, Dagdelenler et al. [57] explored the applicability of DHNN in assessing the weathering degree of granitic rocks, and the results indicate that the developed model is efficient. Afterward, a DHNN model was established by Monjezi et al. [58] to forecast the uniaxial compressive strength of rock.

SOMANN is a competitive learning ANN algorithm without supervision, and it can map data from high-dimension spaces to low-dimension spaces. SOMANN consists of input and competitive layers, and the neurons in the input and competitive layers are interconnected [59]. SOMANN is widely adopted in geotechnical engineering to settle problems about prediction, categorization, and visualization. Firstly, a SOMANN model was established by Ferentinou and Sakellariou [60] to evaluate slope stability under static and dynamic loadings. The results show that the model can make precise estimations of the stability of slopes under different loadings. Then, Chauhan et al. [61] proposed that the SOMANN skill is useful in establishing 2D segmented pictures to analyze the microstructures of rock cores. Subsequently, Huang et al. [62] combined SOMANN and extreme learning machine (ELM) techniques to predict landslides. The investigation demonstrates that the combined model has higher accuracy in forecasting the susceptibility of landslides than the SOMANN or ELM models. Afterward, Mokarram et al. [63] proposed that SOMANN is a reliable tool to visualize data, and it can precisely categorize soil according to soil fertility evaluation results.

2.3. DT

The structure of DT, which can be used conduct classification and prediction operations, is composed of nodes and directed edges, as seen in Figure 3 [64]. There are three main strengths of DT: (1) its principle is easily understood; (2) the number of needed specimen data points for modeling is not many; and (3) the performance of DT is convenient to validate with static tests [65].

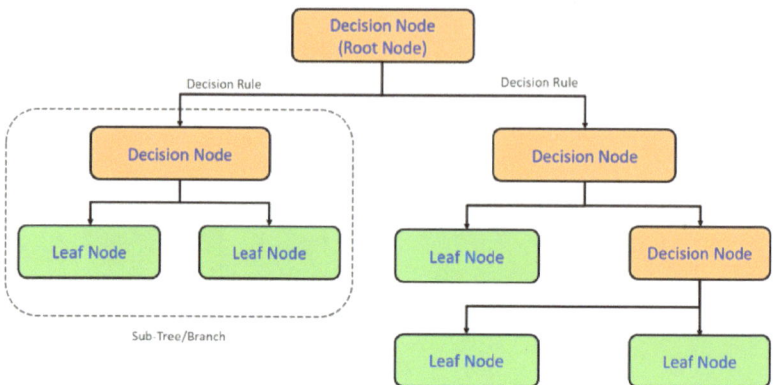

Figure 3. The typical structure of decision trees.

DT is extensively used in settling the issues of geomaterial categorization and pattern recognition. Juang et al. [66] first combined the analysis of fuzzy sets and DT to classify slope failure potentials for establishing a slope hazard map. The study demonstrates that the established model can evaluate the slope failure potentials precisely. Then, Scull et al. [67] applied DT to classify the types of soil, which was proved to be an effective method. After that, Shahriar et al. [68] employed DT to divide rock under different ground conditions on account of the tunnel boring machine data. The categorization outcomes were verified by the results of field tests, indicating that the established model can divide rock effectively. Subsequently, Jin et al. [69] researched the applicability of DT in dividing the types of soil according to the freeze states of soil, and the outcomes indicated that the precision of DT is high in recognizing the types of soil. Afterward, according to soil parent materials, Lacoste et al. [70] constructed a DT model to forecast and categorize soil parent materials. The outcomes indicate that the established soil parent material maps can represent superficial soil more precisely than the maps gained via conventional approaches. Afterwards, Gandomi et al. [71] established a DT model to evaluate soil liquefaction by adopting standard penetration test data. The outcomes indicate that the DT model has a higher accuracy than that of the model that was established by logistic regression. Following that, Liang et al. [72] adopted DT to classify rock according to rock strength, and the outcomes show that DT has a higher forecasting accuracy than that of multiple regressions.

DT is also extensively adopted in geotechnical engineering to settle problems related to complicated and non-linear modeling. Zmazek et al. [73] first used DT, linear regression, and instance regression to analyze soil radon data, and proposed that DT has a higher predictive accuracy than the other models. Then, Geissen et al. [74] applied DT to predict soil erosion, and the results show that the forecasting performance of DT is satisfactory. After that, Sikder and Munakata [75] combined the rough sets and the DT model to recognize the most significant variables of earthquake activity. The research indicates that the joint usage of rough sets and DT can obtain more precise forecasting results. Subsequently, Pham et al. [76] compared the performance of two machine learning skills, bagging-based DT and logistic regression, in constructing landslide susceptibility maps. The forecasting precision was verified using statistical approaches, and the outcomes show that the bagging-based DT model has a higher accuracy.

2.4. Other Machine Learning Algorithms

Except for the aforementioned three machine learning techniques, other machine learning algorithms have been extensively adopted in geotechnical areas, regarding the classification and prediction of the characteristics of soil. Firstly, Bhattacharya and Solomatine [77] and Bhargavi and Jyothi [78] used constraint clustering and classification to classify the type of soil. The outcomes were verified by the results of physical tests. The study indicates that the established approach can classify the kind of soil efficiently, which is consistent with the experimental results. Then, Bhargavi and Jyothi [75] classified the type of agricultural soil according to naïve Bayes and conventional statistic approaches. The research indicates that machine learning skills can classify the type of soil when sufficient data are available, and that the predictive precision is higher than that for conventional methods. Regarding dividing and forecasting the properties of rock, Simpson and Priest [79] established a GA-based model to recognize the maximum discontinuity frequency inside complex rock structures. The outcomes demonstrate that the constructed model can obtain the optimum solution, and the predicted accuracy is high. For the usage of machine learning skills in earthquake analysis, firstly, with the aim of earthquake early warning, Oh et al. [80] used the Bayesian learning technique with an automatic relevance determination prior to categorize earthquake ground motion data into near and far sources. The outcomes show that the established model has superior classification precision to that of conventional approaches, with superior generalizing. Then, Alimoradi and Beck [81] constructed a model according to Gaussian regression to conduct analysis and carry out the simulation of the ground motion under an earthquake. The outcomes demonstrate that the established model can effectively assess the ground motion, particularly in regions that are well instrumented.

3. Comparing Diverse Machine Learning Algorithms

The algorithm is the key to machine learning techniques, and every machine learning algorithm has its own superior and inferior fields because of the inherent structure features of different algorithms. For a specific geotechnical issue, it is vital to determine the applicable machine learning algorithms, which can remarkably improve the prediction performance. Thus, this section summarizes comparison studies regarding the applicability of diverse machine learning algorithms in settling different geotechnical problems, and for a given matter the corresponding best-matched algorithm is given.

3.1. Soil Classification

Soil categorization is significant for the design, building, and maintenance of geotechnical engineering applications. The comparative research about the use of machine learning algorithms in classifying soil types is summarized in Table 1.

Table 1. The performances of different machine learning algorithms in categorizing soil.

Authors' Name	Time	Algorithm	Classification Performance
			Kappa statistics κ
Kovačević et al. [37]	(2009)	SVM	0.52
		Multinomial Naïve Bayes (MNB)	0.51
			Fitting of degree R2
Ahmad et al. [82]	(2009)	SVM	0.51
		BPANN	0.42
		Multinomial Logistic Regression (MLR)	0.39
			Regression coefficient
Duro et al. [83]	(2011)	SVM	89.26%
		RF	89.67%
		DT	87.6%
			Classification accuracy
Heung et al. [38]	(2015)	DT	67%
		k-nearest neighbor	72%
		MLR	37%
		BPANN	26%

Table 1. *Cont.*

Authors' Name	Time	Algorithm	Classification Performance
Heung et al. [38]	(2015)	RF	68%
		SVM	72%
			Kappa statistics κ
Brungard et al. [51]	(2014)	RF	0.55
		MLR	0.37
		DT	0.27
		SVM	0.46
		BPANN	0.41
			Classification accuracy
Ardakani et al. [50]	(2015)	BPANN	97.2%
		SVM	100%
		DT	96.3%

Table 1 shows six different comparison studies about machine learning algorithms in soil classification, which all involve the usage of SVM. Among them, there are four studies conducted by Ahmad et al. [82], Heung et al. [38], Ardakani and Kohestani [50], and Kovačević et al. [37] that show that SVM has the optimal performance in the classification of soil types. The other two comparison studies implemented by Duro et al. [83] and Brungard et al. [51] involve the comparison of SVM and RF, indicating that RF has better classification accuracy than SVM. Thus, based on the collective relevant research, SVM has higher precision than ANN, DT and MLR in sorting soil types, but when compared with RF, the accuracy of SVM is lower.

3.2. Rock Classification

Rock classification is also a significant study area in geotechnical engineering. Some comparative research has been conducted in this research area to explore the applicability of different machine learning algorithms, as listed in Table 2.

Table 2. The performances of machine learning approaches in categorizing rock.

Authors' Name	Time	Algorithm	Performance Parameters
			Classification accuracy
Qiu et al. [40]	(2010)	SVM	100%
		BPANN	67.7%
			Classification accuracy
Seng et al. [39]	(2009)	MNB	95%
		BPANN	96%
		SVM	99%
			Classification accuracy
Chauhan et al. [84]	(2016)	SOMANN	95%
		BPANN	97%
		SVM	90%
			R^2
Liang et al. [72]	(2016)	DT	0.801
		MNB	0.77

Table 2 lists four different comparison studies about the use of machine learning modeling in sorting rock types. Three of the studies involve the usage of BPANN and SVM, conducted by Qiu [40], Seng and Chen [39], and Chauhan et al. [84], respectively, all showing that SVM has better classification performance when compared with BPANN, MNB, and SOMANN. Thus, based on the collective studies, compared with BPANN, MNB, and SOMANN, it is recommended to adopt SVM to sort rock types.

3.3. Forecasting the Deformation of Rock

The deformation of rock has a large impact on the safety of engineering applications. However, the deformation of rock has remarkable non-linearity and plasticity, which makes it highly difficult to predict via adopting conventional approaches. Thus, a rising number of scholars have used machine learning approaches to address these kinds of issues. The existing relevant research compares the applicability of DT, SVM, and BPANN in predicting the deformation of rock, which is summarized in Figure 4 [85].

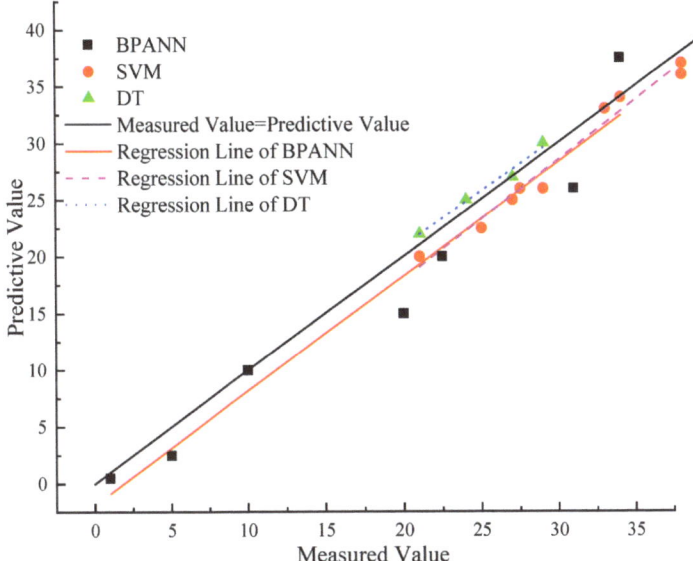

Figure 4. The comparison of DT, SVM, and BPANN in forecasting the deformation of rock.

In Figure 4, if the predictive points fall on the black straight line ($y = x$), this represents that the observed value equals the predictive value. Thus, the distance between the data points and the line reflects the predictive accuracy. Based on Figure 4, in general, the data points obtained by SVM are closer to the black line. To conduct quantitative analysis and draw comparisons on the prediction precision for the three machine learning approaches, the data points gained by adopting diverse approaches, as shown in Figure 1, are fitted by Equation (1) to obtain the regression coefficients, as shown in Table 3.

$$y = Ax + B \qquad (1)$$

where A and B are constants, respectively.

Table 3. Regression coefficients (DT, SVM, and BPANN).

Algorithm	DT	SVM	BPANN
R	0.96	0.99	0.92

As listed in Table 3, the regression coefficients of the three machine learning algorithms are all above 0.90. Among them, the regression coefficient of SVM is highest, at 0.99. Thus, based on the collective research, compared to DT and BPANN, it is recommended to adopt SVM to forecast the deformation of rock.

3.4. Predicting the Compressive Strength of Rock

Correctly evaluating the compressive strength of rock determines the stability of the engineering applications that are built on rock foundations. Since there are multiple influencing factors affecting the compressive strength of rock, it is tough to use traditional methods to predict the compressive strength. Thus, several investigators have utilized machine learning techniques to assess compressive strength. The existing research compared the applicability of BPANN, Hopfield ANN, and DT in predicting the compressive strength of rock, which is summarized in Figure 5 [86].

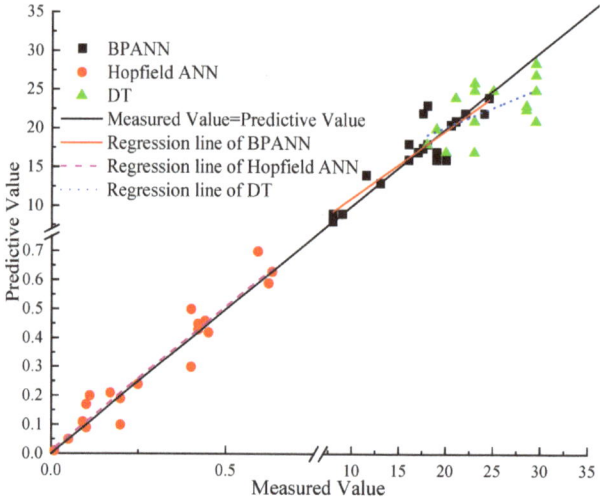

Figure 5. The comparison of BPANN, Hopfield ANN, and DT in forecasting the rock compressive strength.

As above, in Figure 5, the black straight line ($y = x$) indicates that the observed value equals the predicted value. In general, the data points obtained by BPANN are closer to the line. To analyze and compare the forecasting precision of the three machine learning algorithms, the data points in Figure 2 were fitted by using Equation (1) to obtain the regression coefficients, as listed in Table 4.

Table 4. Regression coefficients (Hopfield ANN, DT, and BPANN).

Algorithm	Hopfield ANN	DT	BPANN
R	0.96	0.92	0.99

According to Table 4, the regression coefficients of the three machine learning algorithms are all above 0.90. Among them, the regression coefficient of BPANN is the highest, at 0.99. Thus, based on the collective research, compared to Hopfield ANN and DT, it is recommended to adopt BPANN to assess the compressive strength of rock.

3.5. Landslide Susceptibility

The analysis of landslide susceptibility can offer guidance for geotechnical engineers to adopt steps to prevent landslides happening and protect the safety of the public. Some researchers compared the applicability of different machine learning techniques in analyzing the susceptibility of landslides, as listed in Table 5.

Table 5 lists six different comparison studies about the applicability of diverse machine learning algorithms in predicting landslide susceptibility, five of which involve the usage of SVM. The comparison investigations conducted by Yao et al. [87], Pham et al. [88], Marjanović et al. [89], and Huang and Zhao [90] all show that SVM has the best performance in forecasting landslide susceptibility when compared with linear regression, BPANN, and DT. However, the comparison research implemented by Micheletti et al. [91], and Zhang et al. [92] indicates that compared with RF, SVM has a lower predictive accuracy. Overall, based on the collective research, SVM has a higher precision than DT and BPANN in assessing landslide susceptibility, but when compared to RF, the forecasting accuracy of SVM is lower.

Table 5. The performances of machine learning algorithms in forecasting landslide susceptibility.

Authors' Name	Time	Algorithm	Predictive Performance
			Predictive precision
Yao [87]	(2007)	SVM	90.39%
		Linear regression	77.29%
			Predictive accuracy
Micheletti [91]	(2014)	SVM	92%
		RF	93%
			Kappa statistics κ
Marjanović [89]	(2011)	SVM	0.43
		Linear regression	0.23
		DT	0.34
			Predictive accuracy
Pham [88]	(2016)	SVM	79.65%
		DT	79.10%
			Predictive accuracy
Huang [90]	(2017)	BPANN	84.25%
		SVM	87.37%
			Predictive accuracy
Pham [88]	(2017)	Linear regression	88%
		DT	90%

3.6. Prediction of Soil Settlement

Some researchers have compared the performance of diverse machine learning algorithms in forecasting soil settlement. The existing research compared the applicability of Hopfield ANN and multiple layer perceptron (MLP) models in assessing soil settlement, which is shown in Figure 6 [93–98].

As above, in Figure 6, the black straight line ($y = x$) indicates that observations equal predictions. In general, the data points obtained by Hopfield ANN are closer to the black line. To conduct quantitative analysis and draw comparisons on the prediction precision for the two machine learning methods, Equation (1) is used to fit the data points in Figure 6; the regression coefficients are listed in Table 6.

Table 6. Regression coefficients (Hopfield ANN and MLP).

Algorithm	Hopfield ANN	MLP
R	0.99	0.90

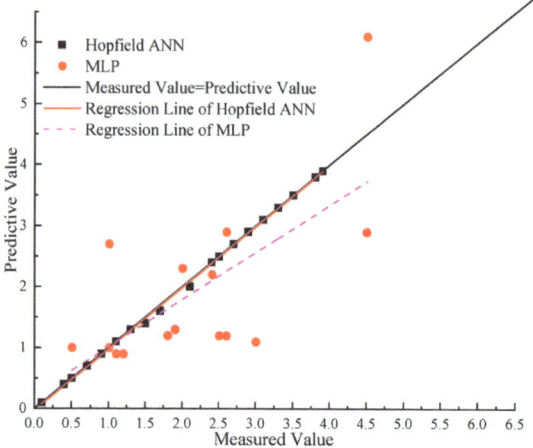

Figure 6. The comparison of Hopfield ANN and MLP in predicting soil settlement.

According to Table 6, both of the regression coefficients for the two machine learning algorithms are above 0.90. Compared to MLP, Hopfield ANN has a higher regression coefficient, at 0.99, indicating the more accurate results obtained by using Hopfield ANN. Thus, based on the collective research, Hopfield ANN is recommended to predict soil settlement over MLP.

4. Conclusions

This paper reviews the applications of machine learning techniques in geotechnical engineering, and a comparison of the applicability of different machine learning algorithms in settling special geotechnical issues is summarized. The following are the main conclusions: Firstly, ANN, SVM, and DT are among the most popular machine learning algorithms used in geotechnical engineering, addressing various geotechnical issues. Based on collective research, RF is recommended for soil type classification over SVM, ANN, and DT. Additionally, SVM is preferred for rock type classification and deformation prediction over BPANN and DT. Moreover, BPANN is recommended for assessing rock compressive strength over HPANN and DT, as shown in Table 7. Lastly, for soil settlement prediction, Hopfield ANN is favored over MLP, as indicated by the collective research.

Table 7. The strengths and weaknesses of three ML techniques (ANN, SVM, and DT).

Algorithm	Strength	Weakness
ANN	1. Wide applicability, suitable for various types of problems such as image recognition, regression analysis, etc. 2. Capable of learning complex nonlinear relationships, excels in handling complex data and tasks. 3. Can utilize parallel computing to accelerate the training process.	1. High training complexity. 2. Difficulty in selecting hyperparameters. 3. Risk of overfitting when data are insufficient.
SVM	1. Performs well with high-dimensional data and is suitable for tasks such as text classification and image classification. 2. Different kernel functions can be used to adapt to various types of data. 3. Overfitting can be controlled by adjusting the regularization parameter.	1. For large-scale datasets, SVMs have high training time and memory requirements. 2. Multiclass problems require the use of a one-vs.-all or one-vs.-one strategy. 3. Performance is highly dependent on parameter selection, necessitating processes such as cross-validation for tuning.

Table 7. *Cont.*

Algorithm	Strength	Weakness
DT	1. Easy to visualize and explain. 2. Capable of handling numerical and categorical features. 3. Exhibits a certain level of robustness against missing data or outliers.	1. Pruning and other methods are needed to reduce the risk of overfitting. 2. There is instability, as minor changes in data may lead to the generation of different tree structures. 3. The process of generating decision trees uses a greedy algorithm, which may lead to getting stuck in local optimal solutions.

In the future, researchers can choose appropriate machine learning algorithms and perform model parameter tuning to find the best models. Consideration can also be given to using ensemble learning methods to improve model performance and enhance prediction accuracy. Furthermore, researchers should explore the potential of deep learning techniques in geotechnical engineering, utilizing deep learning algorithms such as convolutional neural networks (CNNs) and recurrent neural networks (RNNs) for more complex problem modeling and prediction. Attention should also be given to research on the interpretability of machine learning models, allowing engineers and decision-makers to understand the models' prediction results and reasoning processes.

Author Contributions: Conceptualization, W.S.; investigation, W.Y. and Y.Z. (Ye Zhang); resources, Z.C. and X.F.; data curation, W.S. and W.Y.; writing—original draft, Z.C. and X.F.; writing—review and editing, Z.C., H.W. and W.Y.; visualization, W.S., T.Z. and Y.Z. (Ye Zhang); software, W.Y., X.F. and Y.Z. (Yutong Zhang), supervision, Y.D. and X.F.; funding acquisition, Z.C. All authors have read and agreed to the published version of the manuscript.

Funding: This research was funded by the consistent support of the National Natural Science Foundation of China (No. 52301327). The paper is also sponsored by the 2022 Open Project of Failure Mechanics and Engineering Disaster Prevention, Key Lab of Sichuan Province (No. FMEDP202209), and the Shanghai Sailing Program (No. 22YF1415800, No. 23YF1416100). Finally, this project is also funded by the Shanghai Natural Science Foundation (No. 23ZR1426200), the China Postdoctoral Science Foundation (No. 2023M730929, No. 2023TQ0025), the Shanghai Soft Science Key Project (No. 23692119700), the Key Laboratory of Ministry of Education for Coastal Disaster and Protection, Hohai University (No. 202302), and the Key Laboratory of Estuarine & Coastal Engineering, Ministry of Transport (No. KLECE202302).

Data Availability Statement: In this paper, all data, models, and code used during the study appear in the submitted article.

Conflicts of Interest: The authors declare no conflict of interest.

References

Chao, Z.; Shi, D.; Fowmes, G.; Xu, X.; Yue, W.; Cui, P.; Hu, T.; Yang, C. Artificial intelligence algorithms for predicting peak shear strength of clayey soil-geomembrane interfaces and experimental validation. *Geotext. Geomembr.* **2023**, *51*, 179–198. [CrossRef]

Meng, K.; Cui, C.; Liang, Z.; Li, H.; Pei, H. A new approach for longitudinal vibration of a large-diameter floating pipe pile in visco-elastic soil considering the three-dimensional wave effects. *Comput. Geotech.* **2020**, *128*, 103840. [CrossRef]

Cui, C.; Xu, M.; Xu, C.; Zhang, P.; Zhao, J. An ontology-based probabilistic framework for comprehensive seismic risk evaluation of subway stations by combining Monte Carlo simulation. *Tunn. Undergr. Space Technol.* **2023**, *135*, 105055. [CrossRef]

Cui, C.; Meng, K.; Xu, C.; Liang, Z.; Li, H.; Pei, H. Analytical solution for longitudinal vibration of a floating pile in saturated porous media based on a fictitious saturated soil pile mode. *Comput. Geotech.* **2021**, *131*, 103942. [CrossRef]

Chao, Z.M.; Shi, D.; Fowmes, G. Mechanical behaviour of soil under drying-wetting cycles and vertical confining pressure. *Environ. Geotech.* **2023**, 1–9. [CrossRef]

Chao, Z.; Wang, M.; Sun, Y.; Xu, X.; Yue, W.; Yang, C.; Hu, T. Predicting stress-dependent gas permeability of cement mortar with different relative moisture contents based on hybrid ensemble artificial intelligence algorithms. *Constr. Build. Mater.* **2020**, *348*, 128660. [CrossRef]

Zhang, W.; Shi, D.; Shen, Z.; Wang, X.; Gan, L.; Shao, W.; Tang, P.; Zhang, H.; Yu, S. Effect of calcium leaching on the fracture properties of concrete. *Constr. Build. Mater.* **2023**, *365*, 130018. [CrossRef]

8. Li, D.; Jiang, Z.; Tian, K.; Ji, R. Prediction of hydraulic conductivity of sodium bentonite GCLs by machine learning approach. *Environ. Geotech.* **2023**, 1–17. [CrossRef]
9. Chao, Z.; Gong, B.; Yue, W.; Xu, X.; Shi, D.; Yang, C.; Hu, T. Experimental study on stress-dependent gas permeability and porosity of artificially cracked cement mortar. *Constr. Build. Mater.* **2022**, *359*, 129290. [CrossRef]
10. Zainab, B.; Wireko, C.; Li, D.; Tian, K.; Abichou, T. Hydraulic conductivity of bentonite-polymer geosynthetic clay liners to coal combustion product leachates. *Geotext. Geomembr.* **2022**, *49*, 1129–1138. [CrossRef]
11. Li, D.; Zainab, B.; Tian, K. Effect of effective stress on hydraulic conductivity of bentonite–polymer geosynthetic clay liners to coal combustion product leachates. *Environ Geotech.* **2021**, *40*, 1–12. [CrossRef]
12. Cui, C.Y.; Meng, K.; Wu, Y.J.; Chapman, D.; Liang, Z.M. Dynamic response of pipe pile embedded in layered visco-elastic media with radial inhomogeneity under vertical excitation. *Geomech. Eng.* **2018**, *16*, 609–618.
13. Zhao, S.; Zhang, J.; Feng, S.J. The era of low-permeability sites remediation and corresponding technologies: A review. *Chemosphere* **2022**, *313*, 137264. [CrossRef]
14. Li, D.; Tian, K. Effects of prehydration on hydraulic conductivity of bentonite-polymer geosynthetic clay liner to coal combustion product leachate. *Geo-Congress* **2022**, *2022*, 568–577.
15. Cui, C.; Liang, Z.; Xu, C.; Xin, Y.; Wang, B. Analytical solution for horizontal vibration of end-bearing single pile in radial heterogeneous saturated soil. *Appl. Math. Model.* **2023**, *116*, 65–83. [CrossRef]
16. Cui, C.; Meng, K.; Xu, C.; Wang, B.; Xin, Y. Vertical vibration of a floating pile considering the incomplete bonding effect of the pile-soil interface. *Comput. Geotech.* **2022**, *150*, 104894. [CrossRef]
17. Zhang, W.; Shi, D.; Shen, Z.; Zhang, J.; Zhao, S.; Gan, L.; Li, Q.; Chen, Y.; Tang, P. Influence of chopped basalt fibers on the fracture performance of concrete subjected to calcium leaching. *Theor. Appl. Fract. Mech.* **2023**, *125*, 103934. [CrossRef]
18. Erofeev, A.; Orlov, D.; Ryzhov, A.; Koroteev, D. Prediction of porosity and permeability alteration based on machine learning algorithms. *Transp. Porous Med.* **2019**, *128*, 677–700. [CrossRef]
19. Chao, Z.; Fowmes, G. Modified stress and temperature-controlled direct shear apparatus on soil-geosynthetics interfaces. *Geotext. Geomembr.* **2021**, *49*, 825–841. [CrossRef]
20. Cui, C.Y.; Zhang, S.P.; Yang, G.; Li, X.F. Vertical vibration of a floating pile in a saturated viscoelastic soil layer overlaying bedrock. *J. Cent. South Univ.* **2016**, *23*, 220–232. [CrossRef]
21. Cui, C.; Zhang, S.; Chapman, D.; Meng, K. Dynamic impedance of a floating pile embedded in poro-visco-elastic soils subjected to vertical harmonic loads. *Geomech. Eng.* **2018**, *15*, 793–803.
22. Dong, Y.; Cui, L.; Zhang, X. Multiple-GPU parallelization of three-dimensional material point method based on single-root complex. *Int. J. Numer. Methods Eng.* **2022**, *123*, 1481–1504. [CrossRef]
23. Zhang, W.; Shi, D.; Shen, Z.; Shao, W.; Gan, L.; Yuan, Y.; Tang, P.; Zhao, S.; Chen, Y. Reduction of the calcium leaching effect on the physical and mechanical properties of concrete by adding chopped basalt fibers. *Constr. Build. Mater.* **2023**, *365*, 130085. [CrossRef]
24. Zhang, Y.; Zang, W.; Zheng, J.; Cappietti, L.; Zhang, J.; Zheng, Y.; Fernandez-Rodriguez, E. The influence of waves propagating with the current on the wake of a tidal stream turbine. *Appl. Energy* **2021**, *290*, 116729. [CrossRef]
25. Kumar, S.; Basudhar, P.K. A neural network model for slope stability computations. *Geotech. Lett.* **2018**, *8*, 149–154. [CrossRef]
26. Chao, Z.; Dang, Y.; Pan, Y.; Wang, F.; Wang, M.; Zhang, J.; Yang, C. Prediction of the shale gas permeability: A data mining approach. *Geomech. Energy Environ.* **2023**, *33*, 100435. [CrossRef]
27. Zhang, Z.; Zhang, Y.; Zheng, Y.; Zhang, J.; Fernandez-Rodriguez, E.; Zang, W.; Ji, R. Power fluctuation and wake characteristics of tidal stream turbine subjected to wave and current interaction. *Energy* **2023**, *264*, 126185. [CrossRef]
28. Chao, Z.; Fowmes, G. The short-term and creep mechanical behaviour of clayey soil-geocomposite drainage layer interfaces subjected to environmental loadings. *Geotext. Geomembr.* **2022**, *50*, 238–248. [CrossRef]
29. Zhao, G.; Wu, T.; Ren, G.; Zhu, Z.; Gao, Y.; Shi, M.; Ding, S.; Fan, H. Reusing waste coal gangue to improve the dispersivity and mechanical properties of dispersive soil. *J. Clean. Prod.* **2023**, *404*, 136993. [CrossRef]
30. Shi, D.; Niu, J.; Zhang, J.; Chao, Z.; Fowmes, G. Effects of particle breakage on the mechanical characteristics of geogrid-reinforced granular soils under triaxial shear: A DEM investigation. *Geomech. Energy Environ.* **2023**, *34*, 100446. [CrossRef]
31. Dong, Y.; Wang, D.; Randolph, M.F. Investigation of impact forces on pipeline by submarine landslide using material point method. *Ocean Eng.* **2017**, *146*, 21–28. [CrossRef]
32. Fan, N.; Jiang, J.; Nian, T.; Dong, Y.; Guo, L.; Fu, C.; Tian, Z.; Guo, X. Impact action of submarine slides on pipelines: A review of the state-of-the-art since 2008. *Ocean Eng.* **2023**, *286*, 115532. [CrossRef]
33. Samui, P. Application of statistical learning algorithms to ultimate bearing capacity of shallow foundation on cohesionless soil. *Int. J. Numer. Anal. Methods Geomech.* **2012**, *36*, 100–110. [CrossRef]
34. Zhou, J.; Shi, X.; Du, K.; Qiu, X.; Li, X.; Mitri, H.S. Feasibility of random-forest approach for prediction of ground settlements induced by the construction of a shield-driven tunnel. *Int. J. Geomech.* **2017**, *17*, 04016129. [CrossRef]
35. Shao, W.; Xiong, Y.; Shi, D.; Xu, X.; Yue, W.; Soomro, M.A. Time dependent analysis of lateral bearing capacity of reinforced concrete piles combined with corrosion and scour. *Ocean Eng.* **2023**, *282*, 115065. [CrossRef]
36. Shu, Z.; Ning, B.; Chen, J.; Li, Z.; He, M.; Luo, J.; Dong, H. Reinforced moment-resisting glulam bolted connection with coupled long steel rod with screwheads for modern timber frame structures. *Earthq. Eng. Struct. Dyn.* **2023**, *52*, 845–864. [CrossRef]

- Kovačević, M.; Bajat, B.; Gajić, B. Soil type classification and estimation of soil properties using support vector machines. *Geoderma* **2010**, *154*, 340–347. [CrossRef]
- Heung, B.; Ho, H.C.; Zhang, J.; Knudby, A.; Bulmer, C.E.; Schmidt, M.G. An overview and comparison of machine-learning techniques for classification purposes in digital soil mapping. *Geoderma* **2016**, *265*, 62–77. [CrossRef]
- Seng, D.; Chen, W. Application of RS Theory and SVM in the Ore-rock Classification. In Proceedings of the 2009 International Conference on Computational Intelligence and Software Engineering, Wuhan, China, 11–13 December 2009; IEEE: Piscataway, NJ, USA, 2009; pp. 1–4.
- Qiu, D.; Li, S.; Zhang, L.; Xue, Y. Application of GA-SVM in classification of surrounding rock based on model reliability examination. *Min. Sci. Technol.* **2010**, *20*, 428–433. [CrossRef]
- Yao, X.; Tham, L.G.; Dai, F.C. Landslide susceptibility mapping based on support vector machine: A case study on natural slopes of Hong Kong, China. *Geomorphology* **2008**, *101*, 572–582. [CrossRef]
- Xu, C.; Dai, F.; Xu, X.; Lee, Y.H. GIS-based support vector machine modeling of earthquake-triggered landslide susceptibility in the Jianjiang River watershed, China. *Geomorphology* **2012**, *145*, 70–80. [CrossRef]
- Pham, B.T.; Tien Bui, D.; Dholakia, M.B.; Prakash, I.; Pham, H.V. A comparative study of least square support vector machines and multiclass alternating decision trees for spatial prediction of rainfall-induced landslides in a tropical cyclones area. *Geotech. Geol. Eng.* **2016**, *34*, 1807–1824. [CrossRef]
- Pham, B.T.; Pradhan, B.; Bui, D.T.; Prakash, I.; Dholakia, M.B. A comparative study of different machine learning methods for landslide susceptibility assessment: A case study of Uttarakhand area (India). *Environ. Model. Softw.* **2016**, *84*, 240–250. [CrossRef]
- Wang, H.; Li, L.; Li, J.; Sun, D.A. Drained expansion responses of a cylindrical cavity under biaxial in situ stresses: Numerical investigation with implementation of anisotropic S-CLAY1 model. *Can. Geotech. J.* **2022**, *60*, 198–212. [CrossRef]
- Zhai, Y.; Thomasson, J.A.; Boggess III, J.E.; Sui, R. Soil texture classification with artificial neural networks operating on remote sensing data. *Comput. Electron. Agric.* **2006**, *54*, 53–68. [CrossRef]
- Wang, Z.L.; Li, Y.C.; Shen, R.F. Correction of soil parameters in calculation of embankment settlement using a BP network back-analysis model. *Eng. Geol.* **2007**, *91*, 168–177. [CrossRef]
- Saito, H.; Nakayama, D.; Matsuyama, H. Comparison of landslide susceptibility based on a decision-tree model and actual landslide occurrence: The Akaishi Mountains, Japan. *Geomorphology* **2009**, *109*, 108–121. [CrossRef]
- Samui, P.; Sitharam, T.G. Machine learning modelling for predicting soil liquefaction susceptibility. *Nat. Hazard. Earth Sys.* **2011**, *11*, 1–9. [CrossRef]
- Ardakani, A.; Kohestani, V.R. Evaluation of liquefaction potential based on CPT results using C4. 5 decision tree. *J. AI Data Min.* **2015**, *3*, 85–92.
- Brungard, C.W.; Boettinger, J.L.; Duniway, M.C.; Wills, S.A.; Edwards, T.C., Jr. Machine learning for predicting soil classes in three semi-arid landscapes. *Geoderma* **2015**, *239*, 68–83. [CrossRef]
- Cooner, A.J.; Shao, Y.; Campbell, J.B. Detection of urban damage using remote sensing and machine learning algorithms: Revisiting the 2010 Haiti earthquake. *Remote Sens.* **2016**, *8*, 868. [CrossRef]
- Zang, W.; Zheng, Y.; Zhang, Y.; Lin, X.; Li, Y.; Fernandez-Rodriguez, E. Numerical investigation on a diffuser-augmented horizontal axis tidal stream turbine with the entropy production theory. *Mathematics* **2022**, *11*, 116. [CrossRef]
- Ambrožič, T.; Turk, G. Prediction of subsidence due to underground mining by artificial neural networks. *Comput. Geosci.* **2003**, *29*, 627–637. [CrossRef]
- Tiryaki, B. Estimating rock cuttability using regression trees and artificial neural networks. *Rock Mech. Rock Eng.* **2009**, *42*, 939–946. [CrossRef]
- Yao, B.Z.; Yang, C.Y.; Yao, J.B.; Sun, J. Tunnel surrounding rock displacement prediction using support vector machine. *Int. J. Comput. Int. Sys.* **2010**, *3*, 843–852.
- Dagdelenler, G.; Sezer, E.A.; Gokceoglu, C. Some non-linear models to predict the weathering degrees of a granitic rock from physical and mechanical parameters. *Expert Syst. Appl.* **2011**, *38*, 7476–7485. [CrossRef]
- Monjezi, M.; Amini Khoshalan, H.; Razifard, M. A neuro-genetic network for predicting uniaxial compressive strength of rocks. *Geotech. Geol. Eng.* **2012**, *30*, 1053–1062. [CrossRef]
- Rizzo, R.; Allegra, M.; Fulantelli, G. Hypertext-like structures through a SOM network. In Proceedings of the 10th ACM Conference on Hypertext and Hypermedia: Returning to our Diverse Roots, Darmstadt, Germany, 21–25 February 1999; pp. 71–72.
- Ferentinou, M.D.; Sakellariou, M.G. Computational intelligence tools for the prediction of slope performance. *Comput. Geotech.* **2007**, *34*, 362–384. [CrossRef]
- Chauhan, S.; Rühaak, W.; Khan, F.; Enzmann, F.; Mielke, P.; Kersten, M.; Sass, I. Processing of rock core microtomography images: Using seven different machine learning algorithms. *Comput. Geotech.* **2016**, *86*, 120–128. [CrossRef]
- Huang, F.; Yin, K.; Huang, J.; Gui, L.; Wang, P. Landslide susceptibility mapping based on self-organizing-map network and extreme learning machine. *Eng. Geol.* **2017**, *223*, 11–22. [CrossRef]
- Mokarram, M.; Najafi-Ghiri, M.; Zarei, A.R. Using self-organizing maps for determination of soil fertility (case study: Shiraz plain). *Soil Water Res.* **2018**, *13*, 11–17. [CrossRef]
- Freund, Y.; Mason, L. The alternating decision tree learning algorithm. *icml* **1999**, *99*, 124–133.

65. Magerman, D.M. Statistical decision-tree models for parsing. In Proceedings of the 33rd Annual Meeting on Association for Computational Linguistics, Cambridge, MA, USA, 26–30 June 1995; Association for Computational Linguistics: Stroudsburg, PA, USA, 1995.
66. Juang, C.H.; Lee, D.H.; Sheu, C. Mapping slope failure potential using fuzzy sets. *J. Geotech. Eng.* **1992**, *118*, 475–494. [CrossRef]
67. Scull, P.; Franklin, J.; Chadwick, O.A. The application of classification tree analysis to soil type prediction in a desert landscape. *Ecol. Model.* **2005**, *181*, 1–15. [CrossRef]
68. Shahriar, K.; Sharifzadeh, M.; Hamidi, J.K. Geotechnical risk assessment based approach for rock TBM selection in difficult ground conditions. *Tunn. Undergr. Space Technol.* **2008**, *23*, 318–325. [CrossRef]
69. Jin, R.; Li, X.; Che, T. A decision tree algorithm for surface soil freeze/thaw classification over China using SSM/I brightness temperature. *Remote Sens. Environ.* **2009**, *113*, 2651–2660. [CrossRef]
70. Lacoste, M.; Lemercier, B.; Walter, C. Regional mapping of soil parent material by machine learning based on point data. *Geomorphology* **2011**, *133*, 90–99. [CrossRef]
71. Gandomi, A.H.; Fridline, M.M.; Roke, D.A. Decision tree approach for soil liquefaction assessment. *Sci. World J.* **2013**, *2013*, 346285. [CrossRef]
72. Liang, M.; Mohamad, E.T.; Faradonbeh, R.S.; Jahed Armaghani, D.; Ghoraba, S. Rock strength assessment based on regression tree technique. *Eng. Comput.* **2016**, *32*, 343–354. [CrossRef]
73. Zmazek, B.; Todorovski, L.; Džeroski, S.; Vaupotič, J.; Kobal, I. Application of decision trees to the analysis of soil radon data for earthquake prediction. *Appl. Radiat. Isot.* **2003**, *58*, 697–706. [CrossRef]
74. Geissen, V.; Kampichler, C.; López-de Llergo-Juárez, J.J.; Galindo-Acántara, A. Superficial and subterranean soil erosion in Tabasco, tropical Mexico: Development of a decision tree modeling approach. *Geoderma* **2007**, *139*, 277–287. [CrossRef]
75. Sikder, I.U.; Munakata, T. Application of rough set and decision tree for characterization of premonitory factors of low seismic activity. *Expert Syst. Appl.* **2009**, *36*, 102–110. [CrossRef]
76. Pham, B.T.; Tien Bui, D.; Prakash, I. Landslide susceptibility assessment using bagging ensemble based alternating decision trees, logistic regression and J48 decision trees methods: A comparative study. *Geotech. Geol. Eng.* **2017**, *35*, 2597–2611. [CrossRef]
77. Bhattacharya, B.; Solomatine, D.P. Machine learning in soil classification. *Neural Netw.* **2006**, *19*, 186–195. [CrossRef] [PubMed]
78. Bhargavi, P.; Jyothi, S. Applying naive bayes data mining technique for classification of agricultural land soils. *Int. J. Comput. Sci. Net.* **2009**, *9*, 117–122.
79. Simpson, A.R.; Priest, S.D. The application of genetic algorithms to optimisation problems in geotechnics. *Comput. Geotech.* **1993**, *15*, 1–19. [CrossRef]
80. Oh, C.K.; Beck, J.L.; Yamada, M. Bayesian learning using automatic relevance determination prior with an application to earthquake early warning. *J. Eng. Mech.* **2008**, *134*, 1013–1020. [CrossRef]
81. Alimoradi, A.; Beck, J.L. Machine-learning methods for earthquake ground motion analysis and simulation. *J. Eng. Mech.* **2015**, *141*, 04014147. [CrossRef]
82. Ahmad, S.; Kalra, A.; Stephen, H. Estimating soil moisture using remote sensing data: A machine learning approach. *Adv. Water Resour.* **2010**, *33*, 69–80. [CrossRef]
83. Duro, D.C.; Franklin, S.E.; Dubé, M.G. A comparison of pixel-based and object-based image analysis with selected machine learning algorithms for the classification of agricultural landscapes using SPOT-5 HRG imagery. *Remote Sens. Environ.* **2012**, *118*, 259–272. [CrossRef]
84. Chauhan, V.K.; Dahiya, K.; Sharma, A. Problem formulations and solvers in linear SVM: A review. *Artif. Intell. Rev.* **2019**, *52*, 803–855. [CrossRef]
85. Martins, F.F.; Miranda, T.F. Estimation of the rock deformation modulus and RMR based on Data Mining techniques. *Geotech. Geol. Eng.* **2012**, *30*, 787–801. [CrossRef]
86. Kim, T.H.; Ko, T.Y.; Park, Y.S.; Kim, T.K.; Lee, D.H. Prediction of uniaxial compressive strength of rock using shield TBM machine data and machine learning technique. *Tunn. Undergr. Space Technol.* **2020**, *30*, 214–225.
87. Yao, Y.; Liu, Y.; Yu, Y.; Xu, H.; Lv, W.; Li, Z.; Chen, X. K-SVM: An Effective SVM Algorithm Based on K-means Clustering. *Comput.* **2013**, *8*, 2632–2639. [CrossRef]
88. Pham, B.T.; Jaafari, A.; Prakash, I.; Bui, D.T. A novel hybrid intelligent model of support vector machines and the MultiBoost ensemble for landslide susceptibility modeling. *Bull. Eng. Geol. Environ.* **2019**, *78*, 2865–2886. [CrossRef]
89. Marjanović, M.; Kovačević, M.; Bajat, B.; Voženílek, V. Landslide susceptibility assessment using SVM machine learning algorithm. *Eng. Geol.* **2011**, *123*, 225–234. [CrossRef]
90. Huang, Y.; Zhao, L. Review on landslide susceptibility mapping using support vector machines. *Catena* **2018**, *165*, 520–529. [CrossRef]
91. Micheletti, N.; Foresti, L.; Kanevski, M.; Pedrazzini, A.; Jaboyedoff, M. Landslide susceptibility mapping using adaptive support vector machines and feature selection. *Geophys. Res. Abstr.* **2011**, *13*.
92. Zhang, P.; Wu, H.N.; Chen, R.P.; Chan, T.H. Hybrid meta-heuristic and machine learning algorithms for tunneling-induced settlement prediction: A comparative study. *Tunn. Undergr. Space Technol.* **2020**, *99*, 103383. [CrossRef]
93. Wang, F.; Zhang, D.; Huang, H.; Huang, Q. A phase-field-based multi-physics coupling numerical method and its application in soil-water inrush accident of shield tunnel. *Tunn. Undergr. Space Technol.* **2023**, *140*, 105233. [CrossRef]

54. Wang, F.; Huang, H.; Zhang, D.; Zhou, M. Cracking feature and mechanical behavior of shield tunnel lining simulated by a phase-field modeling method based on spectral decomposition. *Tunn. Undergr. Space Technol.* **2022**, *119*, 104246. [CrossRef]
55. Wang, F.; Zhou, M.; Shen, W.; Huang, H.; He, J. Fluid-solid-phase multi-field coupling modeling method for hydraulic fracture of saturated brittle porous materials. *Eng. Fract. Mech.* **2023**, *286*, 109231. [CrossRef]
56. Cai, X.; Yuan, J.; Zhou, Z.; Pi, Z.; Tan, L.; Wang, P.; Wang, S.; Wang, S. Effects of hole shape on mechanical behavior and fracturing mechanism of rock: Implications for instability of underground openings. *Tunn. Undergr. Space Technol.* **2023**, *141*, 105361. [CrossRef]
57. Zhou, Z.; Wang, P.; Cai, X.; Cao, W. Influence of Water Content on Energy Partition and Release in Rock Failure: Implications for Water-Weakening on Rock-burst Proneness. *Rock Mech. Rock Eng.* **2023**, *56*, 6189–6205. [CrossRef]
58. Zhou, Z.; Cai, X.; Li, X.; Cao, W.; Du, X. Dynamic response and energy evolution of sandstone under coupled static–dynamic compression: Insights from experimental study into deep rock engineering applications. *Rock Mech. Rock Eng.* **2020**, *53*, 1305–1331. [CrossRef]

Disclaimer/Publisher's Note: The statements, opinions and data contained in all publications are solely those of the individual author(s) and contributor(s) and not of MDPI and/or the editor(s). MDPI and/or the editor(s) disclaim responsibility for any injury to people or property resulting from any ideas, methods, instructions or products referred to in the content.

Article

Numerical Investigation on the Performance of Horizontal Helical-Coil-Type Backfill Heat Exchangers with Different Configurations in Mine Stopes

Bo Zhang *, Long Shi, Wenxuan Zhang, Chao Huan, Yujiao Zhao and Jingyu Wang

College of Energy Engineering, Xi'an University of Science and Technology, Xi'an 710054, China
* Correspondence: bozhang@xust.edu.cn

Abstract: The application of ground heat exchanger technology in backfill mines can actualize subterranean heat storage, which is one of the most effective solutions for addressing solar energy faults such as intermittence and fluctuation. This paper provides a 3D unsteady heat transfer numerical model for full-size horizontal backfill heat exchangers (BFHEs) with five configurations in a mining layer of a metal mine by using a COMSOL environment. In order to ensure the fairness of the comparative analysis, the pipes of BFHEs studied have the same heat exchange surface area. By comparing and evaluating the heat storage/release characteristics of BFHEs in continuous operation for three years, it was discovered that the helical pipe with serpentine layout may effectively enhance the performance of BFHEs. Compared with the traditional SS BFHEs, the heat storage capacity of the S-FH type is significantly increased by 21.7%, followed by the SA-FH type, which is increased by 11.1%, while the performances of U-DH and SH type are considerably lowered. Also, the impact of the critical structural factors (pitch length and pitch diameter) was further studied using the normalized parameters C_1 and C_2 based on the inner diameter of the pipe. It is discovered that BFHEs should be distributed in a pipe with a lower C_1, and increasing C_2 encourages BFHEs to increase the storaged/released heat of BFHEs. By comparatively analysing the effect of thermal conductivity, it is found that the positive effects of thermal conductivity on the performance of SH, U-DH, SA-FH, and S-FH type BFHEs are found to decrease successively. This work proposes a strategy for improving the heat storage and release potential of BFHEs in terms of optimal pipe arrangement.

Keywords: backfill heat exchangers; horizontal helical pipe; thermal energy storage; heat storage and release performance

MSC: 80M10

1. Introduction

The rapid growth increase in the world's energy demand has led to the development of solar energy as it is a sustainable and clean source of energy, and it is expected that solar technology will provide about 70% of the world's energy consumption by the year 2100 [1]. However, the biggest dilemma of solar energy is that it is unstable and cannot be matched in real-time with user demand, which severely limits its utilization efficiency. Thermal energy storage (TES, thermal energy storage) is an effective technological solution that stores solar energy and extracts it for utilization at the time of need, thus considering both the demand side and the supply side at different time scales [2,3].

The hollow area formed after mining provides a huge, utilizable space for underground heat storage and energy storage. Some researchers have combined geothermal exploitation with underground space in order to realize the secondary usage of underground space, in addition to doing research on the stability of subterranean space, rock damage, and rock-burst suppression ect. [4–6]. Ghoreishi et al. [7] first applied the underground pipe heat transfer technology to the backfilling mine to exploit the deep mine geothermal energy by using the backfilling body as the heat storage medium, and the results of the study elucidated its feasibility and good economic benefits. Guo Pingye et al. [8] concluded that the use of underground space for anti-seasonal cyclic energy storage can realize efficient heating and cooling in winter and summer seasons, significantly reduce the carbon dioxide emission coefficient, and enhance economic benefits. Li et al. [9] used numerical methods to evaluate the thermal storage performance of the backfilling quarry with pre-buried heat exchanger pipes, and the results showed that a 3 km long underground backfilling quarry of a typical coal mine could provide 23 GWh of thermal energy per year. Therefore, based on the academic theoretical foundation of functional mine backfilling, the process method of deposit-geothermal synergistic mining [10] can be adopted, and the heat exchanger pipelines can be buried into the backfilling body during the back backfilling process of the mine to construct the BFHEs, and then form the underground heat storage and energy storage system of the backfilling mine (as shown in Figure 1) to store the solar energy, etc., in the form of thermal energy. Solar energy is stored in the form of thermal energy in the underground backfilling body, realizing cross-seasonal storage and solving the contradiction of imbalance between the supply and demand of thermal energy.

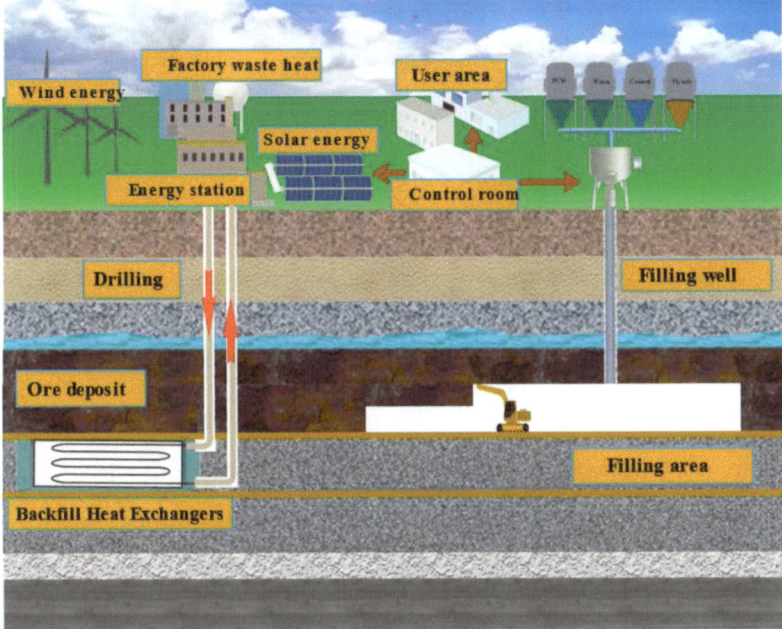

Figure 1. Schematic diagram of heat storage/release system with BFHEs in mine stopes.

BFHEs, as the core component of downhole thermal energy storage, whose heat exchanger pipe arrangement is reasonable or not, will inevitably have a great impact on the performance of downhole thermal energy storage systems. Sivasakthivel et al. [11] experimentally compared the heat transfer performance of single U and double U buried pipes and found that the latter has higher heat transfer performance in both heat storage/release modes. Zhao et al. [12] experimentally investigated and comparatively analyzed the effect of heat transfer performance of serpentine, single U, and double U-shaped buried pipes based on a similar theory, and the results showed that the serpentine arrangement has the highest performance with the total efficiency of 46.1%. Liang Pu et al. [13] simulated the heat transfer performance of double-layer serpentine buried pipe and found that when the relative offset displacement (D/S) is greater than 1/3, the heat transfer performance of the staggered arrangement is better than that of the down-row arrangement.

In the design of buried pipes, their geometrical structure is also continuously innovated and developed, and helix pipe is widely used due to its advantages of large heat exchange area, small occupied space, and easy assembly [14,15]. Zhao et al. [16] comprehensively analyzed the transient heat transfer process of U,W-type, and helix pipe-type heat exchangers and found that helix pipes have better heat transfer performance in both the long- and short-term. Saeidi et al. [17] constructed a 1D–3D unsteady state model of helix buried pipes heat exchangers by using COMSOL simulation software, and the study found that the pitch length of screws has a great influence on the heat transfer performance. Kim et al. [18] investigated the heat transfer performance of helix and slink-type buried pipes heat exchangers through thermal response experiments (TPTs), and the results showed that the form of heat exchanger pipe arrangement is one of the main influencing factors of buried pipes heat exchangers, and the heat transfer performance of helix type is better than slink type. Javadi et al. [19] compared eight types of buried pipes heat exchangers with a helix arrangement and single U type and found that single U-type has the worst heat transfer performance, although the pressure drop is small. Serageldin et al. [20] used numerical simulation to compare the heat transfer performance of single U-type and double helix-type buried pipes heat exchangers at two different flow rates and found that the thermal efficiency and heat transfer power of the double helix-type increased by 40.8% and 44.1%, respectively, compared with that of single U-type, and that the effect of helix pitch diameter in the structural parameters was the most significant. Jalaluddin et al. [21] comparatively studied the heat transfer power and pressure drop per meter drilled for different pitch lengths of the helix GHE and U-type GHE with different pitch lengths in terms of heat transfer power and pressure drop per meter of drilled holes and analyzed from the point of view of energy efficiency, the use of helix pipe in ground source heat pump system has a better performance than the use of U-type pipe. Shi et al. [22] compared and analyzed the heat transfer performance of four arrangements of GHE, namely, Slinky, helix, tandem U-type, and tiled, and concluded that the tandem U-type has the best performance and that the performance of tandem U-type is the best for the helix pipe increasing the center diameter and decreasing the pitch length reduces its economic efficiency. Dinh et al. [23] investigated two types of pipes, Horizontal U-pipe and Horizontal helix pipe, in terms of economic and heat transfer performance, and the results showed that although the total initial installation cost of helix type of GHE is 30% higher, its high annual heat exchange leads to shorter payback period and higher internal rate of return.

Helix-buried pipes heat exchanger is very popular for their advantages of small footprint, simple installation, and high concentration of heat exchanger pipes, and extensive research has been carried out in the technical evaluation and optimization of its heat transfer performance [24], but the heat storage carriers are mostly soils and sandy soils, and there are fewer researches on the performance of helix heat exchanger with mine backfiller as the heat storage medium. Therefore, this paper constructs four arrangement forms of helix and traditional U-type filled body buried pipes heat exchangers and numerically simulates their heat storage/release performance using COMSOL simulation software to provide a theoretical basis for the optimal design of inter-seasonal heat storage and energy storage system based on the backfilling mine.

2. Numerical Modeling

2.1. Physical Model

In this paper, with reference to the quarry dimensions of the Jinchuan II mine in Jinchang City, Gansu Province, China [25], BFHEs are constructed in a backfill sublayer (4 m × 6 m × 60 m) as shown in Figure 2. The buried pipes are arranged in the form of traditional Serpentine Straight-pipes (SS), Single Helix-pipes (SH), U-type Double Helix-pipes (U-DH), Serpentine-type four helix-pipes (S-FH), and Square Array-type four helix-pipes (SA-FH), as shown in Figure 3.

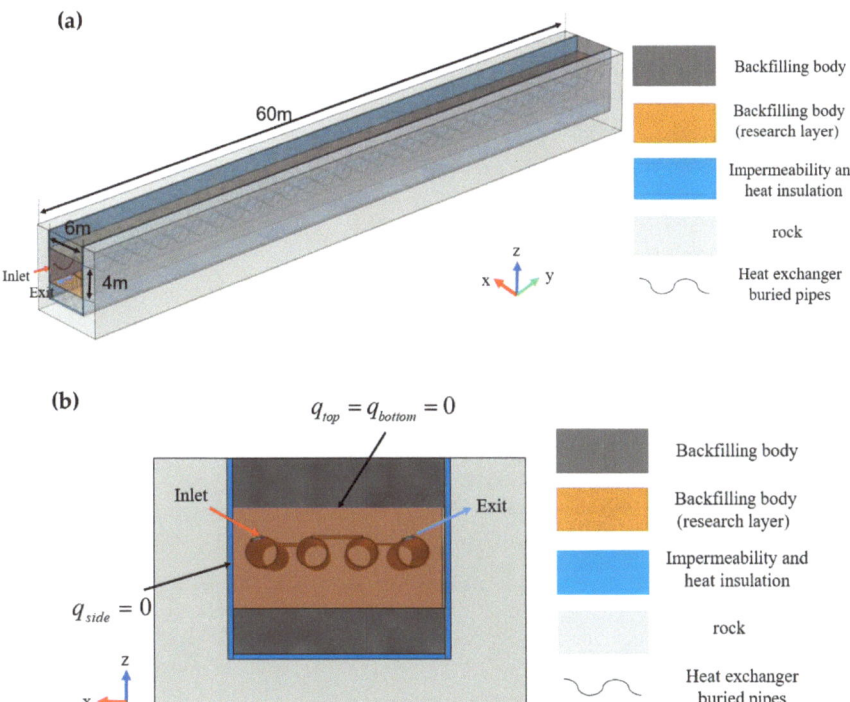

Figure 2. Physical model diagram of BFHEs. (**a**) Axonometric view; (**b**) Front view.

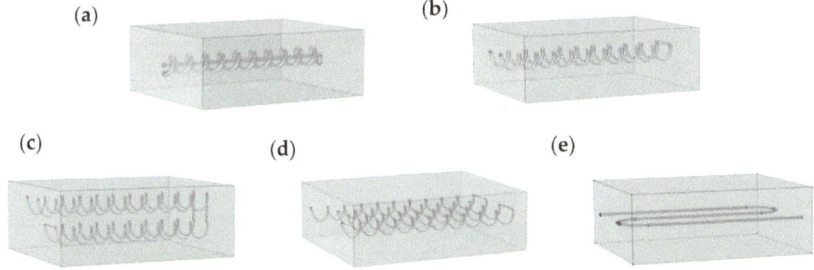

Figure 3. Schematic of different configurations for BFHEs. (**a**) SH; (**b**) U-DH; (**c**) SA-FH; (**d**) S-FH; (**e**) SS.

The heat exchange surface area of buried pipe is the key factor in determining the heat exchange capacity of BFHEs; in order to ensure the fairness of the comparative analysis, the studied BFHEs with different buried pipe arrangement forms and structural parameters keep the same heat exchange internal surface area of the buried pipe. The inner diameter of the buried pipes, the pitch diameter, and the pitch length of the helix buried pipes are selected with reference to the relevant literature and combined with the actual size of the backfilling body [26–28] and the geometrical parameters of the BFHEs with different forms of pipe arrangement and the related material thermo-physical parameters are shown in Tables 1 and 2, respectively.

Table 1. Geometric parameters of BFHEs with different configurations.

Pipe Distribution Form	Pipe Inner Diameter /m	Pipe Length /m	Total Surface Area of Pipe Inner Wall /m²	Pitch Diameter /m	Helix Pitch /m
SH	0.038	183.7	21.75		
U-DH	0.028	248.0	21.80	0.8	1.4
S-FH/SA-FH	0.016	433.4	21.77		
SS *	0.038	182.3	21.75	/	

* Note: Pipe spacing is 2 m [9].

Table 2. Thermophysical properties of BFHEs materials [29].

Material	Density (m³/kg)	Thermal Conductivity W/(m·K)	Specific Heat Capacity J/(kg·K)
Backfill body	1709	0.6	1235
Copper	8500	110	393.6
Rock	2400	2.5	2000

2.2. Mathematical Model

In BFHEs, the process of storing and releasing heat is a complicated three-dimensional unstable heat transfer. The thermophysical parameters of the heat transfer fluid are listed in Table 3. The following hypotheses are used in the numerical simulation process to make the calculation simpler [20,30]:

(1) The backfilling body is homogeneous and isotropic;
(2) Neglect the contact thermal resistance between the buried pipe wall and the backfilling body and the contact thermal resistance between the backfilling body and the surrounding rock;
(3) The influence of underground seepage is not considered;
(4) The heat transfer fluid is an incompressible fluid, and the temperature and velocity are uniform in any radial section;
(5) The thermo-physical properties of materials are temperature-independent.

Table 3. Thermophysical parameters of heat transfer fluids.

Type	Parameter	Value
Heat transfer fluid (water)	$Q_{f,in}$ (inlet volume flow rate)	3.5×10^{-4} m³/s
	ρ (density of water)	998 m³/kg
	λ (thermal conductivity of water)	0.6 W/(m·k)
	c_p (specific heat of water)	4182 J/(kg·K)

2.2.1. Governing Equation

(1) Backfill body region

Energy equation:

$$\frac{\partial T}{\partial \tau} = \frac{\lambda_b}{\rho_b c_{p,b}} \left(\frac{\partial^2 T}{\partial x^2} + \frac{\partial^2 T}{\partial y^2} + \frac{\partial^2 T}{\partial z^2} \right) \tag{1}$$

(2) Backfill Heat Exchangers region

The energy equation for the heat transfer fluid inside a heat exchanger buried pipes [31]:

$$\rho_f A_p c_f \frac{\partial T_f}{\partial \tau} + \rho_f A_p c_f u \cdot \nabla T_f = \nabla \cdot \left(A_p k_f \nabla T_f \right) \frac{1}{2} f_D \frac{\rho_f A_p}{d_h} |u|^3 + Q + Q_{wall} \tag{2}$$

$$Q_{\text{wall}} = (hZ)_{\text{eff}}(T_{\text{ext}} - T_f) \tag{3}$$

$$(hZ)_{\text{eff}} = \frac{2\pi}{\frac{1}{r_0 h_{\text{int}}} + \frac{\ln \frac{r_1}{r_0}}{\lambda}} \tag{4}$$

Momentum equation:

$$\rho_f \frac{\partial u}{\partial \tau} + \rho_f u \cdot \nabla u = -\nabla p_f - f_D \frac{\rho_f}{2d_h} u|u| \tag{5}$$

The continuity equation:

$$\frac{\partial \rho_f}{\partial \tau} + \nabla \cdot (\rho_f u_f) = 0 \tag{6}$$

2.2.2. Boundary Condition

The heat transfer fluid, the backfilling body, and the heat transfer buried pipe are the main components of the model under consideration. During the simulation, the relevant boundary conditions are set as follows:

(1) BFHEs are provided with impermeable and thermal insulation on both sides of the backfilling body (as shown in Figure 2), so both sides are set to be adiabatic in the simulation:

$$q_{\text{side}} = 0 \tag{7}$$

(2) Based on geometric symmetry, the top and bottom of the backfilling of BFHEs are adiabatic surfaces:

$$q_{\text{top}} = q_{\text{bottom}} = 0 \tag{8}$$

(3) Inlet temperature of heat exchanger buried pipe:

$$T_f(x, \tau)|_{x=0} = T_{f,\text{in}} \tag{9}$$

where $T_{f,\text{in}}$ is the temperature of the heat transfer fluid at the inlet of the heat transfer buried pipes, the heat storage phase is taken as 90 °C, and the heat release phase is taken as 20 °C [9].

(4) Buried pipe inlet volume flow rate:

$$Q_f(x, \tau)|_{x=0} = Q_{f,\text{in}} = A_p \times \frac{\pi d_h^2}{4} \tag{10}$$

In the formula, $Q_{f,\text{in}}$ for the heat transfer fluid in the buried pipe inlet volume flow rate to the pipe inner diameter of 38 mm, the flow rate of 0.3 m/s as the basis for the calculation of the default value of 3.5×10^{-4} m^3/s, and to ensure that all the conditions of the inlet volume flow rate are the same.

2.2.3. Initial Conditions

Heat storage phase:

$$T_f = T_b = T_p = T_0 \tag{11}$$

Heat release phase:

$$T_f = T_b = T_p = T_e \tag{12}$$

where T_0 is the initial temperature of BFHEs, which is taken as 45 °C [32,33]; T_e is the initial temperature of BFHEs in the heat release phase, which is the same as the temperature distribution at the moment of the end of heat storage.

3. Numerical Simulation and Verification

3.1. Geometric Modeling and Meshing

Due to the intricacy of the heat transfer mechanism at the intersection of the backfilling body and the underground pipe, geometric modeling and meshing of the BFHEs are performed using COMSOL software prior to numerical simulation computations. The grid is locally encrypted in the vicinity of the heat transfer buried pipe (As shown in the red box), as shown in Figure 4, to increase calculation accuracy.

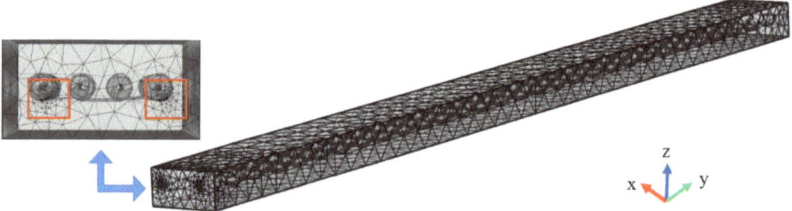

Figure 4. Meshing division diagram of BFHEs (Taking S-FH, for example).

3.2. Grid and Time-Step Independence Verification

It is vital to select a reasonable number of grids and time steps in order to guarantee the correctness of the calculations while also reducing the cost of computational time. For the 240th day of thermal storage for S-FH type BFHEs, the variation of the body-averaged temperature with the number of grids is shown in Figure 5a. As can be observed, there are more grids overall (from 375,105 to 866,340), yet the change in body temperature is only 0.2 °C. Figure 5b shows the variation of the outlet temperature of the heat transfer fluid of the S-FH type BFHEs for 240 d of heat storage at different time steps. It can be seen that the temperature difference between time steps 1 d and 0.5 d is tiny, with a change value of less than 0.1%, but the temperature difference with 5 d is greater than 5%. The number of grids is selected as 375,105 with a time step of 1 d for comprehensive consideration.

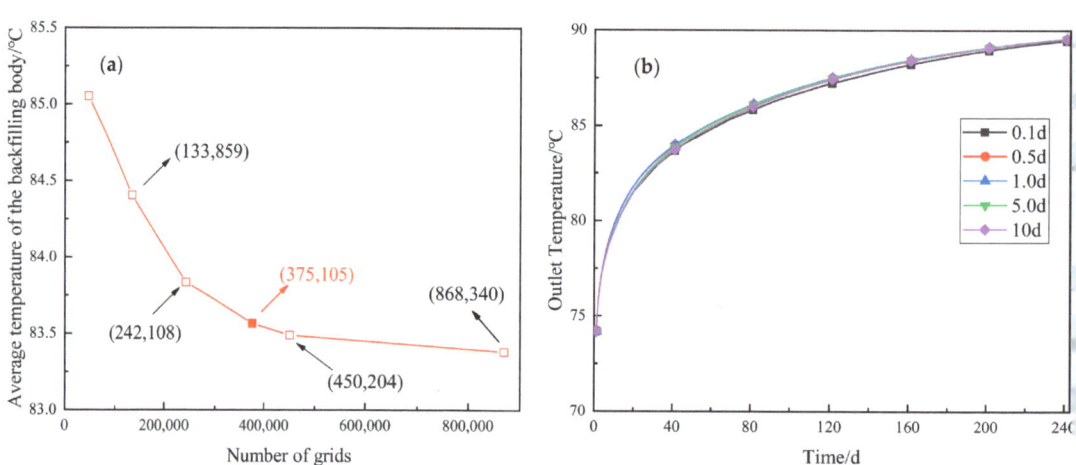

Figure 5. Mathematical model independence verification: (a) Grid independence verification; (b) Time step independence verification.

3.3. Model Validation

In this paper, the experimental data of Dehghan B.B. [34] and Dinh B.H. et al. [23] are used to confirm the precision of the established mathematical model. The validation model's geometrical parameters, boundary conditions, beginning circumstances, and operational conditions are maintained in accordance with previous research, details of the parameters are shown in Table 4. According to Figure 6, the difference between the simulated value of the inlet and outlet temperatures of the heat transfer fluid and the experimental value of Dinh et al. is less than 10%, and the error between the simulated value of the heat transfer rate and the experimental value of Dehghan B. is within 10%. It demonstrates that the numerical model developed in this publication has good accuracy and can be used moving forward for additional research.

Table 4. Model parameters for Dinh B.H. [23] and Dehghan B.B. [34].

Model		Dinh B.H.	Dehghan B.B.
Geometric dimensions of models		$5 \times 1 \times 1$ m	$6 \times 6 \times 4$ m
Backfill materials	Density	1782 m^3/kg	2100 m^3/kg
	Thermal conductivity	1.62 W/(m·k)	1.8 W/(m·k)
	Specific heat	860 J/(kg·K)	900 J/(kg·K)
Heat transfer fluid (water)	Volume flow rate	4 L/min	15 L/min
	Inlet temperature	change over time	50 °C
Operation time		1600 min	150 h

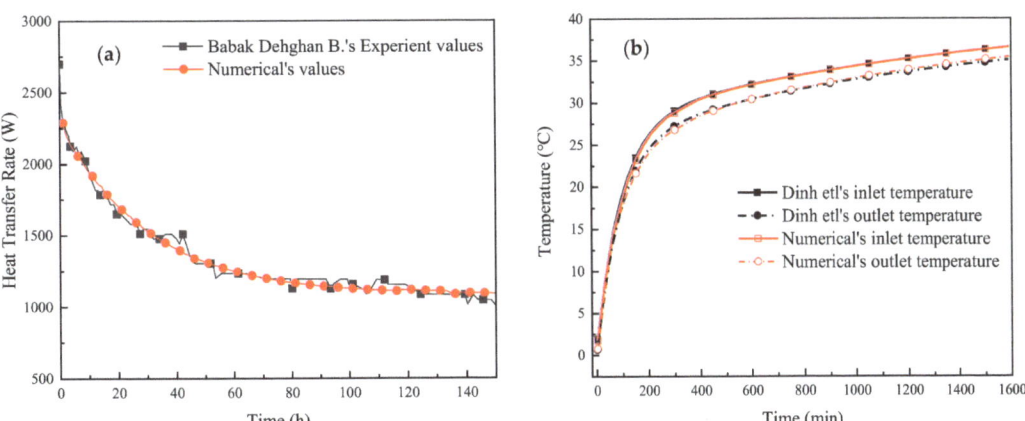

Figure 6. Accuracy verification of mathematical model. (**a**) Compared with Dehghan's experimental results; (**b**) Compared with Dinh's measured values.

4. Evaluation Indicators

4.1. Accumulated Heat Storage/Release and Heat Storage/Release Rate

Accumulated heat storage/release refers to the cumulative heat stored or released by BFHEs after a τ time period, calculated from the initial moment of the heat storage or release phase, respectively, reflecting their overall heat storage/release capacity.

The heat storage/release rate, which reflects the BFHEs' actual heat storage/release capacity, is the amount of heat that they store and release per unit of time. The equations are as follows:

$$Q = \int_0^\tau m_f c_{pf}(T_{i,f} - T_{o,f}) d\tau \tag{13}$$

$$\Phi = \frac{dQ}{d\tau} = m_f c_{pf}(T_{i,f} - T_{o,f}) \tag{14}$$

4.2. Total Heat Storage and Release Efficiency

The total heat storage-release efficiency is the ratio of the effective cumulative heat release to the cumulative heat storage of the BFHEs in a heat storage-release cycle and is calculated as follows [35]:

$$\eta_{\text{BFHEs}} = \frac{|Q_r|}{|Q_s|} = \frac{\int_0^{\tau_2} m_f c_{pf}(T_{o,f} - T_{i,f}) d\tau}{\int_0^{\tau_1} m_f c_{pf}(T_{i,f} - T_{o,f}) d\tau} \tag{15}$$

where τ_1 and τ_2 are the heat storage time and heat release time of a heat storage-release cycle, s.

4.3. Comprehensive Heat Transfer Performance

A comprehensive evaluation of the thermal performance of BFHEs needs to consider its heat transfer efficiency and flow resistance, this paper takes the SS-type BFHEs with the same buried pipe heat transfer area as the reference and introduces the comprehensive heat transfer performance TPC for evaluation and the specific calculation formula is as follows [20]:

$$TPC = \frac{\varphi/\varphi_0}{f/f_0} \tag{16}$$

The average combined heat transfer performance of a heat storage and release cycle is calculated by the following equation:

$$TPC_{\text{ave}} = \frac{\int_0^\tau TPC d\tau}{\tau} \tag{17}$$

where φ_0 and f_0 are the heat transfer efficacy and friction coefficient of SS-type BFHEs, respectively; φ and f are the heat transfer efficacy and friction coefficient of helix BFHEs, respectively;

The heat transfer efficiencies of the BFHEs are calculated as follows:

$$\varphi = \frac{T_{i,f} - T_{o,f}}{T_{i,f} - T_{\text{ave},b}} \tag{18}$$

where $T_{\text{ave},b}$ is the average temperature of the filled body storage/release initial body. The heat storage is T_0 and the heat release is T_e, °C.

The friction coefficient f is calculated as follows [20]:

$$f = \frac{\Delta P}{\frac{1}{2}\rho_f u^2} \cdot \frac{d_h}{L_T} = \frac{2 d_h \Delta P}{\rho_f u^2 L_T} \tag{19}$$

where d_h is the diameter of heat transfer buried pipe, m; ΔP is the pressure drop between the inlet and outlet of the heat transfer buried pipe, Pa; ρ_f is the density of heat transfer fluid, kg/m³;

The formula for calculating the pipe length of helix pipe is as follows [20]:

$$L_T = \frac{H_h}{P_h}\sqrt{(\pi D_h)^2 + P_h^2} \tag{20}$$

5. Simulation Results and Analysis

5.1. Comparative Analysis of the Heat Storage/Release Characteristics of BFHEs in Five Arrangement Forms

The capacity of BFHEs to storage and release heat can be readily observed in the backfilling body's average body temperature change. Figure 7 displays the average temperature variation for traditional serpentine BFHEs and helix pipe BFHEs over a period of three years. As seen in Figure 7, the average body temperature of the S-FH type reached 85.9 °C and 37.7 °C at the end of heat storage/release, respectively. The temperature change range is the largest, reaching 48.2 °C, which was 21.7% higher than that of the SS type. The average body temperature change range of the SA-FH type is second, increased by 11.1%. This suggests that when the heat exchange area of the buried pipe is the same, the heat storage/release capacity of S-FH BFHEs is greatly increased. The SA-FH type's heat storage/release capability is lower than that of the S-FH type as a result of the pipe group's interlayer thermal interference. The thermal resistance of the backfilling body affects the SH type, so it has the lowest capacity for heat storage/release.

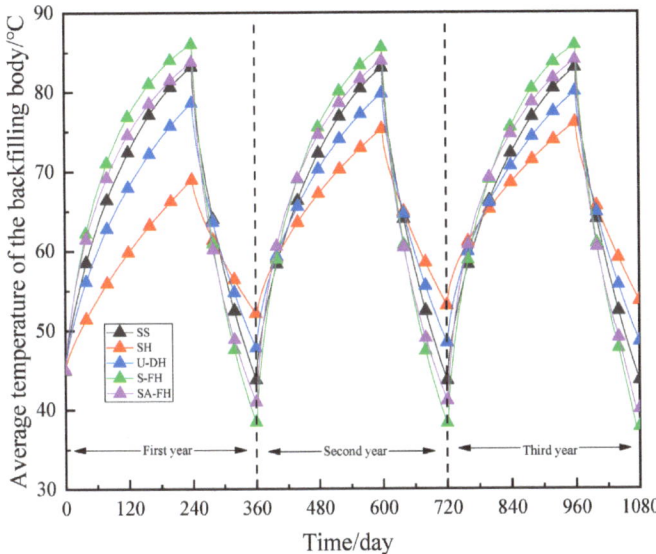

Figure 7. Variations in bulk temperature of helical BFHEs with different arrangements during 3 years of continuous operation.

Figure 8 shows the change in heat storage/release rate between helix BFHEs and traditional serpentine BFHEs with different arrangements for 3 years of continuous operation. It can be seen from the figure that BFHEs have a high rate of heat storage/release at the beginning of the heat storage/release phase, which then decreases rapidly and gradually slows down. It is found that at the beginning of heat storage/release, the heat storage/release rate of SA-FH type and S-FH type is slightly higher than that of SS type by 3~6%, while the U-DH type and SH type are significantly lower than that of SS type, about 43% and 35%, respectively. In the early phase of the heat storage/release phase, the heat storage rate of Ss-type decreases faster, and the heat storage/release rates of both SA-FH-type and S-FH-type are significantly higher than those of SS-type, with the maximum difference reaching about 15 kW, while in the late phase, they are slightly lower than those of SS-type, with the maximum difference not exceeding 0.4 kW. Due to the initial low rate of heat storage/release, the U-DH and SH types are essentially lower than the SS type throughout the storage/release period. The rate of heat storage/heat release of BFHEs organized in five varied greatly at the beginning of heat storage/release but only slightly at the end, between 1.5 and 2.5 kW and 4.0 and 7.5 kW, respectively. The rate of heat storage/release of BFHEs arranged by S-FH, SA-FH, SS, U-DH, and SH decreases consecutively throughout the entire storage/release period.

Figure 9 displays the cumulative heat storage/release variance for three years of continuous operation for helix BFHEs with various arrangements. The S-FH type of the four-helix BFHEs has the highest cumulative heat storage/release, which is much higher than that of the SS type, as can be seen from the figure. This demonstrates how the serpentine-shaped helix buried pipe may effectively increase the heat storage/release capacity of BFHEs by better matching the backfilling body's internal heat transfer. The heat transfer between the helix buried pipe and the backfilling body is too concentrated in the SH type, resulting in a decrease in the heat storage/release capacity of BFHEs, which is much lower than that of the SS type, and the U-DH type has a significant improvement over the SH type. The SA-FH type is affected by the thickness of the backfilling body, the smaller spacing of the pipe rows, and the intensification of thermal interference, resulting in a poorer heat storage/release capacity than the S-FH type, although it is much improved over the U-DH type.

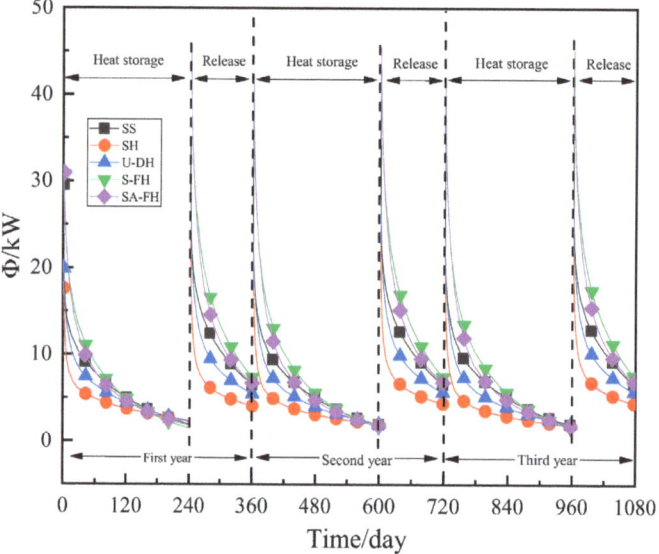

Figure 8. Variations in heat storage/release rate of helical BFHEs with different arrangements during 3 years of continuous operation.

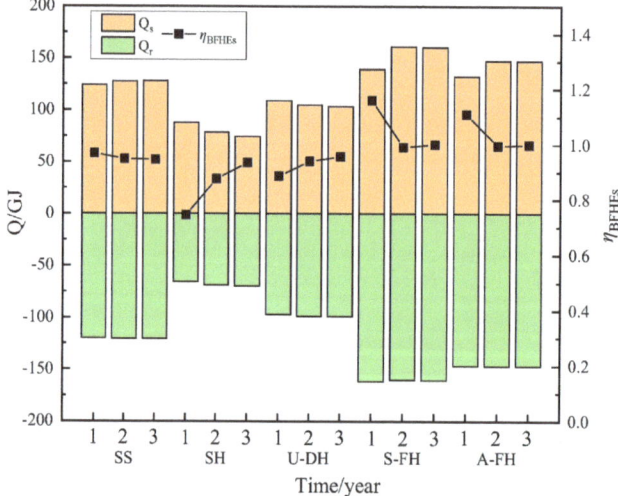

Figure 9. Changes in cumulative heat storage/release of helical BFHEs with different arrangements during 3 years of continuous operation.

The total efficiency of SS-type storage/release heat fluctuates around 0.95, according to Figure 9's variation in the total efficiency of storage-heat release, while the total efficiency of U-DH type in the second year is 0.94, which is comparable to that of SS-type. The total efficiency of the S-FH type and SA-FH type in the second year of operation has reached 0.99, and the storage/release of heat has basically reached equilibrium, reflecting a good storage-release of heat stabilization, while the SH type is 0.87 storage-release of heat stabilization of the worst ability.

Figure 10 displays the TPCs of variously arranged helix BFHEs in their third year of operation. TPC larger than 1 denotes that the overall heat transfer performance of this helix BFHEs is superior to that of the SS type and vice versa. The figure shows that the TPC of the SA-FH type decreases rapidly in the early phase of heat storage, and the TPC of the S-FH type starts to be less than 1 on the 96th and 50th days, respectively. The TPC of the S-FH type is 1.63 and 1.67 at the beginning of heat storage and decreases to 0.30 and 0.40 at the end as the heat storage progressed, which demonstrates that the S-FH type and SA-FH type have better overall heat transfer performance than the SS type in the early phases of heat storage. However, as heat storage capacity decreases, the negative effects of increased resistance brought on by the reduction in heat exchange pipe diameter gradually become apparent. As a result, the comprehensive heat transfer performance is lower than the SS type in the middle and late phases of heat storage, and the gap widens. At the start and end of heat storage, the TPC of SH type and U-DH type is comparable to that of SS type, and the TPC is lower than 1 while heat storage is taking place, indicating that their overall heat transfer performance is inferior to that of SS type. It can also be found from the figure that the comprehensive heat transfer performance of SH type and U-DH type is also lower than that of SS type in the heat release phase, but S-FH and SA-FH type are significantly improved, and they are better than SS type in the whole heat release phase.

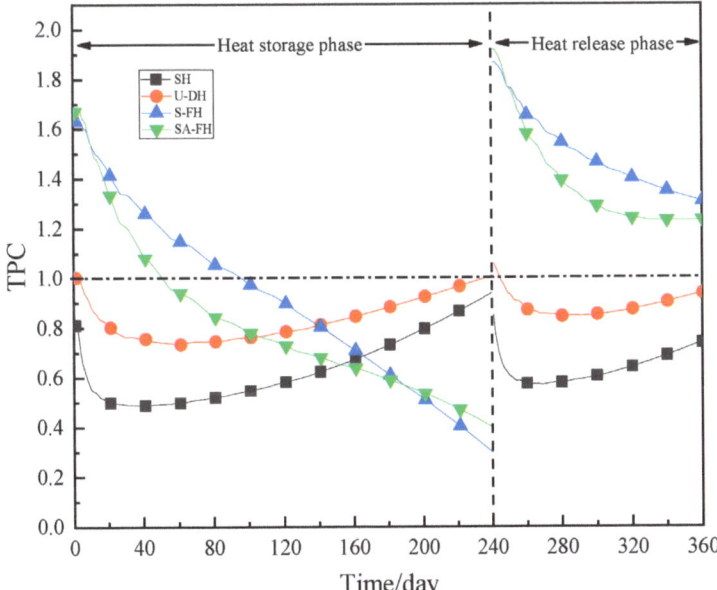

Figure 10. Changes in TPC of four helical BFHEs in the third year of operation.

The average TPC variation of helix BFHEs over three years of operation in various configurations is shown in Figure 11. The average comprehensive heat transfer performance of heat storage is marginally better than that of SS type, but the average comprehensive heat transfer performance of heat release is significantly better compared with that of SS type, as can be seen from the fact that in the second and third years of the storage-release cycle, the S-FH type heat storage TPC_{ave} is about 1.10, and the heat release TPC_{ave} is about 1.51. The average comprehensive heat transfer performance of the heat storage phase is slightly worse than that of the SS type, but the heat release phase is significantly stronger, according to the TPC_{ave} of the SA-FH type in the heat storage and release phases, which are about 0.96 and 1.39, respectively. The average complete heat transfer performance is the worst, with the TPC_{ave} of the storage/release phase of U-DH ranking third at about 0.85 and the TPC_{ave} value of the SH type being around 0.64.

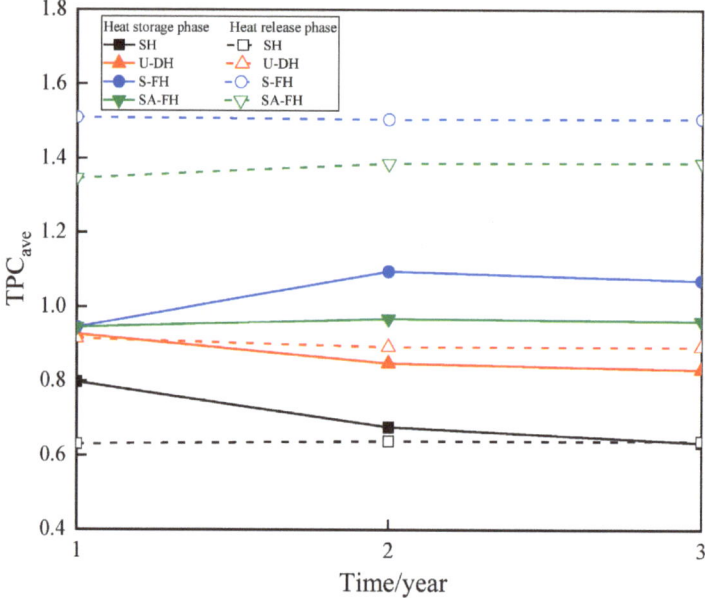

Figure 11. Changes in TPC_{ave} of four helical BFHEs in the third year of operation.

Figure 12 depicts the change in the BFHEs cross-sectional temperature cloud at y = 30 m during heat storage/heat release in five pipe shapes. The cloud diagram shows that the temperature distribution of SS-type BFHEs is relatively uniform along the X-direction at the end of the heat storage/release process and close to the temperature around the buried pipe. However, the distribution along the Z direction is less uniform and has a larger temperature gradient, which reduces the heat storage/release capacity of SS-type BFHEs, thus affecting its performance. The combination of serpentine and helix S-FH inherits the advantages of uniform temperature distribution in the X direction of SS and improves the temperature distribution in the Z direction significantly, and the temperature at the boundary of the backfilling body at the end of heat storage/release is very close to that of the peripheral area of the heat exchanger pipe, so its heat storage/release capacity is most significantly improved. SA-FH further improves the temperature distribution in the Z-direction, but the rectangular cross-section of backfilling body, the difference in the temperature distribution along the X-direction increases, so its heat storage/release capacity is reduced compared with that of S-FH. The heat transfer surface of the SH type is too concentrated in the center of the cross-section of the backfilling body, and the temperature distribution uniformity is the worst, and the temperature distribution of U-DH is still inferior to that of the SS type, although it has a more obvious improvement than that of SH type, resulting in the heat storage/release capacity of both SH type and U-DH type being lower than that of SS type.

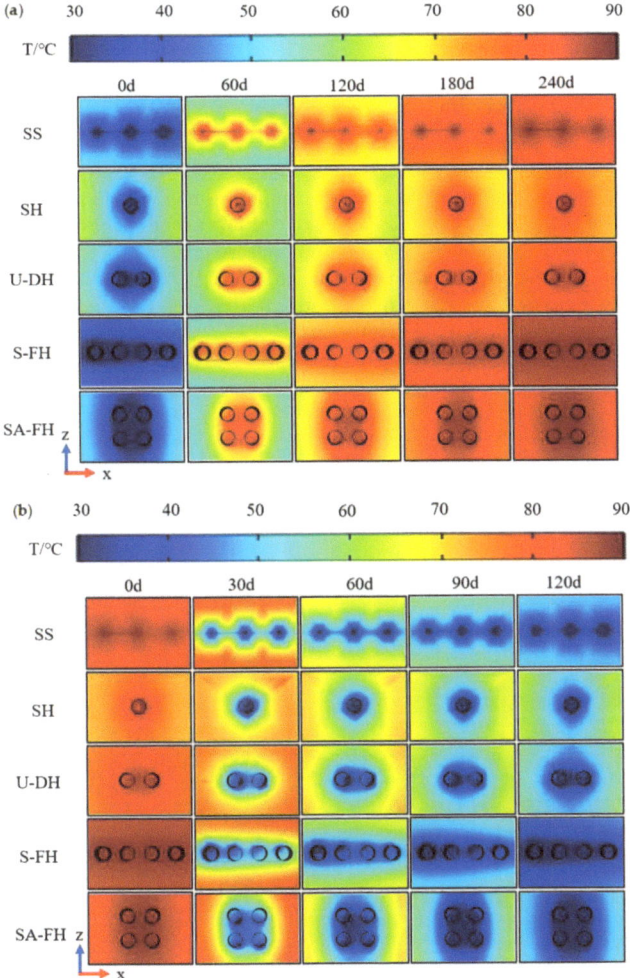

Figure 12. Temperature cloud diagram of the cross-section of BFHEs with five configurations at y = 30 m. (**a**) Heat storage process; (**b**) Heat release process.

5.2. The Influence of Helix Pitch Length and Pitch Diameter

The helix pitch length, pitch diameter, and inner diameter of the buried pipe have important effects on the heat transfer performance of the helix buried pipe [7,20,36]. In this paper, five commonly used buried pipes (with inner diameters of 20 mm, 25 mm, 32 mm, 38 mm, and 48 mm, respectively) are selected, and the four-helix BFHEs in the paper are arranged by varying the helix pitch length and pitch diameter, respectively, with the pitch diameter of 0.8 m and the pitch length of 1.4 m as the default dimensions. The arrangement process ensured that the total internal surface of the buried pipe was 21.75 m² (as shown in Table 1), with a maximum of 1.5% inaccuracy.

In order to facilitate the study of the effect of pitch length and pitch diameter on the heat transfer performance of these four helical buried pipes BFHEs, in this paper, the pitch length and pitch diameter are normalized with the diameter of the buried pipes to form two dimensionless parameters:

$$C_1 = \frac{P_h}{d_h} \tag{21}$$

$$C_2 = \frac{D_h}{d_h} \tag{22}$$

5.2.1. The Influence of Helix Pitch Length

Figure 13 shows the heat storage/release characteristics of the four-helix pipe forms of BFHEs at different C_1. Figure 13a shows that the initial storage/release rates of BFHEs with different C_1 differ significantly, but the difference is very small at the end of the storage/release period. The larger the C_1 is, the lower the initial storage/release rates of SH-type and U-DH-type, which results in lower storage/release rates in most phases of the storage/release period. The initial heat storage rate of SA-FH and S-FH BFHEs do not exhibit a monotonic trend with C_1. As seen in Figure 13a, the SA-FH and S-FH types' initial heat storage/release rates are not the greatest at a C_1 value of 875. However, they rise rather than decrease as heat is stored/released, and the average heat storage/release rate is not the highest.

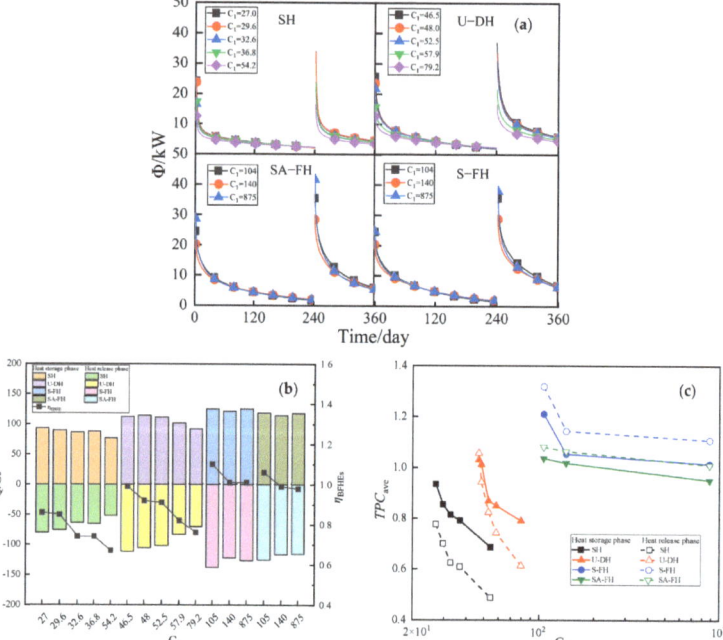

Figure 13. Thermal performance of helical BFHEs with different configurations for different C_1. (a) Heat storage/release rate Φ; (b) Accumulated heat storage/release Q and total heat storage-release efficiency η_{BFHEs}; (c) TPC_{ave}.

According to Figure 13b, the cumulative heat storage/release of BFHEs of the SH and U-DH types is significantly lowering with respect to C_1. The cumulative heat storage-release of S-FH and SA-FH types is comparatively stable, with the same amount of heat storage/release for larger values of C_1, and the total efficiency of heat storage-release near 1, which is essentially in a stable state. In contrast, the cumulative heat storage-release of SH and U-DH types decreases more than the cumulative heat release with an increase in C_1, leading to a decreasing trend of the total heat storage-release efficiency of BFHEs in the first year.

The average integrated heat transfer performance of BFHEs degrades monotonically with C_1, with the TPC_{ave} for SH and U-DH types degrading more noticeably. This is seen in Figure 13c. Therefore, when the flow resistance and heat transfer capacity are thoroughly taken into account, the BFHEs should be selected with a smaller C_1 in the form of piping. The sequential decline in TPC_{ave} of the S-FH, SA-FH, U-DH, and SH types is also evident in Figure 13c. It is not advised to choose the SH type because, in the range of C_1 values examined, all of its TPC_{ave} are smaller than 1, reflecting its less effective overall heat transmission than the SS type. U-DH type, which is superior to SS type, is only marginally over 1.0 at smaller C_1. The improvement in overall heat transfer performance is particularly pronounced in S-FH and SA-FH types, where the TPC_{ave} is essentially more than 1.0.

5.2.2. The Influence of Pitch Diameter

Figure 14 shows the heat storage/release characteristics of the four helical BFHEs at different C_2. Figure 14a shows that the differences in the storage/release heat rates of BFHEs at different C_2 are very obvious. Increasing the C_2, the initial storage/release rates of SH and U-DH types are elevated, and therefore, the overall higher storage/release rates were observed. However, the change of C_2 has a relatively small effect on the storage/release rates of SA-FH and S-FH BFHEs, and the smaller the C_2, the smaller the difference in storage/release rates.

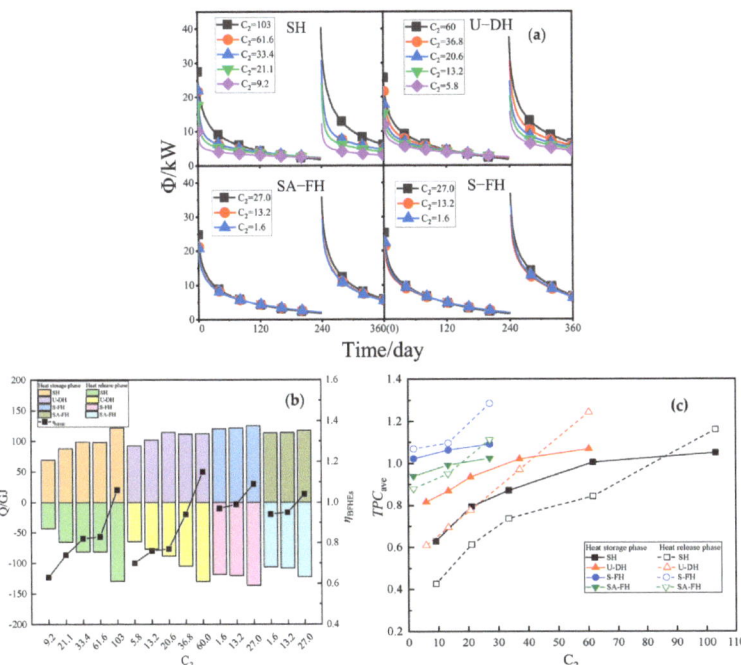

Figure 14. Thermal performance of helical BFHEs with different configurations for different C_2. (a) Heat storage/release rate Φ; (b) Accumulated heat storage/release Q and total heat storage-release efficiency η_{BFHEs}; (c) TPC_{ave}.

As shown in Figure 14b, increasing C_2 is beneficial to improving the cumulative heat storage/release of BFHEs, especially for SH and U-DH types. In addition, it can be found from Figure 14b that the total accumulation-release heat efficiency increases significantly with C_2, indicating that increasing C_2 can enhance the heat release capacity of BFHEs more effectively.

Figure 14c shows that the average integrated heat transfer efficiency TPC_{ave} of the four helix BFHEs monotonically increases with C_2, where the TPC_{ave} increase is more pronounced in the heat release phase. Therefore, the BFHEs should be selected with a larger C_2 in the form of piping when the flow resistance and heat exchange capacity are considered comprehensively. It is found that the TPC_{ave} of the S-FH BFHEs is better than that of the other three helix pipe arrangements and is always greater than 1 within the range of C_2 studied, which further indicates that the serpentine and helix pipe arrangement combination is the best option.

5.3. The Influence of Thermal Conductivity

Figure 15 illustrates the changes in the thermal storage/release performance of the four-helix BFHEs with different thermal conductivity of the backfilling body. From Figure 15a, it can be seen that increasing the thermal conductivity of the backfilling body can effectively strengthen the heat storage/release rate of the BFHEs, but for the U-DH, SA-FH, and S-FH types, at the later phase of the heat storage phase, due to the small temperature difference between the heat transfer fluid in the pipe and the backfilling body, the heat storage rate will instead be reduced, which leads to differences in the degree of strengthening. The thermal conductivity of the backfilling body is enhanced from 0.4 W/(m·k) to 0.8 W/(m·k), and the thermal storage rate of BFHEs of SH, U-DH, SA-FH, and S-FH types is enhanced by 46%, 34%, 25%, and 22% on average. Due to the short duration of the heat release phase, the heat release rate enhancement was even more pronounced, with average enhancements of 78%, 67%, 40%, and 39%.

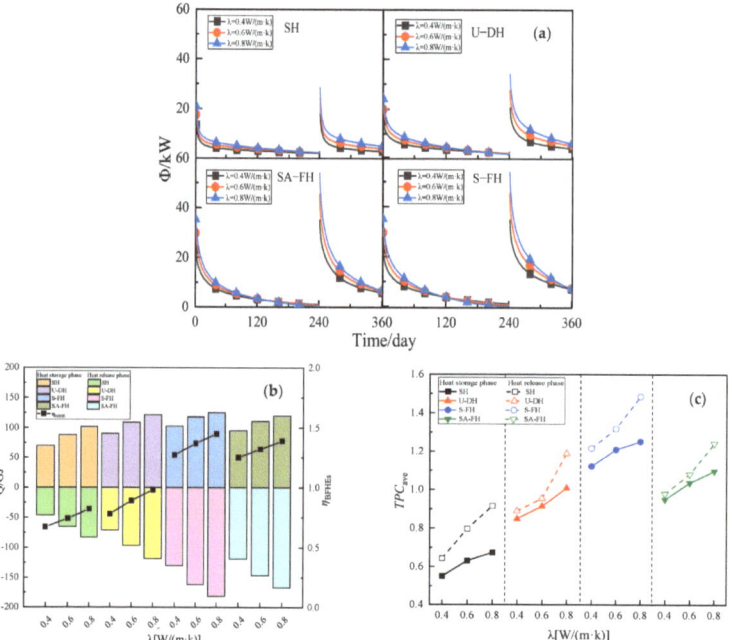

Figure 15. Thermal performance of helical BFHEs with different configurations under different thermal conductivity of backfill body. (**a**) Heat storage/release rate Φ; (**b**) Accumulated heat storage/release Q and total efficiency η_{BFHEs}; (**c**) TPC_{ave}.

Figure 15b demonstrates that the total heat storage-release efficiency and cumulative heat storage/release efficiency of the four helical BFHEs increase linearly with the backfilling body's thermal conductivity, with the increase in total heat storage-release efficiency indicating that the backfilling body's improved thermal conductivity results in better utilization of the total heat stored there.

The average TPC of the four helical BFHEs increases with an increase in thermal conductivity, as shown in Figure 15c because an increase in thermal conductivity improves the heat storage/release rate of BFHEs. The figure shows that the TPC_{ave} of the SH, U-DH,

SA-FH, and S-FH type BFHEs decreases in line with the increase in thermal conductivity. This is mostly caused by the variable impact of the backfilling body's thermal conductivity resistance on the heat transfer of BFHEs. Since the SH type's buried pipes arrangement is highly centralized and the backfilling body's thermal conductivity resistance has the greatest impact on heat transfer performance, improving thermal conductivity has the most obvious positive impact on the SH type's storage/release capacity. The backfilling body's influence on the S-FH type buried pipes arrangement's thermal conductivity resistance is minimized by optimal dispersion and matching, and the improvement brought about by an increase in thermal conductivity occurs naturally, thermal conductivity naturally reduces as it gets better.

6. Conclusions

The numerical simulation of the performance of the full-size horizontal BFHEs used in metal backfilling mines is performed in this work. A three-dimensional unsteady heat transfer model of BFHEs is established by COMSOL software, and its accuracy is validated. Considering the same inner surface of the heat exchange pipe, the helical pipe BFHEs with four different arrangements are compared with the traditional SS-type BFHEs for the three years of continuous operation and the influence of main parameters (pitch length, pipe diameter and thermal conductivity of backfill body) on the heat storage/release performance of the helical pipe BFHEs is analyzed, and the following conclusions can be reached:

(1) Compared with the conventional Serpentine Straight-pipes (SS), the Serpentine-type four helix-pipes (S-FH) have the best fit with the internal heat transfer of the backfill body in the mining layer of the metal mine, and the internal temperature distribution of the backfill body is the most uniform throughout the processes of heat storage/release. And it can increase the capacity of heat storage/release of BFHEs by a large amount of 21.7%. The next best configuration, with an improvement of 11.1%, is the Square Array-type four helix-pipes (SA-FH). The Single Helix-pipes (SH) and U-type Double Helix-pipes (U-DH) layouts, which have fallen by 19.9% and 42.7%, respectively, are both subpar.

(2) The pipe configuration significantly affects the change in the heat storage/release rate of BFHEs, especially in the early phase of the heat storage/release processes. With a maximum increase of roughly 15 kW, S-FH and SA-FH have much higher heat storage/release rates than SS, but U-DH and SH have significantly lower rates.

(3) Given the flow resistance, the pipe configuration distinctly influences the thermal performance capability of helical BFHEs. When BFHEs are operating steadily, S-FH and SA-FH have TPC_{ave} in the heat storage phase that is similar to that of SS at roughly 1.10 and 0.96 and in the heat release phase that is substantially higher at 1.51 and 1.39. The TPC_{ave} of U-DH and SH, at roughly 0.85 and 0.64, respectively, is significantly lower than that of SS during the heat storage/release phase.

(4) To enhance the thermal performance and heat storage/release capacity of helical BFHEs, it is advantageous to decrease the pitch length to pipe diameter ratio (C_1) and increase the pitch diameter to pipe diameter ratio (C_2).

(5) The thermal performance of helical BFHEs can be effectively improved by increasing the backfill body's thermal conductivity, with SH experiencing the greatest improvement and S-FH experiencing the least improvement. The average increases in the heat storage/release rates of SH, U-DH, SA-FH, and S-FH are 46%/78%, 34%/67%, 25%/40%, and 22%/39%, respectively, when the thermal conductivity is raised from 0.4 W/(m·k) to 0.8 W/(m·k).

Author Contributions: Conceptualization, methodology, B.Z. and C.H.; software, validation, L.S. and W.Z.; formal analysis, L.S.; data curation, W.Z.; writing—original draft preparation, B.Z., L.S., and C.H.; writing—review and editing, J.W. and W.Z.; funding acquisition, B.Z. and Y.Z. All authors have read and agreed to the published version of the manuscript.

Funding: This research was funded by the National Natural Science Foundation of China (Grant Nos. 52274063, 52004207, 52104148), Natural Science Basic Research Plan of Shaanxi Province of China (2022JM-173, 2022JQ-401).

Data Availability Statement: No applicable.

Conflicts of Interest: The authors declare no conflict of interest.

Nomenclature

Symbols

A_p	cross-section area of pipe (m^2)
c_p	specific thermal capacity (kJ/(kg·K))
d_h	buried pipe diameter (m)
D_h	pitch diameter (m)
f	friction coefficient
f_D	Darcy friction factor
h_{ext}	outer wall of the heat transfer coefficient (W/(m^2·k))
H_h	helix height (m)
h_{int}	inlet wall of the heat transfer coefficient (W/(m^2·k))
L_T	total length of the heat transfer buried pipe (m)
m	the mass flow rate of heat transfer fluid (kg/s)
p	head pressure inside the pipe (Pa)
P_h	pitch length (m)
ΔP	pressure drop of the heat transfer buried pipe (Pa)
Q	cumulative heat storage/release of BFHEs (kJ)
$Q_{f,in}$	Volume flow rate of the heat transfer fluid (m^3/s)
Q_r	total heat exchange in heat release phase (kJ)
Q_s	total heat exchange in heat storage phase (kJ)
Q_{wall}	heat flow through the wall of the heat exchanger pipe (W/m)
r_0	inner radius of the heat exchanger buried pipes [m]
r_i	outer radius of the heat exchanger buried pipes [m]
T	Temperature (°C)
T_0	initial temperature of BFHEs in the heat storage phase (°C)
T_e	initial temperature of BFHEs in the heat release phase (°C)
$T_{f,in}$	inlet temperature of the heat transfer fluid (°C)

Greek Letters

ρ	Density (kg/m^3)
ϑ	flow rate of heat transfer fluid (m/s)
υ	kinematic viscosity (m^2/s)
Φ	storage/release of heat rate of BFHEs (kW)
η	ratio of the effective cumulative heat release to the heat storage
∇	the gradient: $\nabla = \left(\frac{\partial}{\partial x}, \frac{\partial}{\partial y}, \frac{\partial}{\partial z}\right)^T$

Subscripts

τ	time (s)
b	backfilling body
p	heat transfer buried pipes
f	heat transfer fluid

Abbreviations

BFHEs	Backfill heat exchangers
TPC	Thermal performance coefficient

References

1. Rasih, R.A.; Sidik, N.A.C.; Samion, S. Recent progress on concentrating direct absorption solar collector using nanofluids. *Therm. Anal. Calorim.* **2019**, *137*, 903–922. [CrossRef]
2. Memme, S.; Boccalatte, A.; Brignone, M. Simulation and design of a large thermal storage system: Real data analysis of a sma polygeneration micro grid system. *Appl. Therm. Eng.* **2022**, *201*, 117789. [CrossRef]
3. Li, G.; Li, M.; Taylor, R. Solar energy utilisation: Current status and roll-out potential. *Appl. Therm. Eng.* **2022**, *209*, 11828 [CrossRef]

Cai, X.; Yuan, J.; Zhou, Z.; Pi, Z.; Tan, L.; Wang, P.; Wang, S.; Wang, S. Effects of hole shape on mechanical behavior and fracturing mechanism of rock: Implications for instability of underground openings. *Tunn. Undergr. Space Technol.* **2023**, *141*, 105361. [CrossRef]

Zhou, Z.; Wang, P.; Cai, X.; Cao, W. Influence of Water Content on Energy Partition and Release in Rock Failure: Implications for Water-Weakening on Rock-burst Proneness. *Rock Mech. Rock Eng.* **2023**, *56*, 6189–6205. [CrossRef]

Zhou, Z.; Cai, X.; Li, X.; Cao, W.; Du, X. Dynamic Response and Energy Evolution of Sandstone Under Coupled Static–Dynamic Compression: Insights from Experimental Study into Deep Rock Engineering Applications. *Rock Mech. Rock Eng.* **2020**, *53*, 1305–1331. [CrossRef]

Ghoreishi-Madiseh, S.A.; Hassani, F.; Abbasy, F. Numerical and experimental study of geothermal heat extraction from backfilled mine stopes. *Appl. Therm. Eng.* **2015**, *90*, 1119–1130. [CrossRef]

Guo, P.; Wang, M.; Sun, X.; He, M. Study on off-season cyclic energy storage in underground space of abandoned mine. *J. China Coal Soc.* **2022**, *47*, 2193–2206. [CrossRef]

Li, B.; Zhang, J.; Ghoreishi-Madiseh, S.A.; de Brito, M.A.R.; Deng, X.; Kuyuk, A.F. Energy performance of seasonal thermal energy storage in underground backfilled stopes of coal mines. *J. Clean. Prod.* **2020**, *275*, 122647. [CrossRef]

Zhang, B.; Xue, P.; Liu, L.; Huan, C.; Wang, M.; Zhao, Y.; Qin, X.; Yang, Q. Exploration on the method of ore deposit-geothermal energy synergetic mining in deep backfill mine. *J. China Coal Soc.* **2021**, *46*, 2824–2837. [CrossRef]

Zhao, Y.; Liu, L.; Wen, D.; Zhang, B.; Zhang, X.; Huan, C.; Wang, M.; Wang, X. Experimental study of horizontal ground heat exchangers embedded in the backfilled mine stopes. *Geothermics* **2022**, *100*, 102344. [CrossRef]

Sivasakthivel, T.; Philippe, M.; Murugesan, K. Experimental thermal performance analysis of ground heat exchangers for space heating and cooling applications. *Renew. Energ.* **2017**, *113*, 1168–1181. [CrossRef]

Pu, L.; Xu, L.; Qi, D.; Li, Y. Structure optimization for horizontal ground heat exchanger. *Appl. Therm. Eng.* **2018**, *136*, 131–140. [CrossRef]

Larwa, B.; Teper, M.; Grzywacz, R.; Kupiec, K. Study of a slinky-coil ground heat exchanger—Comparison of experimental and analytical solution. *Int. J. Heat Mass Transf.* **2019**, *142*, 118438. [CrossRef]

Yoon, S.; Lee, S.R.; Go, G.H. Evaluation of thermal efficiency in different types of horizontal ground heat exchangers. *Energy Build.* **2015**, *105*, 100–105. [CrossRef]

Zhao, Q.; Chen, B.; Liu, F. Study on the thermal performance of several types of energy pile ground heat exchangers: U-shaped, W-shaped and helix-shaped. *Energy Build.* **2016**, *133*, 335–344. [CrossRef]

Saeidi, R.; Noorollahi, Y.; Esfahanian, V. Numerical simulation of a novel helix type ground heat exchanger for enhancing heat transfer performance of geothermal heat pump. *Energy Convers. Manag.* **2018**, *168*, 296–307. [CrossRef]

Kim, M.J.; Lee, S.R.; Yoon, S.; Go, G.H. Thermal performance evaluation and parametric study of a horizontal ground heat exchanger. *Geothermics* **2016**, *60*, 134–143. [CrossRef]

Javadi, H.; Ajarostaghi, S.S.M.; Pourfallah, M.; Zaboli, M. Performance analysis of helical ground heat exchangers with different configurations. *Appl. Therm. Eng.* **2019**, *154*, 24–36. [CrossRef]

Serageldin, A.A.; Radwan, A.; Katsura, T.; Sakata, Y.; Nagasaka, S.; Nagano, K. Parametric analysis, response surface, sensitivity analysis, and optimization of a novel helix-double ground heat exchanger. *Energy Convers. Manag.* **2021**, *240*, 114251. [CrossRef]

Jalaluddin; Miyara, A. Thermal performance and pressure drop of helix-pipe ground heat exchangers for ground-source heat pump. *Appl. Therm. Eng.* **2015**, *90*, 630–637. [CrossRef]

Shi, Y.; Cui, Q.; Song, X.; Xu, F.; Song, G. Study on thermal performances of a horizontal ground heat exchanger geothermal system with different configurations and arrangements. *Renew. Energ.* **2022**, *193*, 448–463. [CrossRef]

Dinh, B.H.; Kim, Y.S.; Yoon, S. Experimental and numerical studies on the performance of horizontal U-type and helix-coil-type ground heat exchangers considering economic aspects. *Renew. Energ.* **2022**, *186*, 505–516. [CrossRef]

Rashidi, S.; Bakhshi, N.; Rafee, R. Progress and challenges of helical-shaped geothermal heat exchangers. *Environ. Sci. Pollut. Res.* **2021**, *28*, 28965–28992. [CrossRef] [PubMed]

Lu, W.; Wang, W.; Zou, L.; Kou, Y. Parameters Optimizaion of Stoping Drift Under Massive Backfill Based on Combined Weighting. *Min. Res. Dev.* **2022**, *42*, 15–21. [CrossRef]

Park, S.; Sung, C.; Jung, K.; Sohn, B.; Chauchois, A.; Choi, H. Constructability and heat exchange efficiency of large diameter cast-in-place energy piles with various configurations of heat exchange pipe. *Appl. Therm. Eng.* **2015**, *90*, 1061–1071. [CrossRef]

Liang, B.; Chen, M.; Fu, B.A.; Guan, J. Thermal and flow characteristics in a vertical helix-type ground heat exchanger based on linear non-equilibrium thermodynamic principle. *Energy Build.* **2022**, *266*, 112111. [CrossRef]

Zhang, H.; Yu, Y.; Hu, C. Selection of pipe diameter for ground-source heat pump system. *J. Heat. Vent. Air Cond.* **2012**, *42*, 114–117.

Zhang, X.; Xu, M.; Liu, L.; Huan, C.; Zhao, Y.; Qi, C.; Song, K.I. Experimental study on thermal and mechanical properties of cemented paste backfill with phase change material. *J. Clean. Prod.* **2020**, *9*, 2164–2175. [CrossRef]

Zhang, B.; Yang, Z.; Liu, L.; Zhao, Y.; Huan, C.; Wang, M.; Tu, B. Study on the thermal interference of backfill heat exchangers in heat storage/release processes in deep mines. *J. China Coal Soc.* **2023**, *48*, 1155–1168. [CrossRef]

Li, C.; Cleall, P.J.; Mao, J.; Muñoz-C, J.J. Numerical simulation of ground source heat pump systems considering unsaturated soil properties and groundwater flow. *Appl. Therm. Eng.* **2018**, *139*, 307–316. [CrossRef]

32. Wu, L.; Kang, T.; Yin, B.; Du, M. Microcalorimetric test and analysis of hydration heat of fly ash paste-filling material. *J. Chin. Coal Soc.* **2015**, *40*, 2801–2806. [CrossRef]
33. Gan, D.; Sun, H.; Xue, Z.; Yan, Z.; Liu, Z. Flow Characteristics of Slurry Conveying Pipe with Large Flow under High Temperature Environment. *Met. Mine* **2021**, *539*, 43–49. [CrossRef]
34. Dehghan, B.B. Experimental and computational investigation of the helix ground heat exchangers for ground source heat pump applications. *Appl. Therm. Eng.* **2017**, *121*, 908–921. [CrossRef]
35. Zhang, H.; Hou, H.; Han, J.; Zhang, Q.; Jin, T. Simulation and Analysis of Performance of Seasonal Borehole Thermal Energy Storage. *J. Eng. Thermophys.* **2022**, *43*, 1148–1154.
36. Yang, W.; Xu, R.; Wang, F.; Chen, S. Experimental and numerical investigations on the thermal performance of a horizontal helix-coil ground heat exchanger. *J. Eng. Thermophys.* **2022**, *147*, 979–995. [CrossRef]

Disclaimer/Publisher's Note: The statements, opinions and data contained in all publications are solely those of the individual author(s) and contributor(s) and not of MDPI and/or the editor(s). MDPI and/or the editor(s) disclaim responsibility for any injury to people or property resulting from any ideas, methods, instructions or products referred to in the content.

Article

Research on Precursor Information of Brittle Rock Failure through Acoustic Emission

Weiguang Ren [1,2], Chaosheng Wang [3,4,*], Yang Zhao [2] and Dongjie Xue [5]

1. China Institute of Coal Science, Beijing 100013, China; rwgjszsj@outlook.com
2. China Coal Research Institute, Beijing 100013, China; zhao_no1@126.com
3. School of Civil Engineering and Architecture, Henan University of Science and Technology, Luoyang 471023, China
4. Engineering Technology Research Center of Safety and Protection of Buildings of Henan Province, Luoyang 471023, China
5. School of Mechanics and Civil Engineering, China University of Mining and Technology Beijing, Beijing 100083, China; xuedongjie@163.com
* Correspondence: 9905755@haust.edu.cn

Abstract: Dynamic failure of surrounding rock often causes many casualties and financial losses. Predicting the precursory characteristics of rock failure is of great significance in preventing and controlling the dynamic failure of surrounding rock. In this paper, a triaxial test of granite is carried out, and the acoustic emission events are monitored during the test. The fractal characteristics of acoustic emission events' energy distribution and time sequence are analyzed. The correlation dimension and the b value are used to study the size distribution and sequential characteristics. Furthermore, a rock failure prediction method is proposed. The correlation dimension is chosen as the main index and the b value is chosen as a secondary index for the precursor of granite failure. The study shows that: (1) The failure process can be divided into an initial stage, active stage, quiet stage, and failure stage. (2) The b value and correlation dimension both can describe the process of rock failure. There is a continuous decline before failure. Because of the complexity of the field, it is difficult to accurately estimate the stability of surrounding rock using a single index. (3) The combination of the b value and correlation dimension to establish a new method, which can accurately represent the stability of the surrounding rock. When the correlation dimension is increasing, the surrounding rock is stable with stress adjusting. When the correlation dimension is decreasing and the b value remains unchanged after briefly rising, the surrounding rock is stable, and stress is finished adjusting. When the correlation dimension and b value are both decreasing, the surrounding rock will be destroyed.

Keywords: granite; AE; b value; correlation dimension; precursor information

MSC: 74L10

---

1. Introduction

With the burial depth of underground engineering gradually increasing, underground engineering faces a complex geological environment, such as high geostress, high temperature, high pore pressure, and intense excavation disturbance, which lead to an irreversible development of internal defects within the rock. Brittle rock is a common rock in deep underground engineering. With damage accumulating, the surrounding brittle rock is prone to dynamic disasters such as rock bursts, which can seriously impact construction progress and project safety, and even result in numerous casualties and financial losses [1,2]. Revealing prospective predictions and implementing prompt measures constitute effective approaches to prevent and manage subterranean dynamic disasters in the surrounding geological formations [3–5]. Therefore, it is of great significance to study the precursor information of brittle rocks in order to prevent engineering disasters.

Acoustic emission (AE) is a phenomenon of transient elastic waves generated by the rapid release of energy from local sources in materials. AE can characterize the damage and pore-fracture evolution of rock samples under stress. The characteristics of AE can reflect the damage and failure state of rock. Therefore, acoustic emission technology is often used to monitor rock damage and failure in underground engineering [6,7]. The AE characteristics are closely related to the failure state of the rock, which indicates that the failure state of the rock can be predicted using AE characteristic parameters [8]. The analysis of AE signal characteristics mainly includes AE event number, energy and count, spatial localization, and fractal characteristics [9–11].

Many scholars revealed rock damage and failure characteristics based on AE characteristics. Vishal et al. [10] studied the mechanical behavior of coal under fluid saturation using AE characteristics. Moradian et al. [12] found that AE events could be used to describe the failure levels of brittle rocks. Shkuratnik et al. [13] studied the changes in the AE spectra of coal under uniaxial and triaxial compression tests and found that the AE spectral patterns vary greatly at the coal pre-failure stage under uniaxial compression tests. Abbas et al. [14] investigated the impact of high attenuation on rock AE mapping failure and then proposed a new method to monitor the rock failure position based on the AE events. Yang et al. [15] analyzed AE characteristics and fractal features of disc samples during splitting failure in relation to the loading rate. Holcomb [16] evaluated the stress state of surrounding rock based on the Kaiser effect principle of acoustic emission and applied AE event number to rock damage evaluation. Kusunose et al. [17] investigated the spatial distribution of acoustic emission events under triaxial testing conditions for two different texture distributions of granite.

Since Mandelbrot proposed the concept of fractal, fractal theory has attracted more and more attention from scientists and technologists in various fields [18]. Xie [19] expounded and proved fractures of rocks from microcracks to broken all have fractal characteristics, and the fractal dimension gradually reduces in the process of failure. So, the fractal method also received attention in the analysis of AE. Scholars have conducted AE experiments on the loading and unloading of rocks under various stress conditions and analyzed the fractal characteristics of AE events during the process of rock failure. Then, the fractal characteristic of AE events was applied to analyze the stress state or stable state of rock. The most common characterizing parameters are the AE b-value [20–23] and correlation dimension [24–26]. Many scholars have conducted extensive experimental research on the evolution of the b-value and correlation dimension under various stress conditions. The b value is related to the stress state of rocks, and it is negatively correlated with stress [27]. The fractal dimensions are lower in initial loading stages and increase gradually along with stress; about at 40% of the strength, fractal values begin to fall down [28]. With the development of research on fractal theory in AE, it has been verified that fractal parameters of AE can describe the precursor information of rock instability and failure. Virkar et al. [29] found that the b value could be used to predict rock failure and analyze rock damage. Hayakawa et al. [30] researched the AE fractal characteristic of cold forging tool damage during forming operation and calculated the AE fractal dimension of deformation and fracture, which verified that fractal dimension can be used to describe cold forging tool failure as an effective indicator. In summary, many domestic and foreign scholars have extensively investigated AE characteristics and precursor characteristics of rock failure. They proposed many methods to predict rock failure. But the methods cannot accurately predict the failure of rocks. Therefore, precursor characteristics based on the b value and correlation dimension under different confining pressures were investigated. The fractal characteristics of AE events' energy distribution and time sequence were analyzed. The application of laboratory experiment results in field construction was further discussed.

2. Samples and Experiment Method

2.1. Granite Samples

The samples were taken from the underground research laboratory (URL) of the Beishan preselected area of China's high-level radioactive waste geological repository (Figure 1). The samples are classified into granodiorite, which is intact with a hard texture and has partial development of fissures. The Beishan granodiorite displays a hue ranging from white to grayish red. The rock mass remains undeformed or displays limited deformation. The rock mass primarily consists of a grained granite structure, exhibiting irregular and blocky textures. The main minerals in the samples are plagioclase (30–40%), potash feldspar (10–20%), quartz (20–30%), biotite (2–8%) and hornblende (1–3%) [31,32].

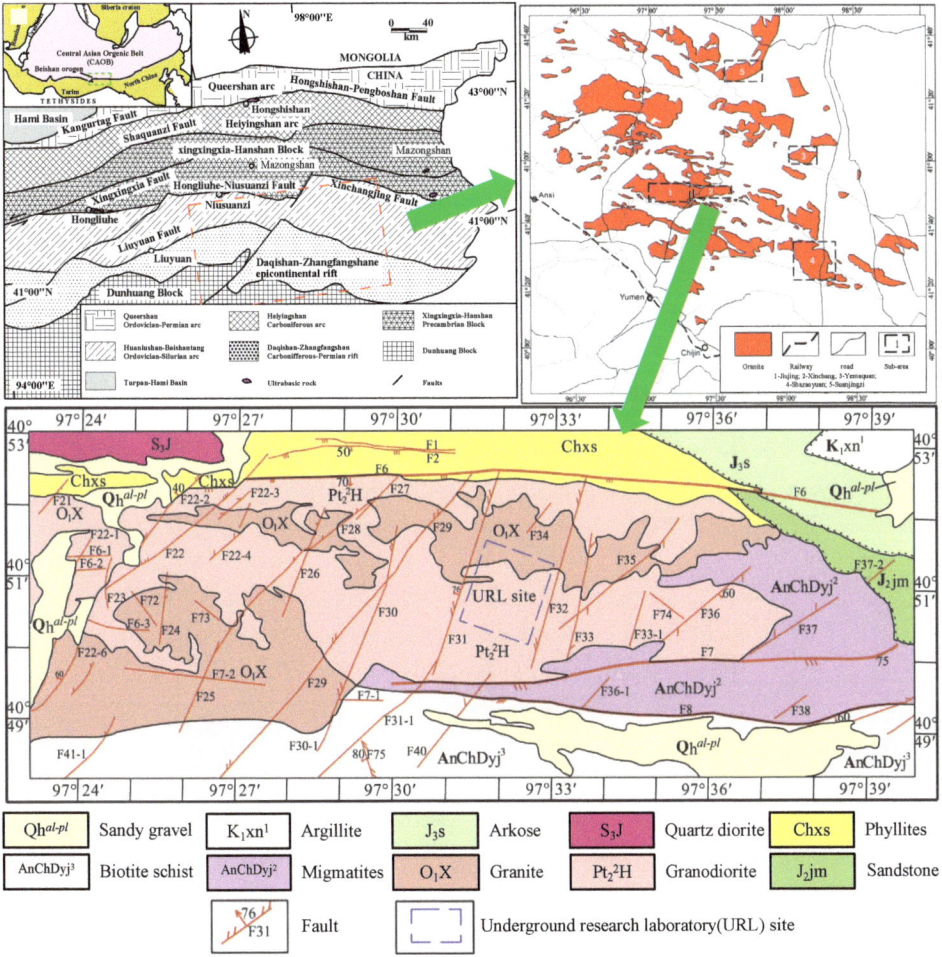

Figure 1. Geological map of the sampling site (URL site) [31,32].

The core cuttings were used for X-ray fluorescence spectroscopy analysis (XRF). Detailed information on the samples is listed in Table 1. According to XRF results, the samples contain SiO_2, Al_2O_3, Fe_2O_3, MgO, CaO, Na_2O, K_2O, MnO, TiO_2, P_2O_5, LOI, and FeO. The highest content is SiO_2, which varies from 69.77% to 70.99%. The content of Al_2O_3 varies from 14.78% to 15.19%. The content of Na_2O, K_2O, CaO, Fe_2O_3, and FeO are all less than

5%, varying from 3.66% to 4.77, 2.94% to 4.13%, 2.25% to 2.56%, 2.00% to 2.21%, and 1.57% to 1.70%, respectively. The content of MgO, LOI, TiO_2, P_2O_5, and MnO are all less than 1%, varying from 0.77% to 0.81%, 0.66% to 0.89%, 0.323% to 0.376%, 0.091% to 0.100%, and 0.037% to 0.038%, respectively.

Table 1. Major elements in the samples/%.

Sample ID	SiO_2	Al_2O_3	Fe_2O_3	MgO	CaO	Na_2O	K_2O	MnO	TiO_2	P_2O_5	LOI	FeO
A	70.99	14.78	2.00	0.79	2.25	3.66	4.13	0.037	0.323	0.100	0.89	1.63
B	70.89	15.19	2.14	0.77	2.56	4.31	2.94	0.038	0.376	0.092	0.66	1.70
C	69.77	15.15	2.21	0.81	2.41	4.77	3.57	0.037	0.371	0.091	0.75	1.57

2.2. Experimental Detail

The triaxial compression experiments were conducted using an MTS815 Flex Test GT rock mechanics test system (Figure 2) manufactured in the United States. The AE events were recorded using a PCI-II Acoustic Apparatus manufactured by American Acoustics Company in the process of the experiment. The acquisition frequency of AE sensors was set to 200 kHz. The threshold value for signal acquisition was set to 26 dB. The layout of the AE sensors is shown in Figure 3. Each specimen is symmetrically arranged with 8 AE sensors. The eight AE sensors are evenly arranged on the upper and lower sections of the specimen. The center of the four AE sensors arranged on the bottom surface is the coordinate origin, with the z-axis direction upward and the x-axis and y-axis in the horizontal direction. The coordinates of each sensor are shown in Table 2.

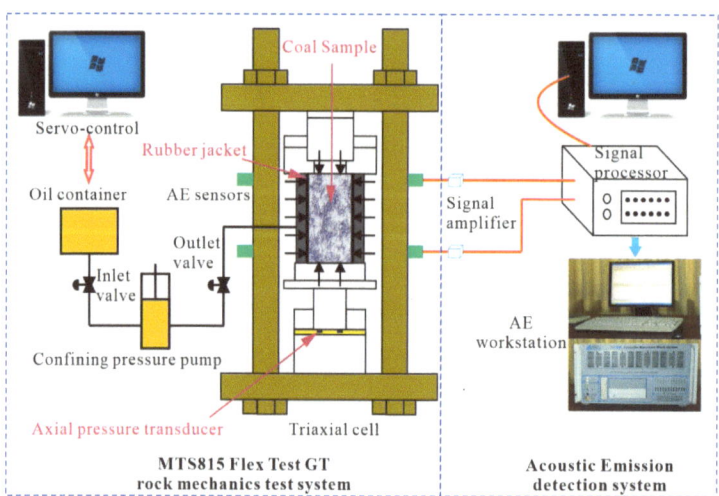

Figure 2. MTS815 Flex Test GT rock mechanics test system and the AE detection system.

Table 2. The coordinates of AE sensors.

Numbers	1	2	3	4	5	6	7	8
x (mm)	0	180	0	−180	0	180	0	−180
y (mm)	180	0	−180	0	180	0	−180	0
z (mm)	140	140	140	140	0	0	0	0

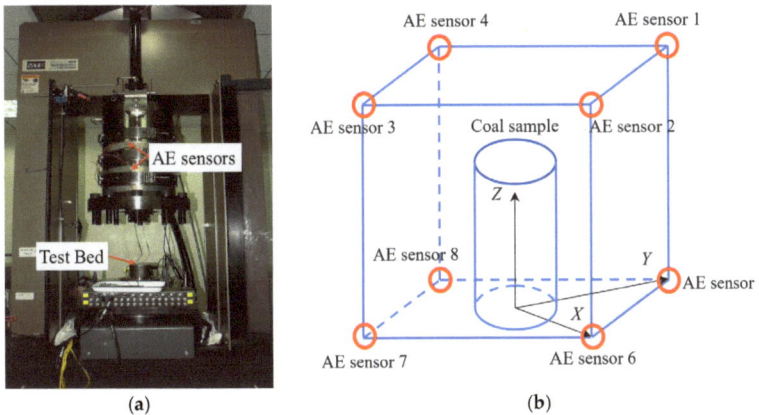

Figure 3. The layout of AE sensors: (**a**) experimental equipment and (**b**) spatial position of AE sensors.

Axial stress and circumferential deformation were combined to control loading. The specific experimental steps are as follows: (1) Axial force was applied to the sample with axial stress control at 30 KN/min. (2) The loading control changed from axial stress control to circumferential deformation control when the inflection point of the volume strain curve appeared. (3) Axial force was applied to the sample with circumferential deformation control at 0.02 mm/min until the specimen was damaged. During the experiments, the confining pressure was set to 5, 10, 15, and 30 MPa, respectively, according to the stress characteristics of Beishan and the depth of the underground laboratory.

2.3. AE Localization

The AE localization algorithm primarily consists of the simplex algorithm [33] and the Geiger algorithm [34]. Both algorithms calculate the position of an AE event by the time difference in sound emission signals received from different location sensors [35]. In this study, the Geiger algorithm is used to determine the location of the AE event for specimen failure. In the experiment, eight AE sensors are fixed in certain spatial positions, and their coordinates were assumed to be S_i (x_i, y_i, z_i) (i = 1, 2, 3, 4, 5, 6, 7, 8). The relative time difference in picking up P-waves with different position sensors is measured to achieve spatial localization of the AE event. For an AE event, given the focal coordinates (x, y, z), the initial time of the AE event t, and the arrival time t_i (i = 1, 2, 3, 4, 5, 6, 7, 8) of P-wave received by sensor S_i, the location of the AE event can be calculated using the following equation.

$$(x_i - x)^2 + (y_i - y)^2 + (z_i - z)^2 = v^2(t_i - t)^2 \quad (1)$$

where v is the velocity of the P-wave in the travel path. In Equation (1), there exist four unknown variables (x, y, z, t), which required at least four AE sensors triggered to determine the four unknown variables.

3. Experiment Results and Analysis

3.1. Experiment Results

Figure 4 shows stress–strain curves of the specimens under different confining pressures. The confining pressure of the 1–6, 1–7, 1–10, and 1–11 specimens were 5, 10, 15, and 30 MPa, respectively. The peak strength of the 1–6, 1–7, 1–10, and 1–11 specimens were 172.4, 218.8, 264.3, and 358.0 MPa, respectively. With the confining pressure increasing, the peak strength significantly increases. The specimens exhibit obvious shear failure (Figure 5). As the confining pressure increases, the specimen destruction is more intense, which means the energy release is more severe.

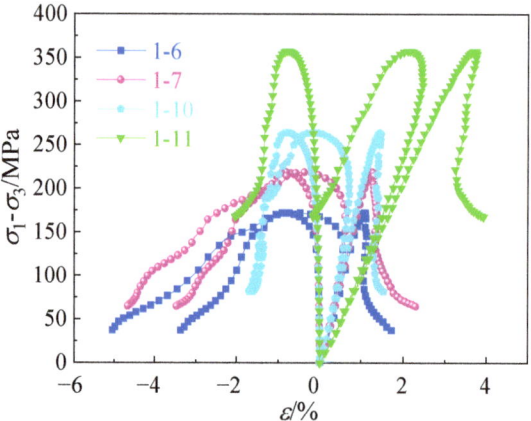

Figure 4. Stress—strain curves of specimen under different confining pressures.

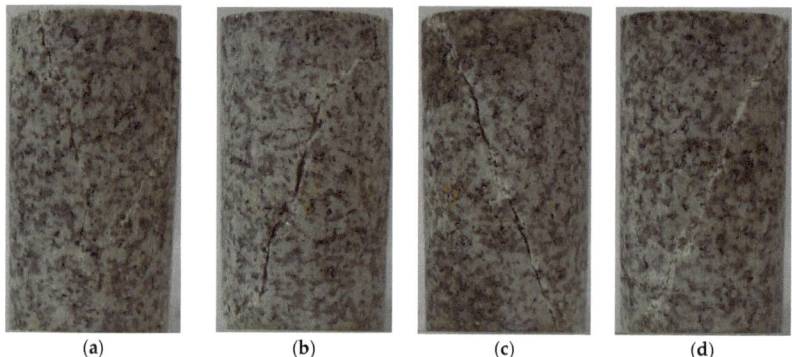

Figure 5. Image of failure specimens: (**a**) 1–6; (**b**) 1–7; (**c**) 1–10; and (**d**) 1–11.

3.2. Characteristics of AE

Figure 6 shows curves of AE hits, amplitude, and stress with time. The confining pressure of the 1–6, 1–7, 1–10, and 1–11 specimens were 5, 10, 15, and 30 MPa, respectively. According to the number of AE events, the failure process is divided into the initial stage, active stage, quiet stage, and failure stage (Figure 3, respectively, with I, II, III, IV).

The initial stage runs through the stage of compaction and elastic deformation of the specimen. AE events show a sporadic distribution and the number of AEs is small, so few fractures occur, and AEs mainly come from the original crack closing. The active stage begins with the stress being about 40% of the peak stress and finishes with stress reaching 98% of the peak stress. During this stage, a large number of fractures are generated, expanded, and connected, which is the main stage of crack generation and propagation. AE events in the quiet phase decreased sharply, mainly because more cracks had been already generated and the stress was redistributed at the crack tip. During this period, the expansion of cracks is primarily driven by small-scale fractures.. During the failure stage, stress concentrates on the rupture surface, and the fracture further expands so that AE events rapidly increase.

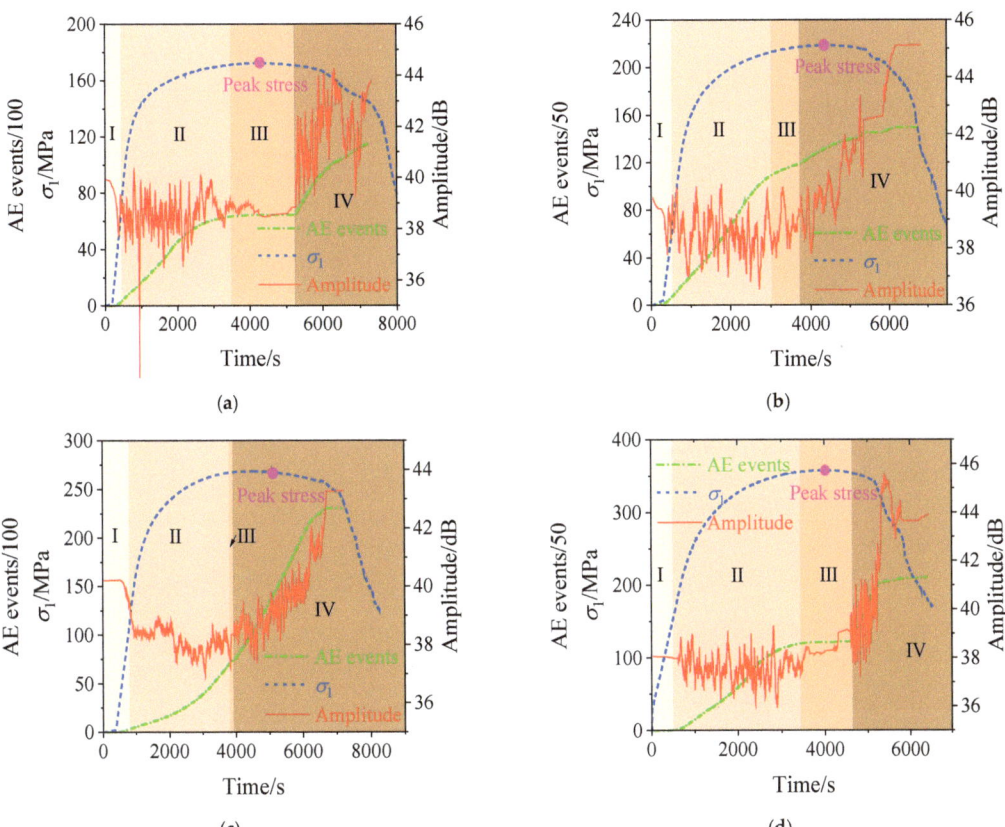

Figure 6. Curves of AE hits, AE amplitude, and stress with time: (**a**) 1–6; (**b**) 1–7; (**c**) 1–10; and (**d**) 1–11.

As shown in Figure 5, the amplitude of each specimen showed a stable decrease in the initial stage and its fluctuation was not obvious. The amplitude in the active stage fluctuated obviously, but the overall trend in amplitude remained constant. In the quiet stage, the amplitude fluctuation of the 1–6, 1–10, and 1–11 specimens disappeared, and their size basically remained stable, which was obviously different from the active phase. However, the amplitude of specimen 1–7 in the calm stage showed little difference from that in the active stage.

In summary, AEs in the process of failure can be divided into four stages, AEs in different stages have different characteristics, and the quiet period can provide some reference for rock failure. Due to the inhomogeneity in the rock, AE characteristics in the quiet stage are not obvious at times, such as the AE event number of the 1–7 specimen. So, it is hard to capture the quiet stage before failure because the duration of the quiet period is very short. Therefore, AE characteristics can provide some references for rock failure, but they cannot provide an accurate destruction of precursor information.

3.3. Research on the b Value

In this paper, the G-R relationship and the G-P algorithm [36] are used to study the distribution characteristics and sequential features of AE energy, respectively. The method for calculating the AE b value using the G-R relationship is shown in Equation (2).

$$\lg N = a - b \lg Q \tag{2}$$

where Q is absolute energy contained in an AE event, N is the number of AE events whose energy is greater than or equal to Q, a and b are constants, and the physical meaning of the AE b value is a measure of development of the crack. b values and their change trends are closely related to the development of cracks in the rock.

When the b value decreases, the proportion of small AE events decreases, and the proportion of large AE events increases. On the contrary, the proportion of small events increases. When the b value changes slowly or its amplitude is small, the number of large events and small events is stable, and crack development is a gradual and stable expansion. A significant reduction in b indicates that the evolution of cracks is drastic and is a symbol of dramatic increasing in AE events, which may cause damage to the rock. In this paper, the b value was counted every 500 AE events, and $\lg N$ and $\lg Q$ were fitted to linear (Figure 7).

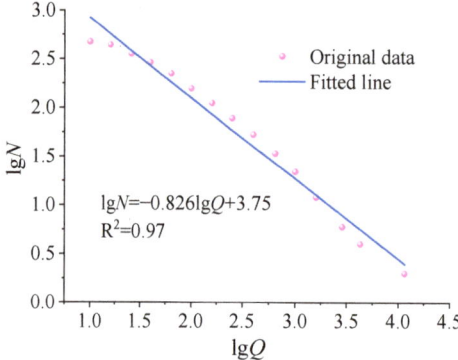

Figure 7. Fitting curve of lgN and lgQ.

The relationship between the b value, stress, and time is shown in Figure 8 and Table 3. From Figure 8 and Table 3, it can be seen that the b value of AE basically shows an upward trend before the stress reaches damage stress, which indicates AE events are dominated by small events and the fracture propagates slowly. In the unstable crack expansion stage, the b value begins to fluctuate, indicating that small AE events and large events alternately occupy the leading position; therefore, the rapid expansion of large fractures and the slow expansion of small fractures alternately dominate the internal rock fracture expansion. However, in the process, the b value does not change much, which shows that the fractures gradually and steadily expand inside the rock. In the later stage of unstable fracture expansion, the b value generally showed a steady downward trend, and the specimen quickly reached the peak and failure, which shows that the proportion of AE events increased, and large cracks developed rapidly before failure.

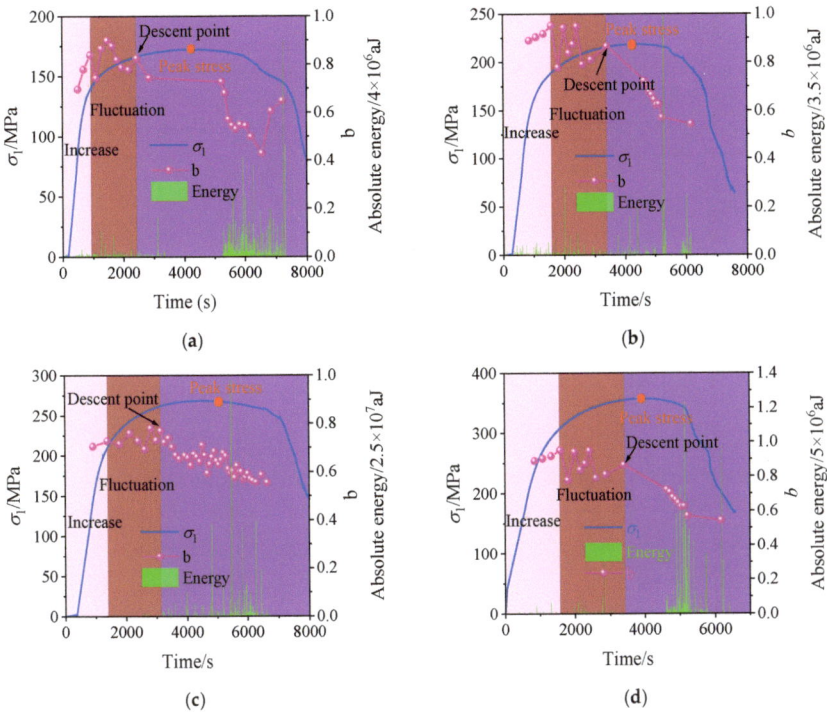

Figure 8. Curves of the b value, AE energy, and stress with time: (**a**) 1–6; (**b**) 1–7; (**c**) 1–10; and (**d**) 1–11.

Table 3. Relationship between b and time.

Number	b Value	Time/s	Stress/MPa
1–6	increase	0–913	0–139.88
	fluctuation	913–250	139.88–166.80
	descent point	2500	166.80
1–7	increase	0–1393	0–182.83
	fluctuation	1393–3300	182.83–215.32
	descent point	3300	215
1–10	increase	0–1214	0–194
	fluctuation	1214–3150	194.21–262.85
	descent point	3150	262
1–11	increase	0–1582	0–308.14
	fluctuation	1582–3400	308.14–353.42
	descent point	3400	353.42

The peak stress of specimens 1–6, 1–7, 1–10, and 1–11 appear at 4260, 4310, 5060, and 3900 s, respectively, and the b-value descent point is 1760, 1110, 1910, and 500 s earlier than the peak stress. The b-value descent point is in the later stage of unstable crack expansion, the stress of the b-value descent point is relatively large, but it is less than peak stress. Therefore, the b-value steady descent point can be chosen as a precursor of rock failure.

3.4. Research on the Correlation Dimension

The AE correlation dimension is an AE fractal dimension calculated using the G-P relationship [36]. In this method, a multi-dimensional space is reconstructed based on the temporal feature of the AE parameter. Considering the coordinates p_i of AE events as individual elements and arranging the AE events in a time sequence, a coordinate set of AE events can be obtained.

$$\begin{cases} A = \{p_1, p_2, \cdots, p_n\} \\ p_i = \{x_i, y_i, z_i\} \end{cases} \quad (3)$$

Select a positive integer m ($m < n$). Then, an m-dimensional phase space for AE events in the time sequence can be established.

$$\begin{cases} P_1 = \{p_1, p_2, \cdots, p_m\} \\ P_2 = \{p_2, p_3, \cdots, p_{m+1}\} \\ \cdots \\ P_{n-m+1} = \{p_{n-m+1}, p_{n-m+2}, \cdots, p_n\} \end{cases} \quad (4)$$

For the constructed m-dimensional phase space, the correlation function can be defined under a given scale r.

$$C(r) = \frac{1}{N^2} \sum_{i=1}^{N} \sum_{j=1}^{N} H(r - \langle P_i - P_j \rangle) \quad (5)$$

where $H(x)$ is the Heaviside function. $<P_i - P_j>$ represents the distance between two m-dimensional phase space points.

$$H(x) = \begin{cases} 1, & x > 0 \\ 0, & x \leq 0 \end{cases} \quad (6)$$

$$\langle P_i - P_j \rangle = \left[\sum_{t=1}^{m} (P_{i,t} - P_{j,t})^2 \right]^{\frac{1}{2}} \quad (7)$$

The correlation function represents the proportion of AE events with spatial distance less than the scale r in the total. The scale r can be obtained using the following equation.

$$r = k \frac{1}{N^2} \sum_{i=1}^{N} \sum_{j=1}^{N} \langle P_i - P_j \rangle \quad (8)$$

where k is the proportional coefficient. In this study, k was selected as 0.1, 0.2, 0.3, 0.4, 0.5, 0.6, 0.7, 0.8, 0.9, 1.0, 1.1, 1.2. N is the number of m-dimensional phase space points.

The correlation dimension can be determined using the correlation function and the scale. Applying logarithms to the correlation function and the scale, there is a linear relationship between lg$C(r)$ and lg$r$. The slope is the correlation dimension.

$$D = \lim_{r \to 0} \frac{\lg C(r)}{\lg r} \quad (9)$$

where D is the correlation dimension, which represents the concentration of AE events in the reconstructed multi-dimensional space. The larger the D value is, the more concentrated the AE events are in the reconstructed multi-dimensional space. In this paper, the dimension value m of the phase space was 15, and the delay time was 1 s. The correlation dimension was calculated every 500 s. The linear fitting of lg$r$ and lg$C(r)$ is shown in Figure 9.

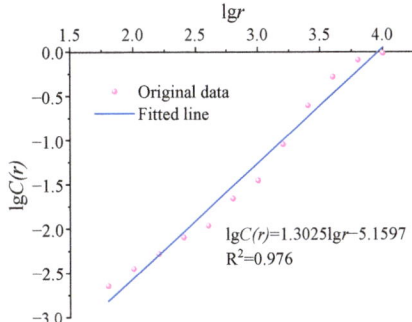

Figure 9. Fitting curve of lg$r$ and lg$C(r)$.

The correlation dimension initially rises and then falls throughout the experiment (Table 4 and Figure 10), which can be divided into two distinct stages: rising and falling. The maximum correlation dimensions for specimens 1–6, 1–7, 1–10, and 1–11 occurred at time points of 3500 s, 3500 s, 3500 s, and 3000 s, respectively. The rising stage encompasses the period from the beginning of loading to reaching the maximum correlation dimension. During this stage, there is an increase in the ratio of AE event pairs with short distances, indicating a progressive concentration of AE events in the reconstructed multi-dimensional space. Additionally, the stable AE energy rate suggests a stable expansion of cracks within the granite sample. Subsequently, the correlation dimension reaches its peak value before continuously declining during the falling stage, which extends from reaching a maximum correlation dimension to sample failure. In this stage, there is an increase in the ratio of AE event pairs with long distances, signifying the dispersion of AE events in the reconstructed multi-dimensional space. Notably, both the value and time sequence of AE energy rate exhibit significant fluctuations during this period suggesting unstable expansion behavior of cracks within granite.

Table 4. Relationship between correlation dimension and time.

Number	Correlation Dimension	Time/s	Stress/MPa
1–6	Rising	0–3500	0–171.23
	Maximum	3500	171.23
	Falling	3500–7000	171.23–156.87
1–7	Rising	0–3500	0–216.54
	Maximum	3500	216.54
	Falling	3500–6500	216.54–179.62
1–10	Rising	0–3500	0–265.41
	Maximum	3500	265.41
	Falling	3500–6700	265.41–256.18
1–11	Rising	0–3000	0–351.72
	Maximum	3000	351.72
	Falling	3000–6500	351.72–175.31

The correlation dimension continuously declines during the falling stage. In this stage, main failures initially appeared locally, resulting in abnormal AE energy rates in terms of both numerical values and time sequences. Consequently, the correlation dimension declines. Subsequently, microcracks form and connect these localized main failures. During this period, the number and energy rate of AE events are relatively low, leading to a continuous decline in the correlation dimension. Finally, as the connectivity between localized main failures increases, cracks rapidly expand and form a major failure surface in the specimen. The AE events generated during this period exhibit abrupt timing and high energy rates. The correlation dimension continues to decrease accordingly. The maximum correlation dimensions of 1–6, 1–7, 1–10, and 1–11 appear at 3500 s (760 s earlier than the peak stress point), 3500 s (830 s earlier than the peak stress point), 3500 s (1560 s earlier than the peak stress point), and 3000 s (900 s earlier than the peak stress point), respectively. Therefore, the correlation dimension can also be considered as precursor information for rock failure.

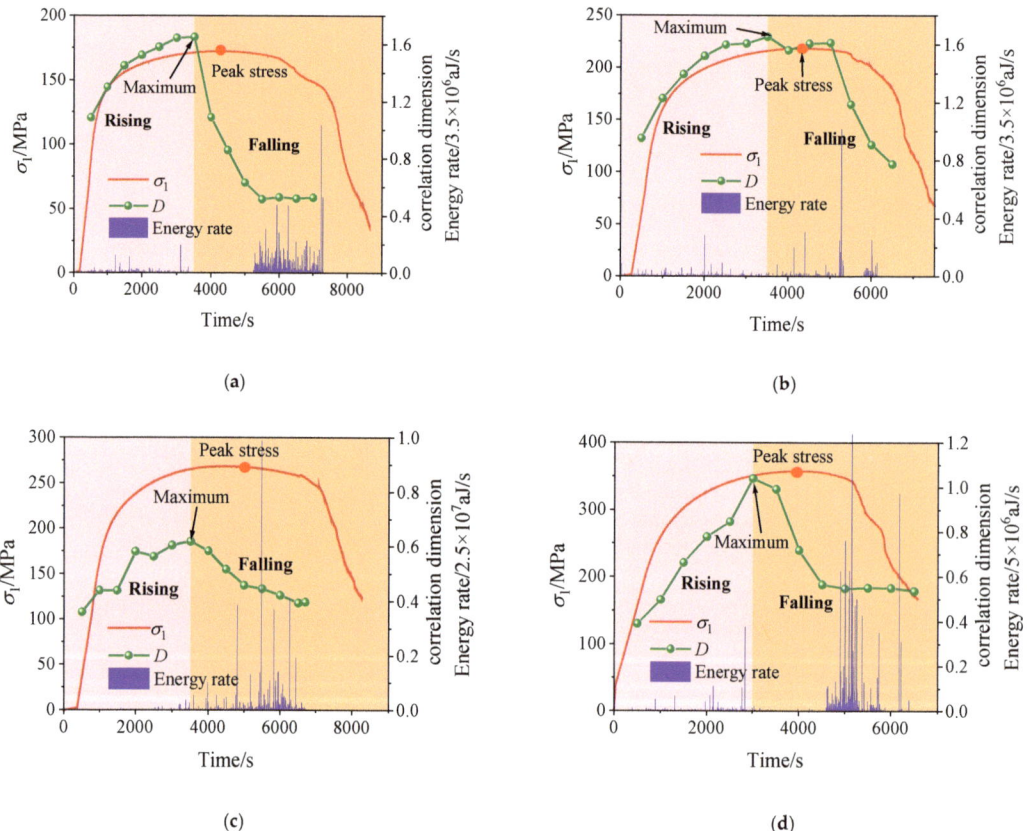

Figure 10. Curves of the correlation dimension, energy rate, and stress with time: (**a**) 1–6; (**b**) 1–7; (**c**) 1–10; and (**d**) 1–11.

4. Discussion

The b value and correlation dimension calculated based on AE events both can well describe the fracture propagation and failure process in rock. They all decrease before specimen destruction, which indicates that rock failure is a process of dimension reduction and dissipation. The b value and correlation dimension both can be used as effective indicators to evaluate the stability of rock masses and provide advanced warning signals. The b value fluctuates for a long time before continuously falling, so it is difficult to determine the decent point. The change in the correlation dimension is relatively simple, which only has rising and falling stages in the entire destruction process. However, a sudden increase or decrease in the AE energy rate can lead to the correlation dimension decreasing, and the reason for the decrease usually cannot be determined. In summary, the correlation dimension is chosen as the main index, and the b value is chosen as a secondary index for the precursor of rock failure. The surrounding rock stability state has the following three kinds of situations (Figure 11).

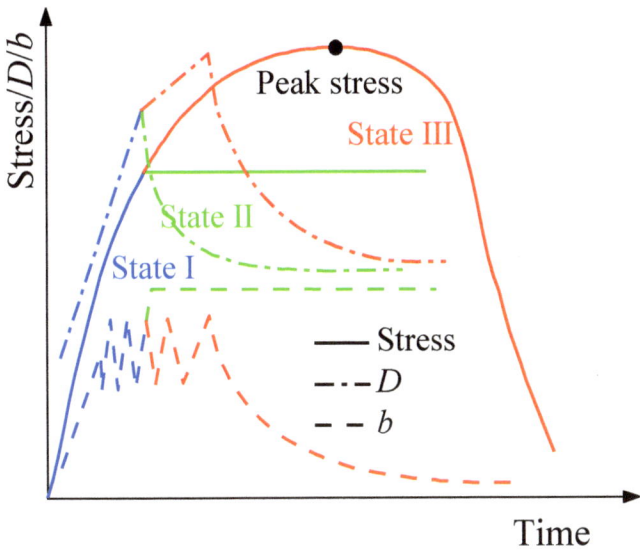

Figure 11. Sketch of the relationship between stable state, fractal dimension, b, and stress.

(1) Surrounding rock stress is redistributing, and damage continuously increases with increasing stress, which is similar to the active stage in laboratory experiments. In this situation, the correlation dimension continually increases, and the b value keeps fluctuating after a short increase (State I in Figure 11).

(2) Stress redistribution has been completed. But the surrounding rock is still in a stable state and does not produce AE events anymore. Most AE events received during this state are high-frequency noise events. Both the AE energy rate and events are reduced suddenly, and the proportion of small events increases. The correlation dimension suddenly drops, but the b value remains unchanged after a short rise (State II in Figure 11).

(3) The surrounding rock stress is redistributing again. As the stress increases, the surrounding rock is gradually destroyed, which is similar to a complete laboratory experiment. This situation has a significant impact on engineering safety. Therefore, it is necessary to predict the stability of the surrounding rock in advance before the surrounding rock destruction. The correlation dimension and b value continuously decrease before rock failure, which has been validated using laboratory experiments. So, it is necessary to take some measures to avoid the occurrence of dynamic disasters when the correlation dimension and b value both decrease (State III in Figure 11).

In summary, the comprehensive correlation dimension and b value can simply and accurately characterize the different stability of the surrounding rock and further warn of the destruction of the surrounding rock. It is necessary to calculate the correlation dimension and b value from time to time and always pay attention to their change during tunneling. When the correlation dimension remains unchanged or increases, the surrounding rock is still in the process of stress adjustment and is in a stable state. When the correlation dimension and the b value decrease at the same time, the surrounding rock will be destroyed, and protective measures need to be taken. When the correlation dimension decreases and the b value remains stable after a brief rise, the stress adjustment in the surrounding rock is complete, and the surrounding rock is still in a relatively stable state.

5. Limitations and Future Works

In this paper, the AE characteristics of specimens are studied in detail. However, the physical properties and the deformation characteristics of specimens were not mentioned, which is important to study rock failure [37]. In this paper, the correlation dimension is chosen as the main index, and the b value is chosen as the secondary index for the precursor of granite failure. However, the method is still in the laboratory stage and has not been verified on-site. In future works, the physical properties and the deformation characteristics will be studied using theoretical analysis, physical experiments, and numerical simulation, focusing on the investigation of failure evolution in a specimen, which can be studied using nuclear magnetic resonance, micro-X-ray computed tomography, and so on. In future works, the method for the precursor of granite failure proposed in this article will be verified and applied in an engineering site. Based on the experimental results of the engineering site, the predictive indicators will be further quantified and analyzed. Then, quantitative indicators will be proposed.

6. Conclusions

This study conducted triaxial compressive tests of granite specimens and monitored AE signals during the experiments. AE fractal characteristic parameters were studied. The AE b value and correlation dimension were calculated using the G-P algorithm, which was used to predict the precursor information of rock failure. The conclusions are as follows.

(1) The rock failure process can be divided into the initial stage, active stage, quiet stage, and failure stage based on the characteristics of AE events. During the quiet stage, the number of AE events is very few and the amplitude remains in a constant state. The quiet stage can be selected as a precursor information of rock failure.

(2) The AE b value and correlation dimension both can describe the rock failure process and show a continuous decline before destruction. But the b value fluctuates for a long time before continuously falling. A sudden increase or decrease in the AE energy rate can lead to a decrease in the correlation dimension, and the reason for the decrease usually cannot be determined.

(3) Regarding the comprehensive correlation dimension and b value, the correlation dimension is chosen as the main index, and the b value is chosen as the secondary index for the precursor of rock failure, which can simply and accurately evaluate the different stability of the surrounding rock and further warn of the destruction of the surrounding rock.

Author Contributions: Conceptualization, W.R.; methodology, W.R. and C.W.; validation, Y.Z. and D.X.; formal analysis, C.W.; investigation, Y.Z. and D.X.; resources, W.R. and C.W.; data curation, C.W. and Y.Z.; writing—original draft preparation, W.R.; writing—review and editing, C.W.; visualization, Y.Z.; supervision, W.R. and D.X.; project administration, Y.Z.; funding acquisition, W.R., C.W., Y.Z. and D.X. All authors have read and agreed to the published version of the manuscript.

Funding: This work was supported by the National Natural Science Foundation of China (Grant Nos. 52104082), the Science and Technology Development Fund Project of China Coal Research Institute (Grant Nos. 2021CX-II-12 and 2022CX-I-04), Science and Technology Project of China Energy Investment Corporation (CEIC) (GJNY2030XDXM-19-01.2, GJNY-21-42) and the Open Fund of State Key Laboratory of Water Resource Protection and Utilization in Coal Mining (GJNY-20-113-04).

Data Availability Statement: Not applicable.

Conflicts of Interest: The authors declare no conflict of interest.

References

1. Akdag, S.; Karakus, M.; Nguyen, G.D.; Taheri, A.; Bruning, T. Evaluation of the propensity of strain burst in brittle granite base on post-peak energy analysis. *Undergr. Space* **2019**, *6*, 1–11. [CrossRef]
2. Zhou, Z.; Cai, X.; Li, X.; Cao, W.; Du, X. Dynamic Response and Energy Evolution of Sandstone Under Coupled Static–Dynamic Compression: Insights from Experimental Study into Deep Rock Engineering Applications. *Rock Mech. Rock Eng.* **2020**, *5*, 1305–1331. [CrossRef]

Xie, H.; Gao, F.; Ju, Y. Research and development of rock mechanics in deep ground engineering. *Chin. J. Rock Mech. Eng.* **2015**, *34*, 2161–2178.

Bieniawski, Z.T. Mechanism of brittle rock fracture: Part 1—Theory of the fracture process. *Int. J. Rock Mech. Min. Sci. Geomech. Abstr.* **1967**, *4*, 395–406. [CrossRef]

Sueyoshi, K.; Kitamura, M.; Lei, X.; Katayama, I. Identification of fracturing behavior in thermally cracked granite using the frequency spectral characteristics of acoustic emission. *J. Mineral. Petrol. Sci.* **2023**, *118*, 221014. [CrossRef]

Lockner, D.A.; Byerlee, J.D.; Kuksenko, V.; Ponomarev, A.; Sidorin, A. Quasi-static fault growth and shear fracture energy in granite. *Nature* **1991**, *359*, 39–42. [CrossRef]

Thompson, B.D.; Young, R.P.; Lockner, D.A. Observations of premonitory acoustic emission and slip nucleation during a stick slip experiment in smooth faulted Westerly granite. *Geophys. Res. Lett.* **2005**, *32*, 10304. [CrossRef]

Vilhelm, J.; Vladimír, R.; Tomáš, L.; Živor, R. Application of autocorrelation analysis for interpreting acoustic emission in rock. *Int. J. Rock Mech. Min. Sci.* **2008**, *45*, 1068–1081. [CrossRef]

Rudajev, V.; Vilhelm, J.; Lokajcek, T. Laboratory studies of acoustic emission prior to uniaxial compressive rock failure. *Int. J. Rock Mech. Min. Sci.* **2000**, *37*, 699–704. [CrossRef]

Vishal, V.; Ranjith, P.G.; Singh, T.N. An experimental investigation on behaviour of coal under fluid saturation, using acoustic emission. *J. Nat. Gas Sci. Eng.* **2015**, *22*, 428–436. [CrossRef]

Ishida, T.; Kanagawa, T.; Kanaori, Y. Source distribution of acoustic emissions during an in-situ direct shear test: Implications for an analog model of seismogenic faulting in an inhomogeneous rock mass. *Eng. Geol.* **2010**, *110*, 66–76. [CrossRef]

Moradian, Z.; Einstein, H.H.; Ballivy, G. Detection of cracking levels in brittle rocks by parametric analysis of the acoustic emission signals. *Rock Mech. Rock Eng.* **2016**, *49*, 785–800. [CrossRef]

Shkuratnik, V.L.; Nikolenko, P.V.; Koshelev, A.E. Spectral characteristic of acoustic emission in loaded coal specimens for failure prediction. *J. Min. Sci.* **2017**, *53*, 818–823. [CrossRef]

Abbas, H.A.; Mohamed, Z.; Kudus, S.A. Anisotropic AE Attenuation in Mapping of Composite Specimen Progressive Failure under Unconfined Loading. *Int. J. Geomech.* **2023**, *23*, 04023005. [CrossRef]

Yang, J.; Zhao, K.; Song, Y.; Yan, Y.; He, Z.; Zhou, Y.; Gu, S. Acoustic emission characteristics and fractal evolution of rock splitting and failure processes under different loading rates. *Arab. J. Geosci.* **2022**, *15*, 265. [CrossRef]

Holcomb, D.J. General theory of the Kaiser effect. *Int. J. Rock Mech. Min. Sci. Geomech. Abstr.* **1993**, *30*, 929–935. [CrossRef]

Kusunose, K.; Lei, X.; Nishizawa, O.; Satoh, T. Effect of grain size on fractal structure of acoustic emission hypocenter distribution in granitic rock. *Phys. Earth Planet. Inter.* **1991**, *67*, 194–199. [CrossRef]

Mandelbrot, B.B. *The Fractal Geometry of Nature*; Freeman: San Francisco, CA, USA, 1983.

Heping, X. *Introduction to Fractal Rock Mechanics*; Science Press: Beijing, China, 1996.

Gutenberg, B.; Richter, C.F. Frequency of earthquakes in California. *Bull. Seismol. Soc. Am.* **1944**, *34*, 185–188. [CrossRef]

Dong, L.; Zhang, L.; Liu, H.; Du, K.; Liu, X. Acoustic Emission b Value Characteristics of Granite under True Triaxial Stress. *Mathematics* **2022**, *10*, 451. [CrossRef]

Smith, W.D. The b-value as an earthquake precursor. *Nature* **1981**, *289*, 136–139. [CrossRef]

Schroeder, M. *Fractals, Chaos, Power Laws: Minutes from an Infinite Paradise*; W. H. Freeman: New York, NY, USA, 1991.

Costin, L.S. A microcrack model for the deformation and failure of brittle rock. *J. Geophys. Res. Solid Earth* **1983**, *88*, 9485–9492. [CrossRef]

Kong, X.; Wang, E.; Hu, S.; Shen, R.; Li, X.; Zhan, T. Fractal characteristics and acoustic emission of coal containing methane in triaxial compression failure. *J. Appl. Geophys.* **2016**, *124*, 139–147. [CrossRef]

Carpinteri, A.; Lacidogna, G.; Niccolini, G. Fractal analysis of damage detected in concrete structural elements under loading. *Chaos Solitons Fractals* **2009**, *42*, 2047–2056. [CrossRef]

Scholz, C. The frequency-magnitude relation of microfracturing in rock and its relation to earthquakes. *Bull. Seismol. Soc. Am.* **1968**, *58*, 399–415. [CrossRef]

Yin, X.G.; Li, S.L.; Tang, H.Y.; Pei, J.L. Study on quiet period and its fractal characteristics of rock failure acoustic emission. *Chin. J. Rock Mech. Eng.* **2009**, *28*, 3383–3390.

Virkar, Y.; Clauset, A. Power-Law Distributions in Empirical Data. *Siam Rev.* **2009**, *51*, 661–703. [CrossRef]

Hayakawa, K.; Nakamura, T.; Yonezawa, H.; Tanaka, S. Detection of damage and fracture of forging die by fractal property of acoustic emission. *Mater. Trans.* **2004**, *45*, 3136–3141. [CrossRef]

Shan, L. *Triassic Granitoids in Beishan-Inner Mongolia, China and Its Tectonic Implications*; Chinese Academy of Geological Sciences: Beijing, China, 2013.

Wang, J.; Chen, L.; Su, R.; Zhao, X. The Beishan underground research laboratory for geological disposal of high-level radioactive waste in China: Planning, site selection, site characterization and in situ tests. *J. Rock Mech. Geotech. Eng.* **2018**, *10*, 411–435. [CrossRef]

Nelder, J.A.; Mead, R. A Simplex Method for Function Minimization. *Comput. J.* **1964**, *7*, 308–313. [CrossRef]

Geiger, L. Probability method for the determination of earthquake epicenters from the arrival time only. *Bull. St. Louis Univ.* **1912**, *8*, 60–71.

Spence, W. Relative epicenter determination using P-wave arrival-time differences. *Bull. Seismol. Soc. Am.* **1980**, *70*, 171–183.

36. Grassberger, P.; Procaccia, I. Characterization of strange attractors. *Phys. Rev. Lett.* **1983**, *50*, 346–349. [CrossRef]
37. Cai, X.; Yuan, J.; Zhou, Z.; Tan, L.; Wang, P.; Wang, S.; Wang, S. Effects of hole shape on mechanical behavior and fracturing mechanism of rock: Implications for instability of underground openings. *Tunn. Undergr. Space Technol.* **2023**, *141*, 105360. [CrossRef]

Disclaimer/Publisher's Note: The statements, opinions and data contained in all publications are solely those of the individual author(s) and contributor(s) and not of MDPI and/or the editor(s). MDPI and/or the editor(s) disclaim responsibility for any injury to people or property resulting from any ideas, methods, instructions or products referred to in the content.

Time-Frequency Response of Acoustic Emission and Its Multi-Fractal Analysis for Rocks with Different Brittleness under Uniaxial Compression

Jianchun Ou [1], Enyuan Wang [2,*] and Xinyu Wang [2]

[1] State Key Laboratory for Fine Exploration and Intelligent Development of Coal Resources, China University of Mining and Technology, Xuzhou 221116, China; oujianchun@cumt.edu.cn
[2] School of Safety Engineering, China University of Mining and Technology, Xuzhou 221116, China; wxytopcumt@cumt.edu.cn
* Correspondence: eywangcumt@163.com or weytop@cumt.edu.cn

Abstract: The occurrence of rock burst hazards is closely related to the brittleness of rocks. Current research has paid less attention to the in-depth relationship between rock brittleness and acoustic emission (AE) signal characteristics and precursor information caused by rock fracture. Therefore, in order to further improve the accuracy of the AE monitoring of rockburst hazards, uniaxial compression tests were carried out and AE were monitored for rocks with different brittleness (yellow sandstone, white sandstone, marble, and limestone) in this paper. The relationship between the mechanical properties and the time-frequency characteristics of the AE was analyzed. In addition, the multi-fractal theory was introduced to further deconstruct and mine the AE signals, and the multi-fractal characteristics of AE from rocks with different brittleness were investigated. The results show that the stronger the brittleness of the rock, the higher the main frequency and main frequency amplitude of the AE. Brittleness is positively correlated with the multi-fractal parameter $\Delta \alpha$ (uniformity of data distribution) and negatively correlated with Δf (frequency difference between large and small data). In addition, the dynamics of $\Delta \alpha$ and Δf provide new indicators for AE monitoring of rock stability, and their abrupt changes can be regarded as precursors of failure. The weaker the brittleness of the rock, the earlier the failure precursor is and the more significant it is. This has potential engineering application value, which can help identify rockburst precursors and take timely protective measures to ensure engineering safety.

Keywords: rockburst; brittleness; acoustic emission; multi-fractal

MSC: 37F05

1. Introduction

With the depletion of shallow coal resources, coal mining worldwide is gradually moving into the deeper parts of the earth [1,2]. Concerning the rupture of rock under high-stress environments, in deep underground conditions, it is very easy to induce a rock burst disaster, which seriously threatens the safety of the project [3–6]. Acoustic emission (AE), which is generated by microcrack propagation, is a ubiquitous phenomenon associated with brittle fracture and reflects a wealth of information about rock fracture [7]. AE is widely used in engineering as well as in laboratories as a favorable tool for rockburst monitoring [8–10]. An in-depth understanding of AE signal characteristics, identification of precursor information of rock failure, and timely adoption of risk avoidance means are crucial to reducing the risk of rock burst disasters.

Research on the characteristics of AE signals during rock loading has been carried out extensively. He et al. [11] investigated the AE characteristics of strainbursts under true triaxial unloading conditions, including the time series parameters and frequency characteristics of the signals. Brittle fracture processes in rocks during uniaxial compression testing were identified and characterized by combined AE and strain gauge monitoring by Eberhardt et al. [12]. Dong et al. [13] studied the AE b-value characteristics of granite under true triaxial compression conditions, and the decrease in AE b-value can be used as a precursor of rock instability. Li et al. [14] studied the AE response and AE weakening mechanism under uniaxial compression of sandstones with different water contents. Du et al. [15] carried out a series of rock tests to determine the fracture patterns and hence elucidate the microcracking characteristics of the rocks through AE RA/AF values.

In fact, the disaster occurrence of a rock burst is closely related to the inherent properties of the rock itself, such as strength and brittleness [16–18]. Due to the complexity of the strata, it is important to study the AE characteristics of different types of rocks to improve the accuracy of monitoring. In addition, fractal theory has been proposed to describe the existence of irregularities and complex systems in nature and has been widely used in the field of rock mechanics [19]. Several studies have been conducted to show that signals such as acoustic emission and electromagnetic radiation during rock fracture have fractal characteristics [14,20]. Therefore, in this paper, uniaxial compression tests and AE monitoring were carried out on four rocks (yellow sandstone, white sandstone, marble, and greywacke) with different brittleness. The relationship between brittleness and AE time-frequency characteristics is analyzed. Importantly, the multi-fractal theory was introduced to further explore the AE signal characteristics. The results of this study can provide new indicators for the AE monitoring of rock mass stability and further improve the effectiveness of disaster warnings.

2. Experimental Materials and Procedures

2.1. Sample Preparation

Four rocks were selected for the follow-up study, which were yellow sandstone, white sandstone, marble, and limestone. Their densities were 1.8 g/cm^3, 2.7 g/cm^3, 3.1 g/cm^3, and 2.4 g/cm^3, respectively. They were machined into standard samples with a diameter of 50 mm and a height of 100 mm for uniaxial compression testing according to the standards of the International Society of Rock Mechanics (ISRM). They were tested and analyzed by X-ray diffraction (XRD) in order to clarify their material composition. Figure 1 shows the physical objects of the four specimens as well as their XRD spectra. The mineral compositions obtained from the analyses are specifically listed in Table 1. The mineral components of the yellow sandstone are quartz (59.5%), k-feldspar (37.5%), calcite (0.8%), and clay (2.1%). The mineral components of the white sandstone are quartz (32%), k-feldspar (4.5%), plagioclase (52.8%), calcite (0.5%), and clay (10.3%). The mineral component of the marble is calcite (100%). The mineral components of the limestone are quartz (1.1%), calcite (96.1%), and clay (2.8%).

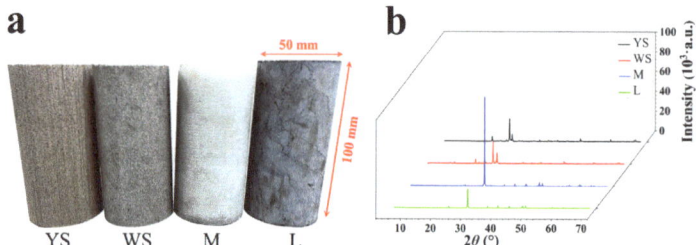

Figure 1. Physical specimens (**a**) and their XRD spectra (**b**).

Table 1. Mineral components.

Mineral Composition \ Rock Type	Yellow Sandstone	White Sandstone	Marble	Limestone
Quartz (%)	59.5	32	0	1.1
K-feldspar (%)	37.5	4.5	0	0
Plagioclase (%)	0	52.8	0	0
Calcite (%)	0.8	0.5	100	96.1
Clay (%)	2.1	10.3	0	2.8

2.2. Test Scheme

The test system consists of a press and an AE monitoring instrument. The physical object is shown in Figure 2. The press adopted the new SANS microcomputer-controlled electro-hydraulic servo pressure testing machine. The AE monitoring instrument adopted the 24-channel Micro-II type AE monitoring host of the American Physical Acoustics Corporation with a NANO-30 AE probe and a preamplifier. The loading rate of the press was set to 500 N/s. The AE acquisition parameters, including threshold, amplification, and acquisition frequency, were set to 40 dB, 40 dB, and 2×10^6/s, respectively. The AE probe was affixed to the surface of the sample by means of a special coupling agent. The instrument was connected, and the AE was calibrated. Afterwards, loading and AE acquisition were synchronized until the specimen was completely destroyed. Three replicate experiments were performed for each rock type, totaling 12 samples. The mechanical test results of all specimens are shown in Table 2.

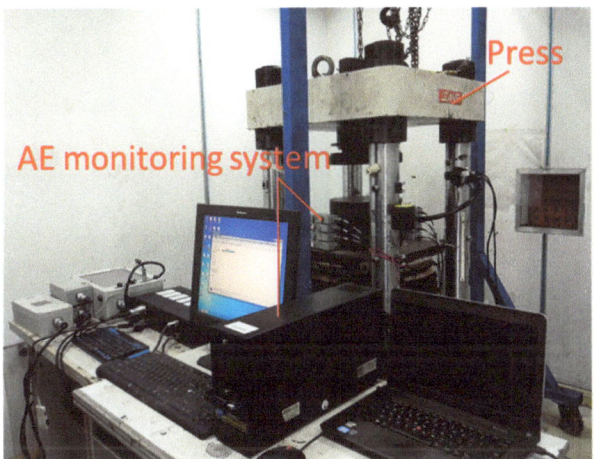

Figure 2. Physical test system.

Table 2. Mechanical test results.

Rock Types	USC (MPa) Value	USC (MPa) Average	E (GPa) Value	E (GPa) Average	B_I Value	B_I Average
Yellow sandstone	38.3		6.0		0.68	
	36.6	38.0	5.4	5.8	0.66	0.67
	39.1		6.2		0.68	
White sandstone	69.8		11.3		0.87	
	68.3	70.1	10.3	11.3	0.89	0.88
	72.1		12.3		0.87	

Table 2. Cont.

Rock Types	USC (MPa)		E (GPa)		B_I	
	Value	Average	Value	Average	Value	Average
Marble	52.3 49.3 53.1	51.6	13.3 12.4 14.2	13.3	0.62 0.60 0.59	0.60
Limestone	45.1 48.2 43.2	45.5	8.8 8.1 9.0	8.6	0.71 0.70 0.71	0.71

3. Mechanical Properties of Different Rocks

Figure 3a shows typical stress–strain curves for a set of different rocks. The curve of the yellow sandstone (YS) sample in the figure is used as an example for annotation. All samples went through four stages [21]: compaction (o-a), elastic deformation (a-b), crack propagation (b-c), and ultimate failure (c-d). The curve in the compaction stage showed an upward concave shape due to the closure of the original pores and cracks. The stress in the elastic deformation stage increased linearly with strain. After the end of elastic deformation, the crack inside the specimen developed and expanded. The damage intensified and the curve gradually became non-linear. Strain-hardening behavior was exhibited. Massive propagation and penetration of cracks within the specimen occurs when the stress is loaded to the limit of the specimen's capacity, i.e., the uniaxial compressive strength UCS of the specimen. This leads to a reduction in the load-carrying capacity of the specimen, which is shown in the stress–strain curve by an increase in strain and a gradual fall in stress.

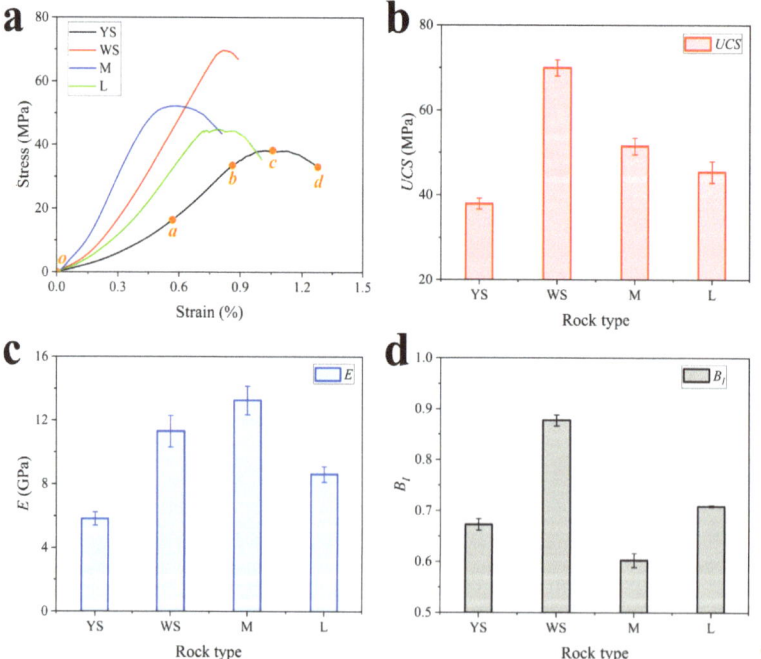

Figure 3. Mechanical properties: (a) stress–strain curves; (b) uniaxial compressive strength; (c) elastic modulus; (d) brittleness index.

The *UCS*, elastic modulus *E*, and brittleness of all samples are statistically presented in Figure 3b–d. Among them, the brittleness was characterized using a classical index B_I [22]:

$$B_I = U^{ep}/U^p = \frac{UCS^2}{2E} / \int_0^{\varepsilon^p} \sigma d\varepsilon \tag{1}$$

where U^{ep} is the elastic energy stored at peak stress, U^p is the total amount of work done by the outside world at peak stress, and ε^p is the strain at peak stress. It reflects the energy storage capacity of the material. The *UCS* of yellow sandstone, white sandstone, marble, and limestone averaged 38 MPa, 70.1 MPa, 51.6 MPa, and 45.5 MPa, respectively, whereas the *E* were 5.8 GPa, 11.3 GPa, 13.3 GPa, and 8.6 GPa, respectively. Furthermore, the order of brittleness of the four rocks from largest to smallest was white sandstone, limestone, yellow sandstone, and marble.

4. AE Time-Frequency Response of Different Rocks

4.1. Time-Series Variation of AE Energy

Figure 4 shows the time series of changes in AE energy during the loading process of different rock samples. Usually, the change in AE energy reflects the deformation and fracture process of the specimen well. In the early stage of loading, due to the randomness of the original cracks and pores, there were some fluctuations in the AE energy during the compaction stage. During the elastic deformation stage, there was basically no fracture inside the specimen [21], so the AE was not very active, and the energy value remained at a very low level. In the later loading stage, a large number of cracks propagated and penetrated inside the specimen, resulting in a strong AE response and high energy values. In addition, after loading to peak stress, the AE energy also reached its peak when failure occurred. The sudden increase in AE energy of the white sandstone sample during the later stage of loading was more sudden and violent, due to its higher strength and brittleness. The brittleness of marble was the weakest, so its sudden increase in AE was more advanced due to its greater damage and energy dissipation before peak stress.

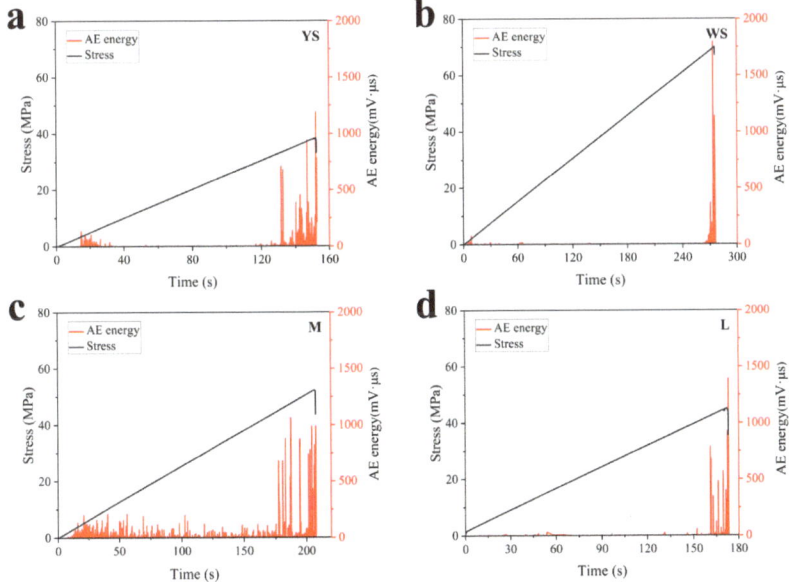

Figure 4. AE energy variations characteristics: (**a**) yellow sandstone; (**b**) white sandstone; (**c**) marble; (**d**) limestone.

4.2. AE Frequency Domain Characteristics

The frequency domain characteristics of AE were investigated by time-frequency transforming the AE hits at different stress level points (including at 20%, 60%, and 100% of the peak stress) during the loading process. The classical fast Fourier transform (FFT) method was used for the time-frequency transformation, and the spectrum obtained after the transformation is shown in Figure 5. The maximum amplitude of the AE signal and the corresponding frequency (i.e., the dominant frequency) were mainly explored. The dominant frequencies and dominant amplitudes for different rocks are summarized in Figure 6. In general, the amplitude of the AE signal gradually increased with increasing stress, while the frequency gradually decreased [23]. In terms of frequency specifically, the main frequency of the acoustic emission signal was above 250 KHz at the beginning of loading, while at the peak stress moments, the frequencies of the signals were all below 40 KHz. This is related to the scale of the crack, that is, the size of the crack. In the early stages of rock loading, the scale of the crack within the rock is small and tends to be a grain-wide fracture. Later in the loading period, a large number of cracks propagate and penetrate, and macroscopic cracks visible to the naked eye will appear. In general, large-scale cracks correspond to low-frequency, high-amplitude signals, while the opposite is true for small-scale cracks [23]. The evolution of AE signals during the loading process of all rocks has a basically similar law, i.e., it evolves from high-frequency, low-energy signals to low-frequency, high-energy signals with the increase of the fracture scale. The dominant frequency of the AE and its amplitude were correlated with the brittleness of the material when comparing different rocks. Specifically, the more brittle the rock, the higher the dominant frequency and the higher the amplitude of the signal, regardless of the stress level. White sandstone was the most brittle, and it had the highest dominant frequency and amplitude. Marble was the least brittle and had the lowest dominant frequency and amplitude.

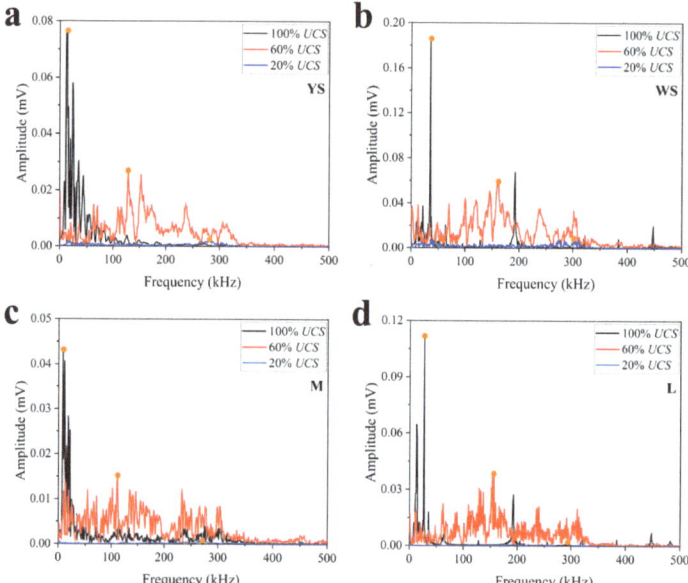

Figure 5. Frequency spectrum characteristics of AE at different stress levels: (**a**) yellow sandstone; (**b**) white sandstone; (**c**) marble; (**d**) limestone.

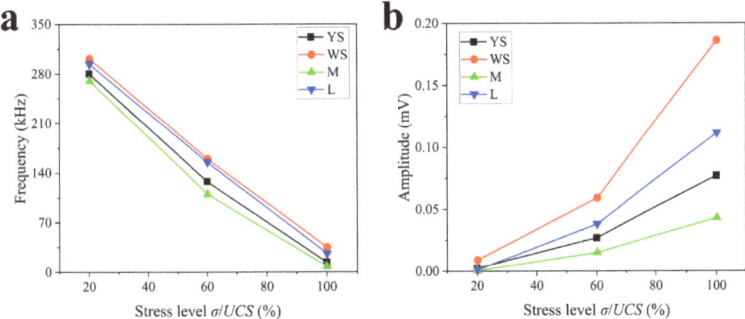

Figure 6. (a) AE dominant frequency and (b) dominant frequency amplitude for different stress levels.

5. AE Multi-Fractal Analysis of Different Rocks

5.1. Multi-Fractal Theory

In order to further reveal the AE characteristics of different brittle rocks, multi-fractal theory was introduced to deconstruct and analyze the AE energy data sequence. According to Hu et al. [20], the multi-fractal map α–$f(\alpha)$ can reflect the uneven distribution characteristics of the data. The width of the spectrum $\Delta\alpha$ ($\Delta\alpha = \alpha_{max} - \alpha_{min}$) reflects the uniformity of the data distribution. The larger the width of the spectrum, the more diverse the data and the more pronounced the multi-fractal characteristics. The Δf value ($\Delta f = f(\alpha_{max}) - f(\alpha_{min})$) of the spectrum reflects the relationship between the occurrence frequency of big data and small data. A smaller value of Δf means that big data occurs more frequently, and a larger value means that small data occurs more frequently. Moreover, $\Delta f > 0$ indicates that small data is dominant; $\Delta f < 0$ indicates that big data is dominant. It should be noted that big data refers to higher AE energy values, which usually imply large-scale rock fracturing events, while small data refers to lower AE energy values, which often imply small-scale rock fracturing events.

In this paper, the box dimension method is used to calculate the multi-fractal spectrum [14,20]. The AE energy data sequence is divided into N subsets, each of size k. The probability distribution $\{P_i(k)\}$ is calculated for each subset:

$$X_q(k) \equiv \sum P_i(k)^q \sim k^{\tau(q)} \tag{2}$$

$$\tau(q) = \lim_{k \to 0} \frac{\ln X_q(k)}{\ln k} \tag{3}$$

$$\alpha = \frac{d(\mu(q))}{dq} = \frac{d}{dq}\left(\lim_{k \to 0} \frac{\ln X_q(k)}{\ln k}\right) \tag{4}$$

$$f(\alpha) = \alpha q - \tau(q) \tag{5}$$

where i is a time stamp reflecting the amount of data. The $X_q(k)$ is the defined partition function, i.e., the statistical moments. $\tau(q)$ is the quality index, $\infty < q < +\infty$. α is a constant called the singularity index that controls the singularity of $\{P_i(k)\}$. It reflects the inhomogeneity of the subset of $\{x_i\}$ probabilities for different k. The $f(\alpha)$ denotes the frequency of the subset represented by α over all subsets, and it is also the fractal dimension of the subset α.

5.2. Multi-Fractal Feature

Figure 7 shows the multi-fractal maps of the AE energy sequences for a set of different rocks for the whole loading process. The values of the multi-fractal parameters $\Delta\alpha$ and Δf for all specimens of different rocks are counted in Figure 8. The white sandstone has the largest Δα value and the widest multi-fractal spectrum, which means that it has the most inhomogeneous distribution of the AE energy, with obvious multi-fractal features. The order of Δα value size is white sandstone, limestone, yellow sandstone, and marble. In terms of Δf values, all rocks have an Δf greater than 0. This suggests that it is the smaller AE energy data that occur more frequently and that their performance is dominant. The order of size of Δf value is marble, yellow sandstone, limestone, and white sandstone. This is the exact reverse of the situation with the Δα value. White sandstone has excellent AE signals for large energy values. Marble has excellent AE signals for small energy values. Figure 9 shows the relationship between the brittleness index B_I and the multi-fractal parameter, B_I is positively proportional to Δα and inversely proportional to Δf. The following significant linear relationship exists between them:

$$\Delta\alpha = 4.81 B_I - 2.34 \quad R^2 = 0.9 \tag{6}$$

$$\Delta f = -0.46 B_I - 0.65 \quad R^2 = 0.93 \tag{7}$$

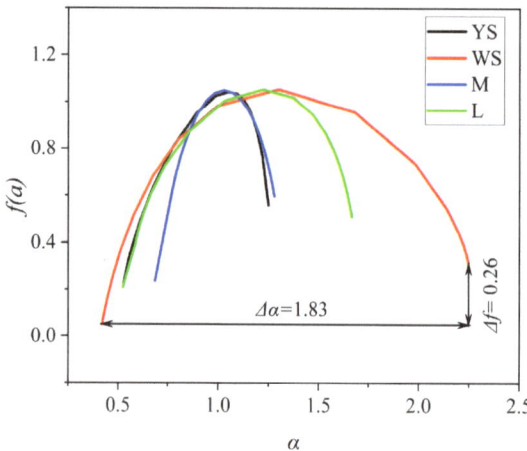

Figure 7. Multi-fractal spectrum.

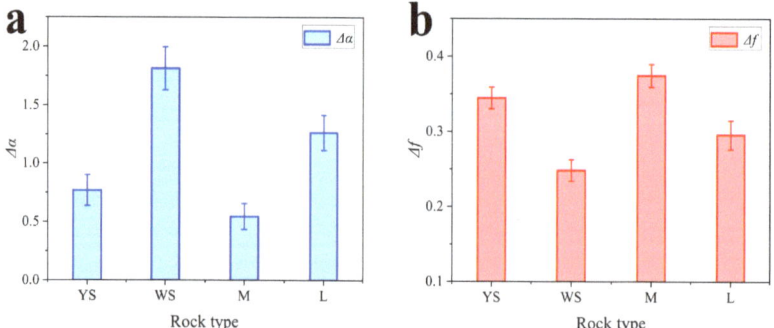

Figure 8. Multi-fractal parameters for different rocks: (**a**) Δα; (**b**) Δf.

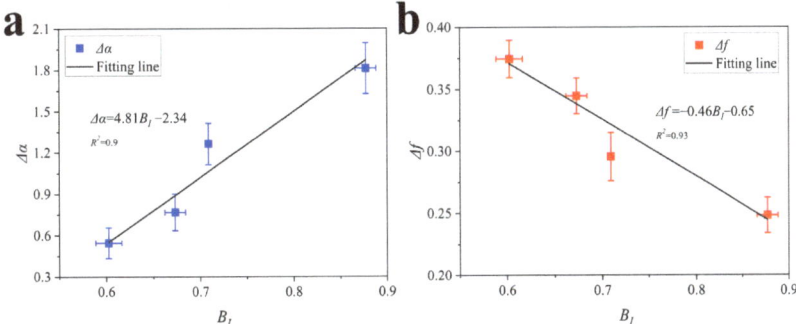

Figure 9. Relationship between brittleness index and multi-fractal parameters: (**a**) Δa; (**b**) Δf.

This means that the more brittle the rock, the more heterogeneous the AE distribution and the more dominant the AE signal produced by large fractures.

5.3. Time-Varying Multi-Fractal

In order to explore the dynamics of the data characteristics of the AE energy during the loading process, dynamic multi-fractal parameters can be calculated [14,20]. Therefore, we assume that the time series of AE is $\{y_i\}$ and the total time length of AE is T. In the time window l_t, if the sampling interval is Δt, then the set of AE sequences X_m in l_t is as follows:

$$X_m = \{x_i = y_i | y_i = nm\Delta t; (l_t + nm\Delta t)\}, m = 0, \cdots, \frac{T - l_t}{n\Delta t} \tag{8}$$

where n is a positive integer. Then, at time $T_m = l_t + nm\Delta t$, the dynamic multi-fractal parameters are as follows:

$$\alpha_m = \frac{d(\tau_m(q))}{dq} = \frac{d}{dq}\left(\lim_{\varepsilon \to 0} \frac{\ln X_q(\varepsilon)}{\ln \varepsilon}\right) \tag{9}$$

$$f_m(\alpha) = \alpha_m q - \tau_m(q) \tag{10}$$

The calculated results for different rocks are shown in Figure 10. The evolution of the multi-fractal parameters for different rocks has a similar pattern. In the early stage of loading, the rock is essentially undamaged, with only some microfractures, and the AE signals are all low, so Δa is also maintained at a low level, while Δf is high. In the later stages of loading, large ruptures occur, AE increases abruptly, and the signal becomes more complex, so the Δa value increases. When a large rupture occurs, the large-energy AE signals excel, so Δf falls abruptly. In addition, the dynamically varying multi-fractal parameters can provide new and referable indicators for AE monitoring of rock stability. The sudden increase in Δa value and the sudden decrease in Δf value can be used as a precursor of rock failure and instability, which is potentially valuable for engineering applications. Moreover, rocks that are less brittle have more energy dissipation and more fracture before peak stress, i.e., before failure, and their precursors are more advanced and significant. Therefore, some means of material modification, such as water injection, to reduce the brittleness of the rock and enhance its plastic characteristics [14,24–27] is not only conducive to reducing the risk of dynamic hazards, such as rock bursts, but also conducive to the identification of precursors and early warning of rock instability.

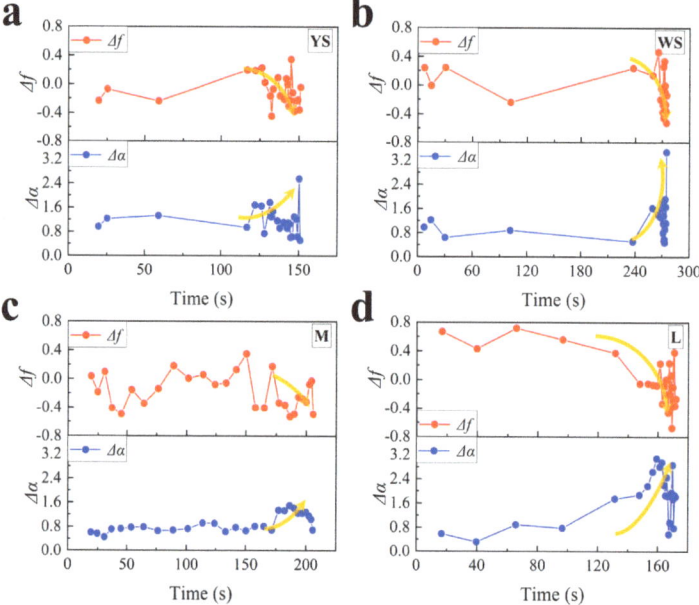

Figure 10. Time-series variation of multi-fractal parameters: (**a**) yellow sandstone; (**b**) white sandstone; (**c**) marble; (**d**) limestone.

Moreover, The AE response of rocks is not only related to the properties of the rock itself but also to the loading mode and conditions, the water content of the rock, the temperature, and other factors. In this paper, we have only investigated the effect of the rock's own properties by controlling the variables. More research will be conducted in the future to investigate the effects of more types of rocks and other mining conditions.

6. Conclusions and Summary

In this paper, uniaxial compression tests were carried out on rock materials with different brittleness, including yellow sandstone, white sandstone, marble, and limestone. Moreover, the monitoring of AE signals was also carried out. The correlation between their mechanical properties and the time-frequency characteristics of the AE was analyzed.

Strongly brittle rocks show a more abrupt and violent increase in AE during failure, while weakly brittle rocks have a richer AE precursor prior to failure. During the loading process, the main frequency of AE gradually decreases, and the main frequency amplitude increases. The brittleness of the rock is directly proportional to the main frequency of the AE, which is also directly proportional to the amplitude of the main frequency.

The multi-fractal theory was introduced to further data mining and deconstruction of the acoustic emission signals, and the multi-fractal features of acoustic emission from different brittle rocks were explored. It is found that rock brittleness is positively proportional to the multi-fractal parameter Δa (uniformity of data distribution) and inversely proportional to the parameter Δf (frequency difference between large and small data). In addition, the dynamic change of Δa and Δf can provide new indicators for the AE monitoring of rock stability, and their abrupt change can be regarded as a precursor of rock failure.

The new indicators are further deconstructed and analyzed from the AE data, which have potential engineering value and provide referable precursor information for an early warning of rockburst disasters. Promptly taking protective measures after sudden changes in indicators can ensure project safety. Moreover, the results in terms of signal frequency can also guide the selection of AE monitoring frequency bands in the project.

Author Contributions: Conceptualization, J.O. and E.W.; writing—original draft, J.O.; project administration, J.O. and E.W.; investigation, J.O. and X.W. All authors have read and agreed to the published version of the manuscript.

Funding: This work was supported by the National Natural Science Foundation of China (51974305).

Data Availability Statement: The related data used to support the findings of this study are included within the article.

Conflicts of Interest: The authors declare no conflict of interest.

References

1. Cai, X.; Yuan, J.; Zhou, Z.; Pi, Z.; Tan, L.; Wang, P.; Wang, S.; Wang, S. Effects of hole shape on mechanical behavior and fracturing mechanism of rock: Implications for instability of underground openings. *Tunn. Undergr. Space Technol.* **2023**, *141*, 105361. [CrossRef]
2. Xie, H.P.; Li, C.; He, Z.Q.; Li, C.B.; Lu, Y.Q.; Zhang, R.; Gao, M.Z.; Gao, F. Experimental study on rock mechanical behavior retaining the in situ geological conditions at different depths. *Int. J. Rock Mech. Min. Sci.* **2021**, *138*, 104548. [CrossRef]
3. Li, C.X.; Li, D.J.; Liu, X.L. Experimental study on the influence of intermediate principal stress on failure characteristics of strain rock burst for granite. *Bull. Eng. Geol. Environ.* **2023**, *82*, 340. [CrossRef]
4. Li, J.Y.; Liu, D.Q.; He, M.C.; Guo, Y.P. True Triaxial Experimental Study on the Variation Characteristics of Rockburst with the Number of Fast Unloading Surfaces. *Rock Mech. Rock Eng.* **2023**, *56*, 5585–5606. [CrossRef]
5. Li, H.R.; He, M.C.; Qiao, Y.F.; Cheng, T.; Xiao, Y.M.; Gu, Z.J. Mode I fracture properties and energy partitioning of sandstone under coupled static-dynamic loading: Implications for rockburst. *Theor. Appl. Fract. Mech.* **2023**, *127*, 104025. [CrossRef]
6. Li, H.R.; Qiao, Y.F.; He, M.C.; Shen, R.X.; Gu, Z.J.; Cheng, T.; Xiao, Y.M.; Tang, J. Effect of water saturation on dynamic behavior of sandstone after wetting-drying cycles. *Eng. Geol.* **2023**, *319*, 1070105. [CrossRef]
7. Lockner, D. The role of acoustic emission in the study of rock fracture. *Int. J. Rock Mech. Min. Sci. Geomech. Abstr.* **1993**, *30*, 883–899. [CrossRef]
8. Li, X.L.; Chen, S.J.; Liu, S.M.; Li, Z.H. AE waveform characteristics of rock mass under uniaxial loading based on Hilbert-Huang transform. *J. Cent. South Univ.* **2021**, *28*, 1843–1856. [CrossRef]
9. Di, Y.Y.; Wang, E.Y.; Huang, T. Identification method for microseismic, acoustic emission and electromagnetic radiation interference signals of rock burst based on deep neural networks. *Int. J. Rock Mech. Min. Sci.* **2023**, *170*, 105541. [CrossRef]
10. Lu, C.P.; Liu, G.J.; Liu, Y.; Zhang, N.; Xue, J.H.; Zhang, L. Microseismic multi-parameter characteristics of rockburst hazard induced by hard roof fall and high stress concentration. *Int. J. Rock Mech. Min. Sci.* **2015**, *76*, 18–32. [CrossRef]
11. He, M.C.; Miao, J.L.; Feng, J.L. Rock burst process of limestone and its acoustic emission characteristics under true-triaxial unloading conditions. *Int. J. Rock Mech. Min. Sci.* **2010**, *47*, 286–298. [CrossRef]
12. Eberhardt, E.; Stead, D.; Stimpson, B. Quantifying progressive pre-peak brittle fracture damage in rock during uniaxial compression. *Int. J. Rock Mech. Min. Sci.* **1999**, *36*, 361–380. [CrossRef]
13. Dong, L.J.; Zhang, L.Y.; Liu, H.N.; Du, K.; Liu, X.L. Acoustic Emission b Value Characteristics of Granite under True Triaxial Stress. *Mathematics* **2022**, *10*, 451. [CrossRef]
14. Li, H.R.; Qiao, Y.F.; Shen, R.X.; He, M.C.; Cheng, T.; Xiao, Y.M.; Tang, J. Effect of water on mechanical behavior and acoustic emission response of sandstone during loading process: Phenomenon and mechanism. *Eng. Geol.* **2021**, *294*, 106386. [CrossRef]
15. Du, K.; Li, X.F.; Tao, M.; Wang, S.F. Experimental study on acoustic emission (AE) characteristics and crack classification during rock fracture in several basic lab tests. *Int. J. Rock Mech. Min. Sci.* **2020**, *133*, 104411. [CrossRef]
16. Meng, F.Z.; Wong, L.N.Y.; Zhou, H. Rock brittleness indices and their applications to different fields of rock engineering: A review. *J. Rock Mech. Geotech. Eng.* **2021**, *13*, 221–247. [CrossRef]
17. Tang, H.M.; Wen, T.; Wang, Y.K. Brittleness evaluation based on the energy evolution throughout the failure process of rocks. *J. Pet. Sci. Eng.* **2020**, *194*, 107361. [CrossRef]
18. Xue, Y.; Liu, J.; Ranjith, P.G.; Gao, F.; Zhang, Z.Z.; Wang, S.H. Experimental investigation of mechanical properties, impact tendency, and brittleness characteristics of coal mass under different gas adsorption pressures. *Geomech. Geophys. Geo-Energy Geo-Resour.* **2022**, *8*, 131. [CrossRef]
19. Xie, H.; Pariseau, W.G. Fractal character and mechanism of rock bursts. *Int. J. Rock Mech. Min. Sci. Geomech. Abstr.* **1993**, *30*, 343–350. [CrossRef]
20. Hu, S.B.; Wang, E.Y.; Li, Z.H.; Shen, R.X.; Liu, J. Time-Varying Multifractal Characteristics and Formation Mechanism of Loaded Coal Electromagnetic Radiation. *Rock Mech. Rock Eng.* **2014**, *47*, 1821–1838. [CrossRef]
21. Cai, M.; Kaiser, P.K.; Tasaka, Y.; Maejima, T.; Morioka, H.; Minami, M. Generalized crack initiation and crack damage stress thresholds of brittle rock masses near underground excavations. *Int. J. Rock Mech. Min. Sci.* **2004**, *41*, 833–847. [CrossRef]
22. Hucka, V.; Das, B. Brittleness determination of rocks by different methods. *Int. J. Rock Mech. Min. Sci. Geomech. Abstr.* **1974**, *11*, 389–392. [CrossRef]
23. Jiang, R.C.; Dai, F.; Liu, Y.; Li, A.; Feng, P. Frequency Characteristics of Acoustic Emissions Induced by Crack Propagation in Rock Tensile Fracture. *Rock Mech. Rock Eng.* **2021**, *54*, 2053–2065. [CrossRef]

24. Cai, X.; Cheng, C.Q.; Zhao, Y.; Zhou, Z.L.; Wang, S.F. The role of water content in rate dependence of tensile strength of fine-grained sandstone. *Arch. Civ. Mech. Eng.* **2022**, *22*, 58. [CrossRef]
25. Li, H.R.; Shen, R.X.; Qiao, Y.F.; He, M.C. Acoustic emission signal characteristics and its critical slowing down phenomenon during the loading process of water-bearing sandstone. *J. Appl. Geophys.* **2021**, *194*, 104458. [CrossRef]
26. Li, H.R.; Qiao, Y.F.; Shen, R.X.; He, M.C. Electromagnetic radiation signal monitoring and multi-fractal analysis during uniaxial compression of water-bearing sandstone. *Measurement* **2022**, *196*, 111245. [CrossRef]
27. Ma, Q.; Liu, X.; Tan, Y.; Elsworth, D.; Shang, J.; Song, D.; Liu, X.; Yan, F. Numerical study of mechanical properties and microcrack evolution of double-layer composite rock specimens with fissures under uniaxial compression. *Eng. Fract. Mech.* **2023**, *289*, 10940. [CrossRef]

Disclaimer/Publisher's Note: The statements, opinions and data contained in all publications are solely those of the individual author(s) and contributor(s) and not of MDPI and/or the editor(s). MDPI and/or the editor(s) disclaim responsibility for any injury to people or property resulting from any ideas, methods, instructions or products referred to in the content.

Article

Dynamic Evolution of Coal Pore-Fracture Structure and Its Fractal Characteristics under the Action of Salty Solution

Min Wang [1], Yakun Tian [1,*], Zhijun Zhang [1], Qifeng Guo [2] and Lingling Wu [1]

[1] School of Resource & Environment and Safety Engineering, University of South China, Hengyang 421001, China; wangmin@usc.edu.cn (M.W.); 2003000550@usc.edu.cn (Z.Z.); 2013000541@usc.edu.cn (L.W.)

[2] School of Civil and Resource Engineering, University of Science and Technology Beijing, Beijing 100083, China; guoqifeng@ustb.edu.cn

* Correspondence: 2017000012@usc.edu.cn

Abstract: The instability and failure of coal pillars is one of the important factors leading to the catastrophic consequences of coal mine goaf collapse. Coal mine water has the characteristics of high salinity. Long-term mine water erosion can easily deform the coal pillar structure, eventually leading to instability and damage. This study carried out tests on coal samples soaked in salt solutions with different concentrations, and the nuclear magnetic resonance (NMR) method was used to obtain the dynamic evolution of the pore-fracture structure of coal. On the basis of fractal theory, the changes in fractal dimension of pore structure during the soaking process were discussed. The damage variable based on the pore fractal dimension was defined and the evolution relationship between the damage variable and immersion time was characterized. The findings demonstrated that the porosity change rate has an exponentially increasing relationship with the immersion time, and with the increasement of concentration of salt solution, the porosity change rate also shows increasing trends. The number of seepage pores and total pores increased with the immersion time. While, with the extension of soaking time, the number of adsorption pores first increased and then decreased. The connectivity between pores was enhanced. The relationship between the fractal dimension and the immersion time is linearly decreasing. The damage variable showed an increasing trend with the immersion time. As the concentration of salt solution increased, the damage of coal increased. The research results are of great significance for rationally evaluating the stability of coal pillars and ensuring the safe operation of underground engineering.

Keywords: coal; pore-fracture structure; salt solution; fractal characteristics

MSC: 74L10

1. Introduction

During the underground mining process of coal mines, the coal pillars are reserved in the goaf area as the main load-bearing structure. When a mine is closed, groundwater flows into the goaf and gradually floods the underground structure. Mine water is characterized by high salinity and is rich in Cl^- and SO_4^{2-} plasma components [1,2]. The coal pillars reserved in the goaf have been exposed to the environment of concentrated salt mine water for a long time. Under the long-term erosion of mine water, coal pillars are prone to water softening, including chemical erosion, dissolution, and expansion. The number of internal pores and fractures increases and the structure undergoes severe deformation, leading to instability of the coal pillar and ultimately causing disasters of surface subsidence. Change in the pore-fracture structure is an important reason for the instability and failure of coal pillars. Therefore, it is necessary to carry out quantitative analysis of the time-dependent changes in the internal pore-fracture structure of coal under the action of salt solution, which is of great significance for evaluating the stability of underground coal pillars.

When exposed to mine water for a long time, the hydrochemical reaction will change the mineral composition and matrix structure of coal, causing changes in physical properties, which eventually bring great uncertainty to the safety and stability of the coal pillar. Previous studies [3–10] indicated that the physical and mechanical properties of rock materials not only depend on their own characteristics such as mineral composition and pore-fracture network, but are also affected by external factors. Among them, the action of hydrochemicals has a significant impact on the physical properties and mechanical strength of rocks. Extensive research on water-coal interactions has been carried out [11–19]. Under the action of water immersion, soluble organic matter and inorganic matter in coal will dissolve in water, causing certain physical and chemical changes. The redistribution of chemical elements and changes in microstructure will ultimately lead to differences in coal properties. Ai et al. [11] carried out water saturation tests on coal and the mechanism of water on the microstructure of coal was analyzed by means of NMR, SEM, and XRD. It was found that the porosity gradually increases with soaking time. Liu et al. [14] found that the increase in water content intensifies the pore alteration of the ultrasonic stimulated coal, and the change in pore structure promoted the diffusion of gas in the pore-fracture channel. Yao et al. [18] studied the spatiotemporal distribution of water content and the crack expansion characteristics in coal before and after water immersion. The results of NMR test showed that the water content in the coal increases exponentially with the soaking time, and the presence of water promotes the development and expansion of pores. Wang et al. [19] demonstrated that the presence of water significantly changed the permeability characteristics of coal and the permeability of saturated water coal was two orders of magnitude lower than that of dry coal. When the chemical solution interacts with the coal, complex physical and chemical reactions occur within the coal matrix, which significantly change the properties of the coal. Previous researchers have elucidated that the porosity, permeability, and dissolution degree of mineral components of coal increase with the prolongation of chemical corrosion time [20–26]. The physical and mechanical properties of underground coal pillars change significantly under the action of concentrated salt mine water. However, there are few reports on the evolution characteristics of the internal pore-fracture structure of coal under the action of salt solution.

Coal is a complex heterogeneous and anisotropic porous rock. In addition to small pores, there are also complex discontinuities or joint networks inside the coal. The pores or fissures are filled with different mineral particles. When the water or chemical solution flows into the coal matrix, a series of physical and chemical effects will occur on the mineral composition and pore structure. The physical and chemical interaction changes the microstructure of coal matrix, which eventually affects the macroscopic properties. The damage evolution at micro scale is of great significance for understanding the deformation and failure mechanism of large-scale rock. With the development of science and technology, testing methods such as X-ray computed tomography (CT) [27], nuclear magnetic resonance (NMR) [28], scanning electron microscopy (SEM) [29], mercury intrusion [30], and nitrogen adsorption [31] have been used to characterize the microstructure of rocks. Among them, NMR is widely used because of its short test period, no damage to the primary pore structure, and large pore size test range. Many scholars have studied the evolution of coal pore structure and its fractal characteristics under different external factors by using NMR method. Zhou et al. [32] quantitatively analyzed the fractal characteristics of pore-fracture structure of low-rank coal by using nuclear magnetic resonance technology and established a permeability model based on the pore fractal. Liu et al. [33] used NMR to obtain the changes in pore structure and permeability of coal under different water pressure conditions, and built a fractal permeability model of coal. It is confirmed that the internal pore structure of water injected coal is complex and it has fractal characteristics. Chen et al. [34] quantitatively analyzed the dynamic changing characteristics of the pore structure in coal under the effect of stress. It found that when the confining pressure increased, the pore structure was compacted, and the fractal characteristics of the seepage space gradually became significant. Lei et al. [35] carried out a study on the fractal characteristics of low-rank coal under the action of liquid nitrogen freeze-thaw cycle and quantitatively evaluated the complexity of coal pore structure. It indicated that the fractal dimension of seepage pores and open pores was negatively correlated with the number of freeze-thaw cycles. The pore structure of coal has fractal characteristics, and it is more complicated and inhomogeneous than that of other types of rocks such as sandstone, carbonate and shale [36]. The above research reveals the complexity of evolution of coal pore structure under the action of different external factors, but there are few studies on the fractal characteristics of coal pore structure under the action of salt solution and the relationship between pore fractal and the coal damage.

This paper aims to study the damage effect of salt solution immersion on the pore-fracture structure of coal. The coal samples were immersed in salt solutions of different concentrations, and then NMR measurements were carried out on the coal samples immersed in salt solutions for different times. The relationship between the porosity change rate and immersion time and salt solution concentration was discussed. The evolution characteristics of pore size and the number of different types of pores were analyzed. After that the fractal dimensions of pore spaces were calculated using fractal theory. The relationship between fractal dimension and immersion time and porosity was discussed. Damage variables based on pore fractal dimension were defined, and the evolution of damage variables with immersion time under the action of salt solutions was discussed. Finally, the damage mechanism of coal under the action of salt solutions was analyzed. The results of this study are helpful to quantitatively characterize the change in pore structure in coal pillar under the action of concentrated salt mine water, which is of great significance for stability research of coal pillar in underground mine.

2. Materials and Methods

2.1. Coal Sample Preparation

The coal selected for the experiment were taken from Ningdong mining area, China. In order to analyze the mineral composition of the raw coal, the retrieved coal was firstly ground into a powder of about 200 mesh by a grinder. The elements contained in the coal were detected by X-ray fluorescence spectrometer, and X-ray diffraction analysis was further carried out based on the measured element content. The inorganic components of coal are kaolinite, quartz and siderite, whose contents are 51.3%, 41.9%, and 6.8%, respectively (as shown in Figure 1).

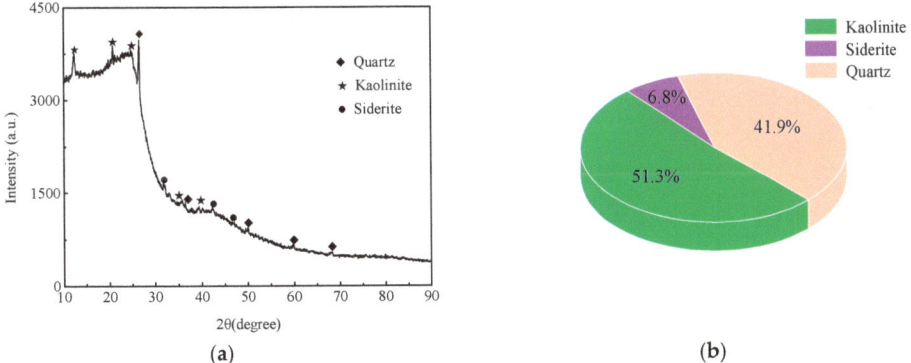

Figure 1. Mineral composition analysis. (**a**) X-ray diffraction curve; (**b**) mineral content.

The coal blocks retrieved from the site were wrapped in plastic wrap and transported to the laboratory for processing. First, a rock coring machine was used to drill a cylindrical coal sample with a diameter of 50 mm, and then the rock cutting machine was applied to cut the core into a sample with a height of 100 mm, and finally the upper and lower end faces of the sample were polished smooth with sandpaper to form a standard cylindrical specimen with a specification of Φ50 × 100 mm. According to the ISRM rock preparation standard, the unevenness of the two end faces should not exceed 0.02 mm. The parallelism of the end faces should not exceed 0.005 mm. The verticality of the shaft should not exceed 0.001° and the surrounding is smooth. In order to ensure the relative uniformity of samples used in the test, the coal samples were drilled from the same block.

2.2. Salt Solution Preparation and Test Procedures

Mine water is usually weakly acidic or alkaline, mostly containing Na^+, K^+, Cl^-, and SO_4^{2-} plasma components, which has the characteristics of high salinity. The ion composition of mine water from Ningdong mining area was determined in laboratory. The chemical test results showed that the main ion components of the mine water are Na^+, SO_4^{2-}, and Cl^- and the calculated concentration ratio is about 5:1:3. Therefore, the cation in the salt solution in this study is Na^+ and the anion are SO_4^{2-} and Cl^-. The concentration ratio of ion in salt solution is the same as that in mine water. An experimental study on the time-dependent evolution of pore and fracture structure of coal under action of salt solution immersion with different concentrations was carried out. Meanwhile, coal samples soaked in distilled water were prepared as a control group. Under the natural condition, the physical and chemical action of mine water on coal is a slow process. Due to the limitation of test time, the means of increasing the acidity and alkalinity of salt solution and increasing the concentration of ions in solution were adopted to accelerate the physical and chemical action of salt solution on coal samples. The pH value of the prepared salt solution is 1, and the concentrations of the salt solution are 0.1 mol/L, 0.5 mol/L, and 1 mol/L. The volume of solution in each immersion group was 10 L. The experiments were carried out at normal temperature and pressure. The pretest showed [37] that the quality of coal samples tends to be stable after soaking for about 30 days, so the soaking period was 30 days.

After the processing of the samples, the longitudinal wave velocity of the coal samples was tested first. The longitudinal wave velocity range of the samples was 1.8 km/s–2.0 km/s. The samples with large differences were excluded, and the remaining samples were immersed in distilled water and salt solution with different concentration, respectively. After soaking for 1 day, 3 days, 5 days, 7 days, 10 days, 15 days, 20 days, and 30 days, the coal samples were taken for NMR test. The MesoMR23-060H-I low-field NMR instrument produced by Suzhou Niumag Electronic Technology Co., Ltd. (Suzhou, China) was used for NMR test. The parameters of NMR were set to RF signal center frequency (SF) of 21 MHz, echo spacing (TE) of 0.2 ms, repeat sampling interval time (TW) of 1000 ms, sampling starting point (RFD) of 0.25 ms, and echo numbers of 2000. The experimental process and equipment are shown in Figure 2.

2.3. The NMR Theory

Nuclear magnetic resonance (NMR) has been widely used as a new technique to detect micro-structures such as rock pores and fractures, which has the advantages of fast, non-destructive and simple operation. Low field NMR mainly uses hydrogen proton in pore water as the signal source for detection. When water is injected into the pores, the relaxation time and initial magnetization vector of the different sizes pores can be obtained through the special CPMG sequence. The distribution curve of the transverse relaxation time (T_2) of the pore structure can be obtained through the inversion of the hydrogen ion attenuation signal. For fluid in rocks pores, there are three different relaxation mechanisms, and when these three actions exist simultaneously, the relaxation time T_2 of water in the pores can be expressed as:

$$\frac{1}{T_2} = \frac{1}{T_{2S}} + \frac{1}{T_{2B}} + \frac{1}{T_{2D}} = \rho \left(\frac{S}{V}\right)_{pore} + 3\left(\frac{T_k}{298\eta}\right) + \frac{D(\gamma G T_E)^2}{12} \tag{1}$$

where T_{2S} is the surface relaxation time of the pore fluid; T_{2B} is the volume relaxation time of the fluid; T_{2D} is the relaxation time of pore fluid caused by gradient magnetic field diffusion; ρ is the T_2 relaxation strength of the particle surface; $(S/V)_{pore}$ is the ratio of pore surface area to fluid volume; T_k is the Kelvin temperature; η is the liquid viscosity; G is the field intensity gradient; and T_E is the echo interval.

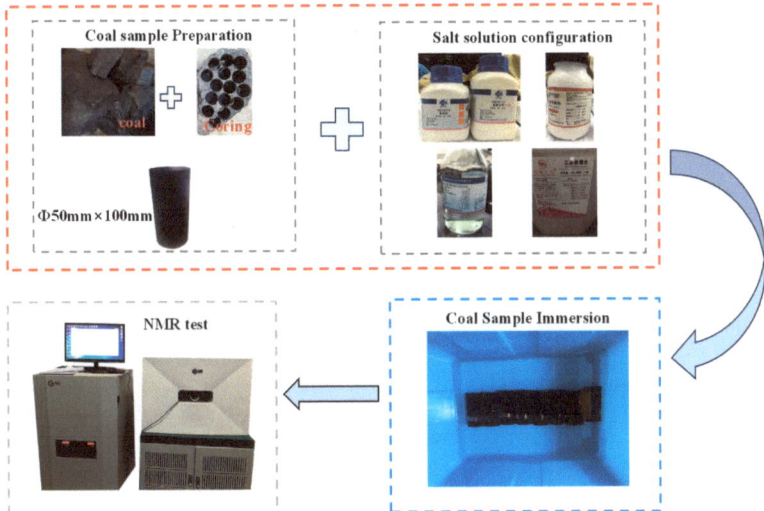

Figure 2. Experimental process and equipment.

According to Formula (1), the free relaxation time is mainly affected by the fluid characteristics, and its value is negligible compared with the surface relaxation time. The diffusion relaxation time is affected by field gradient and echo interval. For coal, the values of G and T_E are small, so the diffusion relaxation time can be ignored. Therefore, Formula (1) can be simplified as:

$$\frac{1}{T_2} \approx \rho \left(\frac{S}{V}\right)_{pore} = F_S(\rho/r) \qquad (2)$$

where F_S is the pore shape parameter, and the shape parameters of fracture, tubular pore and spherical pore are 1, 2, and 3, respectively; and r is the pore size.

According to Formula (2), the relaxation time T_2 is proportional to the pore size. The internal pore size distribution, pore number, connectivity and other parameters of the tested sample can be obtained from the T_2 spectra.

3. Results
3.1. Time-Dependent Changes in Porosity

Coal porosity is an important parameter to characterize the degree of development of internal defects, which is defined as the ratio of the volume of defects such as pores and fractures to the volume of coal sample. In order to analyze the degree of change in the coal porosity under the action of salt solution immersion, the porosity change rate $\Delta\varphi_p$ was defined to characterize the evolution of the coal porosity. The expression is as follows:

$$\Delta\varphi_p = \frac{\varphi_{pt} - \varphi_{p0}}{\varphi_{p0}} \times 100\% \qquad (3)$$

where φ_{p0} is the porosity of coal before immersion; and φ_{pt} is the porosity of coal after immersion t days.

The porosity and porosity change rate of coal obtained from the NMR test under the action of salt solution are shown in Table 1.

Table 1. φ_p and $\Delta\varphi_p$ of coal samples at different immersion time.

Immersion Time (Days)	Distilled Water		0.1 mol/L Salt Solution		0.5 mol/L Salt Solution		1 mol/L Salt Solution	
	φ_p (%)	$\Delta\varphi_p$ (%)	φ_p (%)	$\Delta\varphi_p$ (%)	φ_p (%)	$\Delta\varphi_p$ (%)	φ_p (%)	$\Delta\varphi_p$ (%)
0	20.29		19.83		16.64		19.41	
1	20.87	2.86	20.66	4.19	17.34	4.21	20.47	5.46
3	21.35	5.22	21.52	8.52	18.39	10.52	21.98	13.24
5	21.90	7.94	22.81	15.03	19.69	18.33	23.72	22.21
10	22.08	8.82	23.30	17.50	20.17	21.21	24.90	28.28
15	22.12	9.02	23.74	19.72	20.92	25.72	25.56	31.69
20	22.20	9.41	23.95	20.78	21.47	29.03	26.84	38.28
30	22.33	10.05	24.13	21.68	22.02	32.33	27.47	41.53

Table 1 shows that the porosity of coal samples increases with the increasing immersion time. In the initial state, the porosity of coal samples in distilled water, 0.1 mol/L, 0.5 mol/L, and 1 mol/L salt solution is 20.29%, 19.83%, 16.64%, and 19.41%, respectively. After 30 days of immersion, φ_p and $\Delta\varphi_p$ of the corresponding coal samples are 22.33% and 10.054%, 24.13% and 21.684%, 22.02% and 32.332%, 27.47% and 41.525%, respectively. There are some differences in the coal porosity at the initial state, which is caused by the number and distribution of the primary pores in different coal samples. After 30 days of immersion, the porosity change rate of coal samples soaked in 1 mol/L salt solution is the highest. The $\Delta\varphi_p$ increases with the increase in salt solution concentration. It indicated that the effect of high concentration salt solution can promote the expansion of primary pores and the initiation of new fractures, which eventually lead to a relatively large growth rate of total pore volume in the coal matrix.

The porosity change rate of coal samples varies with immersion time and salt solution concentration are shown in Figures 3 and 4. Under different immersion time and salt solution concentration, there are different changing rules between the porosity change rate and soaking variables. There was an exponential correlation between the porosity change rate and immersion time (Table 2). When the concentration of salt solution is constant, the longer the soaking time, the greater the change in porosity. While there is a linear correlation between the porosity change rate and the salt solution concentration (Table 3). With the same immersion time, the porosity change rate shows an increasing trend with the increase in salt solution concentration. Under the action of salt solution, pore expansion, crack widening, penetration and extension eventually lead to the increase in porosity, thus aggravating the deterioration of macro-properties of coal samples.

Table 2. Relationship between porosity change rate and immersion time.

Concentration of Salt Solution (mol/L)	Fit Function	a	b	R^2
0	$y = a \times (1 - e^{-b \times x})$	9.513	0.3065	0.986
0.1		21.17	0.2015	0.988
0.5		31.30	0.1358	0.979
1		40.79	0.1285	0.983

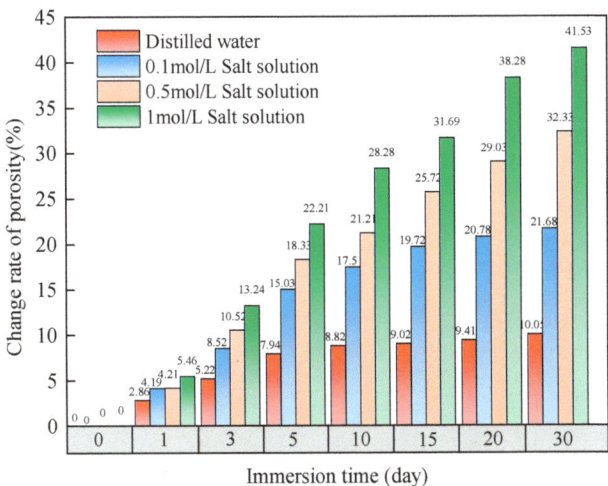

Figure 3. The porosity change rate varies with immersion time.

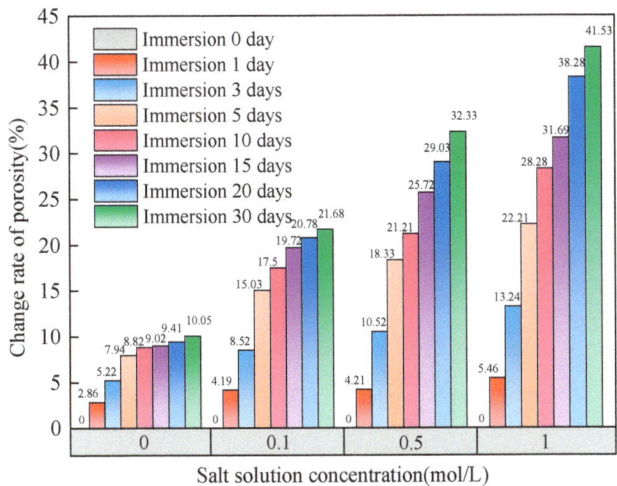

Figure 4. The porosity change rate varies with the concentration of salt solution.

Table 3. Relationship between porosity change rate and salt solution concentration.

Immersion Time (Days)	Fit Function	a	b	R^2
1	$y = a + b \times x$	3.344	2.090	0.895
3		6.567	7.019	0.838
5		11.06	12.05	0.730
10		12.30	16.63	0.806
15		13.76	19.45	0.755
20		14.13	25.60	0.849
30		15.03	28.43	0.858

3.2. Evolution of Pore-Fracture Structure

3.2.1. Evolution Characteristics of Pore Size

It can be seen from Formula (2) that the T_2 spectra obtained from NMR can better reflect the characteristics of the internal pore structure in coal sample. The pore size is positively correlated with the transverse relaxation time T_2. Large pore sizes correspond to larger T_2 values, and conversely, small pore sizes correspond to smaller T_2 values. The size of the amplitude of the T_2 spectrum represents number of pores corresponding to a particular size, that is, the smaller the amplitude, the smaller the number of pores, and vice versa. The T_2 spectra of coal samples soaked by distilled water and salt solutions are shown in Figure 5. It can be seen from Figure 5 that the transverse relaxation time (T_2) is divided into three relaxation peaks in the attenuation range. Since the attenuation constant is proportional to the pore size, the three relaxation peaks from left to right correspond to micropores (pore size < 100 nm), mesopore (100 nm < 10,000 nm), macropores or fractures (pore size > 10,000 nm). Research indicated that the pore structure can be classified according to the pore size based on the T_2 curve [38]. In this study, two points T_2 = 2.5 ms and T_2 = 50 ms were used to classify the pore structure. Areas with T_2 values less than 2.5 ms correspond to small pores, areas with T_2 values between 2.5 ms and 50 ms correspond to medium pores and areas with T_2 values greater than 50 ms correspond to large pores or fractures. Among them, the small pores are defined as the adsorption pore. The middle pores and the large pores are defined as the seepage pore, which is the channel for fluid to move freely.

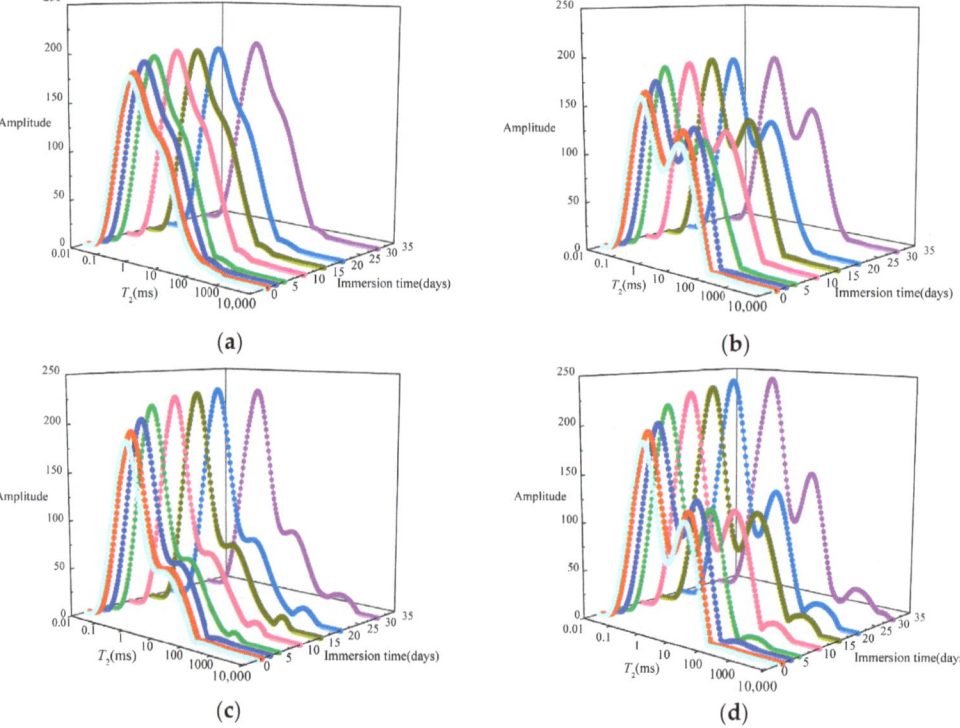

Figure 5. T_2 spectra of coal samples under the action of salt solution. (**a**) Distilled water; (**b**) 0.1 mol/L salt solution; (**c**) distilled water; (**d**) 1 mol/L salt solution.

By observing the T_2 spectra of coal samples, it can be found that the amplitude of the first peak is the largest, followed by the second peak, and the amplitude of the third peak is the lowest, indicating that the number of small pores in coal matrix is large and well-developed, and the number of large pores is small and poorly developed. For the same sample, with the increase in soaking time, the amplitude of three relaxation peaks is significantly enhanced. The location of the relaxation peak is related to the pore size, and the amplitude of the peak is related to the number of corresponding pores. The increase in the T_2 spectra amplitude indicates that the number of pores in the coal matrix increases with the prolongation of soaking time, while the transverse relaxation time range becomes wider, indicating that pores with smaller or larger sizes have been generated. By comparing the T_2 spectra of samples soaked in distilled water and salt solution of different concentrations, it can be seen that the number of pores and fractures in coal increased after salt solution immersion, and the number of large pores in coal treated with high concentration increased the most. With the increase in soaking time, the originally isolated peaks gradually connected, indicating that the connectivity between pores of different sizes was enhanced, and salt solution immersion promoted the opening of closed pores, which accelerating the connection between pores and fractures.

3.2.2. Variation in Pore Number

Under the physical and chemical action of salt solution, the minerals inside the coal sample are dissolved and softened, resulting in the change in pore structure. The increasing number of pores and fractures aggravated the damage of coal samples. The area of T_2 spectra obtained by NMR reflects the number of pores with different size [24]. The sum of the amplitude of the T_2 spectra under different relaxation times is defined as the area of the T_2 spectra. The number of total pores (S_T) is the total area of the T_2 spectra. The number of adsorption pores (S_{T1}) is the curve area with T_2 value less than 2.5 ms, and the number of seepage pores (S_{T2}) is the curve area with T_2 value greater than 2.5 ms.

The relationship berween immersion time and the number of different types of pores in coal under the action of distilled water and salt solutions are shown in Figure 6. In general, the number of different types of pores increased to different degrees after 30 days of immersion in distilled water and salt solution. After soaking for 30 days, the number of adsorption pores in distilled water, 0.1 mol/L salt solution, 0.5 mol/L salt solution and 1 mol/L salt solution increased by 1.34%, 7.56%, 9.65%, and 16.62%, respectively. The number of seepage holes increased by 35.66%, 34.03%, 75.03%, and 72.27%, respectively. The total pore number increased by 12.59%, 18.23%, 26.45%, and 35.72%, respectively. The number of seepage pores and total pores increased with soaking time. However, the number of adsorption pores increased first and then decreased with soaking time. The main reason for this phenomenon is that the small pores are gradually connected to form larger pores in the late stage of immersion. The pore structure in the coal matrix provides storage space for water immersion. Under the same saturated water condition, the amount of water entering the coal matrix is affected by pore parameters such as pore number and pore connectivity. There are relatively many mineral particles in the coal with small degree of dissolution, which affects the openness of pore space and the saturation degree of pore water. The seepage space contains large pores and fractures. The increase in the number of seepage pores means the increase in large pores or cracks, which is the main reason for the weakening of coal properties.

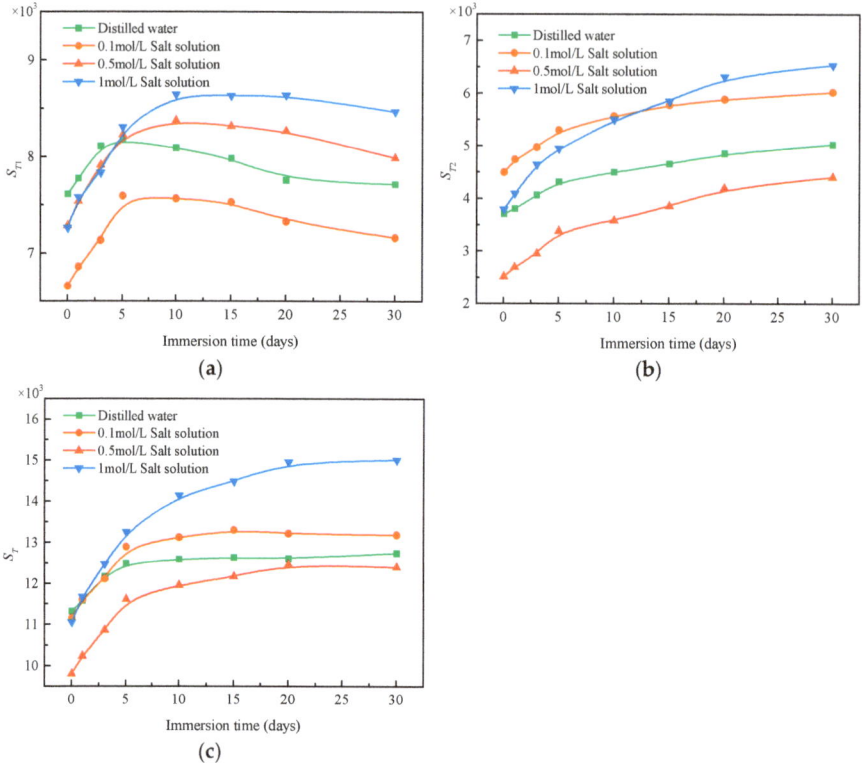

Figure 6. The relationship between immersion time and pore number of coal under the action of salt solution. (**a**) Adsorption pore; (**b**) seepage pore; (**c**) total pore.

4. Discussion
4.1. Fractal Characteristics

According to the fractal theory [39,40], if the pore structure in the coal sample follows the fractal law, the relationship between the pores number and the radius is the following power function:

$$N(>r) = \int_r^{r_{\max}} P(r)dr = ar^{-D} \tag{4}$$

where $r_{\max}$ is the maximum pore radius of coal; $P(r)$ is the probability density function of the pore size distribution; a is the proportional coefficient; and D is the fractal dimension of the pore structure.

The expression of the probability density function can be obtained by derivation of Formula (4):

$$P(r) = \frac{dN(r)}{dr} = -Dar^{-D-1} \tag{5}$$

The cumulative pore volume with a pore radius less than r can be expressed as:

$$V(<r) = \int_{r_{\min}}^{r} P(r)V_0 dr \tag{6}$$

where V_0 is the volume of a single pore, r^3 for square pores and $4\pi r^3/3$ for spherical pores, and $r_{\min}$ is the minimum pore radius.

It can be obtained by integrating Formula (5) into Formula (6):

$$V(<r) = a'\left(r^{3-D} - r_{min}^{3-D}\right) \tag{7}$$

Then the total pore volume inside the coal sample is:

$$V(<r_{max}) = a'\left(r_{max}^{3-D} - r_{min}^{3-D}\right) \tag{8}$$

The pore volume fraction with pore radius less than r in the coal sample is

$$S_v = \frac{V(<r)}{V(<r_{max})} = \frac{r^{3-D} - r_{min}^{3-D}}{r_{max}^{3-D} - r_{min}^{3-D}} \tag{9}$$

Since the minimum pore radius (r_{min}) is much smaller than the maximum pore radius (r_{max}), Formula (9) can be simplified as

$$S_v = \frac{r^{3-D}}{r_{max}^{3-D}} \tag{10}$$

In NMR theory, the transverse relaxation time T_2 can be expressed as:

$$\frac{1}{T_2} = \frac{1}{T_{2B}} + \rho\left(\frac{S}{V}\right) + \frac{1}{T_{2D}} \tag{11}$$

where T_{2B} is the volume relaxation time of the fluid; S is the surface area of the pore; V is the pore volume; ρ is the T_2 relaxation strength of the particle surface; and T_{2D} is the relaxation time of pore fluid caused by gradient magnetic field diffusion.

Usually, T_{2B} is between 2 and 3 s, which is much larger than T_2. In addition, when the magnetic field is uniform (the corresponding magnetic field strength is very low) and the echo time is short enough, T_{2D} can also be ignored. Therefore, the Formula (11) can be simplified as:

$$\frac{1}{T_2} = \rho\left(\frac{S}{V}\right) = F_s\frac{\rho}{r} \tag{12}$$

where F_s is the geometric parameter related to the pore shape, for spherical pores, $F_s = 3$, for cylindrical pores, and $F_s = 2$; r is the pore radius.

Substituting Formula (12) into Formula (10)

$$S_v = \left(\frac{T_2}{T_{2max}}\right)^{3-D} \tag{13}$$

where S_v is the percentage of the cumulative pore volume with transverse relaxation time less than T_2 in the total pore volume.

Taking the logarithm of both sides of Formula (13), a fractal theoretical model characterized by the value of T_2 can be obtained:

$$\lg(S_v) = (3-D)\lg(T_2) + (D-3)\lg(T_{2max}) \tag{14}$$

According to Formula (14), the linear relationship between $\lg(S_v)$ and $\lg(T_2)$ indicates that the pore structure has fractal characteristics. By fitting the experimental data, the linear relationship between $\lg(S_v)$ and $\lg(T_2)$ was obtained as Formula (15).

$$\lg(S_v) = a\lg(T_2) + b \tag{15}$$

The expression of fractal dimension can be obtained by Formula (16):

$$D = 3 - a \tag{16}$$

Figure 7 and Table 4 show the fractal dimension characteristics of coal sample calculated based on T_2 spectra. The logarithmic relationship between S_v and T_2 can be divided into two sections. As mentioned above, with $T_2 = 2.5$ ms as the node, the pores in coal sample are divided into adsorption pores and seepage pores. The fractal dimensions based on adsorption pore and seepage pore were calculated in the left and right sections of $T_2 = 2.5$ ms.

According to the fractal theory, it is meaningful that the fractal dimension of coal pore structure is between 2 and 3. The fractal dimension based on adsorption pores is less than 2, so it does not meet the fractal characteristics, and it will not be discussed in this paper. The fractal dimension based on the total pores ranges from 2.51 to 2.57, and the fractal dimension of seepage pores ranges from 2.93 to 2.98, which shows fractal characteristics. The linear fitting correlation coefficient based on the fractal dimension of the seepage pore (0.59–0.788) is larger than that based on the total pore (0.502–0.542), indicating that the pore distribution of the seepage pore has more obvious fractal characteristics.

The fractal dimension of the pore reflects the complexity of the structure, and the higher the fractal dimension, the stronger the anisotropy and more complex of the pore structure, and vice versa. Figure 8 reveals that the fractal dimension of pore structure of coal sample is related to immersion parameter. The fractal dimension is negatively correlated with the immersion time. The longer the immersion time, the lower the fractal dimension of pores. Under the same immersion time, the fractal dimension of pore structure of coal samples immersed in salt solution decreases faster than that immersed in distilled water. It shows that the damage effect of salt solution immersion on coal sample is greater than that of distilled water.

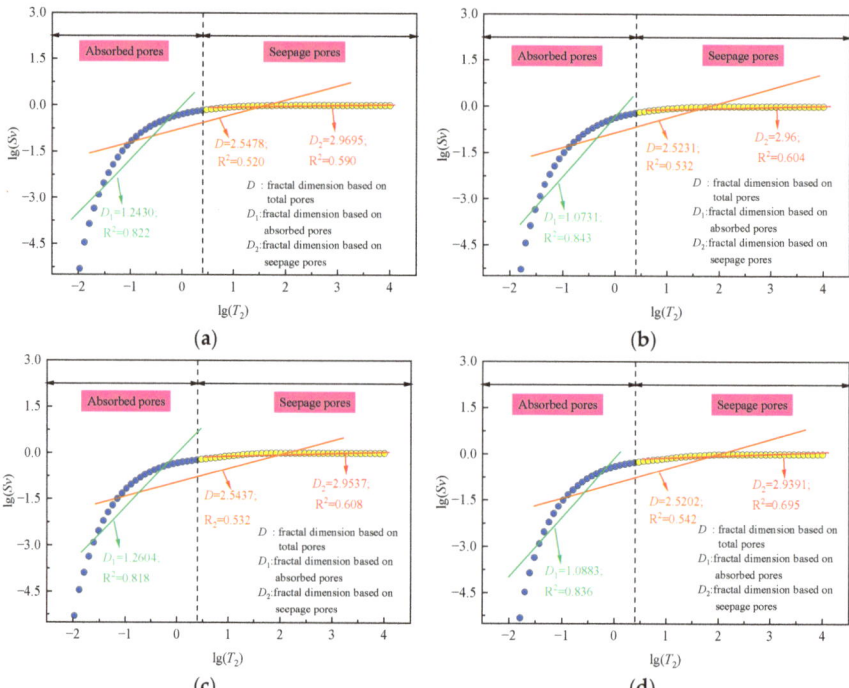

Figure 7. Cont.

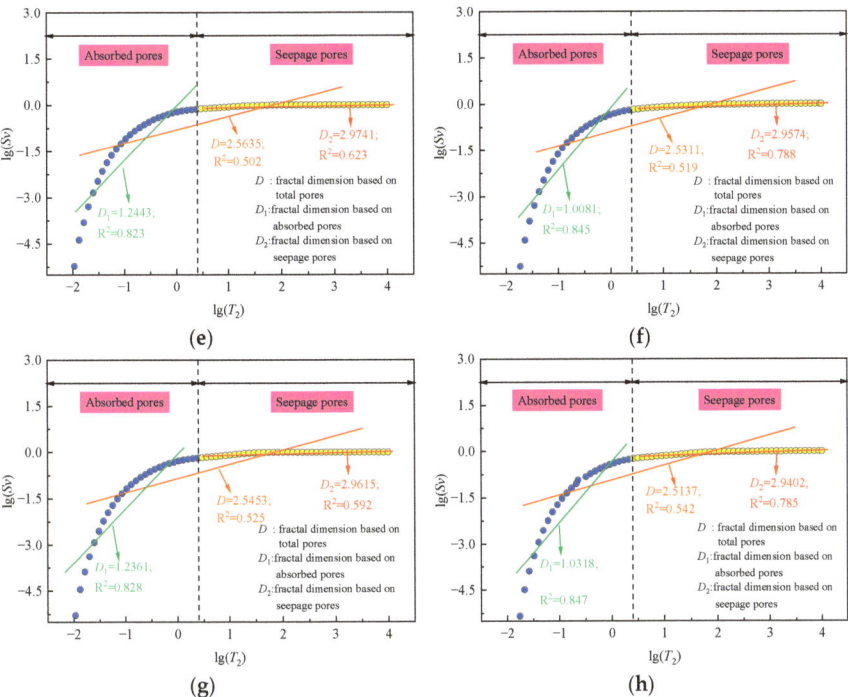

Figure 7. Fractal dimension of pore structure of coal sample. (**a**) Immersed in distilled water for 0 day; (**b**) Immersed in distilled water for 30 days; (**c**) immersed in 0.1 mol/L salt solution for 0 day; (**d**) immersed in 0.1 mol/L salt solution for 30 days; (**e**) immersed in 0.5 mol/L salt solution for 0 day; (**f**) immersed in 0.5 mol/L salt solution for 30 days; (**g**) immersed in 1 mol/L salt solution for 0 day; (**h**) immersed in 1 mol/L salt solution for 30 days.

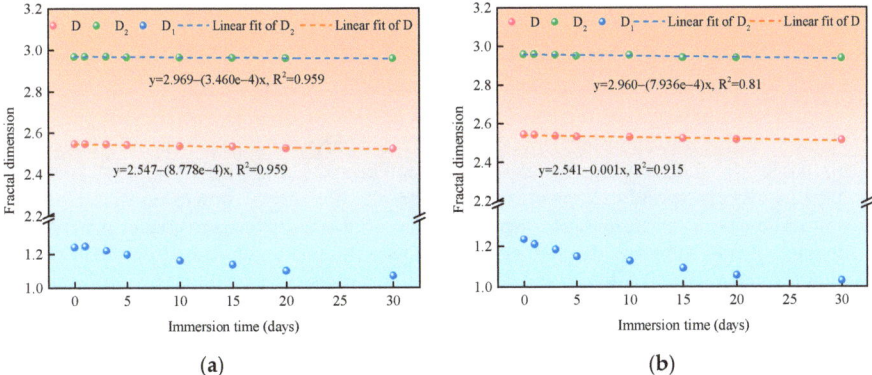

Figure 8. Relationship between fractal dimension and immersion time. (**a**) Immersed in distilled water; (**b**) immersed in 1 mol/L salt solution.

Table 4. Fractal dimension of coal pore structure.

Immersion Solution Type	Immersion Time (Days)	Adsorption Pore		Seepage Pore		Total Pores	
		D_1	R^2	D_2	R^2	D	R^2
Distilled water	0	1.2430	0.822	2.9695	0.590	2.5478	0.520
	1	1.2475	0.822	2.9692	0.595	2.5466	0.520
	3	1.2218	0.824	2.9692	0.575	2.5458	0.521
	5	1.1989	0.827	2.9673	0.583	2.5433	0.522
	7	1.1626	0.832	2.9657	0.587	2.5364	0.526
	15	1.1398	0.832	2.9639	0.592	2.5352	0.525
	20	1.1033	0.840	2.9613	0.605	2.5266	0.531
	30	1.0731	0.843	2.9600	0.604	2.5231	0.532
0.1 mol/L salt solution	0	1.2604	0.818	2.9537	0.608	2.5437	0.532
	1	1.2590	0.820	2.9541	0.591	2.5418	0.534
	3	1.2315	0.822	2.9523	0.608	2.5418	0.534
	5	1.2136	0.821	2.9484	0.686	2.5393	0.530
	7	1.1820	0.826	2.9461	0.687	2.5353	0.535
	15	1.1514	0.828	2.9441	0.680	2.5309	0.536
	20	1.1163	0.832	2.9408	0.707	2.5250	0.539
	30	1.0883	0.836	2.9391	0.695	2.5202	0.542
0.5 mol/L salt solution	0	1.2443	0.823	2.9741	0.623	2.5635	0.502
	1	1.2166	0.825	2.9729	0.636	2.5602	0.503
	3	1.1934	0.827	2.9717	0.646	2.5579	0.504
	5	1.1394	0.830	2.9676	0.710	2.5531	0.505
	7	1.1098	0.832	2.9660	0.734	2.5500	0.506
	15	1.0773	0.838	2.9640	0.731	2.5434	0.511
	20	1.0398	0.842	2.9607	0.766	2.5367	0.505
	30	1.0081	0.845	2.9574	0.788	2.5311	0.519
1 mol/L salt solution	0	1.2361	0.828	2.9615	0.592	2.5453	0.525
	1	1.2119	0.829	2.9612	0.588	2.5425	0.525
	3	1.1856	0.833	2.9583	0.606	2.5358	0.531
	5	1.1507	0.835	2.9521	0.703	2.5332	0.530
	7	1.1296	0.836	2.9557	0.721	2.5301	0.534
	15	1.0944	0.841	2.9424	0.816	2.5244	0.537
	20	1.0587	0.846	2.9407	0.800	2.5164	0.542
	30	1.0318	0.847	2.9402	0.785	2.5137	0.542

4.2. Relationship between Porosity and Fractal Dimension

The seepage pores and total pores in coal samples show obvious fractal characteristics. Figure 9 shows the relationship between the fractal dimension and the porosity. It is obvious that large fractal dimensions correspond to small porosity, and vice versa, small fractal dimensions correspond to large porosity. The smaller the fractal dimension is, the more uniform the pore structure is. The increase in pore connectivity leads to greater structural damage of coal samples. By comparing the fractal dimension of pore structure of coal samples soaked in salt solution and distilled water, it can be obtained that the decrease in fractal dimension under salt solution immersion is greater than that under distilled water immersion, which indicates that the pore structure anisotropy of coal sample is smaller and the pore connectivity is larger after salt solution immersion.

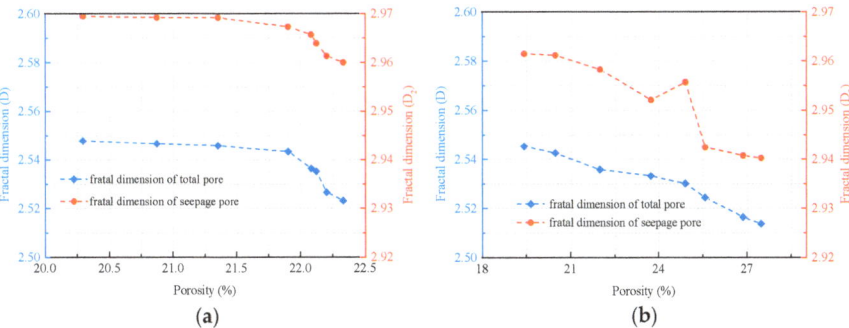

Figure 9. The relationship between fractal dimension and porosity. (**a**) Immersed in distilled water; (**b**) immersed in 1 mol/L salt solution.

4.3. Diachronic Evolution of Damage

Under the physical and chemical action of salt solution, the minerals inside the coal sample are dissolved and softened, leading to the change in pore structure. In Section 4.1, it is explained that the pore space of the total pore and the seepage pore have fractal characteristics, so the fractal dimension of the pore structure will also change. The damage variable δ_i based on the fractal characteristics of the total pore and seepage pore is defined as follows:

$$\delta_i = \frac{D_{i0} - D_{it}}{D_{i0}} \times 100\% \, (i = T, T_2; \, t = 1, 3, 5, \ldots, 30) \tag{17}$$

where D is the fractal dimension; i represents different types of pores, in which T represents total pores, T_2 represents seepage pores; and t is immersion time, days.

The damage variables of coal samples soaked in distilled water and salt solutions of different concentrations are shown in Table 5.

Table 5. Damage variables of coal sample under the action of salt solution.

Immersion Time (Days)	Distilled Water		0.1 mol/L Salt Solution		0.5 mol/L Salt Solution		1 mol/L Salt Solution	
	δ_T (%)	δ_{T2} (%)	δ_T (%)	δ_{T2} (%)	δ_T (%)	δ_{T2} (%)	δ_T (%)	δ_{T2} (%)
0	0.00	0.00	0.00	0.00	0.00	0.00	0.00	0.00
1	0.05	0.01	0.07	−0.01	0.13	0.04	0.11	0.01
3	0.08	0.01	0.07	0.05	0.22	0.08	0.37	0.11
5	0.18	0.07	0.17	0.18	0.41	0.22	0.48	0.32
10	0.45	0.13	0.33	0.26	0.53	0.27	0.60	0.20
15	0.49	0.19	0.50	0.33	0.78	0.34	0.82	0.64
20	0.83	0.28	0.74	0.44	1.05	0.45	1.14	0.70
30	0.97	0.32	0.92	0.49	1.26	0.56	1.24	0.72

With the increase in soaking time, the δ_T and δ_{T2} of coal samples soaked by distilled water and salt solution increase continuously, which indicated that the effect of water and salt solution can aggravate the deterioration of coal structure.

As shown in Figure 10, the damage degree of coal samples represented by different types of pores is positively correlated with soaking time. It directly shows that the longer the soaking time, the more obvious the pore structure changes, and the greater the deterioration degree of mechanical property. Comparing the δ_T of coal samples soaked in distilled water and salt solution with different concentrations, it can be seen that the δ_T value of coal soaked in 1 mol/L salt solution is the largest. In general, the damage degree based on the total pore increased with the increase in concentration. Except there is a slight difference between distilled water and 0.1 mol/L salt solution. The δ_{T2} increases with the increase in the concentration of salt solution, which indicates that the concentration of salt solution has a great influence on the formation and expansion of large pores and fractures. Research shows the development and penetration of large pores and fractures is the main cause of the failure of rock material under external load [41,42]. The fractal characteristics of seepage pores composed of large pores and fractures are more significant than those of total pores. Therefore, in practical engineering, we can use the damage variable represented by the fractal dimension of the seepage pores to analyze and evaluate the stability of coal pillars in underground mine.

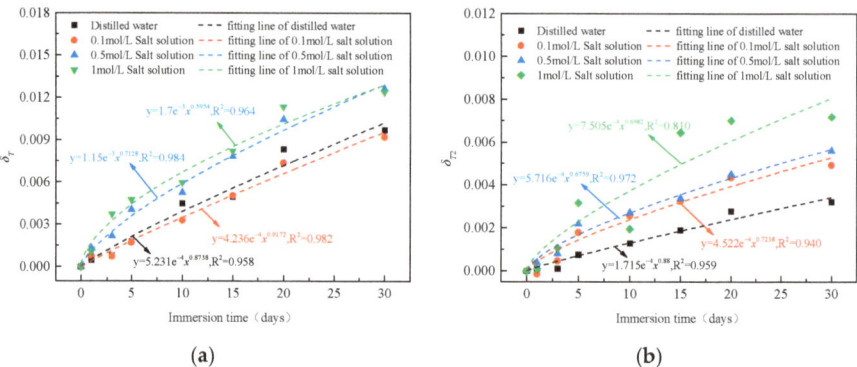

Figure 10. Relationship curves of δ_T, δ_{T2} and soaking time under the action of salt solution. (a) δ_T; (b) δ_{T2}.

The research results provide a theoretical basis for the stability evaluation of coal pillar. In order to improve the stability of coal pillar, the initiation and development of internal pores and fractures should be controlled reasonably. Specific methods are as follows: (1) the anti-seepage treatment of coal pillar can be used to effectively isolate the erosion of ions in mine water; (2) the pores and fractures developed in the coal pillar are reinforced by grouting to enhance the integrity of the coal pillar; (3) setting reasonable coal pillar size; (4) improve the external stress environment and reduce the influence of external load disturbance, among which the leaving waste rocks in the mined-out space [43] and the bolt support controlling the deformation of broken rock strata in the roof are considered to be effective methods to reduce the disturbance of external stress.

4.4. Damage Mechanism

4.4.1. Mechanism of Water Weakening

Complex physical and chemical interactions occur between the liquid and the rock when it immersed in chemical solutions. The physical interaction is when rock minerals dissolve, the lubrication effect produced by the liquid destroys the interconnection between particles. The physical interaction refers to the dissolution reaction of rock minerals and the lubrication produced by the liquid, which finally destroys the interconnection between particles. Additionally, pore water pressure creates uneven stresses within the rock, leading to the reduction in cohesion and friction. Research shows that under the action of external load, water mainly weakens the strength of coal through the following aspects: reducing fracture energy and friction, reducing particle surface tension, increasing pore pressure, and water chemical corrosion [13,44].

The mineral composition of coal is mainly clay minerals, quartz, etc. Water is transmitted into the interior of the coal through porous channels, and the air in the pore space is gradually exhausted, finally, the spaces between the pores are replaced by water. Due to the strong hydrophilicity of clay minerals, a large number of water molecules is easily to be adsorbed to its surface, thus forming a hydration film in the lattice structure of clay minerals. The thickness of the hydration film increases with the increase in water content, resulting in hydration expansion of the mineral. The non-uniform force produced by hydration expansion causes new micro-fractures in coal, and promotes the further expansion of primary fractures. When water diffuses to the surface of minerals, it will exchange ions with the adsorbed ions on the minerals surface, which will change the structure of coal, increase the porosity, and enhance the permeability. In addition, the filling material in the joint will change from solid to liquid when it encounters water, which will eventually lead to structural deterioration.

4.4.2. Mechanism of Chemical Reaction between Coal and H^+ or OH^- in Solution

Chemical reactions are usually caused by the dissolution of rock minerals by chemical solutions. This dissolution causes changes in the microstructure, making the rock softer and weaker and increasing the porosity. The organic functional groups and minerals in coal can be significantly changed by acid and alkali solution. The kaolinite mineral in coal can react with H^+ or OH^- (as shown Formulas (18) and (19)). The quartz mineral is an acidic oxide and can be effectively dissolved in alkaline solution. The chemical reaction between H^+ or OH^- and the minerals in the coal sample dissolves the microstructure surface, resulting in the generation pores and fractures. In order to clarify the effect of salt solution on the microstructure of coal samples, SEM experiments were carried out on the coal samples that in natural state and soaked in 0.1 mol/L salt solution for 30 days. The microscopic morphology of coal samples in natural state and after salt solution immersion is shown in Figure 11. In the natural state, the mineral particles in coal samples are closely connected, and irregularly shaped pores or fractures are scattered on the surface of the structure. After salt solution immersion, there are a small number of mineral particles inside the sample, which distributed in flakes or blocks. Due to the dissolution of the salt solution, the edges of the mineral particles gradually become blurred, and the pore-fracture structure inside the sample changes. The dissolution of the mineral particles gradually reveals the pores that were originally blocked by the particles. Micro-cracks and pores developed and connected to form large pores and fractures. Internal fractures are interconnected, causing the matrix structure to become loose and the number of pores to increase.

$$Al_2O_3 \cdot 2SiO_2 \cdot 2H_2O(Kaolinite) + 14H^+ = 2Al^{3+} + 2Si^{4+} + 9H_2O \tag{18}$$

$$Al_2O_3 \cdot 2SiO_2 \cdot 2H_2O(Kaolinite) + 6OH^- = 2AlO_2^- + 2SiO_3^{2-} + 5H_2O \tag{19}$$

$$SiO_2 + 2OH^- = SiO_3^{2-} + H_2O \tag{20}$$

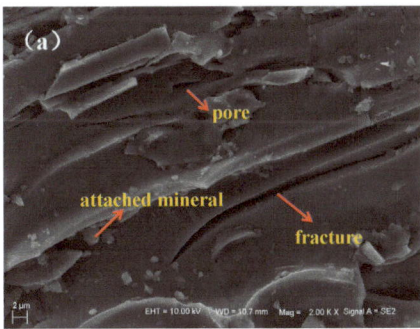 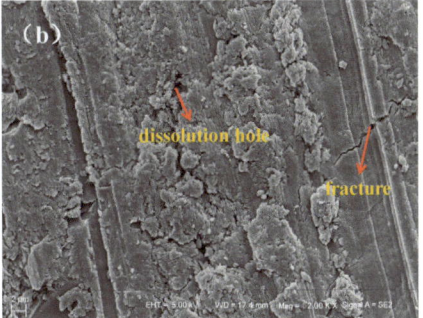

Figure 11. Microscopic morphology of coal samples under the action of salt solution, (**a**) natural state, (**b**) after 0.1 mol/L salt solution immersion.

4.4.3. Interaction Mechanism between Coal and Salt Solution

The strength of coal will deteriorate to a certain extent under the action of salt solution [37,45]. The deterioration of coal strength under the action of salt solution is mainly due to the weakening of cohesion between particles. Only considering the static liquid bridge force, the cohesion between particles is mainly composed of the gravitational attraction between particles (F_a) and the static liquid bridge force (F_{cap}) and the expressions are as follows [46]:

$$F_a = G \frac{m_1 m_2}{(2R_0 + D)^2} \quad (21)$$

$$F_{cap} = 2\pi R_0 \sigma \cos \beta \left[1 - \frac{D}{2R_2 \cos \beta} \right] \quad (22)$$

where m_1, m_2 are the mass of particles; R_0 is the radius of the particle; D is the distance between particles; σ is surface tension; β is the contact angle between liquid and particle; and R_2 is the radius of the liquid bridge neck.

Ni et al. [47] found that the surface tension between liquid and solid particles decreases with the increase in salt solution concentration. It can be seen from Formula (21) that the cohesion between particles in coal is positively correlated with the surface tension, and the increase in surface tension will lead to the increase in cohesion, and vice versa, which indicated that the increase in salt solution will weaken the cohesion between particles, thus resulting in the deterioration of coal strength.

5. Conclusions

In order to study the effect of salt solution on pore structure of coal, salt solution with different concentration was used to soak coal sample and nuclear magnetic resonance measurement was carried out. Firstly, the aging evolution characteristics of porosity and pore structure of coal sample were analyzed. Then, the fractal characteristics of pore structure were discussed on the basis of fractal theory, and the relationship between fractal dimension and immersion parameters was analyzed. Finally, the aging damage variable based on the fractal characteristics of pores was defined, and the hydrochemical damage mechanism of coal under the action of salt solution was analyzed. The main conclusions are summarized as follows:

(1) With the effect of salt solution immersion, the porosity of coal increased with soaking time. The change rate of porosity increased nonlinearly with soaking time and linearly with salt solution concentration.

(2) Under the action of salt solution immersion, the NMR transverse relaxation time range of coal becomes wider, and more pores with larger or smaller size were gradually formed. The number of seepage pores and total pores increased with soaking time. while the number of adsorption pores increased first and then decreased with soaking time. At the later stage of immersion, the pores with small size gradually connect to form larger pores.

(3) The relationship between fractal dimension and soaking time is linearly decreasing. Under the same immersion time, the pore fractal dimension of coal immersed in salt solution decreased more rapidly than that of coal immersed in distilled water. The damage effect of salt solution soaking on coal matrix is greater than that of distilled water. There is a negative correlation between fractal dimension and porosity.

(4) The diachronic damage variables based on pore fractal dimension was defined. The damage variables have a nonlinear increasing relationship with the soaking time, indicating that the longer the soaking time, the more obvious the pore structure changes and the greater the deterioration of coal. The damage mechanism of coal properties was described from three aspects: water corrosion, acid or alkali chemical reaction and interaction between salt and coal.

The deterioration of coal pore structure affects its macroscopic mechanical properties [24]. The essential cause of coal pillar instability failure is the weakening of the ability to resist deformation under external loads. In order to accurately evaluate the stability of coal pillar, it is necessary to establish a direct relationship between the changes in internal pore structure and mechanical properties, which is what we need to further study in the future. In engineering practice, the temperature and flow velocity of mine water are constantly changing. In addition, a coal pillar is subjected to the pressure of overlying rock during the soaking process. To scientifically evaluate the stability of coal pillar, we need to comprehensively consider the coupling effects of multiple factors such as temperature, stress, and seepage to accurately obtain the evolution law of internal pore and fracture structure of coal pillar in natural conditions. This is the focus of future research.

Author Contributions: Conceptualization, M.W. and Y.T.; methodology, M.W.; validation, Y.T.; formal analysis, M.W.; investigation, M.W. and Y.T.; resources, M.W. and Q.G.; data curation, Y.T. and L.W.; writing—original draft preparation, M.W.; writing—review and editing, Y.T. and Z.Z.; supervision, M.W.; project administration, Z.Z.; funding acquisition, M.W., Y.T., L.W. and Z.Z. All authors have read and agreed to the published version of the manuscript.

Funding: This work was supported by the National Natural Science Foundation of China (Grant No. 52274167), the Research Foundation of Education Bureau of Hunan Province (Grant No. 22B0410, 22C0221, 23A0329), the Natural Science Foundation of Hunan Province (Grant No. 2022JJ40374, 2023JJ40549), the Science and Technology Innovation Program of Hunan Province, China (Grant No. 2023RC3171).

Data Availability Statement: The related data used to support the findings of this study are included within the article.

Conflicts of Interest: The authors declare no conflict of interest.

References

1. Shi, J.; Huang, W.; Han, H.; Xu, C. Review on treatment technology of salt wastewater in coal chemical industry of China. *Desalination* **2020**, *493*, 114640. [CrossRef]
2. Hamawand, I.; Yusaf, T.; Hamawand, S. Coal seam gas and associated water: A review paper. *Renew. Sustain. Energy Rev.* **2013**, *22*, 550–560. [CrossRef]
3. Qiao, L.; Wang, Z.; Huang, A. Alteration of mesoscopic properties and mechanical behavior of sandstone due to hydro-physical and hydro-chemical effects. *Rock Mech. Rock Eng.* **2017**, *50*, 255–267. [CrossRef]
4. Zhou, Z.; Wang, P.; Cai, X.; Cao, W. Influence of Water Content on Energy Partition and Release in Rock Failure: Implications for Water-Weakening on Rock-burst Proneness. *Rock Mech. Rock Eng.* **2023**, *56*, 6189–6205. [CrossRef]
5. Noël, C.; Baud, P.; Violay, M. Effect of water on sandstone's fracture toughness and frictional parameters: Brittle strength constraints. *Int. J. Rock Mech. Min.* **2021**, *147*, 104916. [CrossRef]
6. Feng, X.; Chen, S.; Li, S. Effects of water chemistry on microcracking and compressive strength of granite. *Int. J. Rock Mech. Min.* **2001**, *38*, 557–568. [CrossRef]
7. Zhou, Z.; Cai, X.; Cao, W.; Li, X.; Xiong, C. Influence of Water Content on Mechanical Properties of Rock in Both Saturation and Drying Processes. *Rock Mech. Rock Eng.* **2016**, *49*, 3009–3025. [CrossRef]
8. Farquharson, J.; Kushnir, A.; Wild, B.; Baud, P. Physical property evolution of granite during experimental chemical stimulation. *Geotherm. Energy* **2020**, *8*, 14. [CrossRef]
9. Erguler, Z.; Ulusay, R. Water-induced variations in mechanical properties of clay-bearing rocks. *Int. J. Rock Mech. Min.* **2009**, *46*, 355–370. [CrossRef]
10. Chen, S.; Du, Z.; Zhang, Z.; Zhang, H.; Xia, Z.; Feng, F. Effects of chloride on the early mechanical properties and microstruc-ture of gangue-cemented paste backfill. *Constr. Build. Mater.* **2020**, *235*, 117504. [CrossRef]
11. Ai, T.; Wu, S.; Zhang, R.; Gao, M.; Zhou, J.; Xie, J.; Ren, L.; Zhang, Z. Changes in the structure and mechanical properties of a typical coal induced by water immersion. *Int. J. Rock Mech. Min.* **2021**, *138*, 104597. [CrossRef]
12. Gu, H.; Tao, M.; Cao, W.; Zhou, J.; Li, X. Dynamic fracture behaviour and evolution mechanism of soft coal with different porosities and water contents. *Theor. Appl. Fract. Mech.* **2019**, *103*, 102265. [CrossRef]
13. Zhao, Y.; Liu, S.; Jiang, Y.; Wang, K.; Huang, Y. Dynamic Tensile Strength of Coal under Dry and Saturated Conditions. *Rock Mech. Rock Eng.* **2016**, *49*, 1709–1720. [CrossRef]
14. Liu, P.; Fan, L.; Fan, J.; Zhong, F. Effect of water content on the induced alteration of pore morphology and gas sorption/diffusion kinetics in coal with ultrasound treatment. *Fuel* **2021**, *306*, 121752. [CrossRef]
15. Zhang, X.; Gamage, R.; Perera, M.; Ranathunga, A. Effects of Water and Brine Saturation on Mechanical Property Alterations of Brown Coal. *Energies* **2018**, *11*, 1116. [CrossRef]

16. Yao, Q.; Chen, T.; Ju, M.; Liang, S.; Liu, Y.; Li, X. Effects of water intrusion on mechanical properties of and crack propagation in coal. *Rock Mech. Rock Eng.* **2016**, *49*, 4699–4709. [CrossRef]
17. Liu, Y.; Yin, G.; Li, M.; Zhang, D.; Huang, G.; Liu, P.; Liu, C.; Zhao, H.; Yu, B. Mechanical properties and failure behavior of dry and water-saturated anisotropic coal under true-triaxial loading conditions. *Rock Mech. Rock Eng.* **2020**, *53*, 4799–4818. [CrossRef]
18. Yao, Q.; Zheng, C.; Tang, C.; Xu, Q.; Chong, Z.; Li, X. Experimental Investigation of the Mechanical Failure Behavior of Coal Specimens With Water Intrusion. *Front. Earth Sci.* **2020**, *7*, 348. [CrossRef]
19. Wang, S.; Elsworth, D.; Liu, J. Permeability evolution in fractured coal: The roles of fracture geometry and water-content. *Int. J. Coal Geol.* **2011**, *87*, 13–25. [CrossRef]
20. Larsen, J. The effects of dissolved CO_2 on coal structure and properties. *Int. J. Coal Geol.* **2004**, *57*, 63–70. [CrossRef]
21. Balucan, R.; Turner, L.; Steel, K. Acid-induced mineral alteration and its influence on the permeability and compressibility of coal. *J. Nat. Gas. Sci. Eng.* **2016**, *33*, 973–987. [CrossRef]
22. Xu, J.; Zhai, C.; Liu, S.; Qin, L.; Wu, S. Pore variation of three different metamorphic coals by multiple freezing-thawing cycles of liquid CO_2 injection for coalbed methane recovery. *Fuel* **2017**, *208*, 41–51. [CrossRef]
23. Xie, J.; Ni, G.; Xie, H.; Li, S.; Sun, Q.; Dong, K. The effect of adding surfactant to the treating acid on the chemical properties of an acid-treated coal. *Powder Technol.* **2019**, *356*, 263–272.
24. Li, S.; Ni, G.; Wang, H.; Xun, M.; Xu, Y. Effects of acid solution of different components on the pore structure and mechanical properties of coal. *Adv. Powder Technol.* **2020**, *31*, 1736–1747. [CrossRef]
25. Xu, Q.; Liu, R.; Yang, H. Effect of acid and alkali solutions on micro-components of coal. *J. Mol. Liq.* **2021**, *329*, 115518. [CrossRef]
26. Yang, H.; Yu, Y.; Cheng, W.; Rui, J.; Xu, Q. Influence of acetic acid dissolution time on evolution of coal phase and surface morphology. *Fuel* **2021**, *286*, 119464. [CrossRef]
27. Li, Y.; Cui, H.; Zhang, P.; Wang, D.; Wei, J. Three-dimensional visualization and quantitative characterization of coal fracture dynamic evolution under uniaxial and triaxial compression based on μCT scanning. *Fuel* **2020**, *262*, 116568. [CrossRef]
28. Liu, Z.; Liu, D.; Cai, Y.; Yao, Y.; Pan, Z.; Zhou, Y. Application of nuclear magnetic resonance (NMR) in coalbed methane and shale reservoirs: A review. *Int. J. Coal Geol.* **2020**, *218*, 103261. [CrossRef]
29. Nie, B.; Liu, X.; Yang, L.; Meng, J.; Li, X. Pore structure characterization of different rank coals using gas adsorption and scanning electron microscopy. *Fuel* **2015**, *158*, 908–917. [CrossRef]
30. Li, Y.; Song, D.; Liu, S.; Ji, X.; Hao, H. Evaluation of pore properties in coal through compressibility correction based on mercury intrusion porosimetry: A practical approach. *Fuel* **2021**, *291*, 120130. [CrossRef]
31. Ni, G.; Li, S.; Rahman, S.; Xun, M.; Wang, H.; Xu, Y.; Xie, H. Effect of nitric acid on the pore structure and fractal characteristics of coal based on the low-temperature nitrogen adsorption method. *Powder Technol.* **2020**, *367*, 506–516. [CrossRef]
32. Zhou, S.; Liu, D.; Cai, Y.; Yao, Y. Fractal characterization of pore-fracture in low-rank coals using a low-field NMR relaxation method. *Fuel* **2016**, *181*, 218–226. [CrossRef]
33. Liu, Z.; Yang, H.; Wang, W.; Cheng, W.; Xin, L. Experimental Study on the Pore Structure Fractals and Seepage Characteristics of a Coal Sample Around a Borehole in Coal Seam Water Infusion. *Transp. Porous Media* **2018**, *125*, 289–309. [CrossRef]
34. Chen, S.; Tang, D.; Tao, S.; Ji, X.; Xu, H. Fractal analysis of the dynamic variation in pore-fracture systems un-der the action of stress using a low-field NMR relaxation method: An experimental study of coals from western Guizhou in China. *J. Pet. Sci. Eng.* **2019**, *173*, 617–629. [CrossRef]
35. Qin, L.; Zhai, C.; Liu, S.; Xu, J.; Wu, S.; Dong, R. Fractal dimensions of low rank coal subjected to liquid nitrogen freeze-thaw based on nuclear magnetic resonance applied for coalbed methane recovery. *Powder Technol.* **2018**, *325*, 11–20. [CrossRef]
36. Yao, Y.; Liu, D.; Tang, D.; Tang, S.; Huang, W.; Liu, Z.; Che, Y. Fractal characterization of seepage-pores of coals from China: An in-vestigation on permeability of coals. *Comput. Geosci.* **2009**, *35*, 1159–1166. [CrossRef]
37. Wang, M.; Guo, Q.; Tian, Y.; Dai, B. Physical and Mechanical Properties Evolution of Coal Subjected to Salty Solution and Damage Constitutive Model under Uniaxial Compression. *Mathematics* **2021**, *9*, 3264. [CrossRef]
38. Ni, G.; Xie, H.; Li, S.; Sun, Q.; Huang, D.; Cheng, Y.; Wang, N. The effect of anionic surfactant (SDS) on pore-fracture evolution of acidified coal and its significance for coalbed methane extraction. *Adv. Powder Technol.* **2019**, *30*, 940–951.
39. Liu, R.; Li, B.; Jiang, Y. A fractal model based on a new governing equation of fluid flow in fractures for characterizing hydraulic properties of rock fracture networks. *Comput. Geotech.* **2016**, *75*, 57–68. [CrossRef]
40. Li, B.; Liu, R.; Jiang, Y. A multiple fractal model for estimating permeability of dual-porosity media. *J. Hydrol.* **2016**, *540*, 659–669. [CrossRef]
41. Li, P.; Cai, M.; Gao, Y.; Wang, P.; Miao, S.; Wang, Y.; Xi, X. Dynamic mechanical behavior and cracking mechanism of cross-jointed granite containing a hole. *J. Mater. Res. Technol.* **2023**, *22*, 1572–1594. [CrossRef]
42. Cai, X.; Zhou, Z.; Tan, L.; Zang, H.; Song, Z. Fracture behavior and damage mechanisms of sandstone subjected to wetting-drying cycles. *Eng. Fract. Mech.* **2020**, *234*, 107109. [CrossRef]
43. Smoliński, A.; Malashkevych, D.; Petlovanyi, M.; Rysbekov, K.; Lozynskyi, V.; Sai, K. Research into Impact of Leaving Waste Rocks in the Mined-Out Space on the Geomechanical State of the Rock Mass Surrounding the Longwall Face. *Energies* **2022**, *15*, 9522. [CrossRef]
44. Gu, H.; Tao, M.; Wang, J.; Jiang, H.; Li, Q.; Wang, W. Influence of water content on dynamic mechanical properties of coal. *Geomech. Eng.* **2018**, *16*, 85–95.

5. Wang, M.; Xi, X.; Guo, Q. Deterioration Mechanism and Constitutive Model of Coal Subjected to Dry-ing-Wetting Cycles of Salty Mine Water. *Lithosphere* **2022**, *2022*, 7935979. [CrossRef]
6. Pitois, O.; Moucheront, P.; Chateau, X. Liquid Bridge between Two Moving Spheres: An Experimental Study of Viscosity Effects. *J. Colloid Interface Sci.* **2000**, *231*, 26–31. [CrossRef]
7. Ni, G.; Sun, Q.; Xun, M.; Wang, H.; Wang, H.; Cheng, W.; Wang, G. Effect of NaCl-SDS compound solution on the wettability and functional groups of coal. *Fuel* **2019**, *257*, 11607.

Disclaimer/Publisher's Note: The statements, opinions and data contained in all publications are solely those of the individual author(s) and contributor(s) and not of MDPI and/or the editor(s). MDPI and/or the editor(s) disclaim responsibility for any injury to people or property resulting from any ideas, methods, instructions or products referred to in the content.

An Improved Rock Damage Characterization Method Based on the Shortest Travel Time Optimization with Active Acoustic Testing

Jing Zhou [1,2], Lang Liu [1,2,*], Yuan Zhao [3], Mengbo Zhu [1,2], Ruofan Wang [1,2] and Dengdeng Zhuang [1,2]

[1] Energy School, Xi'an University of Science and Technology, Xi'an 710054, China; jingzhou@xust.edu.cn (J.Z.); mengbo_zhu@163.com (M.Z.); ruofan.wang@xust.edu.cn (R.W.); zddeng@126.com (D.Z.)
[2] Key Laboratory of Western Mines and Hazards Prevention, Ministry of Education of China, Xi'an 710054, China
[3] Department of Civil Engineering, School of Human Settlements and Civil Engineering, Xi'an Jiaotong University, Xi'an 712000, China; zhaoyuan92@xjtu.edu.cn
* Correspondence: liulang@xust.edu.cn

Abstract: Real-time evaluation of the damage location and level of rock mass is essential for preventing underground engineering disasters. However, the heterogeneity of rock mass, which results from the presence of layered rock media, faults, and pores, makes it difficult to characterize the damage evolution accurately in real time. To address this issue, an improved method for rock damage characterization is proposed. This method optimizes the solution of the global shortest acoustic wave propagation path in the medium and verifies it with layered and defective media models. Based on this, the relationship between the inversion results of the wave velocity field and the distribution of rock damage is established, thereby achieving quantitative characterization of rock damage distribution and degree. Thus, the improved method is more suitable for heterogeneous rock media. Finally, the proposed method was used to characterize the damage distribution evolution process of rock media during uniaxial compression experiments. The obtained results were compared and analyzed with digital speckle patterns, and the influencing factors during the use of the proposed method are discussed.

Keywords: rock damage; non-destructive testing; inversion of wave velocity field; damage characterization

MSC: 74L10

1. Introduction

Rock is the main supporting material in underground engineering [1–3], and its damage degree evolves with time under the action of external factors such as force [3–6], temperature [7–9], and water [10–12]. Real-time detection and characterization of rock damage location and damage level is the key to preventing underground disasters [13–15]. The commonly used non-destructive characterization methods for rock damage include image method and acoustic method [16,17]. The image method characterizes the damage of rocks by comparing and identifying the images of the rock before and after the damage change [18,19]. The image method relies on high-resolution image acquisition equipment and is limited by lighting conditions and viewing angles. The acoustic wave method mainly analyzes the damage by imaging changes in the velocity of acoustic waves propagating in rocks [20,21]. The characterization method based on acoustic waves has more advantages in revealing the location and mechanism of key fracture damage of rocks and the future development direction of cracks [22,23]. Many studies have been carried out based on this method [24].

The wave velocity of the medium, which is usually obtained from the linear relationship between the acoustic wave test propagation distance and propagation time [25,26], is often associated with the mechanical properties of the medium to analyze its damage changes [27,28]. Madhubabu [29] et al. used multiple linear regression analysis (MVRA) and artificial neural network (ANN) to predict the compressive strength and elastic modulus of carbonate rocks by measuring parameters such as ultrasonic wave velocity and porosity. Hanxin Chen [30] et al. established a nonlinear Lamb wave detection system, analyzed the obtained time domain waveform using fast Fourier transform (FFT), and studied the impact of two types of defects on the non-linear effects of Lamb waves. Umrao [31] et al. proposed an adaptive neural fuzzy inference system (ANFIS) to predict the strength and elastic modulus of sedimentary rocks by measuring P-wave velocity and porosity, considering their heterogeneity. Abbas et al. tested the parameters of ultrasonic wave velocity, amplitude, and energy of composite sand shale and evaluated the macroscopic deformation and crack propagation of the sample. Abbas [32] et al. evaluated the macroscopic deformation and crack propagation of the sample using parameters such as the ultrasonic wave velocity, amplitude, and energy of composite sand shale. Rodríguez [33] et al. analyzed the distribution of damage within rock specimens under diametral compression with P-wave velocity calculation.

The wave velocity field imaging of the medium can be achieved by using multiple acoustic sensors and multiple sets of arrival data, which enables a more accurate analysis of the damage distribution of the rock medium [34,35]. The time-domain inversion calculation of the wave velocity field consists of two interrelated parts: forward and inversion [36]. The forward calculation algorithm determines the propagation model of the acoustic wave in the wave velocity field and obtains the theoretical travel time. In the iterative calculation, the difference between the theoretical and measured travel time data is continuously corrected to obtain the final value [37]. Based on the basic theory used in the inversion calculation, it can be divided into two types: wave velocity field inversion based on ray theory and wave velocity field inversion based on wave theory [38]. Gorbatov [39] et al. calculated the P-wave velocity structure of the Kamchatka Peninsula in the Western Pacific using 5270 shallow- and medium-depth earthquakes recorded in 32 stations of the Russian Geophysical Service Regional Seismic Network. Goodfellow [40] et al. used active and passive ultrasonic methods to study the evolution of the attenuation characteristics of the sandstone sample during true triaxial deformation, calculated the wave velocity field during the stress process of the rock sample, and established a relationship between the wave velocity field and the damage. Caibin Xu et al. [41] pointed out that the scattering behavior between Lamb waves and defects is closely related to wavelength and defect size. They proposed a multi-narrowband fusion method that utilizes Lamb wave information contained in multiple frequency bands to improve the image quality of Lamb wave phased array imaging.

The previous studies indicate that the key to real-time characterization of rock damage based on active acoustic testing is to establish the relationship between wave velocity field imaging results and damage. The shooting method (angle increment method) and bending method are the most basic local forward modeling methods [42], which have high computational efficiency but limited solution accuracy when the ray coverage density is insufficient. The global algorithm has a slower calculation speed but yields a more refined result of inverting the wave velocity field. The presence of layers, holes, and fissures in rock increases the difficulty of characterizing its damage. When the acoustic waves encounter various defects such as faults and holes in the medium, they change their paths. The received waveform information reflects such defect information of the medium [43,44]. Therefore, the rock damage distribution can be characterized by association with the wave velocity field of the rock. The challenge is how to solve the rock wave velocity field accurately and quickly.

An improved method for rock damage characterization based on the shortest travel time optimization with active acoustic testing is proposed. In Section 2, the global shortest travel time optimization based on Bellman–Ford is introduced to solve the distribution of the medium wave velocity field. Then, the connection between the wave velocity field and the rock damage distribution is established. In Section 3, a rock uniaxial compression experiment is used to verify the accuracy of the proposed method in characterizing the evolution of the damage distribution. In Section 4, the influence of emission waveform parameters on the results of the rock damage characterization method based on acoustic wave testing is discussed.

2. Method
2.1. Shortest Path Solution Based on Bellman–Ford Method

The Bellman–Ford algorithm, employed in dynamic programming, excels at finding the shortest path from a single source. Its integration into wave velocity field solutions swiftly yields the globally shortest travel time path, with a key emphasis on efficient relaxation calculations.

Figure 1 is an example of the Bellman–Ford algorithm finding the shortest path from S. Figure 1 illustrates the nodes along the propagation paths and the corresponding propagation times for each sub-path. The initial propagation time is 0. The initial slack involves comparing the propagation paths to all adjacent nodes to identify the shortest propagation time path. Given that $t_1 < t_5$, the shortest path is S-R_1, with a recorded shortest path travel time of 1. In the second slack calculation, considering $t_1 + t_2 < t_5$, the shortest path is revised to S-R_1-R_2, and the recorded shortest travel time is updated to 3. In the third slack calculation, $t_1 + t_2 + t_3 < t_5$ results in the shortest path being S-R_1-R_2-R_3, with a recorded shortest path travel time of 5. Finally, considering $t_1 + t_2 + t_3 + t_4 < t_5$, the fourth slack calculation yields the shortest path as S-R_1-R_2-R_3-R. The steps above can calculate the shortest travel time path from S to R.

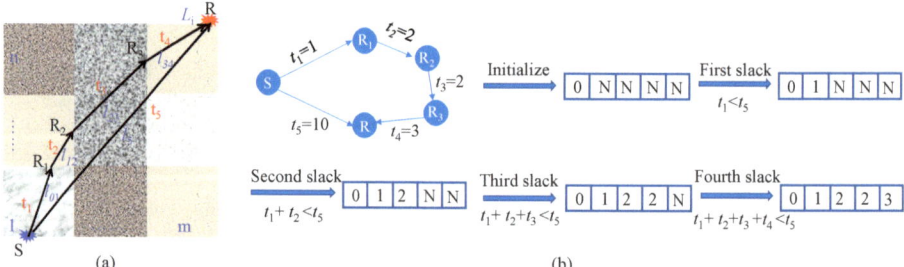

Figure 1. The principle of the shortest path calculation using the Bellman–Ford algorithm. (**a**) is a schematic diagram of the straight line propagation path and the refraction propagation path. (**b**) is the Bellman Ford algorithm to calculate the shortest propagation path considering refraction.

The shortest travel time path algorithm can obtain a path that adheres to Snell's law. It can quickly find the globally shortest path from multiple start nodes to multiple termination nodes. It has more advantages in the wave velocity field calculation of rock materials than the ray tracing method.

We thus used the Bellman–Ford algorithm to solve the shortest travel time path and analyze several common models' global acoustic wave propagation paths in rock damage characterization.

Figure 2a shows a homogeneous medium with a wave velocity of 3000 m/s and 12 sensors. These sensors can transmit and receive acoustic waves. The shortest path solution method based on the Bellman–Ford algorithm obtains the shortest propagation time path in the whole field. The results of the propagation path with the shortest time are shown in Figure 2a. In homogeneous media, the theoretical propagation path with the shortest time is the linear distance between the emission point and the reception point. The solved propagation path with the shortest time conforms to the theoretical results.

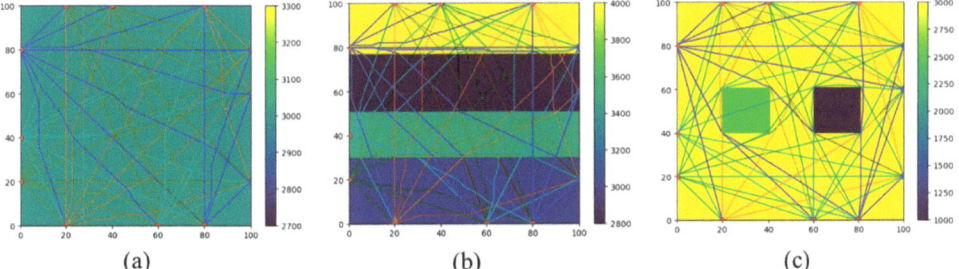

Figure 2. Propagation path with the shortest time of several common models obtained by the Bellman–Ford algorithm. (**a**–**c**) are the propagation path diagrams of the improved algorithm in homogeneous media, layered media and defective media respectively.

Figure 2b shows a layered medium with velocities of 4000 m/s, 2800 m/s, 3500 m/s, and 3000 m/s from top to bottom. The thickness from top to bottom is 24 m, 26 m, 20 m, and 30 m, respectively, and there are 12 sensors for acoustic testing. The propagation path with the shortest time obtained based on the Bellman–Ford algorithm is shown in Figure 2b. Results show that the acoustic wave propagation path refracts at the interface of the layered medium, which is consistent with the hypothetical situation.

Figure 2c shows a medium with a defect area. Its background wave velocity is 3000 m/s, including two defects with different wave velocities. The wave velocity of one defect area is 2500 m/s, which is slightly lower than the background wave velocity. The other is an ultra-low wave velocity zone, with a wave velocity of 1000 m/s.

According to Snell's law, acoustic waves preferentially propagate through areas with higher propagation speeds. Diffraction will occur in the area with ultra-low wave velocity. The propagation time with a straight line is the shortest one corresponding to the area, with little difference from the background wave velocity. The results in Figure 2 are also consistent.

2.2. Wave Velocity Field Calculation

Once the fastest propagation path is determined, the theoretical propagation time for each path is calculated under the assumed initial wave velocity background. This calculation uses the whole field's shortest propagation path solution method based on the Bellman–Ford algorithm. The medium's wave velocity model undergoes continuous refinement based on the arrival time of the received waveform. The wave velocity field of the medium is derived by minimizing errors. The Radon inverse transform is employed to iteratively establish an initial value for calculating the initial wave velocity field, mitigating the influence of the initial value on the calculation results.

As shown in Figure 1a, a medium is divided into m × n units, including several acoustic emission and receiving sensors. The path from one acoustic emission position to the acoustic receiving position is L_i, and its propagation sub-path in each small unit is l_{ij}. The corresponding time of each sub-path is t_{ij}, and the total propagation time is T_i.

The process of the acoustic signal from the acoustic emission point to the acoustic receiving position along the shortest travel time path is Radon positive transformation. The internal information of the inverse medium is the Radon inverse transform. According to Radon changes, the following is true:

$$t_i = \int_{L_i} \frac{1}{v_j(x,y)} dl = \int_{L_i} f_j(x,y) dl, \tag{1}$$

where $v_j(x,y)$ is the wave speed of the jth small unit, and $f_j(x,y)$ is the reciprocal of the jth small unit's wave speed.

When the wave velocity grid of the small element assumed for wave velocity inversion is small enough, the distance can be considered as a constant, and Equation (4) can be changed as follows:

$$t_i = \sum_{j=1}^{m} a_{ij} x_j, \qquad (2)$$

$$\begin{cases} t_1 = a_{11}x_1 + a_{12}x_2 + \cdots + a_{1m}x_m \\ t_2 = a_{21}x_1 + a_{22}x_2 + \cdots + a_{2m}x_m \\ \vdots \\ t_n = a_{n1}x_1 + a_{n2}x_2 + \cdots + a_{nm}x_m \end{cases}, \qquad (3)$$

where t is the monitored arrival time; a is the propagation length obtained by the Bellman–Ford algorithm; x is the slowness of wave velocity.

The back projection algorithm (BPT) is used to solve the problem. We can take the calculation of the wave velocity of cell j in Figure 1a as an example. The wave velocity of cell j is determined by dividing the cumulative time of all paths propagating in cell j by the cumulative path length propagating in cell j. The propagation time of each path in cell j is weighted by the ratio of the propagation path length l_{ij} of the ith acoustic propagation path in cell j to the total length L_i of the ith acoustic propagation path. The ith acoustic propagation path total travel time (T_i) is allocated to each small cell (t_i) of inverse wave velocity. The mathematical expression for solving wave velocity x_i of any grid is as follows:

$$x_i = \sum_{i=1}^{m}\left[T_i\left(\sum_{j=1}^{n} l_{ij}/L_i\right)\right] \Big/ \sum_{i=1}^{m} l_{ij}. \qquad (4)$$

This calculation result is taken as the initial value of the least squares iteration [45]. The error between theoretical travel time and monitoring travel time is illustrated as follows:

$$\begin{cases} \varepsilon_1 = t_1 - a_{11}x_1 + a_{12}x_2 + \cdots + a_{1m}x_m \\ \varepsilon_2 = t_2 - a_{21}x_1 + a_{22}x_2 + \cdots + a_{2m}x_m \\ \vdots \\ \varepsilon_m = t_n - a_{n1}x_1 + a_{n2}x_2 + \cdots + a_{nm}x_m \end{cases}. \qquad (5)$$

Then, the sum of squared errors is as follows:

$$\varepsilon = \varepsilon_1^2 + \varepsilon_2^2 + \cdots + \varepsilon_n^2 \qquad (6)$$

The slow derivation of each wave to be solved is as given:

$$\begin{cases} \frac{\partial \varepsilon}{\partial x_1} = 0 \\ \frac{\partial \varepsilon}{\partial x_1} = 0 \\ \vdots \\ \frac{\partial \varepsilon}{\partial x_m} = 0 \end{cases}. \qquad (7)$$

Substituting into Equation (2), we obtain the following:

$$\begin{cases} -2\sum_{i=1}^{n} a_{i1}[t_i - (a_{11}x_1 + a_{12}x_2 + \cdots + a_{1m}x_m)] = 0 \\ -2\sum_{i=1}^{n} a_{im}[t_i - (a_{11}x_1 + a_{12}x_2 + \cdots + a_{1m}x_m)] = 0 \\ \vdots \\ -2\sum_{i=1}^{n} a_{im}[t_i - (a_{11}x_1 + a_{12}x_2 + \cdots + a_{1m}x_m)] = 0 \end{cases} \qquad (8)$$

We can convert this to the following:

$$\begin{cases} \sum_{i=1}^{n} a_{i1}(a_{11}x_1 + a_{12}x_2 + \cdots + a_{1m}x_m) = \sum_{i=1}^{n} a_{i1}t_i \\ \sum_{i=1}^{n} a_{i2}(a_{11}x_1 + a_{12}x_2 + \cdots + a_{1m}x_m) = \sum_{i=1}^{n} a_{i2}t_i \\ \vdots \\ \sum_{i=1}^{n} a_{im}(a_{11}x_1 + a_{12}x_2 + \cdots + a_{1m}x_m)] = \sum_{i=1}^{n} a_{im}t_i \end{cases} \quad (9)$$

Then, the wave velocity of each unit can be obtained as follows:

$$x = \left[A^T A\right]^{-1} A^T T \quad (10)$$

2.3. Damage Distribution Calculation

In the study of rock damage characterization, the damage factor D used to describe the damage level of the medium is a variable related to the initial and final state of the medium, and its value is between 0 and 1. D is 0 when the rock is undamaged, and D is 1 when it is completely damaged.

Assume that the initial wave velocity before rock damage occurs is V_0, the wave velocity measured under the current damage degree is V_i, and the wave velocity when the rock completely loses its bearing capacity is V_c. The relationship between acoustic wave velocity and rock damage can be established as follows [46]:

$$D = 1 - \left(\frac{V_i}{V_c}\right)^2. \quad (11)$$

In damage mechanics, strain is related to D as follows:

$$D = 1 - \exp\left[-a\left(\frac{\varepsilon_i}{\varepsilon_c}\right)^b\right] \quad (12)$$

where ε_i is the current strain of the rock; ε_c is the strain when the rock is completely damaged.

Since the strain of the rock under load is positively correlated with the wave velocity, the functional relationship between the wave velocity change and the damage level is as follows:

$$D = 1 - \exp\left[-a\left(\frac{\Delta V_i}{\Delta V}\right)^b\right], \quad (13)$$

where ΔV_i is the current wave velocity variation. ΔV is when the rock is completely damaged. Parameters a and b are set according to the range of wave velocity variation of the damaged rock mass.

Assuming the medium is completely damaged, its wave velocity decays to half its original value. The corresponding functional relationship between the damage and the measured wave velocity is shown in Figure 3.

Adjusting parameters a and b in Equation (13) can correct the sensitivity of wave velocity to characterize damage. When it is necessary to discern the minor damage, reduce a and increase b; when minor damage is not noticed, increase a and reduce b.

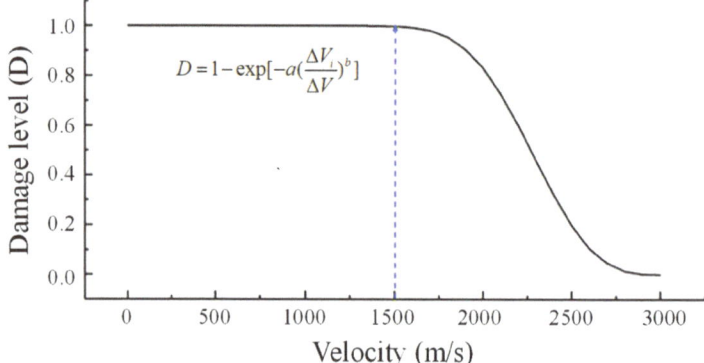

Figure 3. The corresponding functional relationship between the damage and the measured wave velocity.

2.4. Results

The improved method is used to calculate the wave velocity field distribution of the defective model in Figure 2c. The results are shown in Figure 4a. Figure 4b shows the wave velocity field distribution calculated by the initial method. The imaging unit error rate is shown in Figure 5. The newly improved method has slightly higher calculation accuracy than the initial method.

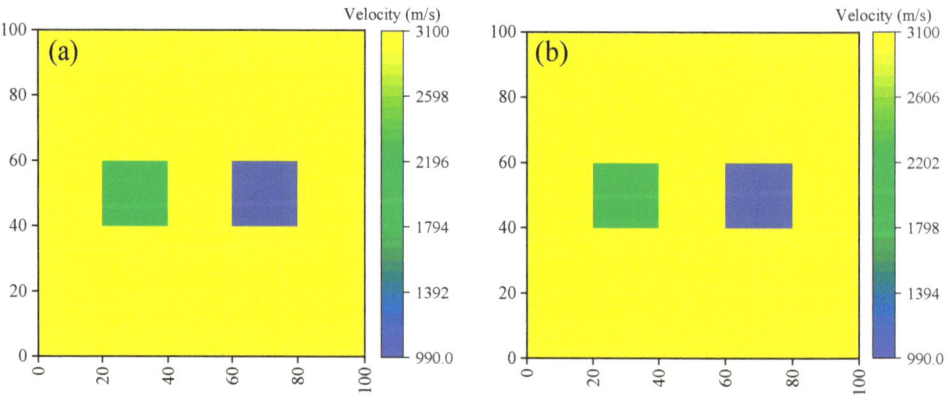

Figure 4. Results of the wave velocity field distribution: (**a**) is obtained by the improved method; (**b**) is obtained by the initial method.

In practical applications, the travel time data obtained from acoustic testing are used as observation values in wave velocity field inversion calculations. The disturbance analysis is of great significance. In the model shown in Figure 2c, a 1% travel time error disturbance is added to two, four, six, and eight paths. Then, the perturbed time shift data are used for wave velocity field inversion calculation. Figure 6 shows the error rate results for each calculation unit. The error rate gradually increases as the number of paths disturbed by travel time errors increases, and the error rate is lower for larger damage. The proposed method is still applicable when the number of paths with travel time error is less than six.

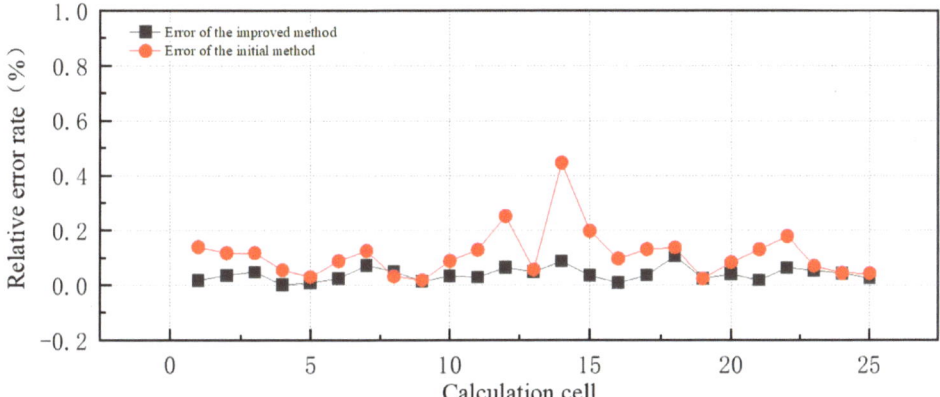

Figure 5. The relative error rate of all the calculation cells.

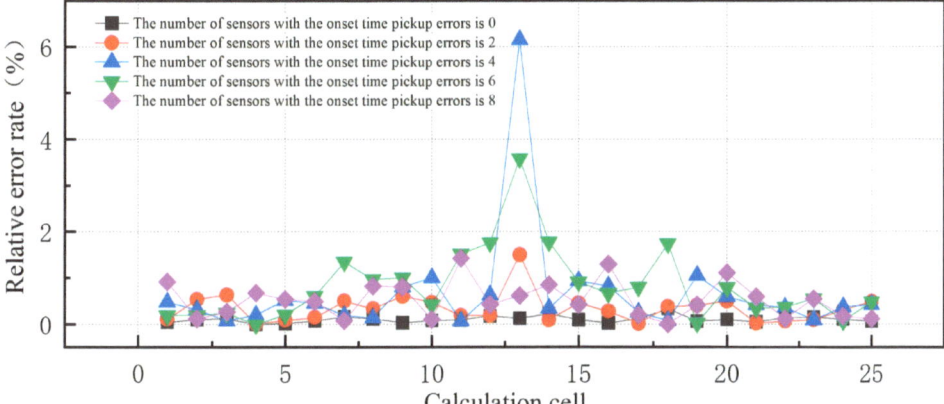

Figure 6. The relative error rate of each calculation unit when the number of measurement error paths is different.

3. Experimental Verification

3.1. Sample and Experiment

The equipment used in the experiment is shown in Figure 7. The uniaxial compression loading equipment provided external force to the rock sample to cause damage. The acoustic emission monitoring equipment was used to monitor the fracture signal of the rock damage process. Moreover, we utilized AST to test the current wave velocity of the rock sample at different stages. The industrial camera was used to take pictures of the damage process of rock samples.

The uniaxial compression equipment is an MTS-322T electro-hydraulic servo control testing machine from the Mechanical Testing Center of Central South University, with a load range of ±500 kN and a load accuracy of ±0.5%. The AE monitoring equipment is the DS5-16C AE acquisition system of Beijing Soft Island Times Technology Co., Ltd. (Beijing, China). It has 16 channels in total, and the range of its sampling frequency is 3 MHz–10 MHz. The matched AE amplifier is adjustable at 20/40/60 dB, and the model of the AE sensor is RS-2A. The industrial camera used in the experiment is the German Basler industrial camera (aca1920-155). Its highest sampling rate is 160 images per second, with a resolution of 5 million pixels.

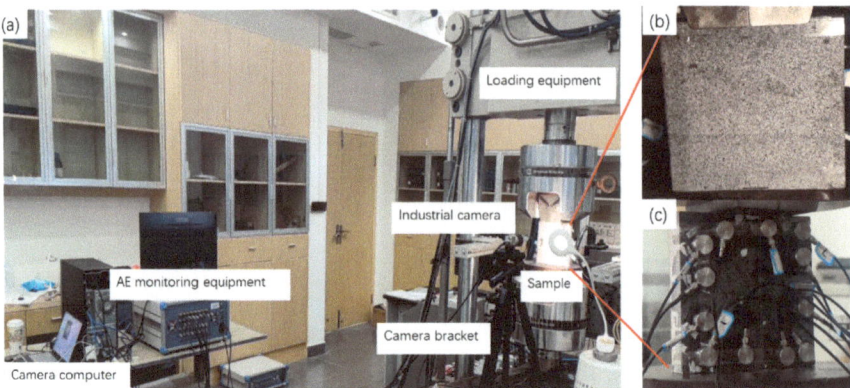

Figure 7. (**a**) is the experimental equipment and samples; (**b**) is one surface of the sample for industrial camera photography; (**c**) is the other surface of the sample for acoustic test and AE monitoring.

The flat granite sample with a side length of 150 mm and a thickness of 20 mm is shown in Figure 7b. The wave velocity of the complete sample is 3916 m/s, and the surface wave velocity is 2672 m/s. The photographing surface and the acoustic testing surface of the sample are shown in Figure 7b,c.

3.2. Experiment Process

The uniaxial compression test was conducted on the servo-hydraulic rock mechanics test system (MTS-322), with a loading rate of 5 kN/min.

Twelve sensors were arranged on the surface of the sample for acoustic testing. Table 1 displays the location coordinates of these sensors. The acoustic wave test transmitted the acoustic wave in turn on the acoustic test surface of the sample by calling the AST function in the DS5-16C AE acquisition system, and the excitation waveform used in the test was a pulse wave. First, an acoustic test was conducted before the experiment. Then, an acoustic test was conducted every 30 kN. Loading was stopped when the sample had visible cracks.

Table 1. Coordinates of the sensor.

	Sensors' Number											
	1	2	3	4	5	6	7	8	9	10	11	12
X	15	60	110	135	135	135	135	90	40	15	15	15
Y	15	15	15	15	60	110	135	135	135	120	90	50

The microfracture signal during uniaxial compression of the rock sample was monitored and collected by the AE monitoring system (DS5-16C), and the AE acquisition sensor was consistent with the acoustic testing sensor. The sampling frequency of the AE monitoring system is 3 MHz, and the signal amplification factor is 40 dB.

The Basler Aca1920-155 industrial camera took pictures of the sample deformation process during the experiment. The photographic surface of the industrial camera was opposite to the acoustic testing surface. The auxiliary white light source was used to illuminate the sample surface, improve brightness, and reduce the camera ISO parameters. The camera shooting resolution is 1920 × 1200 pixels, and the frame rate is 10 fps. These photos were processed by DIC technology. Since the granite sample has small, natural black and white units, and the size met the requirements, the sample surface did not require additional markings.

Figure 8a illustrates the change process of the loading force over time. Before the experiment, the wave velocity of the sample was measured once. Then, an acoustic test was carried out every 30 kN increase in load. After visible cracks appeared, the last acoustic test was carried out. A total of eight acoustic tests were carried out during the experiment. The time of each acoustic test is shown at the arrow positions in Figure 8a.

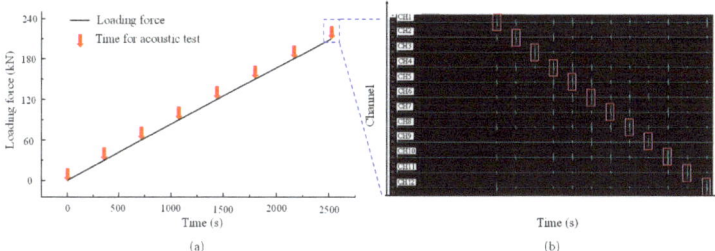

Figure 8. (a) The loading force changes with time and the time of the acoustic wave test; (b) is each channel's transmitted and received waveform. The red box is the excitation signal; the rest are the received signals.

The 12 sensors transmitted pulse waves in turn, and the others received acoustic waves propagating along the sample. The acoustic signals collected in the acoustic test are shown in Figure 8b. From top to bottom, they are the signals received by 12 channels. The red box is the excitation signal; the rest are the received signals.

Sensors at the ends were selected for analysis. The #2 sensor transmitted acoustic waves, and the #8 sensor received the waves propagating along the sample. The waveform received by the #8 sensor is shown in Figure 9.

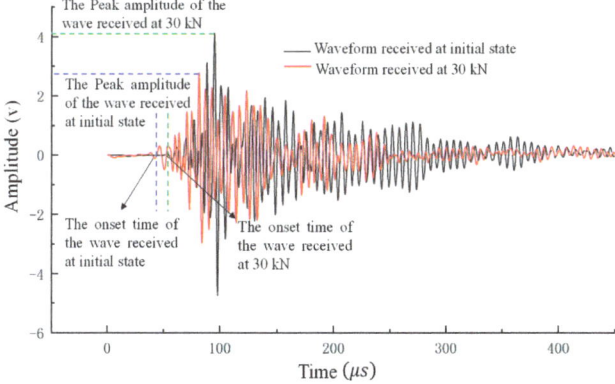

Figure 9. In the initial state and when the loading force is 30 kN, sensor 2 transmits acoustic waves, and sensor 8 receives waveforms.

3.3. Results

In this section, the damage location of the granite sample was characterized by calculating the change in the wave velocity field during the uniaxial compression test. The relationship between the wave velocity field and the damage was also established. The accuracy of the improved method to characterize the damage position was obtained by comparing the change results of the wave velocity field with the sample strain results calculated by DIC.

The size of the plate granite sample is 150 mm × 150 mm. Excluding the diameter of the acoustic emission sensor (18 mm), the size of the wave velocity calculated area in the plate sample is 120 mm × 120 mm. A total of 54 measuring paths could be made up of 12 sensors through the monitoring area. Utilizing the Bellman–Ford algorithm in dynamic programming, the initial velocity field of the plate granite sample was obtained by solving the shortest path within the calculated area. According to the relationship between wave velocity change and damage characterization established in Section 2.3, the damage of the sample during the loading process was characterized. The parameter range is generally set at 0.2~0.8 in rock uniaxial compression experiments. It can be calculated that a and b in Equations (2) and (3) are 3 and 6, respectively. The damage variable D is shown in Figure 10.

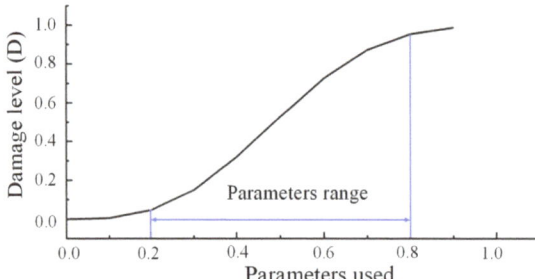

Figure 10. Parameter selection.

Figure 11 illustrates the wave velocity field distribution, damage distribution, and strain field of the rock sample during uniaxial compression. The damaged area identified by the improved method was consistent with the large strain area identified by the DIC technique.

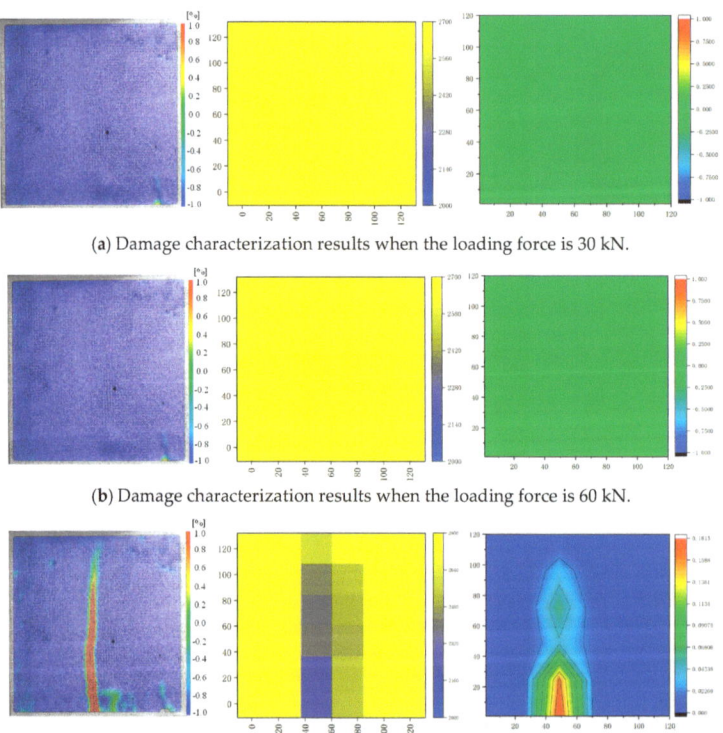

Figure 11. Cont.

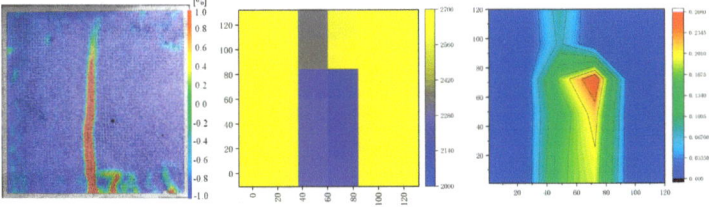

(d) Damage characterization results when the loading force is 120 kN.

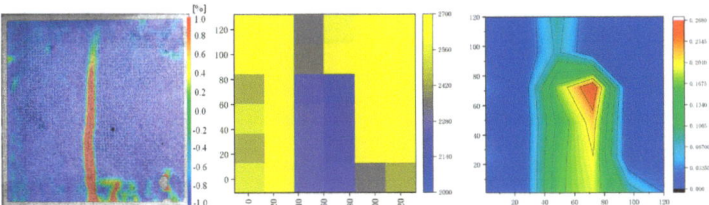

(e) Damage characterization results when the loading force is 150 kN.

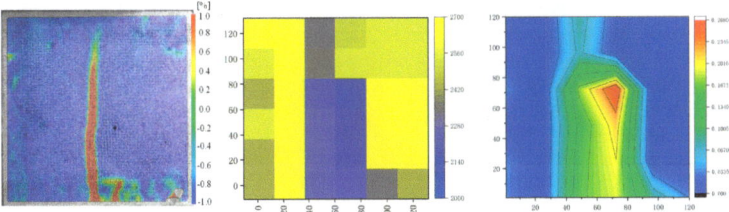

(f) Damage characterization results when the loading force is 180 kN.

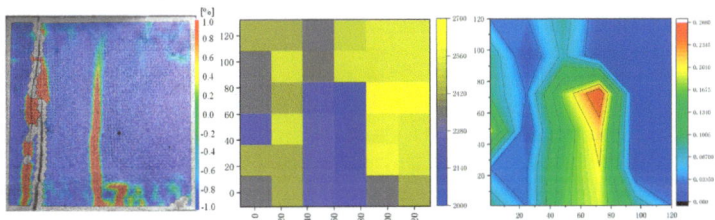

(g) Damage characterization results when the loading force is 210 kN.

Figure 11. Damage characterization results and digital speckle results with different loading forces.

4. Discussion

4.1. Sample and Experiment

The method presented in this paper provides a concise and accurate method for characterizing the damage distribution of rock. In practical applications, the degree of damage increases the internal cracks within the rock. It is thus necessary to analyze the influence of cracks on the acoustic testing method. This section analyzes the influence of waveform type, waveform parameters, and the relative position of a transmitted waveform and defect on the received waveform by the experiment.

The sample used was a granite slab sample with a crack in the center, as shown in Figures 5–10. Its size is 150 mm × 150 mm × 20 mm. The crack is at the center of the sample, as shown in Figure 12. The crack length is 20 mm, and the width is 2 mm.

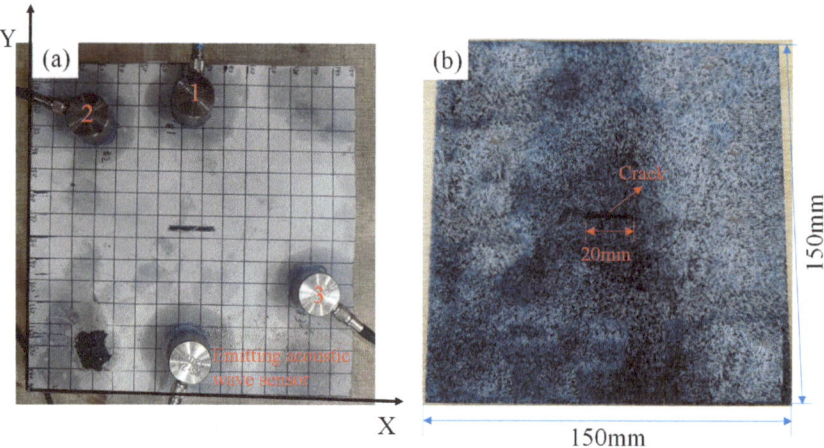

Figure 12. The granite slab sample with a crack. (**a**) is the relative position of the sensor and the crack on the flat sample; (**b**) is the size of the crack and the granite slab sample.

The AE equipment can emit the waveform edited by the user and collect the waveform transmitted through the sample. As shown in Figure 12, four AE sensors were arranged on the sample: one transmitting acoustic wave sensor and the other three receiving acoustic wave sensors. The sensor coordinates are shown in the Table 2.

Table 2. Sensor coordinates.

		AE Location	Sensor #1	Sensor #2	Sensor #3
Coordinates	X	75	75	30	130
	Y	20	130	120.4	50

The straight-line distances between the transmitting acoustic wave sensor and the three receiving acoustic wave sensors were 110 mm, 110.02 mm, and 62.65 mm, respectively. Compared with the position of the crack, the No. 1 sensor and the emitting acoustic wave sensor were located on both sides of the crack, and a straight-line distance passed through the crack. The No. 2 and emitting acoustic wave sensors were located on both sides of the crack, respectively, but the straight-line distance did not pass through the crack. The No. 3 sensor and the transmitting acoustic wave sensor were located on one side of the crack, and the straight-line distance did not pass through the crack.

The influence of the emitted sound wave frequency, different waveforms, and the relative position of the waveform and the defect on the received waveform was studied using this sample.

4.2. The Influence of Transmitting Acoustic Wave Frequency on Receiving Waveform Parameters

When studying the influence of the transmitted acoustic wave frequency on the received waveform, we chose sensor #3 for analysis because it could avoid the influence of cracks on the arrival of the first break. The emitting wave was a half-cycle sine wave with frequencies of 200 kHz, 400 kHz, 600 kHz, 800 kHz, and 1 MHz, respectively. The amplitude of the waveform was 1 V. The duration of the waveform was 2.5, 1.25, 0.833, 0.625, and 0.5, respectively, as shown in Figure 13.

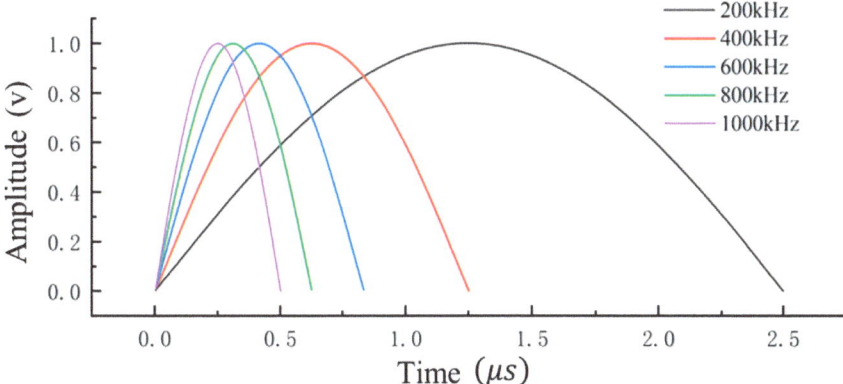

Figure 13. The emitting wave with frequencies of 200 kHz, 400 kHz, 600 kHz, 800 kHz, and 1 MHz, respectively.

We analyzed the waveform received by sensor #3. In Figure 14, (1) to (5) are the spectrum analysis results of the waveform received by sensor #3 when the transmitted waveform was 200 kHz, 400 kHz, 600 kHz, 800 kHz, and 1 MHz.

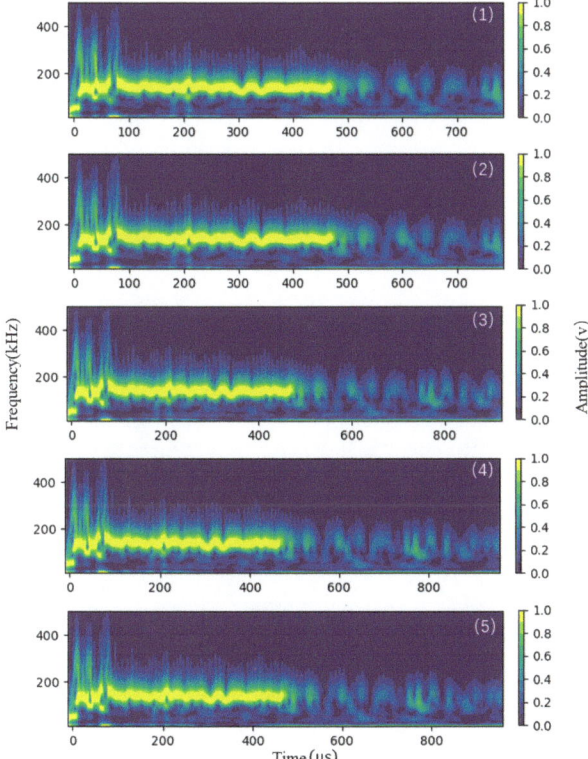

Figure 14. The spectrum analysis results of the waveform received by sensor #3. (**1**)–(**5**) are the spectrum analysis results of the waveform received by sensor #3 when the transmitted waveform was 200 kHz, 400 kHz, 600 kHz, 800 kHz, and 1 MHz.

The onset time, amplitude, and correlation coefficient of the received waveform were obtained for analysis. The correlation coefficient was based on the waveform received at 200 kHz, and the other received waveforms and their correlation coefficients were calculated, respectively. The results are shown in Table 3.

Table 3. The parameters of receiving waveform.

	Frequency of the Emitting Waveform				
	200 kHz	400 kHz	600 kHz	800 kHz	1000 kHz
Onset time (μs)	23.7	23.3	23.3	23.3	23.7
Amplitude (mV)	140.2	139.77	139.16	138.86	138.24
Correlation coefficient	1	0.98	0.97	0.97	0.96

The difference between the obtained parameters is small. The correlation coefficient of the oscillation start time and the waveform does not exhibit a clear change law. Although the amplitude changes are small, they gradually decrease with the frequency increase. That is, the higher the waveform frequency, the faster the attenuation.

4.3. Influence of Different Waveforms on Parameters of Received Waveforms

The half-cycle sine wave, rectangular wave, and triangular wave with a frequency of 1 MHz were used to study the influence of different transmitting waveforms on the parameters of the receiving waveform. The transmitted waveforms are shown in Figure 15; their amplitude was 1 V, and the duration was 0.5 μs.

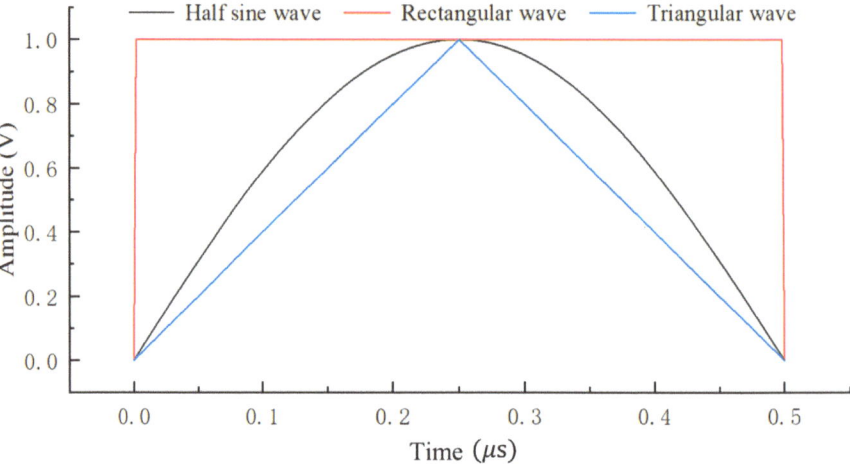

Figure 15. The different emitting waveforms.

We analyzed the waveform received by the No. 3 sensor. The spectrum analysis results of the receiving waveform are shown in Figure 16. The onset time, peak amplitude, and time of peak amplitude are shown in Table 4. The results show that the different types of waveforms do not affect the onset time and the time when the peak amplitude appears. But it does affect the magnitude. For waveforms of the same frequency, the peak amplitude of the rectangular wave is the largest, and the peak amplitude of the sine wave is the smallest. In practical applications, the transmission waveform is rectangular, which is more conducive to the propagation of the excitation waveform.

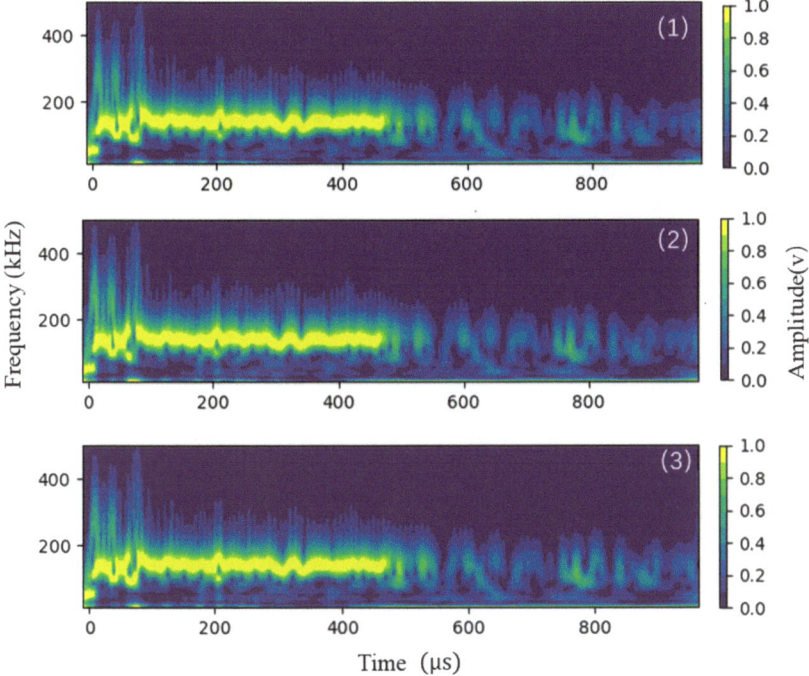

Figure 16. The spectrum analysis results of the receiving waveform. (**1**)–(**3**) are the spectrum diagrams of the received waveforms when the transmitted waveforms are half-cycle sine wave, rectangular wave, and triangular wave respectively.

Table 4. Waveform parameters received with different transmission waveforms.

	Different Transmission Waveforms (1 MHz)		
	Triangular Wave	Half Sine Wave	Rectangular Wave
Onset time (µs)	23.4	23.33	23.33
Amplitude (mV)	142.52	138.24	145.26
Rise time (µs)	168.33	167.33	168.33

4.4. Influence of Wavelength and Relative Position of the Defect on Received Waveform Parameters

The defect detection accuracy in ultrasonic testing is usually half the wavelength. According to Snell's law, the first arrival wave in the acoustic testing of rock materials travels along the shortest path. If the shortest path does not pass through the defect location, the first arrival data obtained at this time cannot reflect the existence of the defect. Therefore, it is necessary to discuss the influence of the transmitted waveform and the relative position between the straight-line path and the defect on the parameters of the received waveform.

The influence of the emission pulse wavelength changes on the received waveform parameters when monitoring a defect of a specific size was studied. Half-cycle sine waves with frequencies of 200 kHz, 400 kHz, 600 kHz, 800 kHz, and 1 MHz were transmitted with defects on one side of the sample. The waveforms corresponding to different frequency waveforms are shown in Table 5. Then, the waveform was received on the other side of the sample. At the same time, another acoustic-wave-receiving sensor was arranged where the straight-line path of the wave did not pass through the defect to study the influence of whether or not the straight-line path passes through the defect on the received waveform parameters. The straight-line path of the waveform received by the No. 1 sensor passed through the defect, as shown in Figure 12. The straight-line path of the waveform received by the No. 2 sensor did not pass through the defect. The distances from the sound source to sensors No. 1 and No. 2 were 110 mm and 109.66 mm, respectively. The emission waveform is shown in Figure 14. The amplitude was 1 V, and the duration was 0.5 μs. From the surface wave velocity of a complete granite sample (2700 m/s), the wavelengths of different frequency emission waveforms can be obtained as follows.

Table 5. The wavelengths of different frequency waveforms propagating on the surface of the sample.

Frequency (Hz)	200 k	400 k	600 k	800 k	1000 k
Wavelength (mm)	13.5	6.75	4.5	3.34	2.7

The waveforms received by No. 1 and No. 2 sensors with different frequencies are shown in Figure 17.

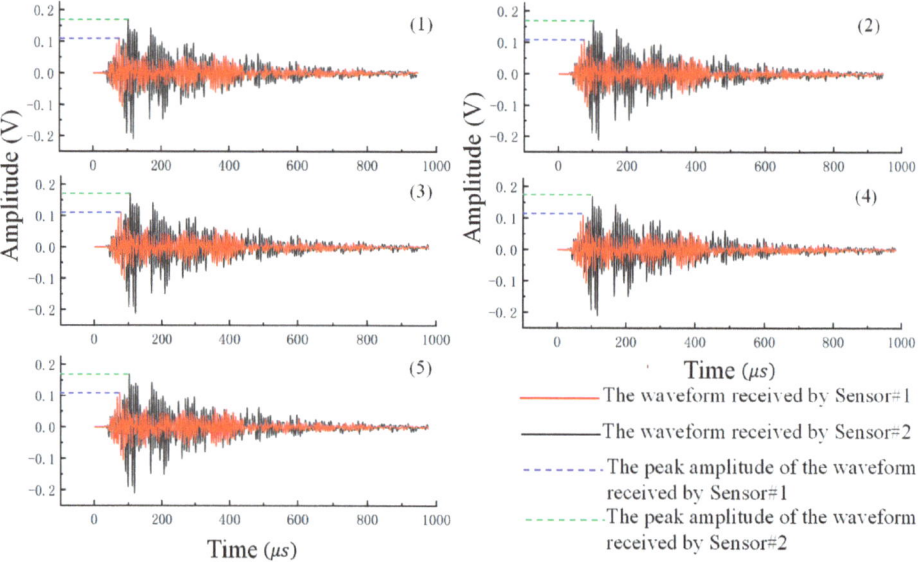

Figure 17. The waveforms received by No. 1 and No. 2 sensors with different frequencies. (1) to (5) represent the received waveforms when the transmitted waveform frequency is 200 kHz, 400 kHz, 600 kHz, 800 kHz, and 1000 kHz.

The spectrum analysis result of the received waveform is shown in Figure 18. In Figure 18, (1) is the spectrum diagram of the waveform of the straight path passing through the defect, and (2) is the spectrum diagram of the waveform of the straight path not passing through the defect. The start-up time and peak amplitude of the received waveforms are listed in Table 6.

Table 6 reveals that although the distances from sensor 1 and sensor 2 to the sound source were the same, the start-up time of sensor 2 was earlier than that of sensor 1. The amplitude of the waveform received by sensor 2 was much larger than that of sensor 1. The reason for the above phenomenon is a defect 2 mm thick on the straight path from the sound source to sensor 2. The defect led to increased propagation paths and energy attenuation of sound waves.

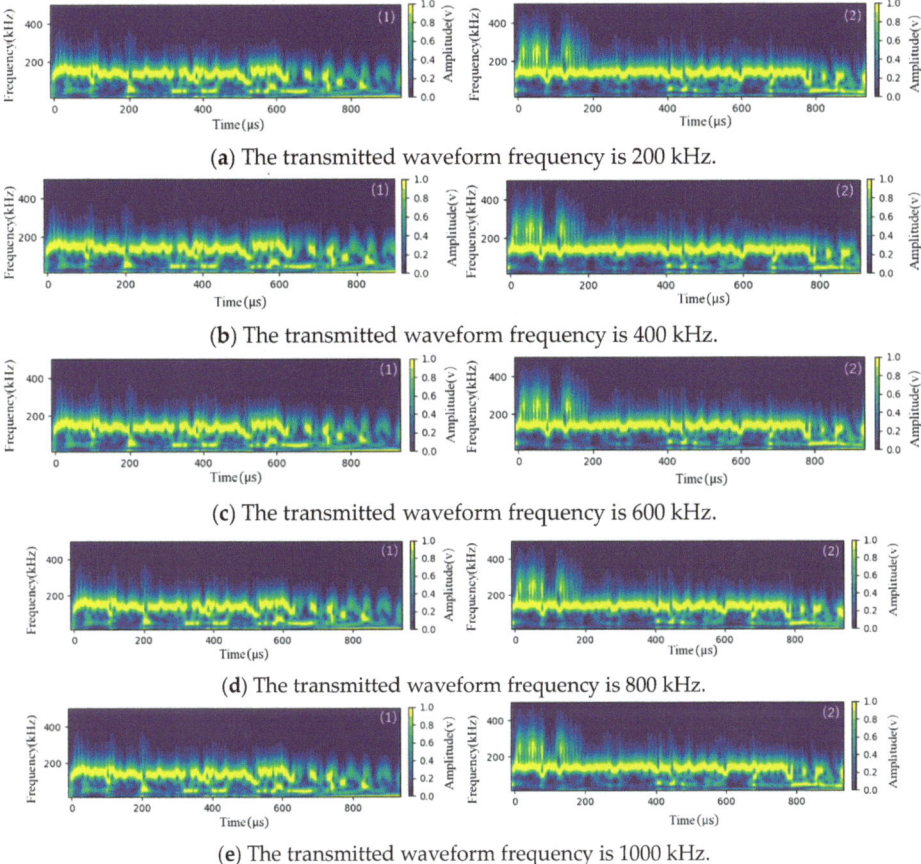

(a) The transmitted waveform frequency is 200 kHz.

(b) The transmitted waveform frequency is 400 kHz.

(c) The transmitted waveform frequency is 600 kHz.

(d) The transmitted waveform frequency is 800 kHz.

(e) The transmitted waveform frequency is 1000 kHz.

Figure 18. The spectrograms of the waves with different source frequencies received by sensor 1 and sensor 2 after propagating in the sample with the defect.

Table 6. The parameters of the waveforms with different source frequencies received by sensor 1 and sensor 2.

	Frequency (Hz)	200 k	400 k	600 k	800 k	1000 k
Start-up time (µs)	Sensor 1	38.33	38	38.66	40	40
	Sensor 2	37.33	38.33	38.33	38.66	38
Peak amplitude (mv)	Sensor 1	109.8	109.2	110.1	110.1	109.5
	Sensor 2	171.2	170.8	170.2	169.3	169.9

Studies have shown that propagation characteristics of acoustic waves are related to the rocks' mechanical properties in acoustic testing. When the wavelength of the sound wave is much larger than the inhomogeneous scale of the rock sample, the sample can be regarded as a homogeneous medium. Otherwise, it should be considered a heterogeneous medium. From the waveform parameters received by sensor 1 in Tables 5 and 6, it can be seen that when the frequency of the transmitted waveform was greater than 600 kHz, the half wavelength was smaller than the width of the crack, and the travel time of the first wave increased significantly. Therefore, in non-destructive testing of rocks, the sensitivity and accuracy are the best when the half wavelength of the transmitted waveform is equal to half the thickness of the defect to be measured.

5. Conclusions

This paper proposes a new method for solving the wave velocity field by optimizing the fastest path search algorithm. The relationship between the wave velocity field and the damage distribution was established to characterize the damage distribution. The improved method was verified with a granite slab sample during uniaxial compression experiments. The damage characterization results obtained using the proposed method were compared with the results obtained using digital speckle patterns methods, demonstrating the accuracy of the proposed method. Finally, the influence of the transmitted wave's waveform on the test result of the acoustic wave was discussed. The main conclusions are presented as follows:

(1) The improved fastest travel path solution was proposed to obtain an accurate propagation path in layered media and media with defects;
(2) A uniaxial compression experiment with granite flat samples was conducted to verify the accuracy of the improved rock damage distribution characterization method. The results of damage distribution characterization with the proposed method were consistent with the strain rate images obtained by the digital image correlation;
(3) The length and shape of the emitted wave affect the accuracy of results in the rock acoustic wave testing. The half wavelength of the emitted wave should be close to the thickness of the defect being measured. Although shortening the wavelength of the transmitted wave can improve the measurement accuracy, it also increases the wave's attenuation. Using a rectangular or sine wave as the transmitted wave is slightly better than using a triangular wave;
(4) When there are large defects in the medium, diffraction will occur during wave propagation, making it difficult to obtain accurate wave velocity fields at the defects using methods based on first-arrival waves. The method proposed in this manuscript is an improved method based on the first arrival wave travel time and will be subject to this limitation. A possible solution is to improve based on the full waveform and introduce coda waves to expand the time-shifted data to overcome this shortcoming.

Author Contributions: Conceptualization, J.Z. and Y.Z.; methodology, J.Z.; software, Y.Z.; validation, L.L., D.Z. and M.Z.; formal analysis, R.W.; investigation, J.Z.; resources, L.L.; data curation, M.Z.; writing—original draft preparation, J.Z.; writing—review and editing, Y.Z.; visualization, J.Z.; supervision, D.Z.; project administration, Y.Z.; funding acquisition, J.Z. All authors have read and agreed to the published version of the manuscript.

Funding: This research was funded by the National Natural Science Foundation of China grant number [52304152], [52222404], [52074212], and [52004206], by China Postdoctoral Science Foundation Funded Project grant number [2023MD744248] and [2023M732793], by Key Research and Development Program of Shaanxi grant number [2023-LL-QY-07], by Shaanxi Province Technology Innovation Guidance Project grant number [2021QFY04-05], and by Shaanxi Province Postdoctoral Research Project grant number [2023BSHYDZZ156].

Data Availability Statement: Data are contained within the article.

Conflicts of Interest: The authors declare no conflict of interest.

References

1. Gautam, P.K.; Dwivedi, R.; Kumar, A.; Kumar, A.; Verma, A.K.; Singh, K.H.; Singh, T.N. Damage Characteristics of Jalore Granite Rocks After Thermal Cycling Effect for Nuclear Waste Repository. *Rock Mech. Rock Eng.* **2021**, *54*, 235–254. [CrossRef]
2. Qian, Q.; Zhou, X. Failure Behaviors and Rock Deformation During Excavation of Underground Cavern Group for Jinping Hydropower Station. *Rock Mech. Rock Eng.* **2018**, *51*, 2639–2651. [CrossRef]
3. Zhao, Y.; Zhao, G.; Xu, L.; Zhou, J.; Huang, X. Mechanical property evolution model of cemented tailings-rock backfill considering strengthening and weakening effects. *Constr. Build. Mater.* **2023**, *377*, 131081. [CrossRef]
4. Zhou, Z.; Cai, X.; Li, X.; Cao, W.; Du, X. Dynamic Response and Energy Evolution of Sandstone Under Coupled Static–Dynamic Compression: Insights from Experimental Study into Deep Rock Engineering Applications. *Rock Mech. Rock Eng.* **2020**, *5*, 1305–1331. [CrossRef]

5. Xie, G.; Liu, L.; Suo, Y.; Zhu, M.; Yang, P.; Sun, W. High-value utilization of modified magnesium slag solid waste and its application as a low-carbon cement admixture. *J. Environ. Manage.* **2024**, *349*, 119551. [CrossRef] [PubMed]
6. Cai, X.; Yuan, J.; Zhou, Z.; Pi, Z.; Tan, L.; Wang, P.; Wang, S.; Wang, S. Effects of hole shape on mechanical behavior and fracturing mechanism of rock: Implications for instability of underground openings. *Tunn. Undergr. Sp. Technol.* **2023**, *141*, 105361. [CrossRef]
7. Guo, Q.; Su, H.; Liu, J.; Yin, Q.; Jing, H.; Yu, L. An experimental study on the fracture behaviors of marble specimens subjected to high temperature treatment. *Eng. Fract. Mech.* **2020**, *225*, 106862. [CrossRef]
8. Fang, Z.; Liu, L.; Zhang, X.; Han, K.; Wang, J.; Zhu, M.; Sun, W.; He, W.; Gao, Y. Carbonation Curing of Modified Magnesium-Coal Based Solid Waste Backfill Material for CO2 Sequestration. *Process Saf. Environ. Prot.* **2023**, *180*, 778–788. [CrossRef]
9. Yin, Q.; Liu, R.; Jing, H.; Su, H.; Yu, L.; He, L. Experimental Study of Nonlinear Flow Behaviors Through Fractured Rock Samples After High-Temperature Exposure. *Rock Mech. Rock Eng.* **2019**, *52*, 2963–2983. [CrossRef]
10. Zhou, Z.; Cai, X.; Cao, W.; Li, X.; Xiong, C. Influence of Water Content on Mechanical Properties of Rock in Both Saturation and Drying Processes. *Rock Mech. Rock Eng.* **2016**, *49*, 3009–3025. [CrossRef]
11. Xie, G.; Suo, Y.; Liu, L.; Yang, P.; Qu, H.; Zhang, C. Pore characteristics of sulfate-activated coal gasification slag cement paste backfill for mining. *Environ. Sci. Pollut. Res.* **2023**, 114920–114935. [CrossRef] [PubMed]
12. Zhou, Z.; Lu, J.; Cai, X.; Rui, Y.; Tan, L. Water saturation effects on mechanical performances and failure characteristics of rock-concrete disc with different interface dip angles. *Constr. Build. Mater.* **2022**, *324*, 126684. [CrossRef]
13. Dai, J.; Liu, J.; Zhou, L.; He, X. Real-Time Ultrasonic Features and Damage Characterization of Deep Shale. *Rock Mech. Rock Eng.* **2023**, *56*, 2535–2550. [CrossRef]
14. Ruan, S.; Liu, L.; Zhu, M.; Shao, C.; Xie, L.; Hou, D. Application of desulfurization gypsum as activator for modified magnesium slag-fly ash cemented paste backfill material. *Sci. Total Environ.* **2023**, *869*, 161631. [CrossRef]
15. Wu, Z.-J.; Wang, Z.-Y.; Fan, L.-F.; Weng, L.; Liu, Q.-S. Micro-failure process and failure mechanism of brittle rock under uniaxial compression using continuous real-time wave velocity measurement. *J. Cent. South Univ.* **2021**, *28*, 556–571. [CrossRef]
16. Zhu, Q.; Li, D.; Li, X.; Han, Z.; Ma, J. Mixed mode fracture parameters and fracture characteristics of diorite using cracked straight through Brazilian disc specimen. *Theor. Appl. Fract. Mech.* **2023**, *123*, 103682. [CrossRef]
17. Zhao, K.; Yang, J.; Yu, X.; Yan, Y.; Zhao, K.; Lai, Y.; Wu, J. Damage evolution process of fiber-reinforced backfill based on acoustic emission three-dimensional localization. *Compos. Struct.* **2023**, *309*, 116723. [CrossRef]
18. Zhang, L.; Zhang, Z.; Chen, Y.; Dai, B.; Wang, B. Crack development and damage patterns under combined dynamic-static loading of parallel double fractured rocks based on DIC technique. *Acta Geotech.* **2023**, *18*, 877–901. [CrossRef]
19. Si, X.; Luo, Y.; Luo, S. Influence of lithology and bedding orientation on failure behavior of "D" shaped tunnel. *Theor. Appl. Fract. Mech.* **2024**, *129*, 104219. [CrossRef]
20. Khoshouei, M.; Bagherpour, R.; Sadeghisorkhani, H.; Jalalian, M.H. A New Look at Hard Rock Abrasivity Evaluation Using Acoustic Emission Technique (AET). *Rock Mech. Rock Eng.* **2022**, *55*, 2425–2443. [CrossRef]
21. Yin, X.C.; Wang, Y.C.; Peng, K.Y.; Bai, Y.L.; Wang, H.T.; Yin, X.F. Development of a new approach to earthquake prediction: Load/unload response ratio (LURR) theory. *Pure Appl. Geophys.* **2000**, *157*, 2365–2383. [CrossRef]
22. Li, X.; Si, G.; Wei, C.; Oh, J.; Canbulat, I. Simulation of ductile fracture propagation using the elastoplastic phase-field damage method calibrated by ultrasonic wave velocity measurement. *Int. J. Rock Mech. Min. Sci.* **2023**, *161*, 105296. [CrossRef]
23. Mei, Y.; Tian, X.; Li, X.; Gepreel, K. Fractal space based dimensionless analysis of the surface settlement induced by the shield tunneling. *Facta Univ. Ser. Mech. Eng.* **2023**, *21*, 737–749.
24. Li, G.; Zhu, C.; He, M.; Zuo, Y.; Gong, F.; Xue, Y.; Feng, G. Intelligent method for parameters optimization of cable in soft rock tunnel base on longitudinal wave velocity. *Tunn. Undergr. Sp. Technol.* **2023**, *133*, 104905. [CrossRef]
25. Weng, L.; Wu, Z.; Wang, Z.; Chu, Z.; Xu, X.; Liu, Q. Acoustic Emission Source Localization in Heterogeneous Rocks with Random Inclusions Using a PRM-Based Wave Velocity Model. *Rock Mech. Rock Eng.* **2023**, *56*, 3301–3315. [CrossRef]
26. Jiang, G.; Zuo, J.; Li, Y.; Wei, X. Experimental Investigation on Mechanical and Acoustic Parameters of Different Depth Shale Under the Effect of Confining Pressure. *Rock Mech. Rock Eng.* **2019**, *52*, 4273–4286. [CrossRef]
27. D'Angiò, D.; Lenti, L.; Martino, S. Microseismic monitoring to assess rock mass damaging through a novel damping ratio-based approach. *Int. J. Rock Mech. Min. Sci.* **2021**, *146*, 1–9. [CrossRef]
28. Zhao, Y.; Yang, T.; Zhang, P.; Zhou, J.; Yu, Q.; Deng, W. The analysis of rock damage process based on the microseismic monitoring and numerical simulations. *Tunn. Undergr. Sp. Technol.* **2017**, *69*, 1–17. [CrossRef]
29. Madhubabu, N.; Singh, P.K.; Kainthola, A.; Mahanta, B.; Tripathy, A.; Singh, T.N. Prediction of compressive strength and elastic modulus of carbonate rocks. *Measurement* **2016**, *88*, 202–213. [CrossRef]
30. Chen, H.; Zhang, G.; Fan, D.; Fang, L.; Huang, L. Nonlinear Lamb wave analysis for microdefect identification in mechanical structural health assessment. *Meas. J. Int. Meas. Confed.* **2020**, *164*, 108026. [CrossRef]
31. Umrao, R.K.; Sharma, L.K.; Singh, R.; Singh, T.N. Determination of strength and modulus of elasticity of heterogenous sedimentary rocks: An ANFIS predictive technique. *Measurement* **2018**, *126*, 194–201. [CrossRef]
32. Abbas, H.A.; Mohamed, Z.; Abdul Kudus, S. Deformation behaviour, crack initiation and crack damage of weathered composite sandstone-shale by using the ultrasonic wave and the acoustic emission under uniaxial compressive stress. *Int. J. Rock Mech. Min. Sci.* **2023**, *170*, 105497. [CrossRef]

33. Rodríguez, P.; Celestino, T.B. Assessment of damage distribution in brittle materials by application of an improved algorithm for three-dimensional localization of acoustic emission sources with P-wave velocity calculation. *Constr. Build. Mater.* **2020**, *231*, 117086. [CrossRef]
34. Liu, B.; Wang, J.; Yang, S.; Xu, X.; Ren, Y. Forward prediction for tunnel geology and classification of surrounding rock based on seismic wave velocity layered tomography. *J. Rock Mech. Geotech. Eng.* **2023**, *15*, 179–190. [CrossRef]
35. Zhang, Y.-B.; Yao, X.-L.; Liang, P.; Wang, K.-X.; Sun, L.; Tian, B.-Z.; Liu, X.-X.; Wang, S.-Y. Fracture evolution and localization effect of damage in rock based on wave velocity imaging technology. *J. Cent. South Univ.* **2021**, *28*, 2752–2769. [CrossRef]
36. Heimann, S.; Vasyura-Bathke, H.; Sudhaus, H.; Isken, M.P.; Kriegerowski, M.; Steinberg, A.; Dahm, T. A Python framework for efficient use of pre-computed Green's functions in seismological and other physical forward and inverse source problems. *Solid Earth* **2019**, *10*, 1921–1935. [CrossRef]
37. Liu, Y.; Hong, X.; Zhang, B. A novel velocity anisotropy probability imaging method using ultrasonic guided waves for composite plates. *Measurement* **2020**, *166*, 108087. [CrossRef]
38. Ivansson, S. Seismic borehole tomography—Theory and computational methods. *Proc. IEEE* **1986**, *74*, 328–338. [CrossRef]
39. Gorbatov, A.; Dominguez, J.; Suarez, G.; Kostoglodov, V.; Zhao, D.; Gordeev, E. Tomographic imaging of the P-wave velocity structure beneath the Kamchatka peninsula. *Geophys. J. Int.* **1999**, *137*, 269–279. [CrossRef]
40. Goodfellow, S.D.; Tisato, N.; Ghofranitabari, M.; Nasseri, M.H.B.; Young, R.P. Attenuation Properties of Fontainebleau Sandstone During True-Triaxial Deformation using Active and Passive Ultrasonics. *Rock Mech. Rock Eng.* **2015**, *48*, 2551–2566. [CrossRef]
41. Xu, C.; Peng, L.; Deng, M. Phased array imaging for damage localization using multi-narrowband Lamb waves. *Mech. Sys Signal Process.* **2023**, *190*, 110134. [CrossRef]
42. Dines, K.A.; Lytle, R.J. Computerized geophysical tomography. *Proc. IEEE* **1979**, *67*, 1065–1073. [CrossRef]
43. Kim, B.; Chen, J.; Kim, J. International Journal of Rock Mechanics and Mining Sciences Relation between crack density and acoustic nonlinearity in thermally damaged sandstone. *Int. J. Rock Mech. Min. Sci.* **2020**, *125*, 104171. [CrossRef]
44. Shirole, D.; Hedayat, A.; Ghazanfari, E.; Walton, G. Evaluation of an Ultrasonic Method for Damage Characterization of Brittle Rocks. *Rock Mech. Rock Eng.* **2020**, *53*, 2077–2094. [CrossRef]
45. Zhou, Z.; Rui, Y.; Cai, X.; Lu, J. Constrained total least squares method using TDOA measurements for jointly estimating acoustic emission source and wave velocity. *Meas. J. Int. Meas. Confed.* **2021**, *182*, 109758. [CrossRef]
46. Yang, J.; Dai, J.; Yao, C.; Jiang, S.; Zhou, C.; Jiang, Q. Estimation of rock mass properties in excavation damage zones of rock slopes based on the Hoek-Brown criterion and acoustic testing. *Int. J. Rock Mech. Min. Sci.* **2020**, *126*, 104192. [CrossRef]

Disclaimer/Publisher's Note: The statements, opinions and data contained in all publications are solely those of the individual author(s) and contributor(s) and not of MDPI and/or the editor(s). MDPI and/or the editor(s) disclaim responsibility for any injury to people or property resulting from any ideas, methods, instructions or products referred to in the content.

MDPI AG
Grosspeteranlage 5
4052 Basel
Switzerland
Tel.: +41 61 683 77 34

Mathematics Editorial Office
E-mail: mathematics@mdpi.com
www.mdpi.com/journal/mathematics

Disclaimer/Publisher's Note: The title and front matter of this reprint are at the discretion of the Guest Editors. The publisher is not responsible for their content or any associated concerns. The statements, opinions and data contained in all individual articles are solely those of the individual Editors and contributors and not of MDPI. MDPI disclaims responsibility for any injury to people or property resulting from any ideas, methods, instructions or products referred to in the content.

www.ingramcontent.com/pod-product-compliance
Lightning Source LLC
LaVergne TN
LVHW072326090526
838202LV00019B/2358